Miliana P7 C315

D1122158

CALIFORNIA

# myPerspectives™

## ENGLISH LANGUAGE ARTS

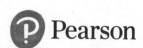 **Pearson**

NEW YORK, NEW YORK • BOSTON, MASSACHUSETTS
CHANDLER, ARIZONA • GLENVIEW, ILLINOIS

Cover image "Birds on Wire" is a combination of illustrations from various artists, and credited to; Rodica Bruma/123RF, Laschi Adrian/123RF, and Peony/Fotolia.

Acknowledgments of third-party content appear on page R81, which constitutes an extension of this copyright page.

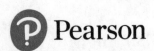 Pearson

ISBN-13: 978-0-13-333957-4
ISBN-10: 0-13-333957-2

12   18

# Welcome!

*my*Perspectives™ *English Language Arts* is a student-centered learning environment where you will analyze text, cite evidence, and respond critically about your learning. You will take ownership of your learning through goal-setting, reflection, independent text selection, and activities that allow you to collaborate with your peers.

Each unit of study includes selections of different genres—including multimedia—all related to a relevant and meaningful Essential Question. As you read, you will engage in activities that inspire thoughtful discussion and debate with your peers allowing you to formulate, and defend, your own perspectives.

*my*Perspectives *ELA* offers a variety of ways to interact directly with the text. You can annotate by writing in your print consumable, or you can annotate in your digital Student Edition. In addition, exciting technology allows you to access multimedia directly from your mobile device and communicate using an online discussion board!

We hope you enjoy using *my*Perspectives *ELA* as you develop the skills required to be successful throughout college and career.

# Authors' Perspectives

myPerspectives is informed by a team of respected experts whose experiences working with students and study of instructional best practices have positively impacted education. From the evolving role of the teacher to how students learn in a digital age, our authors bring new ideas, innovations, and strategies that transform teaching and learning in today's competitive and interconnected world.

> " The teaching of English needs to focus on engaging a new generation of learners. How do we get them excited about reading and writing? How do we help them to envision themselves as readers and writers? And, how can we make the teaching of English more culturally, socially, and technologically relevant? Throughout the curriculum, we've created spaces that enhance youth voice and participation and that connect the teaching of literature and writing to technological transformations of the digital age."

## Ernest Morrell, Ph.D.

is the Macy professor of English Education at Teachers College, Columbia University, a class of 2014 Fellow of the American Educational Research Association, and the Past-President of the National Council of Teachers of English (NCTE). He is also the Director of Teachers College's Institute for Urban and Minority Education (IUME). He is an award-winning author and in his spare time he coaches youth sports and writes poems and plays. Dr. Morrell has influenced the development of myPerspectives in Assessment, Writing & Research, Student Engagement, and Collaborative Learning.

## Elfrieda Hiebert, Ph.D.

is President and CEO of TextProject, a nonprofit that provides resources to support higher reading levels. She is also a research associate at the University of California, Santa Cruz. Dr. Hiebert has worked in the field of early reading acquisition for 45 years, first as a teacher's aide and teacher of primary-level students in California and, subsequently, as a teacher and researcher. Her research addresses how fluency, vocabulary, and knowledge can be fostered through appropriate texts. Dr. Hiebert has influenced the development of *my*Perspectives in Vocabulary, Text Complexity, and Assessment.

> " The signature of complex text is challenging vocabulary. In the systems of vocabulary, it's important to provide ways to show how concepts can be made more transparent to students. We provide lessons and activities that develop a strong vocabulary and concept foundation—a foundation that permits students to comprehend increasingly more complex text."

## Kelly Gallagher, M.Ed.

teaches at Magnolia High School in Anaheim, California, where he is in his thirty-first year. He is the former co-director of the South Basin Writing Project at California State University, Long Beach. Mr. Gallagher has influenced the development of *my*Perspectives in Writing, Close Reading, and the Role of Teachers.

> " The *my*Perspectives classroom is dynamic. The teacher inspires, models, instructs, facilitates, and advises students as they evolve and grow. When teachers guide students through meaningful learning tasks and then pass them ownership of their own learning, students become engaged and work harder. This is how we make a difference in student achievement—by putting students at the center of their learning and giving them the opportunities to choose, explore, collaborate, and work independently."

> " It's critical to give students the opportunity to read a wide range of highly engaging texts and to immerse themselves in exploring powerful ideas and how these ideas are expressed. In *my*Perspectives, we focus on building up students' awareness of how academic language works, which is especially important for English language learners."

## Jim Cummins, Ph.D.

is a Professor Emeritus in the Department of Curriculum, Teaching and Learning of the University of Toronto. His research focuses on literacy development in multilingual school contexts as well as on the potential roles of technology in promoting language and literacy development. In recent years, he has been working actively with teachers to identify ways of increasing the literacy engagement of learners in multilingual school contexts. Dr. Cummins has influenced the development of *my*Perspectives in English Language Learner and English Language Development support.

# UNIT (1) American Voices

INDEPENDENT LEARNING

These selections can be accessed via the Interactive Student Edition.

 PERFORMANCE-BASED ASSESSMENT PREP

 PERFORMANCE-BASED ASSESSMENT

UNIT REFLECTION

 DIGITAL PERSPECTIVES

SCAN FOR MULTIMEDIA

Use the BouncePage app whenever you see "Scan for Multimedia" to access:

- Unit Introduction Videos
- Media Selections
- Modeling Videos
- Selection Audio Recordings

Additional digital resources can be found in:

- Interactive Student Edition
- *my*Perspectives+

UNIT **2** Survival

COMPARE

DIGITAL PERSPECTIVES

 SCAN FOR MULTIMEDIA

Use the BouncePage app whenever you see "Scan for Multimedia" to access:

- Unit Introduction Videos
- Media Selections
- Modeling Videos
- Selection Audio Recordings

Additional digital resources can be found in:

- Interactive Student Edition
- *my*Perspectives+

# UNIT ③ The Literature of Civil Rights

 DIGITAL ⌕
PERSPECTIVES

SCAN FOR MULTIMEDIA

Use the BouncePage app whenever you see "Scan for Multimedia" to access:

- Unit Introduction Videos
- Media Selections
- Modeling Videos
- Selection Audio Recordings

Additional digital resources can be found in:
- Interactive Student Edition
- *my*Perspectives+

# UNIT (4) Star-Crossed Romances

## INDEPENDENT LEARNING

These selections can be accessed via the Interactive Student Edition.

## PERFORMANCE-BASED ASSESSMENT

## UNIT REFLECTION

## DIGITAL PERSPECTIVES

SCAN FOR MULTIMEDIA

Use the BouncePage app whenever you see "Scan for Multimedia" to access:

- Unit Introduction Videos
- Media Selections
- Modeling Videos
- Selection Audio Recordings

Additional digital resources can be found in:
- Interactive Student Edition
- *my*Perspectives+

UNIT **5** Journeys of Transformation

## INDEPENDENT LEARNING

These selections can be accessed via the Interactive Student Edition.

 PERFORMANCE-BASED ASSESSMENT PREP

 ## PERFORMANCE-BASED ASSESSMENT

## UNIT REFLECTION

## DIGITAL PERSPECTIVES

 SCAN FOR MULTIMEDIA

Use the BouncePage app whenever you see "Scan for Multimedia" to access:

- Unit Introduction Videos
- Media Selections
- Modeling Videos
- Selection Audio Recordings

Additional digital resources can be found in:

- Interactive Student Edition
- *my*Perspectives+

UNIT  6 World's End

## DIGITAL ⌕ PERSPECTIVES

 SCAN FOR MULTIMEDIA

Use the BouncePage app
whenever you see "Scan for
Multimedia" to access:

- Unit Introduction Videos
- Media Selections
- Modeling Videos
- Selection Audio Recordings

---

Additional digital resources can be found in:

- Interactive Student Edition
- *my*Perspectives+

# Interactive Student Edition

*my*Perspectives is completely interactive because you can work directly in your digital or print Student Edition.

All activities that you complete in your Interactive Student Edition are saved automatically. You can access your notes quickly so that reviewing work to prepare for tests and projects is easy!

Enter answers to prompts right in your digital Notebook and "turn it in" to your teacher.

The in-line annotation tool allows you to practice close reading by highlighting and adding comments about the text.

Interactivities are available for you to complete and submit directly to your teacher.

Unit 1: Survival › Whole-Class Learning › The Seventh Man

## The Seventh Man
### Haruki Murakami
**ANCHOR TEXT | SHORT STORY**

🗋 Background   👤 Author   ☰ Standards

1  "A huge wave nearly swept me away," said the seventh man, almost whispering. "It happened one September afternoon when I was ten years old."

2  The man was the last one to tell his story that night. The hands of the clock had moved past ten. The small group that huddled in a circle could hear the wind tearing through the darkness outside, heading west. It shook the trees, set the windows to rattling, and moved past the house with one final whistle.

3  "It was the biggest wave I had ever seen in my life," he said. "A strange wave. An absolute giant."

4  He paused.

5  "It just barely missed me, but in my place it swallowed everything that mattered most to me and swept it off to another world. I took years to find it again to recover from the experience—precious years that can never be replaced."

6  The seventh man appeared to be in his mid-fifties. He was a thin man, tall, with a moustache, and next to his right eye he had a short but deep-looking scar that could have been made by the stab of a small blade. Stiff, bristly patches of white marked his short hair. His face had the look you see on people when they can't quite find the words they need. In his case, though, the expression seemed to have been there from long before, as though it were part of him. The man wore a simple blue shirt under a grey tweed coat, and every now and then he would bring his hand to his collar. None of those assembled there knew his name or what he did for a living.

7  He cleared his throat, and for a moment or two his words were lost in silence. The others waited for him to go on.

8  "In my case, it was a wave," he said. "There's no way for me to tell, of course, what it will be for each of you. But in my case it just happened to take the form of a gigantic¹² wave. It presented itself to me all of a sudden one day, without warning. And it was devastating."

9  As you read the selections in this Unit, **identify interesting words** related to the idea of survival and add them to your **Word Network**.

**▼ MAKING MEANING**

**▾ Research**

**Research to Clarify** Choose at least one unfamiliar detail from the text. Briefly research that detail. In what way does the information you learned shed light on an aspect of the story?

📓 Notebook

▸ Close Read the Text
▸ Analyze the Text
▸ Analyze Craft and Structure

**▾ LANGUAGE DEVELOPMENT**

▸ Concept Vocabulary
▾ Word Network

Add interesting survival words from the text to your Word Network

↗ Open activity

🔧 Tool Kit: Word Network Model ›

▸ Word Study
▸ Conventions

the shops in town lowered their shutters in preparation for the storm. Starting early in the morning, my father and brother went around the house nailing shut all the storm-doors, while my mother spent the day in the kitchen cooking emergency provisions. We filled bottles and canteens with water, and packed our most important possessions in rucksacks[2] for possible evacuation. To the adults, typhoons were an annoyance and a threat they had to face almost annually, but to the kids, removed as we were from such practical concerns, it was just a great big circus, a wonderful source of excitement.

12    Just after noon the <u>color of the sky</u> began to change all of a sudden. There was something strange and unreal about it. I stayed outside on the porch, watching the sky, until the wind began to howl and <u>the rain began to beat against the house with a weird dry sound, like handfuls of sand.</u> Then we closed the last storm-door and gathered together in one room of the darkened house, listening to the radio. This particular storm did not have a great deal of rain, it said, but the winds were doing a lot of damage, blowing roofs off houses and capsizing ships. Many people had been killed or injured by flying debris. Over and over again, they warned people against leaving their homes. Every once in a while, <u>the house would creak and shudder as if a huge hand were shaking it,</u> and sometimes there would be a great crash of some heavy-sounding object against a storm-door. My father guessed that these were tiles blowing off the neighbors' houses. For lunch we ate the rice and omelettes my mother had cooked, waiting for the typhoon to blow past.

13    But the typhoon gave no sign of blowing past. The radio said it had lost momentum[3] almost as soon as it came ashore at S. Province, and now it was moving north-east at the pace of a slow runner. The wind kept up its savage howling as it trie̶ ̶ ̶ ̶ ̶ ̶ ̶ ̶ ̶ ̶ stood on land.

14    Perhaps an hour had gone by with the ̶ ̶ ̶ ̶ when a hush fell over everything. All of a ̶ ̶ ̶ could hear a bird crying in the distance. M ̶ ̶ ̶ door a crack and looked outside. The win ̶ ̶ ̶ rain had ceased to fall. Thick, gray clouds ̶ ̶ ̶ ̶ ̶ ̶ ̶ showed here and the ̶ ̶ ̶ ̶ ̶ ̶

*This sentence is leading up to an exciting story.*

**CLOSE READ**

**ANNOTATE:** In paragraph 12, annotate at least four vivid details about the storm. Underline those that compare one thing to another.

**QUESTION:** What is being compared? What picture does each detail create in the reader's mind?

**CONCLUDE:** How do these descriptions help you visualize the typhoon?

*Typhoons are powerful, scary storms that can do a lot of damage.*

Use the close-read prompts to guide you through an analysis of the text. You can highlight, circle, and underline the text right in your print Student Edition.

Respond to questions and activities directly in your book!

THE SEVENTH MAN

## Concept Vocabulary

| desperate | hallucination | profound |
|---|---|---|
| entranced | premonition | meditative |

**Why These Words?** These concept words help to reveal the emotional state of the seventh man. For example, when the wave approaches, the seventh man is *entranced*, waiting for it to attack. After the wave hits, the seventh man believes he sees his friend K. in the wave and claims that this experience was no *hallucination*. Notice that both words relate to experiences that occur only in the mind of the seventh man.

1. How does the concept vocabulary sharpen the reader's understanding of the mental or emotional state of the seventh man?
   *These words are descriptive and precise.*

2. What other words in the selection connect to this concept?
   *ominous, overcome, nightmares*

### Practice

  Notebook The concept vocabulary words appear in "The Seventh Man."

1. Use each concept word in a sentence that demonstrates your understanding of the word's meaning.

2. Challenge yourself to replace the concept word with one or two synonyms. How does the word change affect the meaning of your sentence? For example, which sentence is stronger? Which has a more positive meaning?

## Word Study

**Latin suffix: -tion** The Latin suffix *-tion* often indicates that a word is a noun. Sometimes this suffix is spelled *-ion* or *-ation*. These related suffixes mean "act, state, or condition of." In "The Seventh Man," the word *premonition* means "the state of being forewarned."

1. Record a definition of *hallucination* based on your understanding of its root word and the meaning of the suffix *-tion*.
   *The condition of seeing something that is not real*

2. Look back at paragraphs 37–40 and find two other words that use the suffix *-tion*. Identify the root word that was combined with the suffix. Record a definition for each word.
   *cooperate + -tion—the state of working together*
   *direct + -tion—the state of being guided*

Add interesting survival words from the text to your Word Network.

© Pearson Education, Inc., or its affiliates. All rights reserved.

# Digital Resources

You can access digital resources from your print Student Edition, or from Pearson Realize™.

To watch videos or listen to audio from your print Student Edition, all you need is a device with a camera and Pearson's BouncePages app!

ANCHOR TEXT | SHORT STORY

## The Seventh Man

### Haruki Murakami

SCAN FOR MULTIMEDIA

**BACKGROUND**
Hurricanes that originate in the northwest Pacific Ocean are called typhoons. They can stretch up to 500 miles in diameter and produce high winds, heavy rains, enormous waves, and severe flooding. On average, Japan is hit by three severe typhoons each year due to its location and climatic conditions.

1    "A huge wave nearly swept me away," said the seventh man, almost whispering. "It happened one September afternoon when I was ten years old."

2    The man was the last one to tell his story that night. The hands of the clock had moved past ten. The small group that huddled in

NOTES

**CLOSE READ**
ANNOTATE: Mark details in paragraph 2 that

## How to watch a video or listen to audio:

1. Download Pearson's BouncePages App from the Apple App or Google Play Store.

2. Open the app on your mobile device.

3. Aim your camera so the page from your Student Edition is viewable on your screen.

4. Tap the screen to scan the page.

5. Press the "Play" button on the page that appears on your device.

6. View the video or listen to the audio directly from your device!

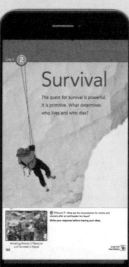

Amazing Stories of Rescues and Survival in Nepal

122

Digital resources, including audio and video, can be accessed in the Interactive Student Edition. Your teacher might also assign activities for you to complete online.

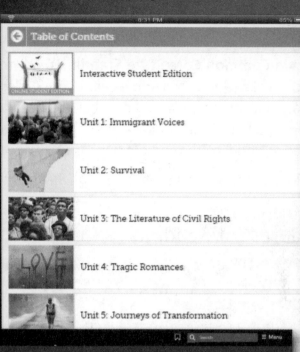

You will also find digital novels, interactive lessons, and games!

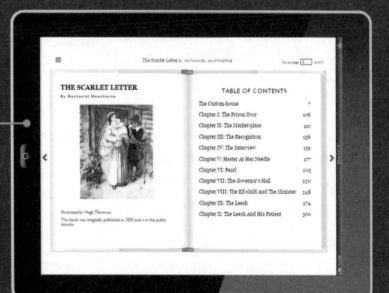

# Standards Overview

**California Common Core State Standards** will prepare you to succeed in college and your future career. The College and Career Readiness Anchor Standards define what you need to achieve by the end of high school, and the grade-specific Standards define what you need to know by the end of your current grade level.

The following provides an overview of the Standards.

## Standards for Reading

| College and Career Readiness Anchor Standards for Reading |
|---|
| **Key Ideas and Details** |
| 1. Read closely to determine what the text says explicitly and to make logical inferences from it; cite specific textual evidence when writing or speaking to support conclusions drawn from the text. |
| 2. Determine central ideas or themes of a text and analyze their development; summarize the key supporting details and ideas. |
| 3. Analyze how and why individuals, events, and ideas develop and interact over the course of a text. |
| **Craft and Structure** |
| 4. Interpret words and phrases as they are used in a text, including determining technical, connotative, and figurative meanings, and analyze how specific word choices shape meaning or tone. |
| 5. Analyze the structure of texts, including how specific sentences, paragraphs, and larger portions of the text (e.g., a section, chapter, scene, or stanza) relate to each other and the whole. |
| 6. Assess how point of view or purpose shapes the content and style of a text. |
| **Integration of Knowledge and Ideas** |
| 7. Integrate and evaluate content presented in diverse formats and media, including visually and quantitatively, as well as in words. |
| 8. Delineate and evaluate the argument and specific claims in a text, including the validity of the reasoning as well as the relevance and sufficiency of the evidence. |
| 9. Analyze how two or more texts address similar themes or topics in order to build knowledge or to compare the approaches the authors take. |
| **Range of Reading and Level of Text Complexity** |
| 10. Read and comprehend complex literary and informational texts independently and proficiently. |

## Grade 9 Reading Standards for Literature

| STANDARD CODE | Standard |
|---|---|
| **Key Ideas and Details** | |
| RL.9–10.1 | Cite strong and thorough textual evidence to support analysis of what the text says explicitly as well as inferences drawn from the text. |
| RL.9–10.2 | Determine a theme or central idea of a text and analyze in detail its development over the course of the text, including how it emerges and is shaped and refined by specific details; provide an objective summary of the text. |
| RL.9–10.3 | Analyze how complex characters (e.g., those with multiple or conflicting motivations) develop over the course of a text, interact with other characters, and advance the plot or develop the theme. |
| **Craft and Structure** | |
| RL.9–10.4 | Determine the meaning of words and phrases as they are used in the text, including figurative and connotative meanings; analyze the cumulative impact of specific word choices on meaning and tone (e.g., how the language evokes a sense of time and place; how it sets a formal or informal tone). (See grade 9–10 Language standards 4–6 for additional expectations.) |
| RL.9–10.5 | Analyze how an author's choices concerning how to structure a text, order events within it (e.g., parallel plots), and manipulate time (e.g., pacing, flashbacks) create such effects as mystery, tension, or surprise. |
| RL.9–10.6 | Analyze a particular point of view or cultural experience reflected in a work of literature from outside the United States, drawing on a wide reading of world literature. |
| **Integration of Knowledge and Ideas** | |
| RL.9–10.7 | Analyze the representation of a subject or a key scene in two different artistic mediums, including what is emphasized or absent in each treatment (e.g., Auden's "Musée des Beaux Arts" and Breughel's *Landscape with the Fall of Icarus*). |
| RL.9–10.8 | (Not applicable to literature) |
| RL.9–10.9 | Analyze how an author draws on and transforms source material in a specific work (e.g., how Shakespeare treats a theme or topic from Ovid or the Bible or how a later author draws on a play by Shakespeare). |
| **Range of Reading and Text Complexity** | |
| RL.9–10.10 | By the end of grade 9, read and comprehend literature, including stories, dramas, and poems, in the grades 9–10 text complexity band proficiently, with scaffolding as needed at the high end of the range. |

# Standards Overview

## Grade 9 Reading Standards for Informational Text

| STANDARD CODE | Standard |
|---|---|
| **Key Ideas and Details** | |
| **RI.9–10.1** | Cite strong and thorough textual evidence to support analysis of what the text says explicitly as well as inferences drawn from the text. |
| **RI.9–10.2** | Determine a central idea of a text and analyze its development over the course of the text, including how it emerges and is shaped and refined by specific details; provide an objective summary of the text. |
| **RI.9–10.3** | Analyze how the author unfolds an analysis or series of ideas or events, including the order in which the points are made, how they are introduced and developed, and the connections that are drawn between them. |
| **Craft and Structure** | |
| **RI.9–10.4** | Determine the meaning of words and phrases as they are used in a text, including figurative, connotative, and technical meanings; analyze the cumulative impact of specific word choices on meaning and tone (e.g., how the language of a court opinion differs from that of a newspaper). (See grade 9–10 Language standards 4–6 for additional expectations.) |
| **RI.9–10.5** | Analyze in detail how an author's ideas or claims are developed and refined by particular sentences, paragraphs, or larger portions of a text (e.g., a section or chapter). |
| **RI.9–10.5.a** | Analyze the use of text features (e.g., graphics, headers, captions) in functional workplace documents. |
| **RI.9–10.6** | Determine an author's point of view or purpose in a text and analyze how an author uses rhetoric to advance that point of view or purpose. |
| **Integration of Knowledge and Ideas** | |
| **RI.9–10.7** | Analyze various accounts of a subject told in different mediums (e.g., a person's life story in both print and multimedia), determining which details are emphasized in each account. |
| **RI.9–10.8** | Delineate and evaluate the argument and specific claims in a text, assessing whether the reasoning is valid and the evidence is relevant and sufficient; identify false statements and fallacious reasoning. |
| **RI.9–10.9** | Analyze seminal U.S. documents of historical and literary significance (e.g., Washington's Farewell Address, the Gettysburg Address, Roosevelt's Four Freedoms speech, King's "Letter from Birmingham Jail"), including how they address related themes and concepts. |
| **Range of Reading and Text Complexity** | |
| **RI.9–10.10** | By the end of grade 9, read and comprehend literary nonfiction in the grades 9–10 text complexity band proficiently, with scaffolding as needed at the high end of the range. |

# Standards for Writing

## College and Career Readiness Anchor Standards for Writing

### Text Types and Purposes

1. Write arguments to support claims in an analysis of substantive topics or texts, using valid reasoning and relevant and sufficient evidence.

2. Write informative/explanatory texts to examine and convey complex ideas and information clearly and accurately through the effective selection, organization, and analysis of content.

3. Write narratives to develop real or imagined experiences or events using effective technique, well-chosen details, and well-structured event sequences.

### Production and Distribution of Writing

4. Produce clear and coherent writing in which the development, organization, and style are appropriate to task, purpose, and audience.

5. Develop and strengthen writing as needed by planning, revising, editing, rewriting, or trying a new approach.

6. Use technology, including the Internet, to produce and publish writing and to interact and collaborate with others.

### Research to Build and Present Knowledge

7. Conduct short as well as more sustained research projects based on focused questions, demonstrating understanding of the subject under investigation.

8. Gather relevant information from multiple print and digital sources, assess the credibility and accuracy of each source, and integrate the information while avoiding plagiarism.

9. Draw evidence from literary or informational texts to support analysis, reflection, and research.

### Range of Writing

10. Write routinely over extended time frames (time for research, reflection, and revision) and shorter time frames (a single sitting or a day or two) for a range of tasks, purposes, and audiences.

## Grade 9 Writing Standards

| STANDARD CODE | Standard |
|---|---|
| **Text Types and Purposes** | |
| W.9–10.1 | Write arguments to support claims in an analysis of substantive topics or texts, using valid reasoning and relevant and sufficient evidence. |
| W.9–10.1.a | Introduce precise claim(s), distinguish the claim(s) from alternate or opposing claims, and create an organization that establishes clear relationships among claim(s), counterclaims, reasons, and evidence. |

# Standards Overview

## Grade 9 Writing Standards

| STANDARD CODE | Standard |
|---|---|
| **Text Types and Purposes (continued)** ||
| W.9–10.1.b | Develop claim(s) and counterclaims fairly, supplying evidence for each while pointing out the strengths and limitations of both in a manner that anticipates the audience's knowledge level and concerns. |
| W.9–10.1.c | Use words, phrases, and clauses to link the major sections of the text, create cohesion, and clarify the relationships between claim(s) and reasons, between reasons and evidence, and between claim(s) and counterclaims. |
| W.9–10.1.d | Establish and maintain a formal style and objective tone while attending to the norms and conventions of the discipline in which they are writing. |
| W.9–10.1.e | Provide a concluding statement or section that follows from and supports the argument presented. |
| W.9–10.2 | Write informative/explanatory texts to examine and convey complex ideas, concepts, and information clearly and accurately through the effective selection, organization, and analysis of content. |
| W.9–10.2.a | Introduce a topic or thesis statement; organize complex ideas, concepts, and information to make important connections and distinctions; include formatting (e.g., headings), graphics (e.g., figures, tables), and multimedia when useful to aiding comprehension. |
| W.9–10.2.b | Develop the topic with well-chosen, relevant, and sufficient facts, extended definitions, concrete details, quotations, or other information and examples appropriate to the audience's knowledge of the topic. |
| W.9–10.2.c | Use appropriate and varied transitions to link the major sections of the text, create cohesion, and clarify the relationships among complex ideas and concepts. |
| W.9–10.2.d | Use precise language and domain-specific vocabulary to manage the complexity of the topic. |
| W.9–10.2.e | Establish and maintain a formal style and objective tone while attending to the norms and conventions of the discipline in which they are writing. |
| W.9–10.2.f | Provide a concluding statement or section that follows from and supports the information or explanation presented (e.g., articulating implications or the significance of the topic). |
| W.9–10.3 | Write narratives to develop real or imagined experiences or events using effective technique, well-chosen details, and well-structured event sequences. |
| W.9–10.3.a | Engage and orient the reader by setting out a problem, situation, or observation, establishing one or multiple point(s) of view, and introducing a narrator and/or characters; create a smooth progression of experiences or events. |
| W.9–10.3.b | Use narrative techniques, such as dialogue, pacing, description, reflection, and multiple plot lines, to develop experiences, events, and/or characters. |
| W.9–10.3.c | Use a variety of techniques to sequence events so that they build on one another to create a coherent whole. |

## Grade 9 Writing Standards

| STANDARD CODE | Standard |
|---|---|
| **Text Types and Purposes (continued)** | |
| **W.9–10.3.d** | Use precise words and phrases, telling details, and sensory language to convey a vivid picture of the experiences, events, setting, and/or characters. |
| **W.9–10.3.e** | Provide a conclusion that follows from and reflects on what is experienced, observed, or resolved over the course of the narrative. |
| **Production and Distribution of Writing** | |
| **W.9–10.4** | Produce clear and coherent writing in which the development, organization, and style are appropriate to task, purpose, and audience. |
| **W.9–10.5** | Develop and strengthen writing as needed by planning, revising, editing, rewriting, or trying a new approach, focusing on addressing what is most significant for a specific purpose and audience. |
| **W.9–10.6** | Use technology, including the Internet, to produce, publish, and update individual or shared writing products, taking advantage of technology's capacity to link to other information and to display information flexibly and dynamically. |
| **Research to Build and Present Knowledge** | |
| **W.9–10.7** | Conduct short as well as more sustained research projects to answer a question (including a self-generated question) or solve a problem; narrow or broaden the inquiry when appropriate; synthesize multiple sources on the subject, demonstrating understanding of the subject under investigation. |
| **W.9–10.8** | Gather relevant information from multiple authoritative print and digital sources, using advanced searches effectively; assess the usefulness of each source in answering the research question; integrate information into the text selectively to maintain the flow of ideas, avoiding plagiarism and following a standard format for citation including footnotes and endnotes. |
| **W.9–10.9** | Draw evidence from literary or informational texts to support analysis, reflection, and research. |
| **W.9–10.9.a** | Apply *grades 9–10 Reading standards* to literature (e.g., "Analyze how an author draws on and transforms source material in a specific work [e.g., how Shakespeare treats a theme or topic from Ovid or the Bible or how a later author draws on a play by Shakespeare]"). |
| **W.9–10.9.b** | Apply *grades 9–10 Reading standards* to literary nonfiction (e.g., "Delineate and evaluate the argument and specific claims in a text, assessing whether the reasoning is valid and the evidence is relevant and sufficient; identify false statements and fallacious reasoning"). |
| **Range of Writing** | |
| **W.9–10.10** | Write routinely over extended time frames (time for research, reflection, and revision) and shorter time frames (a single sitting or a day or two) for a range of tasks, purposes, and audiences. |

# Standards Overview

## Standards for Speaking and Listening

| College and Career Readiness Anchor Standards for Speaking and Listening |
|---|
| **Comprehension and Collaboration** |
| **1.** Prepare for and participate effectively in a range of conversations and collaborations with diverse partners, building on others' ideas and expressing their own clearly and persuasively. |
| **2.** Integrate and evaluate information presented in diverse media and formats, including visually, quantitatively, and orally. |
| **3.** Evaluate a speaker's point of view, reasoning, and use of evidence and rhetoric. |
| **Presentation of Knowledge and Ideas** |
| **4.** Present information, findings, and supporting evidence such that listeners can follow the line of reasoning and the organization, development, and style are appropriate to task, purpose, and audience. |
| **5.** Make strategic use of digital media and visual displays of data to express information and enhance understanding of presentations. |
| **6.** Adapt speech to a variety of contexts and communicative tasks, demonstrating command of formal English when indicated or appropriate. |

| Grade 9 Standards for Speaking and Listening | |
|---|---|
| **STANDARD CODE** | **Standard** |
| **Comprehension and Collaboration** | |
| SL.9–10.1 | Initiate and participate effectively in a range of collaborative discussions (one-on-one, in groups, and teacher-led) with diverse partners on *grades 9–10 topics, texts, and issues,* building on others' ideas and expressing their own clearly and persuasively. |
| SL.9–10.1.a | Come to discussions prepared, having read and researched material under study; explicitly draw on that preparation by referring to evidence from texts and other research on the topic or issue to stimulate a thoughtful, well-reasoned exchange of ideas. |
| SL.9–10.1.b | Work with peers to set rules for collegial discussions and decision-making (e.g., informal consensus, taking votes on key issues, presentation of alternate views), clear goals and deadlines, and individual roles as needed. |
| SL.9–10.1.c | Propel conversations by posing and responding to questions that relate the current discussion to broader themes or larger ideas; actively incorporate others into the discussion; and clarify, verify, or challenge ideas and conclusions. |
| SL.9–10.1.d | Respond thoughtfully to diverse perspectives, summarize points of agreement and disagreement, and, when warranted, qualify or justify their own views and understanding and make new connections in light of the evidence and reasoning presented. |

## Grade 9 Standards for Speaking and Listening

| STANDARD CODE | Standard |
|---|---|
| **Comprehension and Collaboration (continued)** ||
| SL.9–10.2 | Integrate multiple sources of information presented in diverse media or formats (e.g., visually, quantitatively, orally) evaluating the credibility and accuracy of each source. |
| SL.9–10.3 | Evaluate a speaker's point of view, reasoning, and use of evidence and rhetoric, identifying any fallacious reasoning or exaggerated or distorted evidence. |
| **Presentation of Knowledge and Ideas** ||
| SL.9–10.4 | Present information, findings, and supporting evidence clearly, concisely, and logically (using appropriate eye contact, adequate volume, and clear pronunciation) such that listeners can follow the line of reasoning and the organization, development, substance, and style are appropriate to purpose (e.g., argument, narrative, informative, response to literature presentations), audience, and task. |
| SL.9–10.4.a | Plan and deliver an informative/explanatory presentation that: presents evidence in support of a thesis, conveys information from primary and secondary sources coherently, uses domain specific vocabulary, and provides a conclusion that summarizes the main points. (9th or 10th grade) |
| SL.9–10.4.b | Plan, memorize, and present a recitation (e.g., poem, selection from a speech or dramatic soliloquy) that: conveys the meaning of the selection and includes appropriate performance techniques (e.g., tone, rate, voice modulation) to achieve the desired aesthetic effect. (9th or 10th grade) |
| SL.9–10.5 | Make strategic use of digital media (e.g., textual, graphical, audio, visual, and interactive elements) in presentations to enhance understanding of findings, reasoning, and evidence and to add interest. |
| SL.9–10.6 | Adapt speech to a variety of contexts and tasks, demonstrating command of formal English when indicated or appropriate. (See grades 9–10 Language Standards 1 and 3 for specific expectations.) |

# Standards Overview

## Standards for Language

| College and Career Readiness Anchor Standards for Language |
|---|
| **Conventions of Standard English** |
| **1.** Demonstrate command of the conventions of standard English grammar and usage when writing or speaking. |
| **2.** Demonstrate command of the conventions of standard English capitalization, punctuation, and spelling when writing. |
| **Knowledge of Language** |
| **3.** Apply knowledge of language to understand how language functions in different contexts, to make effective choices for meaning or style, and to comprehend more fully when reading or listening. |
| **Vocabulary Acquisition and Use** |
| **4.** Determine or clarify the meaning of unknown and multiple-meaning words and phrases by using context clues, analyzing meaningful word parts, and consulting general and specialized reference materials, as appropriate. |
| **5.** Demonstrate understanding of figurative language, word relationships, and nuances in word meanings. |
| **6.** Acquire and use accurately a range of general academic and domain-specific words and phrases sufficient for reading, writing, speaking, and listening at the college and career readiness level; demonstrate independence in gathering vocabulary knowledge when considering a word or phrase important to comprehension or expression. |

| Grade 9 Standards for Language | |
|---|---|
| **STANDARD CODE** | **Standard** |
| **Conventions of Standard English** | |
| **L.9–10.1** | Demonstrate command of the conventions of standard English grammar and usage when writing or speaking. |
| **L.9–10.1.a** | Use parallel structure. |
| **L.9–10.1.b** | Use various types of phrases (noun, verb, adjectival, adverbial, participial, prepositional, absolute) and clauses (independent, dependent; noun, relative, adverbial) to convey specific meanings and add variety and interest to writing or presentations. |
| **L.9–10.2** | Demonstrate command of the conventions of standard English capitalization, punctuation, and spelling when writing. |
| **L.9–10.2.a** | Use a semicolon (and perhaps a conjunctive adverb) to link two or more closely related independent clauses. |

## Grade 9 Standards for Language

| STANDARD CODE | Standard |
|---|---|
| **Conventions of Standard English (continued)** | |
| L.9–10.2.b | Use a colon to introduce a list or quotation. |
| L.9–10.2.c | Spell correctly. |
| **Knowledge of Language** | |
| L.9–10.3 | Apply knowledge of language to understand how language functions in different contexts, to make effective choices for meaning or style, and to comprehend more fully when reading or listening. |
| L.9–10.3.a | Write and edit work so that it conforms to the guidelines in a style manual (e.g., *MLA Handbook*, Turabian's *Manual for Writers*) appropriate for the discipline and writing type. |
| **Vocabulary Acquisition and Use** | |
| L.9–10.4 | Determine or clarify the meaning of unknown and multiple-meaning words and phrases based on *grades 9–10 reading and content*, choosing flexibly from a range of strategies. |
| L.9–10.4.a | Use context (e.g., the overall meaning of a sentence, paragraph, or text; a word's position or function in a sentence) as a clue to the meaning of a word or phrase. |
| L.9–10.4.b | Identify and correctly use patterns of word changes that indicate different meanings or parts of speech (e.g., *analyze, analysis, analytical; advocate, advocacy*) and continue to apply knowledge of Greek and Latin roots and affixes. |
| L.9–10.4.c | Consult general and specialized reference materials (e.g., college-level dictionaries, rhyming dictionaries, bilingual dictionaries, glossaries, thesauruses), both print and digital, to find the pronunciation of a word or determine or clarify its precise meaning, its part of speech, or its etymology. |
| L.9–10.4.d | Verify the preliminary determination of the meaning of a word or phrase (e.g., by checking the inferred meaning in context or in a dictionary). |
| L.9–10.5 | Demonstrate understanding of figurative language, word relationships, and nuances in word meanings. |
| L.9–10.5.a | Interpret figures of speech (e.g., euphemism, oxymoron) in context and analyze their role in the text. |
| L.9–10.5.b | Analyze nuances in the meaning of words with similar denotations. |
| L.9–10.6 | Acquire and use accurately general academic and domain-specific words and phrases, sufficient for reading, writing, speaking, and listening at the college and career readiness level; demonstrate independence in gathering vocabulary knowledge when considering a word or phrase important to comprehension or expression. |

# American Voices

The people who call the United States home are diverse in their histories and experiences. Is there such a thing as a "correct" way to be "American"?

Define American: Hiep Le

💬 **Discuss It** Is being "American" a matter of geography or choice?

Write your response before sharing your ideas.

SCAN FOR MULTIMEDIA

## UNIT INTRODUCTION

ESSENTIAL QUESTION:

# What does it mean to be "American"?

LAUNCH TEXT
NONFICTION
NARRATIVE MODEL
Music for
My Mother

### WHOLE-CLASS LEARNING

ANCHOR TEXT: ESSAY

**A Quilt of a Country**
Anna Quindlen

ANCHOR TEXT: ESSAY

**The Immigrant Contribution**
*from* A Nation of Immigrants
John F. Kennedy

COMPARE

ANCHOR TEXT: SHORT STORY

**American History**
Judith Ortiz Cofer

### SMALL-GROUP LEARNING

NOVEL EXCERPT

**Rules of the Game**
*from* The Joy Luck Club
Amy Tan

MEDIA: BLOG POST

**The Writing on the Wall**
Camille Dungy

MEMOIR

**With a Little Help From My Friends**
*from* Funny in Farsi
Firoozeh Dumas

POETRY COLLECTION

**Morning Talk**
Roberta Hill Whiteman

**Immigrant Picnic**
Gregory Djanikian

### INDEPENDENT LEARNING

MEMOIR

*from* When I Was Puerto Rican
Esmeralda Santiago

AUTOBIOGRAPHICAL ESSAY

**Finding a Voice: A Taiwanese Family Adapts to America**
Diane Tsai

POETRY

**The New Colossus**
Emma Lazarus

POETRY

**Legal Alien**
Pat Mora

MEDIA: VIDEO

**Grace Abbott and the Fight for Immigrant Rights in America**
BBC

PERFORMANCE TASK

WRITING FOCUS:
Write a Nonfiction Narrative

PERFORMANCE TASK

SPEAKING AND LISTENING FOCUS:
Present a Nonfiction Narrative

PERFORMANCE-BASED ASSESSMENT PREP

Review Evidence for a Nonfiction Narrative

## PERFORMANCE-BASED ASSESSMENT

Narrative: Nonfiction Narrative and Interpretive Reading

PROMPT:

# How is an American identity created?

# Unit Goals

Throughout this unit, you will deepen your understanding of what it means to be "American" by reading, writing, speaking, presenting, and listening. These goals will help you succeed on the Unit Performance-Based Assessment.

Rate how well you meet these goals right now. You will revisit your ratings later when you reflect on your growth during this unit.

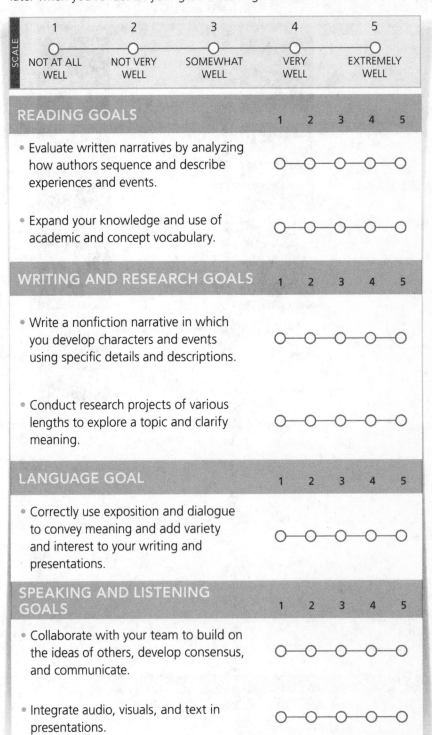

| SCALE | 1 | 2 | 3 | 4 | 5 |
|---|---|---|---|---|---|
| | NOT AT ALL WELL | NOT VERY WELL | SOMEWHAT WELL | VERY WELL | EXTREMELY WELL |

**READING GOALS**

1 2 3 4 5

- Evaluate written narratives by analyzing how authors sequence and describe experiences and events.

- Expand your knowledge and use of academic and concept vocabulary.

**WRITING AND RESEARCH GOALS**

1 2 3 4 5

- Write a nonfiction narrative in which you develop characters and events using specific details and descriptions.

- Conduct research projects of various lengths to explore a topic and clarify meaning.

**LANGUAGE GOAL**

1 2 3 4 5

- Correctly use exposition and dialogue to convey meaning and add variety and interest to your writing and presentations.

**SPEAKING AND LISTENING GOALS**

1 2 3 4 5

- Collaborate with your team to build on the ideas of others, develop consensus, and communicate.

- Integrate audio, visuals, and text in presentations.

## STANDARDS

**L.9–10.6** Acquire and use accurately general academic and domain-specific words and phrases, sufficient for reading, writing, speaking, and listening at the college and career readiness level; demonstrate independence in gathering vocabulary knowledge when considering a word or phrase important to comprehension or expression.

SCAN FOR MULTIMEDIA

# Academic Vocabulary: Narrative Writing

Academic terms appear in all subjects and can help you read, write, and discuss with more precision. Here are five academic words that will be useful to you in this unit as you analyze and write narratives.

**Complete the chart.**

1. Review each word, its root, and the mentor sentences.

2. Use the information and your own knowledge to predict the meaning of each word.

3. For each word, list at least two related words.

4. Refer to a dictionary or other resources if needed.

**TIP**

**FOLLOW THROUGH**
Study the words in this chart, and highlight them or their forms wherever they appear in the unit.

| WORD | MENTOR SENTENCES | PREDICT MEANING | RELATED WORDS |
|---|---|---|---|
| **conflict**<br><br>ROOT:<br>**-flict-**<br>"strike"; "hit" | 1. Alice and Nora resolved their *conflict* by sharing the toy they both wanted.<br><br>2. In the story I'm writing, I want the *conflict* to resolve happily. | | inflict, afflict |
| **description**<br><br>ROOT:<br>**-scrip-**<br>"writing" | 1. Pat Mora's skill with *description* is one reason her poems are so good.<br><br>2. Your comedy routine will be funnier if you include detailed *description* of the scene. | | |
| **dialogue**<br><br>ROOT:<br>**-log-**<br>"word" | 1. Milton has memorized every word of *dialogue* in the film and will gladly recite it.<br><br>2. Greta enjoys writing fiction but has a hard time making *dialogue* sound realistic. | | |
| **exposition**<br><br>ROOT:<br>**-posit-**<br>"sit"; "place"; "put" | 1. The story contains very little *exposition*, so it took me awhile to figure out the characters' relationships.<br><br>2. Kennedy's essay about American identity is a well-organized *exposition* of important ideas. | | |
| **sequence**<br><br>ROOT:<br>**-sequ-**<br>"follow" | 1. A movie director may plan a scene by breaking it into a *sequence* of separate shots.<br><br>2. After Anika finished the experiment, she explained the *sequence* of steps she had followed. | | |

This selection is an example of a **nonfiction narrative,** a type of writing in which an author tells a true story. This is the type of writing you will develop in the Performance-Based Assessment at the end of the unit.

**As you read,** look at the way the writer builds the story. Mark the text to help you answer this question: What details make this narrative vivid and meaningful?

# Music for My Mother

NOTES

1   After dinner my older brother liked to play the guitar. He preferred the music he heard on the radio, but he played the traditional songs for Mama. She enjoyed things that reminded her of home.

2   Her eyes hurt and her fingers would get sore from long hours of work as a seamstress. I remember washing dishes while Pedrito sang: "And seeing myself so lonely and sad like a leaf in the wind, I want to cry . . . from this feeling."

3   He sang in Spanish, which is how the lyrics were written. That song is more than 100 years old now. Mama learned it when she was a girl.

4   Papa tried to nudge Mama out of her nostalgia sometimes. He would answer her in English when she spoke to him in Spanish. His English was not very good at first, but he worked at it until it got better.

5   Mama usually answered him in Spanish. They would go back and forth in either language, talking about work or homesickness or family. Pedrito or I would occasionally correct them or help them finish their sentences in English. Papa would thank us. Mama would just smile and shake her head. But she always repeated the words we

SCAN FOR
MULTIMEDIA

had helped her with. In time her English got better too, but she was far more at ease in her native tongue.

6   I was seven years old when we came to the United States. Pedrito was 11. Papa was a carpenter who also knew a little about plumbing and electricity. From an early age, my brother and I learned how to take care of ourselves in our new home. Our parents worked long hours, and they counted on us to be independent.

7   At first we were almost like guides for Mama and Papa. In big busy places, like the mall or the registry of motor vehicles, they felt uncomfortable, if not overwhelmed. It was easier for us to adjust to environments that were fast-paced and not always friendly. I felt protective of my parents and also proud of how quickly I learned my way around.

8   It would hurt my feelings to see the way some people looked at us. For a while, on Sundays and holidays we would wear our best clothes from home. Before long, we learned to wear casual clothes almost all the time, like most people in this country do. And after a while, our parents became more at ease in stores or government offices. They relaxed a little, I suppose, and we attracted less attention.

9   Mama and Papa live with Pedrito now, in a two-family home outside of Houston. Pedrito is now known as Peter. He runs a construction business that employs 14 men and women.

10  Papa is in his seventies now. Pedrito would like for him to slow down a little and enjoy retirement, but Papa says that Mama wouldn't want him sitting around the house getting in her way. He rises at dawn almost every day and goes to work with Pedrito, building houses.

11  I am a teacher. This summer I will be taking my son, Michael, to visit his grandparents. He is twelve. He wants to learn to play the guitar. I want Mama and his Uncle Peter to teach him a few of the good old songs.

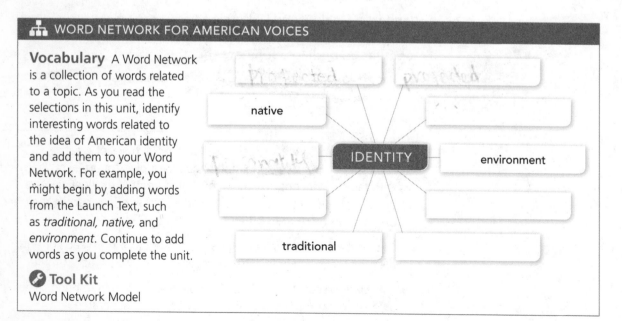

### WORD NETWORK FOR AMERICAN VOICES

**Vocabulary** A Word Network is a collection of words related to a topic. As you read the selections in this unit, identify interesting words related to the idea of American identity and add them to your Word Network. For example, you might begin by adding words from the Launch Text, such as *traditional, native,* and *environment*. Continue to add words as you complete the unit.

protected        projected

native

IDENTITY        environment

traditional

🔧 **Tool Kit**
Word Network Model

## Summary

Write a summary of "Music for My Mother." A **summary** is a concise, complete, and accurate overview of a text. It should not include a statement of your opinion or an analysis.

> What I've read was about an Merican-American
> and how they imgrated to the U.S
> the brother knew how to
> Play the guitar So he learned
> a song that his mother
> knew when she was in
> Mexico. The narritor
> talked about her
> struggles with
> imagrade
> parents

## Launch Activity

**Conduct a Small-Group Discussion** Consider this question: In what ways can music or other creative expression bring people together or, perhaps, separate them?

- Record your feelings on the question and explain your thinking.

  _____

  _____

- Gather in small groups to discuss different examples of creative expression—such as a song, poem, game, or piece of art—you learned with family or friends, at school, or during another experience. As a group, choose an example that you agree either brings people together or separates them from others.

- Gather the small groups and have a representative from each one describe the example they have chosen.

- As a class, discuss the examples. Would each one help to bring people of different backgrounds together or to keep them separated?

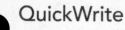

# QuickWrite

Consider class discussions, presentations, the video, and the Launch Text as you think about the prompt. Record your first thoughts here.

PROMPT: **How is an "American" identity created?**

### EVIDENCE LOG FOR AMERICAN VOICES

Review your QuickWrite. Summarize your thoughts in one sentence to record in your Evidence Log. Then, record textual details or evidence from "Music for My Mother" that support your thinking.

Prepare for the Performance-Based Assessment at the end of the unit by completing the Evidence Log after each selection.

**Tool Kit**
Evidence Log Model

Title of Text: _____  Date: _____

| CONNECTION TO PROMPT | TEXT EVIDENCE/DETAILS | ADDITIONAL NOTES/IDEAS |
|---|---|---|
|  |  |  |

How does this text change or add to my thinking?  Date: _____

SCAN FOR
MULTIMEDIA

ESSENTIAL QUESTION:

# What does it mean to be "American"?

America has been described as a "melting pot" of people from different places and cultures—but is that description accurate? Does American identity represent a "melting" or merging of cultures? Or is it more like a salad in which the separate ingredients are still visible? You will work with your whole class to explore the concept of American identity. The selections you are going to read present different perspectives on what it means to be "American."

## Whole-Class Learning Strategies

Throughout your life, in school, in your community, and in your career, you will continue to learn and work in large-group environments.

Review these strategies and the actions you can take to practice them as you work with your whole class. Add ideas of your own for each step. Get ready to use these strategies during Whole-Class Learning.

| STRATEGY | ACTION PLAN |
|---|---|
| Listen actively | • Eliminate distractions. For example, put your cell phone away.<br>• Keep your eyes on the speaker.<br>• |
| Clarify by asking questions | • If you're confused, other people probably are, too. Ask a question to help your whole class.<br>• If you see that you are guessing, ask a question instead.<br>• |
| Monitor understanding | • Notice what information you already know and be ready to build on it.<br>• Ask for help if you are struggling.<br>• |
| Interact and share ideas | • Share your ideas and answer questions, even if you are unsure.<br>• Build on the ideas of others by adding details or making a connection.<br>• |

SCAN FOR
MULTIMEDIA

# CONTENTS

PERFORMANCE TASK

WRITING FOCUS

## Write a Nonfiction Narrative

All three Whole-Class readings deal with issues of cultural diversity and citizenship in the United States. After reading, you will write your own nonfiction narrative about the topic of American identity.

A QUILT OF A COUNTRY

## Comparing Texts

In this lesson, you will read and compare the essay "A Quilt of a Country" and the essay "The Immigrant Contribution." First, complete the first-read and close-read activities for "A Quilt of a Country." The work you do on this selection will help prepare you for the comparing task.

THE IMMIGRANT CONTRIBUTION

### About the Author

**Anna Quindlen** (b. 1953) started working in the newspaper business at the age of 18 as an assistant. After graduating from Barnard College in 1974, she wrote for the *New York Post* and then for the *New York Times*, where her career in journalism began to flourish. She was only the third woman to have a column in the *Times's* Opinion Pages, for which she won a Pulitzer Prize in 1992. Three years later, Quindlen decided to leave the newspaper and pursue her passion for writing fiction. She has written several best-selling novels, as well as nonfiction and children's books.

### 🔧 Tool Kit
First-Read Guide and Model Annotation

### ☰ STANDARDS
**RI.9–10.10** By the end of grade 9, read and comprehend literary nonfiction in the grades 9–10 text complexity band proficiently, with scaffolding as needed at the high end of the range.

# A Quilt of a Country

## Concept Vocabulary

You will encounter the following words as you read "A Quilt of a Country." Before reading, note how familiar you are with each word. Then, rank them each on a scale of 1 (most familiar) to 6 (least familiar).

| WORD | YOUR RANKING |
|------|--------------|
| disparate | |
| discordant | |
| pluralistic | |
| interwoven | |
| diversity | |
| coalescing | |

After completing the first read, return to the concept vocabulary and review your rankings. Mark changes to your original rankings as needed.

## First Read NONFICTION

Apply these strategies as you conduct your first read. You will have an opportunity to complete the close-read notes after your first read.

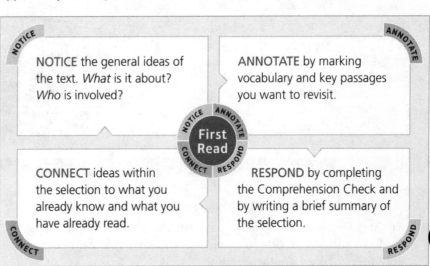

**NOTICE** the general ideas of the text. *What* is it about? *Who* is involved?

**ANNOTATE** by marking vocabulary and key passages you want to revisit.

**CONNECT** ideas within the selection to what you already know and what you have already read.

**RESPOND** by completing the Comprehension Check and by writing a brief summary of the selection.

**First Read**

# A Quilt of a Country

## Anna Quindlen

## BACKGROUND

This essay was published in *Newsweek* magazine about two weeks after the terrorist attacks of September 11, 2001. In New York City, almost 3,000 people were killed when hijackers crashed two airliners into the World Trade Center. In Washington, D.C., 224 people were killed when a hijacked jet crashed into the Pentagon. On hijacked United Airlines Flight 93, passengers tried to regain control of the plane. All 44 people on board died when the aircraft crashed in a field near Shanksville, Pennsylvania.

SCAN FOR
MULTIMEDIA

1    America is an improbable idea. A mongrel nation built of ever-changing **disparate** parts, it is held together by a notion, the notion that all men are created equal, though everyone knows that most men consider themselves better than someone. "Of all the

NOTES

**disparate** (DIHS puhr iht) *adj.*
essentially different in kind

**discordant** (dihs KAWR duhnt)
*adj.* unrelated; out of place

**pluralistic** (plur uh LIHS tihk)
*adj.* having multiple parts or aspects

**CLOSE READ**

**ANNOTATE:** Reread the final sentence in paragraph 2. Mark the repeated adjective in this statement.

**QUESTION:** Why has the author chosen to use the same adjective to describe two very different things?

**CONCLUDE:** What effect does this deliberate use of repetition create?

nations in the world, the United States was built in nobody's image," the historian Daniel Boorstin wrote. That's because it was built of bits and pieces that seem **discordant**, like the crazy quilts that have been one of its great folk-art forms, velvet and calico[1] and checks and brocades.[2] Out of many, one. That is the ideal.

2    The reality is often quite different, a great national striving consisting frequently of failure. Many of the oft-told stories of the most **pluralistic** nation on earth are stories not of tolerance, but of bigotry. Slavery and sweatshops, the burning of crosses and the ostracism of the other. Children learn in social-studies class and in the news of the lynching of blacks, the denial of rights to women, the murders of gay men. It is difficult to know how to convince them that this amounts to "crown thy good with brotherhood," that amid all the failures is something spectacularly successful. Perhaps they understand it at this moment, when enormous tragedy, as it so often does, demands a time of reflection on enormous blessings.

3    This is a nation founded on a conundrum, what Mario Cuomo[3] has characterized as "community added to individualism." These two are our defining ideals; they are also in constant conflict. Historians today bemoan the ascendancy of a kind of prideful apartheid[4] in America, saying that the clinging to ethnicity, in background and custom, has undermined the concept of unity. These historians must have forgotten the past, or have gilded it. The New York of my children is no more Balkanized,[5] probably less so, than the Philadelphia of my father, in which Jewish boys would walk several blocks out of their way to avoid the Irish divide of Chester Avenue. (I was the product of a mixed marriage, across barely bridgeable lines: an Italian girl, an Irish boy. How quaint it seems now, how incendiary then.) The Brooklyn of Francie Nolan's famous tree,[6] the Newark of which Portnoy complained,[7] even the uninflected WASP[8] suburbs of Cheever's[9] characters: they are ghettos, pure and simple. Do the Cambodians and the Mexicans in California coexist less easily today than did the Irish and Italians of Massachusetts a century ago? You know the answer.

4    What is the point of this splintered whole? What is the point of a nation in which Arab cabbies chauffeur Jewish passengers through the streets of New York—and in which Jewish cabbies chauffeur Arab passengers, too, and yet speak in theory of hatred, one for the other? What is the point of a nation in which one part seems to be

---

1. **calico**  *n.* printed cotton cloth
2. **brocades**  *n.* fabrics with raised patterns in gold or silver.
3. **Mario Cuomo**  politician and former New York governor.
4. **apartheid**  (uh PAHR tyd) *n.* system of racial segregation and discrimination.
5. **Balkanized**  *adj.* broken up into smaller, often hostile groups.
6. **Nolan's famous tree . . .**  reference to Betty Smith's novel *A Tree Grows in Brooklyn.*
7. **the Newark of which Portnoy complained . . .**  reference to Philip Roth's novel *Portnoy's Complaint.*
8. **WASP**  short for white Anglo-Saxon Protestant; typically refers to a member of the dominant and most privileged class of people in the United States.
9. **Cheever's**  reference to John Cheever, an American novelist and short story writer.

always on the verge of fisticuffs with another, blacks and whites, gays and straights, left and right, Pole and Chinese and Puerto Rican and Slovenian? Other countries with such divisions have in fact divided into new nations with new names, but not this one, impossibly **interwoven** even in its hostilities.

5      Once these disparate parts were held together by a common enemy, by the fault lines of world wars and the electrified fence of communism. With the end of the cold war there was the creeping concern that without a focus for hatred and distrust, a sense of national identity would evaporate, that the left side of the hyphen— African-American, Mexican-American, Irish-American—would overwhelm the right. And slow-growing domestic traumas like economic unrest and increasing crime seemed more likely to emphasize division than community. Today the citizens of the United States have come together once more because of armed conflict and enemy attack. Terrorism has led to devastation—and unity.

6      Yet even in 1994, the overwhelming majority of those surveyed by the National Opinion Research Center agreed with this statement: "The U.S. is a unique country that stands for something special in the world." One of the things that it stands for is this vexing notion that a great nation can consist entirely of refugees from other nations, that people of different, even warring religions and cultures can live, if not side by side, then on either side of the country's Chester Avenues. Faced with this **diversity** there is little point in trying to isolate anything remotely resembling a national character, but there are two strains of behavior that, however tenuously, abet the concept of unity.

7      There is that Calvinist[10] undercurrent in the American psyche that loves the difficult, the demanding, that sees mastering the impossible, whether it be prairie or subway, as a test of character, and so glories in the struggle of this fractured **coalescing**. And there is a grudging fairness among the citizens of the United States that eventually leads most to admit that, no matter what the English-only advocates try to suggest, the new immigrants are not so different from our own parents or grandparents. Leonel Castillo, former director of the Immigration and Naturalization Service and himself the grandson of Mexican immigrants, once told the writer Studs Terkel proudly, "The old neighborhood Ma-Pa stores are still around. They are not Italian or Jewish or Eastern European any more. Ma and Pa are now Korean, Vietnamese, Iraqi, Jordanian, Latin American. They live in the store. They work seven days a week. Their kids are doing well in school. They're making it. Sound familiar?"

8      Tolerance is the word used most often when this kind of coexistence succeeds, but tolerance is a vanilla-pudding word, standing for little more than the allowance of letting others live

---

10. **Calvinist** *adj.* related to Calvinism, a set of Christian beliefs based on the teachings of John Calvin that stresses God's power, the moral weakness of humans, the idea that one's destiny is set and unchangeable.

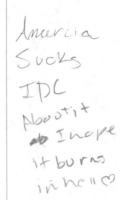

NOTES

**interwoven** (ihn tuhr WOH vuhn) *adj.* intermingled; combined

**diversity** (duh VUR suh tee) *n.* variety of different ethnic or cultural groups

**coalescing** (koh uh LEHS ihng) *n.* coming together in one body or place

Bigbooty
hoe♡

unremarked and unmolested. Pride seems excessive, given the American willingness to endlessly complain about them, them being whoever is new, different, unknown or currently under suspicion. But patriotism is partly taking pride in this unlikely ability to throw all of us together in a country that across its length and breadth is as different as a dozen countries, and still be able to call it by one name. When photographs of the faces of all those who died in the World Trade Center destruction are assembled in one place, it will be possible to trace in the skin color, the shape of the eyes and the noses, the texture of the hair, a map of the world. These are the representatives of a mongrel nation that somehow, at times like this, has one spirit. Like many improbable ideas, when it actually works, it's a wonder. ❧

# Comprehension Check

Complete the following items after you finish your first read.

1. According to Quindlen, what familiar object serves as an ideal representation of America?

2. According to Quindlen, how have people's attitudes about her being a product of a mixed marriage changed over time?

3. What does Quindlen think unified America's diverse ethnic groups before the end of the cold war?

4. According to Quindlen, how have other countries often handled deep ethnic divisions?

5. According to the former head of the Immigration and Naturalization Service, how are today's neighborhood stores similar to and different from the old neighborhood stores?

6. **Notebook** Write a summary of "A Quilt of a Country" to confirm your understanding of the essay.

---

## RESEARCH

**Research to Clarify** Choose at least one unfamiliar detail from the text. Briefly research that detail. In what way does the information you learned shed light on an idea expressed in the essay?

**Research to Explore** Choose something that interests you from the text, and formulate a research question.

A QUILT OF A COUNTRY

## Close Read the Text

1. The model, from paragraph 5 of the essay, shows two sample annotations, along with questions and conclusions. Close read the passage and find another detail to annotate. Then, write a question and your conclusion.

**Close Read**
ANNOTATE — QUESTION — CONCLUDE

ANNOTATE: These phrases make comparisons between people's emotions and physical barriers placed by warring nations.

QUESTION: Why does the author use these comparisons?

CONCLUDE: The comparisons create a sense of danger and clarify the idea of a "common enemy."

ANNOTATE: These words characterize a new concern that arose at the end of the cold war.

QUESTION: What do these words suggest about the nature of the problem?

CONCLUDE: "Creeping" suggests that the problem grew slowly and secretly. "Evaporate" adds that it was hidden and not immediately noticed.

> Once these disparate parts were held together by a common enemy, by the fault lines of world wars and the electrified fence of communism. With the end of the cold war there was the creeping concern that without a focus for hatred and distrust, a sense of national identity would evaporate, that the left side of the hyphen—African-American, Mexican-American, Irish-American—would overwhelm the right.

🔧 **Tool Kit**
Close-Read Guide and
Model Annotation

2. For more practice, go back into the text, and complete the close-read notes.

3. Revisit a section of the text you found important during your first read. Read this section closely, and **annotate** what you notice. Ask yourself **questions** such as "Why did the author choose these words?" What can you **conclude**?

## Analyze the Text

**CITE TEXTUAL EVIDENCE**
to support your answers.

📓 **Notebook** Respond to these questions.

1. (a) **Analyze** Explain Mario Cuomo's conundrum. (b) How does this detail contribute to the development of Quindlen's ideas?

2. (a) **Generalize** Why is Quindlen reluctant to define "anything remotely resembling a national character"? (b) **Connect** What qualities does she propose are essentially American? Explain.

3. (a) **Deduce** At the end of paragraph 3, Quindlen says, "You know the answer." Explain what that answer is. (b) **Interpret** Why do you think she leaves that answer open-ended?

4. **Essential Question:** *What does it mean to be "American"?* What have you learned about American identity from reading this essay?

📋 **STANDARDS**

**RI.9–10.5** Analyze in detail how an author's ideas or claims are developed and refined by particular sentences, paragraphs, or larger portions of a text.

**RI.9–10.6** Determine an author's point of view or purpose in a text and analyze how an author uses rhetoric to advance that point of view or purpose.

# Analyze Craft and Structure

**Purpose and Rhetoric** An **author's purpose** is his or her reason for writing. The four general purposes for writing are to inform, to persuade, to entertain, and to reflect. Writers also have specific purposes for writing that vary with the topic and occasion. A writer may want to explain a particular event or reach a special audience. Those intentions shape the choices the writer makes, including those of structure and **rhetoric**, or language devices.

Anna Quindlen organizes this essay around a central **analogy**—a comparison of two unlike things that works to clarify an idea. Quindlen was moved to write this essay shortly after the terrorist attacks of September 11, 2001. Consider how her purpose and use of analogy reflect the concerns of that moment in history.

## Practice

CITE TEXTUAL EVIDENCE
to support your answers.

📝 **Notebook** Respond to these questions.

1. **(a)** Identify three details in the first paragraph that support Quindlen's idea that America is a mash-up of different cultures. **(b)** According to Quindlen, what "notion" unites American culture into a single whole?

2. For Quindlen, why does the idea of a crazy quilt capture a tension at the heart of American culture?

3. **(a)** Use the chart to explain how each passage adds to Quindlen's analogy of the crazy quilt. **(b)** Select a fourth passage from the essay that you think belongs on the chart. Explain your choice.

| PARAGRAPH | PASSAGE | HOW IT DEVELOPS THE ANALOGY |
|-----------|---------|------------------------------|
| 2 | *Many of the oft-told stories . . . ostracism of the other.* | |
| 4 | *Other countries with such . . . even in its hostilities.* | |
| 8 | *When photographs of the faces . . . a map of the world.* | |
| | | |

4. Why might the analogy of a quilt have seemed fitting at a time that the nation was suffering from a great trauma? Explain.

A QUILT OF A COUNTRY

## Concept Vocabulary

| | | |
|---|---|---|
| disparate | pluralistic | diversity |
| discordant | interwoven | coalescing |

**Why These Words?** These concept words convey unity and fragmentation. For example, at the beginning of the first paragraph, the author describes America as "a mongrel nation built of ever-changing disparate parts." The word *mongrel*, a mixed-breed dog, reinforces the idea of disparate elements that come together to form a unique whole.

1. Which concept vocabulary words contribute to the idea of unity, and which contribute to the idea of fragmentation?

2. What other words in the selection connect to the concepts of unity and fragmentation?

### Practice

📖 **Notebook** The concept vocabulary words appear in "A Quilt of a Country."

1. Use the concept vocabulary words to complete the paragraph.

   America is a _____ society, a nation in which groups of people from many _____ backgrounds come together to live. The members of these groups often raise their voices in disagreement, but their _____ opinions are essential to our democracy. Despite the great _____ of America's population, Americans find ways to bridge their differences, usually by _____ around important social, economic, or political principles. Indeed, the strength of our nation seems to originate from the _____ strands that create its fabric.

2. Write the context clues that help you determine the correct words.

## Word Study

**Latin prefix: *dis-*** The prefix *dis-* shows negation or expresses the idea of being apart or away. In the word *discordant, dis-* combines with the Latin root *-cord-*, meaning "heart." Over time, the word became associated with music that was harsh or out of tune. Today, *discordant* is often used to describe anything that is out of place.

1. Write another word you know that begins with the prefix *dis-*. Explain how the prefix helps you understand the meaning of the word.

2. Reread paragraph 5 of "A Quilt of a Country." Mark a word (other than *disparate*) that begins with the prefix *dis-*. Write a definition for the word.

---

### 🔗 WORD NETWORK

Add interesting words related to American identity from the text to your Word Network.

---

### ⊟ STANDARDS

**RI.9–10.4** Determine the meaning of words and phrases as they are used in a text, including figurative, connotative, and technical meanings; analyze the cumulative impact of specific word choices on meaning and tone.

**L.9–10.4.b** Identify and correctly use patterns of word changes that indicate different meanings or parts of speech and continue to apply knowledge of Greek and Latin roots and affixes.

# Author's Style

**Word Choice** Fiction writers and poets are not the only ones who choose words carefully. Nonfiction writers like Anna Quindlen also use **vivid language**, or strong, precise words, to bring ideas to life and to communicate them forcefully. Strong verbs and precise adjectives make informational writing more interesting and convincing.

> **Ordinary adjective:** We sailed through the *rough* water.
> **Precise adjective:** We sailed though the *churning* water.
>
> **Ordinary verb:** I *fell* into the hole.
> **Strong verb:** I *tumbled* into the hole.

## Read It

Read the passages from "A Quilt of a Country" and identify the precise adjectives and strong verbs in each one. Then, rewrite each passage, changing the vivid word choices to ordinary ones. Explain how Quindlen's original word choices contribute to the accuracy and liveliness of her writing. Use the chart to record your answers.

| PASSAGE | PRECISE ADJECTIVE OR STRONG VERB | REWRITE | EFFECT |
| --- | --- | --- | --- |
| *What is the point of this splintered whole?* (paragraph 4) | | | |
| *Historians today bemoan . . .* (paragraph 3) | | | |
| *. . . but tolerance is a vanilla-pudding word . . .* (paragraph 8) | | | |
| *And there is a grudging fairness among the citizens of the United States . . .* (paragraph 7) | | | |

## Write It

📓 **Notebook** Revise each sentence by replacing verbs or adjectives with stronger, more vivid word choices.

1. The crowd yelled at the player after the game.

2. Eloise was happy when she got her driver's license.

3. The campers carried their gear through the tall grass.

4. The garbage smelled bad after it was in the sun.

A QUILT OF A COUNTRY

## Comparing Texts

You will now read "The Immigrant Contribution," which is a chapter from *A Nation of Immigrants*. First, complete the first-read and close-read activities. Then, compare the author's purpose and use of persuasive techniques in "A Quilt of a Country" with those of "The Immigrant Contribution."

THE IMMIGRANT CONTRIBUTION

### About the Author

Born into a family of politicians, **John F. Kennedy** (1917–1963) did not take schooling seriously and was known as a trickster in the classroom. In his junior year at Harvard University, he developed an interest in political philosophy and became more studious. After school, he served in the U.S. Navy during World War II. In 1961, he became the thirty-fifth president of the United States. Tragically, Kennedy was assassinated on November 22, 1963, in Dallas, Texas.

🔧 **Tool Kit**

First-Read Guide and Model Annotation

☰ **STANDARDS**

**RI.9–10.10** By the end of grade 9, read and comprehend literary nonfiction in the grades 9–10 text complexity band proficiently, with scaffolding as needed at the high end of the range.

# The Immigrant Contribution

## Concept Vocabulary

You will encounter the following words as you read "The Immigrant Contribution." Before reading, note how familiar you are with each word. Then, rank the words in order from most familiar (1) to least familiar (6).

| WORD | YOUR RANKING |
|---|---|
| descendants | |
| stock | |
| minority | |
| naturalization | |
| factions | |
| assimilation | |

After completing the first read, come back to the concept vocabulary and review your rankings. Mark any changes to your original rankings.

## First Read NONFICTION

Apply these strategies as you conduct your first read. You will have an opportunity to complete the close-read notes after your first read.

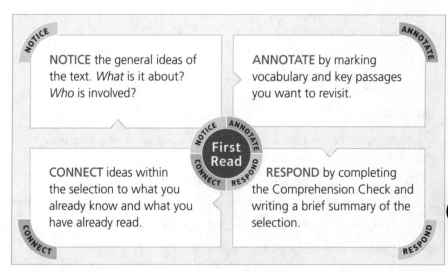

NOTICE the general ideas of the text. *What* is it about? *Who* is involved?

ANNOTATE by marking vocabulary and key passages you want to revisit.

First Read

CONNECT ideas within the selection to what you already know and what you have already read.

RESPOND by completing the Comprehension Check and writing a brief summary of the selection.

# Immigrant Contribution

*from*
## A Nation of Immigrants

### John F. Kennedy

## BACKGROUND

John F. Kennedy wrote the book from which this excerpt was taken when he was a United States senator. He was a prominent supporter of immigrant rights, and ran for president on a platform that included the extension of those rights. He opposed legal distinctions between native-born and naturalized citizens, stating, "There is no place for second-class citizenship in America." He greatly influenced and inspired the immigration reforms of the late twentieth century.

SCAN FOR MULTIMEDIA

1   Oscar Handlin has said, "Once I thought to write a history of the immigrants in America. Then I discovered that the immigrants *were* American history." In the same sense, we cannot really speak of a particular "immigrant contribution" to America because all Americans have been immigrants or the **descendants** of immigrants;

NOTES

**descendants** (dih SEHN duhnts) *n*. people who are the offspring of an ancestor

**stock** (stok) *n.* descendants of a particular individual or ethnic group; family or lineage

**minority** (muh NAWR uh tee) *n.* group of people that differs in some way from the larger population

**naturalization** (NACH uh uh luh ZAY shuhn) *n.* process of becoming a citizen

even the Indians, as mentioned before, migrated to the American continent. We can only speak of people whose roots in America are older or newer. Yet each wave of immigration left its own imprint on American society; each made its distinctive "contribution" to the building of the nation and the evolution of American life. Indeed, if, as some of the older immigrants like to do, we were to restrict the definition of immigrants to the 42 million people who came to the United States *after* the Declaration of Independence, we would have to conclude that our history and our society would have been vastly different if they all had stayed at home.

2    As we have seen, people migrated to the United States for a variety of reasons. But nearly all shared two great hopes: the hope for personal freedom and the hope for economic opportunity. In consequence, the impact of immigration has been broadly to confirm the impulses in American life demanding more political liberty and more economic growth.

3    So, of the fifty-six signers of the Declaration of Independence, eighteen were of non-English **stock** and eight were first-generation immigrants. Two immigrants—the West Indian Alexander Hamilton, who was Washington's Secretary of the Treasury, and the Swiss Albert Gallatin, who held the same office under Jefferson— established the financial policies of the young republic. A German farmer wrote home from Missouri in 1834,

> If you wish to see our whole family living in . . . a country where freedom of speech obtains, where no spies are eavesdropping, where no simpletons criticize your every word and seek to detect therein a venom that might endanger the life of the state, the church and the home, in short, if you wish to be really happy and independent, then come here.

4    Every ethnic **minority**, in seeking its own freedom, helped strengthen the fabric of liberty in American life.

5    Similarly, every aspect of the American economy has profited from the contributions of immigrants. We all know, of course, about the spectacular immigrant successes: the men who came from foreign lands, sought their fortunes in the United States and made striking contributions, industrial and scientific, not only to their chosen country but to the entire world. In 1953 the President's Commission on Immigration and **Naturalization** mentioned the following:

6    Industrialists: Andrew Carnegie (Scot), in the steel industry; John Jacob Astor (German), in the fur trade; Michael Cudahy (Irish), of the meat-packing industry; the Du Ponts (French), of the munitions and chemical industry; Charles L. Fleischmann (Hungarian), of the yeast business; David Sarnoff (Russian), of the radio industry; and William S. Knudsen (Danish), of the automobile industry.

7    Scientists and inventors: Among those whose genius has benefited the United States are Albert Einstein (German), in physics; Michael

^ This photo shows the first Chinese telephone operator in San Francisco in the early part of the twentieth century.

Pupin (Serbian), in electricity; Enrico Fermi (Italian) in atomic research; John Ericsson (Swedish), who invented the ironclad ship and the screw propeller; Giuseppe Bellanca (Italian) and Igor Sikorsky (Russian), who made outstanding contributions to airplane development; John A. Udden (Swedish), who was responsible for opening the Texas oil fields; Lucas P. Kyrides (Greek), industrial chemistry; David Thomas (Welsh), who invented the hot blast furnace; Alexander Graham Bell (Scot), who invented the telephone; Conrad Hubert (Russian), who invented the flashlight; and Ottmar Mergenthaler (German), who invented the linotype machine[1].

8    But the anonymous immigrant played his indispensable role too. Between 1880 and 1920 America became the industrial and agricultural giant of the world as well as the world's leading creditor nation.[2] This could not have been done without the hard labor, the technical skills and the entrepreneurial[3] ability of the 23.5 million people who came to America in this period.

---

1. **linotype machine**  printing machine that sets type in whole lines, instead of letter by letter, in order to print faster.
2. **creditor nation**  country that owes less money to other countries than other countries owe to it.
3. **entrepreneurial**  (on truh pruh NUR ee uhl) *adj.* related to being an entrepreneur, or someone who starts a business and is willing to risk loss in order to make money.

9     Significant as the immigrant role was in politics and in the economy, the immigrant contribution to the professions and the arts was perhaps even greater. Charles O. Paullin's analysis of the *Dictionary of American Biography* shows that, of the eighteenth- and nineteenth-century figures, 20 percent of the businessmen, 20 percent of the scholars and scientists, 23 percent of the painters, 24 percent of the engineers, 28 percent of the architects, 29 percent of the clergymen, 46 percent of the musicians and 61 percent of the actors were of foreign birth—a remarkable measure of the impact of immigration on American culture. And not only have many American writers and artists themselves been immigrants or the children of immigrants, but immigration has provided American literature with one of its major themes.

10     Perhaps the most pervasive influence of immigration is to be found in the innumerable details of life and the customs and habits brought by millions of people who never became famous. This impact was felt from the bottom up, and these contributions to American institutions may be the ones which most intimately affect the lives of all Americans.

11     In the area of religion, all the major American faiths were brought to this country from abroad. The multiplicity of sects established the American tradition of religious pluralism and assured to all the freedom of worship and separation of church and state pledged in the Bill of Rights.

12     So, too, in the very way we speak, immigration has altered American life. In greatly enriching the American vocabulary, it has been a major force in establishing "the American language," which, as H. L. Mencken demonstrated thirty years ago, had diverged materially from the mother tongue as spoken in Britain. Even the American dinner table has felt the impact. One writer has suggested that "typical American menus" might include some of the following dishes: "Irish stew, chop suey, goulash, chile con carne, ravioli, knackwurst mit sauerkraut, Yorkshire pudding, Welsh rarebit, borscht, gefilte fish, Spanish omelet, caviar, mayonnaise, antipasto, baumkuchen, English muffins, Gruyère cheese, Danish pastry, Canadian bacon, hot tamales, wiener schnitzel, petits fours, spumone, bouillabaisse, maté, scones, Turkish coffee, minestrone, filet mignon."

13     Immigration plainly was not always a happy experience. It was hard on the newcomers, and hard as well on the communities to which they came. When poor, ill-educated and frightened people disembarked in a strange land, they often fell prey to native racketeers, unscrupulous businessmen and cynical politicians. Boss Tweed said, characteristically, in defense of his own depredations[4] in New York in the 1870's, "This population is too hopelessly split into races and **factions** to govern it under universal suffrage,[5] except by bribery of patronage, or corruption."

**factions** (FAK shuhnz) *n.* groups of people inside a political party, club, government, etc., working against another group

---

4. **depredations** (dehp ruh DAY shuhnz) *n.* acts of plundering or robbery.
5. **universal suffrage** right to vote for all adults

14 But the very problems of adjustment and **assimilation** presented a challenge to the American idea—a challenge which subjected that idea to stern testing and eventually brought out the best qualities in American society. Thus the public school became a powerful means of preparing the newcomers for American life. The ideal of the "melting pot" symbolized the process of blending many strains into a single nationality, and we have come to realize in modern times that the "melting pot" need not mean the end of particular ethnic identities or traditions. Only in the case of the Negro has the melting pot failed to bring a minority into the full stream of American life. Today we are belatedly, but resolutely, engaged in ending this condition of national exclusion and shame and abolishing forever the concept of second-class citizenship in the United States.

15 Sociologists call the process of the melting pot "social mobility." One of America's characteristics has always been the lack of a rigid class structure. It has traditionally been possible for people to move up the social and economic scale. Even if one did not succeed in moving up oneself, there was always the hope that one's children would. Immigration is by definition a gesture of faith in social mobility. It is the expression in action of a positive belief in the possibility of a better life. It has thus contributed greatly to developing the spirit of personal betterment in American society and to strengthening the national confidence in change and the future. Such confidence, when widely shared, sets the national tone. The opportunities that America offered made the dream real, at least for a good many; but the dream itself was in large part the product of millions of plain people beginning a new life in the conviction that life could indeed be better, and each new wave of immigration rekindled the dream.

16 This is the spirit which so impressed Alexis de Tocqueville,[6] and which he called the spirit of equality. Equality in America has never meant literal equality of condition or capacity; there will always be inequalities in character and ability in any society. Equality has meant rather that, in the words of the Declaration of Independence, "all men are created equal . . . [and] are endowed by their Creator with certain unalienable rights"; it has meant that in a democratic society there should be no inequalities in opportunities or in freedoms. The American philosophy of equality has released the energy of the people, built the economy, subdued the continent, shaped and reshaped the structure of government, and animated the American attitude toward the world outside.

> Immigration is by definition a gesture of faith in social mobility.

**NOTES**

**assimilation** (uh sihm uh LAY shuhn) *n.* process of adapting to the culture of an adopted country

**CLOSE READ**

**ANNOTATE:** Mark nouns and verbs that have positive connotations, or emotional associations, in paragraphs 15 and 16.

**QUESTION:** What common thread of meaning connects these words?

**CONCLUDE:** How do these words add to the author's argument?

6. **Alexis de Tocqueville** (uh LEHK sihs duh TOHK vihl) (1805–1859) French political thinker who traveled through America in 1831. Afterward, he wrote about his experiences in a book called *Democracy in America*.

17  The *continuous* immigration of the nineteenth and early twentieth centuries was thus central to the whole American faith. It gave every old American a standard by which to judge how far he had come and every new American a realization of how far he might go. It reminded every American, old and new, that change is the essence of life, and that American society is a process, not a conclusion. The abundant resources of this land provided the foundation for a great nation. But only people could make the opportunity a reality. Immigration provided the human resources. More than that, it infused the nation with a commitment to far horizons and new frontiers, and thereby kept the pioneer spirit of American life, the spirit of equality and of hope, always alive and strong. "We are the heirs of all time," wrote Herman Melville," and with all nations we divide our inheritance." ❧

# Comprehension Check

Complete the following items after you finish your first read.

1. According to Kennedy, why is it impossible to speak about a particular "immigrant contribution" to the United States?

2. What does Kennedy state are the two main reasons immigrants come to the United States?

3. List five areas in which Kennedy says immigrants have made important contributions to American society.

4. In the case of which minority does Kennedy say the "melting pot" has failed?

5. According to Kennedy, what qualities in American culture impressed Alexis de Tocqueville?

6. 📓 **Notebook** Write a brief summary of "The Immigrant Contribution."

- - - - - - - - - - - - - - - - - - - - - - - - - - - - - - - - - - - - - - - - - - - - - - - - -

## RESEARCH

**Research to Clarify** Choose at least one unfamiliar detail from the text. Briefly research that detail. In what way does the information you learned shed light on an aspect of the essay?

**Research to Explore** Choose one of the immigrant industrialists, scientists, or inventors that Kennedy mentions. Conduct research to learn more about this figure.

THE IMMIGRANT CONTRIBUTION

## Close Read the Text

1. The model, from paragraph 5 of the essay, shows two sample annotations, along with questions and conclusions. Close read the passage and find another detail to annotate. Then, write a question and your conclusion.

**Close Read**
ANNOTATE · QUESTION · CONCLUDE

> ANNOTATE: These words refer to knowledge that "we all" have in common.
>
> QUESTION: Why does the writer make this reference?
>
> CONCLUDE: The reference adds to a sense that the writer and the reader are part of one community.

> ANNOTATE: These verbs all have the same subject, *who*, which refers to "the men."
>
> QUESTION: What is the effect of this string of related verbs and objects?
>
> CONCLUDE: This construction creates a strong sense of forward progress, emphasizing how each action leads to the next.

> We all know, of course, about the spectacular immigrant successes: the men who came from foreign lands, sought their fortunes in the United States and made striking contributions, industrial and scientific, not only to their chosen country but to the entire world.

2. For more practice, go back into the selection, and complete the close-read notes.

3. Revisit a section of the selection you found important during your first read. Read this section closely, and **annotate** what you notice. Ask yourself **questions** such as "Why did the author choose these words?" What can you **conclude**?

## Analyze the Text

**CITE TEXTUAL EVIDENCE**
to support your answers.

📓 **Notebook** Respond to these questions.

1. **Analyze** Does Oscar Hanlin's statement support or refute Kennedy's main idea as it is expressed in the first paragraph of this selection? Explain.

2. (a) What information does Kennedy provide about the immigrant status of some of the signers of the Declaration of Independence?
(b) **Analyze** How does this information connect to his earlier point about all Americans?

3. (a) According to Kennedy, what did the idea of the "melting pot" once mean? (b) **Infer** For Kennedy, how has that ideal changed in modern times? Explain.

4. **Essential Question:** *What does it mean to be "American"?* What have you learned about the nature of American identity from reading this essay?

## STANDARDS

**RI.9–10.1** Cite strong and thorough textual evidence to support analysis of what the text says explicitly as well as inferences drawn from the text.

**RI.9–10.5** Analyze in detail how an author's ideas or claims are developed and refined by particular sentences, paragraphs, or larger portions of a text.

**RI.9–10.6** Determine an author's point of view or purpose in a text and analyze how an author uses rhetoric to advance that point or view or purpose.

# Analyze Craft and Structure

**Purpose and Persuasion** An **author's purpose** is his or her reason for writing. A writer may want to inform or explain, to persuade, to entertain, or to reflect. Writers may also have more than one purpose for creating a particular text. For example, a writer may want to inform readers about a topic while also persuading them to see something in a new way. Those purposes direct the writer's choices, including the types of **persuasive appeals,** or methods of informing and convincing readers, to use. There are three main types of persuasive appeals:

- **Appeals to Authority:** the statements of experts on the topic.
- **Appeals to Reason:** logical arguments based on verifiable evidence, such as facts or data.
- **Appeals to Emotion:** statements intended to affect readers' feelings about a subject. These statements may include **charged language—** words with strong positive or negative associations.

In this essay, John F. Kennedy uses all three types of appeal to great effect. As you read, think about Kennedy's purpose for writing. Ask yourself, "Why does the writer include this information?"

## Practice

CITE TEXTUAL EVIDENCE to support your answers.

📓 **Notebook  Respond to these questions.**

1. Use the chart to record at least two examples of each of the persuasive techniques Kennedy uses in this essay. Explain in what ways each example makes Kennedy's ideas more or less convincing.

| PERSUASIVE TECHNIQUE | EXAMPLES FROM THE TEXT | EFFECTIVE OR INEFFECTIVE? |
|---|---|---|
| Appeal to Authority | | |
| Appeal to Emotion, including charged language | | |
| Appeal to Reason | | |

2. **(a)** Which technique does Kennedy use the most? Explain. **(b)** Why do you think he emphasizes this technique over the others? Explain.

3. Which type of persuasive technique do you find most effective in this essay? Why?

THE IMMIGRANT CONTRIBUTION

## Concept Vocabulary

| descendants | minority | factions |
|---|---|---|
| stock | naturalization | assimilation |

**Why These Words?** These concept words are related to populations and group identities. For example, in the first paragraph of the selection, John F. Kennedy asserts that "all Americans have been immigrants or descendants of immigrants." The word *descendants* refers to the offspring of immigrants.

1. Select two concept vocabulary words other than *descendants*. How does each word relate to ideas about populations and group identities? Explain.

2. What other words in the selection connect to the concepts of populations and group identities?

**WORD NETWORK**

Add interesting words related to American identity from the text to your Word Network.

## Practice

**Notebook** The concept vocabulary words appear in "The Immigrant Contribution." Tell whether each sentence does or does not make sense. Explain your reasoning.

1. Over time, the opinions of certain *factions* may become more popular.

2. American citizens returning from Europe must go through a process of *naturalization*.

3. The U.S. Constitution and Bill of Rights were intended to protect the rights of all American citizens, including those from a *minority* background.

4. Some immigrants may prefer *assimilation* as a way of preserving their cultures of origin.

5. Some historians believe that Native Americans were originally of Asian *stock*.

6. Many third-generation Americans are *descendants* of several different ethnic groups.

## Word Study

**Latin root: -*nat*-** The Latin root -*nat*- means "birth" or "to be born." The root appears in many common words related to populations and group identities.

1. Write a definition of the word *naturalization* that demonstrates your understanding of how the Latin root -*nat*- contributes to its meaning.

2. Reread paragraphs 13 and 14 of "The Immigrant Contribution." Mark two other words that contain the Latin root -*nat*-. Write a definition for each word.

**STANDARDS**

**L.9–10.1.b** Use various types of phrases and clauses to convey specific meanings and add variety and interest to writing or presentations.

**L.9–10.4.b** Identify and correctly use patterns of word changes that indicate different meanings or parts of speech and continue to apply knowledge of Greek and Latin roots and affixes.

# Conventions

**Sentence Structure** Sentences can be classified by the number of independent and dependent clauses they contain. An **independent clause** has a subject and verb and can stand alone as a complete thought. A **dependent,** or **subordinate, clause** also has a subject and verb, but it cannot stand alone as a complete thought. A dependent clause begins either with a subordinating conjunction, such as *when, although, because,* or *while,* or with a relative pronoun, such as *who, whose, which,* or *that.*

This chart shows the four basic sentence structures. Independent clauses are underlined once, and dependent clauses are underlined twice.

**CLARIFICATION**
Refer to the Grammar Handbook to learn more about these terms.

| SENTENCE STRUCTURE | ELEMENTS | EXAMPLE |
|---|---|---|
| simple | a single independent clause | Anand saw the audience for the first time. |
| compound | two or more independent clauses, joined either by a comma and a coordinating conjunction or by a semicolon | The lights came on, and Anand saw the audience for the first time. |
| complex | one independent clause and one or more dependent clauses | When the lights came on, Anand saw the audience for the first time. |
| compound-complex | two or more independent clauses and one or more dependent clauses | When the lights came on, Anand saw the audience for the first time, and he waved to his parents, who were sitting in the front row. |

## Read It

Label each of these sentences from "The Immigrant Contribution" *simple, compound, complex,* or *compound-complex.*

1. This impact was felt from the bottom up, and these contributions to American institutions may be the ones which most intimately affect the lives of all Americans.

2. Immigration provided the human resources.

3. Equality in America has never meant literal equality of condition or capacity; there will always be inequalities in character and ability in any society.

4. We can only speak of people whose roots in America are older or newer.

## Write It

 **Notebook** Write a paragraph containing a simple sentence, a compound sentence, a complex sentence, and a compound-complex sentence.

A QUILT OF A COUNTRY

THE IMMIGRANT CONTRIBUTION

# Writing to Compare

You have read two essays that discuss American cultural diversity. Deepen your understanding of both texts by comparing each writer's diction. **Diction** is a writer's way of using language to create a unique voice.

## Assignment

**Diction** is a writer's choice and arrangement of words and phrases.

- Diction may be formal, informal, ordinary, technical, sophisticated, down-to-earth, old-fashioned, modern, or even slangy.
- The types of diction an author uses reflect the readers, or **audience,** for whom he or she is writing. A writer's diction also reveals his or her **tone,** or attitude.

The essays by Quindlen and Kennedy share a topic, but are very different in diction and tone. Write an **essay** in which you consider how diction and tone reflect each author's purpose, audience, and message.

## Prewriting

**Analyze the Texts** Scan the two texts, and choose two passages from each one that you think use especially interesting language. Describe the type of diction each passage displays. You may use the following categories or add categories of your own. Note that writers may use more than one type of diction in a single passage.

Informal / Formal / Poetic / Ordinary / Sophisticated / Slangy
Technical / Scientific / Concrete / Abstract

**Gather your observations in the chart.**

| PASSAGES | TYPE(S) OF DICTION |
| --- | --- |
| **A Quilt of a Country**<br><br>1.<br><br><br>2. | 1.<br><br><br>2. |
| **The Immigrant Contribution**<br><br>1.<br><br><br>2. | 1.<br><br><br>2. |

🔘 **Notebook** Respond to these questions.

1. For each passage in your chart, explain the tone the diction creates.

2. How does each author's diction and tone reflect his or her purpose for writing and the audience he or she is trying to reach?

## STANDARDS

**RI.9–10.4** Determine the meaning of words and phrases as they are used in a text, including figurative, connotative, and technical meanings; analyze the cumulative impact of specific word choices on meaning and tone.

**W.9–10.2** Write informative/explanatory texts to examine and convey complex ideas, concepts, and information clearly and accurately through the effective selection, organization, and analysis of content.

**W.9–10.9.b** Apply grades 9–10 Reading standards to literary nonfiction.

## Drafting

**Identify Passages and Ideas** Use your Prewriting notes to identify passages to use as examples in your essay. Make sure each passage clearly displays an aspect of Quindlen's or Kennedy's diction that you think offers a clear difference or a clear similarity. Identify the passages, and note the idea you will use each one to support.

Example Passage: _____

    Point It Will Support:

Example Passage: _____

    Point It Will Support:

Example Passage: _____

    Point It Will Support:

Example Passage: _____

    Point It Will Support:

**Write a Thesis** In one sentence, state the central idea you will explore in your essay. As you write, feel free to modify this statement to reflect changes to your ideas.

    Central Idea/Thesis: _____

    _____

**Organize Ideas** Make some organizational decisions before you begin to write. Consider using one of these two structures:

- **Grouping Ideas:** discuss all the similarities in the diction and tone of the two essays and then all of the differences
- **Grouping Texts:** discuss the diction and tone of one essay and then the diction and tone of the other essay

**Elaborate With Examples** Start with a statement, and then add examples.

> **Statement:** Some writers use concrete diction to clarify abstract ideas.
>
> **With Example:** Some writers use concrete diction to clarify abstract ideas. For example, when discussing conflicts in American culture, Quindlen uses concrete terms such as "slavery and sweatshops."

## Review, Revise, and Edit

Once you are done drafting, review your essay. Because your essay is about multiple subjects—the diction and tone of two different texts—clarity and balance are critical. If you see an imbalance or unclear statements, add more analysis, detail, or examples.

**About the Author**

**Judith Ortiz Cofer**
(1952–2016) spent her
childhood in two different
cultures. Born in Puerto Rico,
she moved with her parents
to Paterson, New Jersey,
when she was very young.
She grew up mostly in
Paterson, but she also spent
time in Puerto Rico with her
*abuela* (grandmother). It was
from her grandmother that
Ortiz Cofer learned the art of
storytelling. In her own work,
Ortiz Cofer teaches readers
about the richness and
difficulty of coming of age in
two cultures at once.

🔧 **Tool Kit**
First-Read Guide and
Model Annotation

# American History

## Concept Vocabulary

You will encounter the following words as you read "American History."
Before reading, note how familiar you are with each word. Then, rank the
words in order from most familiar (1) to least familiar (6).

| WORD | YOUR RANKING |
| --- | --- |
| anticipated | |
| infatuated | |
| enthralled | |
| devoted | |
| elation | |
| impulse | |

After completing the first read, return to the concept vocabulary and review
your rankings. Make changes to your original rankings as needed.

## First Read FICTION

Apply these strategies as you conduct your first read. You will have an
opportunity to complete the close-read notes after your first read.

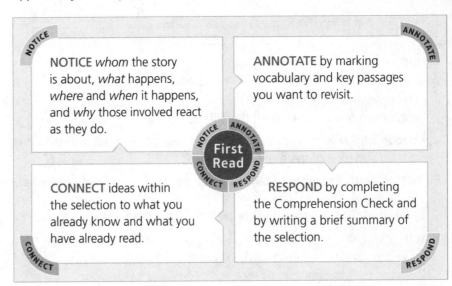

**NOTICE** *whom* the story is about, *what* happens, *where* and *when* it happens, and *why* those involved react as they do.

**ANNOTATE** by marking vocabulary and key passages you want to revisit.

**First Read**

**CONNECT** ideas within the selection to what you already know and what you have already read.

**RESPOND** by completing the Comprehension Check and by writing a brief summary of the selection.

**STANDARDS**

**RL.9–10.10** By the end of grade 9,
read and comprehend literature,
including stories, dramas, and poems,
in the grades 9–10 text complexity
band proficiently, with scaffolding as
needed at the high end of the range.

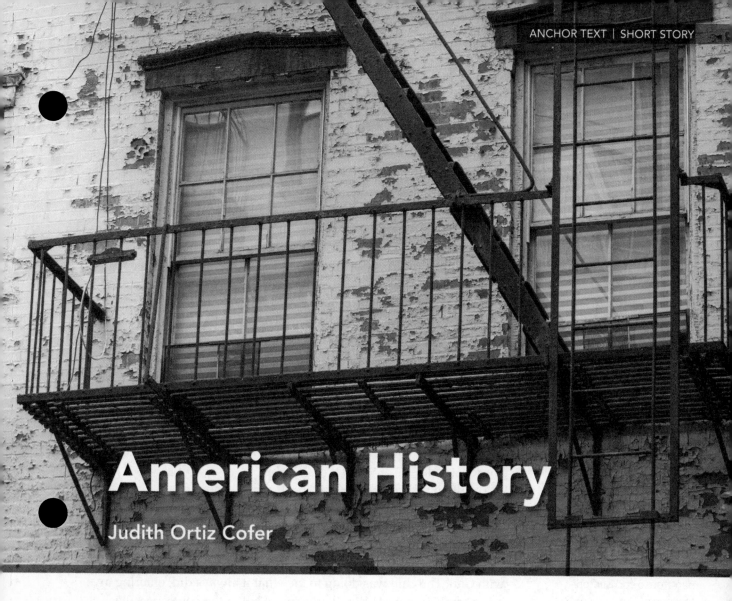

# American History

Judith Ortiz Cofer

## BACKGROUND

On November 22, 1963, President John F. Kennedy was shot and killed in Dallas, Texas, and the United States was plunged into mourning. Most people who lived through that time can still remember where they were when they heard the news. Kennedy's assassination and the nation's grief defined a generation. Key events in this story take place on that fateful day.

SCAN FOR MULTIMEDIA

1   I once read in a "Ripley's Believe It or Not" column that Paterson, New Jersey, is the place where the Straight and Narrow (streets) intersect. The Puerto Rican tenement known as *El Building* was one block up from Straight. It was, in fact, the corner of Straight and Market; not "at" the corner, but *the* corner. At almost any hour of the day, El Building was like a monstrous jukebox, blasting out *salsas*[1] from open windows as the residents, mostly new immigrants just up from the island, tried to drown out whatever they were currently enduring with loud music. But the day President Kennedy was shot there was a profound silence in El Building; even the abusive tongues of viragoes,[2] the cursing of the unemployed, and the screeching of

NOTES

---

1. **salsas** (SAHL suhz) songs written in a particular Latin American musical style.
2. **viragoes** (vih RAH gohz) fierce, irritable women with loud voices.

small children had been somehow muted. President Kennedy was a saint to these people. In fact, soon his photograph would be hung alongside the Sacred Heart and over the spiritist altars that many women kept in their apartments. He would become part of the hierarchy of martyrs they prayed to for favors that only one who had died for a cause would understand.

2    On the day that President Kennedy was shot, my ninth grade class had been out in the fenced playground of Public School Number 13. We had been given "free" exercise time and had been ordered by our P.E. teacher, Mr. DePalma, to "keep moving." That meant that the girls should jump rope and the boys toss basketballs through a hoop at the far end of the yard. He in the meantime would "keep an eye" on us from just inside the building.

3    It was a cold gray day in Paterson. The kind that warns of early snow. I was miserable, since I had forgotten my gloves, and my knuckles were turning red and raw from the jump rope. I was also taking a lot of abuse from the black girls for not turning the rope hard and fast enough for them.

4    "Hey, Skinny Bones, pump it, girl. Ain't you got no energy today?" Gail, the biggest of the black girls had the other end of the rope, yelled, "Didn't you eat your rice and beans and pork chops for breakfast today?"

5    The other girls picked up the "pork chops" and made it into a refrain: "pork chop, pork chop, did you eat your pork chop?" They entered the double ropes in pairs and exited without tripping or missing a beat. I felt a burning on my cheeks and then my glasses fogged up so that I could not manage to coordinate the jump rope with Gail. The chill was doing to me what it always did; entering my bones, making me cry, humiliating me. I hated the city, especially in winter. I hated Public School Number 13. I hated my skinny flat-chested body, and I envied the black girls who could jump rope so fast that their legs became a blur. They always seemed to be warm while I froze.

6    There was only one source of beauty and light for me that school year. The only thing I had **anticipated** at the start of the semester. That was seeing Eugene. In August, Eugene and his family had moved into the only house on the block that had a yard and trees. I could see his place from my window in El Building. In fact, if I sat on the fire escape I was literally suspended above Eugene's backyard. It was my favorite spot to read my library books in the summer. Until that August the house had been occupied by an old Jewish couple. Over the years I had become part of their family, without their knowing it, of course. I had a view of their kitchen and their backyard, and though I could not hear what they said, I knew when they were arguing, when one of them was sick, and many other things. I knew all this by watching them at mealtimes. I could see their kitchen table, the sink, and the stove. During good times, he

## CLOSE READ

**ANNOTATE:** In paragraph 5, mark words and phrases related to temperature.

**QUESTION:** Why is the narrator so focused on feelings of hot and cold?

**CONCLUDE:** How do these details help readers understand Elena's feelings of isolation?

**anticipated** (an TIHS uh payt ihd) *v.* eagerly expected

sat at the table and read his newspapers while she fixed the meals. If they argued, he would leave and the old woman would sit and stare at nothing for a long time. When one of them was sick, the other would come and get things from the kitchen and carry them out on a tray. The old man had died in June. The last week of school I had not seen him at the table at all. Then one day I saw that there was a crowd in the kitchen. The old woman had finally emerged from the house on the arm of a stocky, middle-aged woman, whom I had seen there a few times before, maybe her daughter. Then a man had carried out suitcases. The house had stood empty for weeks. I had had to resist the temptation to climb down into the yard and water the flowers the old lady had taken such good care of.

7    By the time Eugene's family moved in, the yard was a tangled mass of weeds. The father had spent several days mowing, and when he finished, from where I sat, I didn't see the red, yellow, and purple clusters that meant flowers to me. I didn't see this family sit down at the kitchen table together. It was just the mother, a red-headed tall woman who wore a white uniform—a nurse's, I guessed it was; the father was gone before I got up in the morning and was never there at dinner time. I only saw him on weekends when they sometimes sat on lawn chairs under the oak tree, each hidden behind a section of the newspaper; and there was Eugene. He was tall and blond, and he wore glasses. I liked him right away because he sat at the kitchen table and read books for hours. That summer, before we had even spoken one word to each other, I kept him company on my fire escape.

> I saw then that he was blushing deeply. Eugene liked me, but he was shy.

8    Once school started I looked for him in all my classes, but P.S. 13 was a huge, overpopulated place and it took me days and many discreet questions to discover that Eugene was in honors classes for all his subjects; classes that were not open to me because English was not my first language, though I was a straight A student. After much maneuvering, I managed "to run into him" in the hallway where his locker was—on the other side of the building from mine—and in study hall at the library where he first seemed to notice me, but did not speak; and finally, on the way home after school one day when I decided to approach him directly, though my stomach was doing somersaults.

9    I was ready for rejection, snobbery, the worst. But when I came up to him, practically panting in my nervousness, and blurted out: "You're Eugene. Right?" he smiled, pushed his glasses up on his nose, and nodded. I saw then that he was blushing deeply. Eugene liked me, but he was shy. I did most of the talking that day. He nodded and smiled a lot. In the weeks that followed, we walked home together. He would linger at the corner of El Building for a few minutes then walk down to his two-story house. It was not until

Eugene moved into that house that I noticed that El Building blocked most of the sun, and that the only spot that got a little sunlight during the day was the tiny square of earth the old woman had planted with flowers.

10      I did not tell Eugene that I could see inside his kitchen from my bedroom. I felt dishonest, but I liked my secret sharing of his evenings, especially now that I knew what he was reading since we chose our books together at the school library.

11      One day my mother came into my room as I was sitting on the window-sill staring out. In her abrupt way she said: "Elena, you are acting 'moony.'" *Enamorada*[3] was what she really said, that is—like a girl stupidly **infatuated**. Since I had turned fourteen my mother had been more vigilant than ever. She acted as if I was going to go crazy or explode or something if she didn't watch me and nag me all the time about being a *señorita*[4] now. She kept talking about virtue, morality, and other subjects that did not interest me in the least. My mother was unhappy in Paterson, but my father had a good job at the bluejeans factory in Passaic and soon, he kept assuring us, we would be moving to our own house there. Every Sunday we drove out to the suburbs of Paterson, Clifton, and Passaic, out to where people mowed grass on Sundays in the summer, and where children made snowmen in the winter from pure white snow, not like the gray slush of Paterson which seemed to fall from the sky in that hue. I had learned to listen to my parents' dreams, which were spoken in Spanish, as fairy tales, like the stories about life in the island paradise of Puerto Rico before I was born. I had been to the island once as a little girl, to grandmother's funeral, and all I remembered was wailing women in black, my mother becoming hysterical and being given a pill that made her sleep two days, and me feeling lost in a crowd of strangers all claiming to be my aunts, uncles, and cousins. I had actually been glad to return to the city. We had not been back there since then, though my parents talked constantly about buying a house on the beach someday, retiring on the island—that was a common topic among the residents of El Building. As for me, I was going to go to college and become a teacher.

12      But after meeting Eugene I began to think of the present more than of the future. What I wanted now was to enter that house I had watched for so many years. I wanted to see the other rooms where the old people had lived, and where the boy spent his time. Most of all, I wanted to sit at the kitchen table with Eugene like two adults, like the old man and his wife had done, maybe drink some coffee and talk about books. I had started reading *Gone with the Wind*. I was **enthralled** by it, with the daring and the passion of the beautiful girl living in a mansion, and with her **devoted** parents and the slaves who did everything for them. I didn't believe such a world had ever really existed, and I wanted to ask Eugene some questions since he and his

**infatuated** (ihn FACH oo ayt ihd) *adj.* briefly but intensely in love

**enthralled** (ehn THRAWLD) *v.* captivated

**devoted** (dih VOHT ihd) *adj.* loving, loyal, and concerned with another's well-being

---

3. *Enamorada* (ay nah moh RAH dah) Spanish for "enamored; lovesick."
4. *señorita* (seh nyoh REE tah) Spanish for "young lady."

parents, he had told me, had come up from Georgia, the same place where the novel was set. His father worked for a company that had transferred him to Paterson. His mother was very unhappy, Eugene said, in his beautiful voice that rose and fell over words in a strange, lilting way. The kids at school called him "the hick" and made fun of the way he talked. I knew I was his only friend so far, and I liked that, though I felt sad for him sometimes. "Skinny Bones" and the "Hick" was what they called us at school when we were seen together.

13    The day Mr. DePalma came out into the cold and asked us to line up in front of him was the day that President Kennedy was shot. Mr. DePalma, a short, muscular man with slicked-down black hair, was the science teacher, P.E. coach, and disciplinarian at P.S. 13. He was the teacher to whose homeroom you got assigned if you were a troublemaker, and the man called out to break up playground fights, and to escort violently angry teenagers to the office. And Mr. DePalma was the man who called your parents in for "a conference."

14    That day, he stood in front of two rows of mostly black and Puerto Rican kids, brittle from their efforts to "keep moving" on a November day that was turning bitter cold. Mr. DePalma, to our complete shock, was crying. Not just silent adult tears, but really sobbing. There were a few titters from the back of the line where I stood shivering.

15    "Listen," Mr. DePalma raised his arms over his head as if he were about to conduct an orchestra. His voice broke, and he covered his face with his hands. His barrel chest was heaving. Someone giggled behind me.

16    "Listen," he repeated, "something awful has happened." A strange gurgling came from his throat, and he turned around and spat on the cement behind him.

17    "Gross," someone said, and there was a lot of laughter.

18 "The President is dead, you idiots. I should have known that wouldn't mean anything to a bunch of losers like you kids. Go home." He was shrieking now. No one moved for a minute or two, but then a big girl let out a "Yeah!" and ran to get her books piled up with the others against the brick wall of the school building. The others followed in a mad scramble to get to their things before somebody caught on. It was still an hour to the dismissal bell.

19 A little scared, I headed for El Building. There was an eerie feeling on the streets. I looked into Mario's drugstore, a favorite hangout for the high school crowd, but there were only a couple of old Jewish men at the soda-bar talking with the short order cook in tones that sounded almost angry, but they were keeping their voices low. Even the traffic on one of the busiest intersections in Paterson—Straight Street and Park Avenue— seemed to be moving slower. There were no horns blasting that day. At El Building, the usual little group of unemployed men were not hanging out on the front stoop making it difficult for women to enter the front door. No music spilled out from open doors in the hallway. When I walked into our apartment, I found my mother sitting in front of the grainy picture of the television set.

> "You are going out *today*?" The way she said "today" sounded as if a storm warning had been issued.

20 She looked up at me with a tear-streaked face and just said: "*Dios mio,*"[5] turning back to the set as if it were pulling at her eyes. I went into my room.

21 Though I wanted to feel the right thing about President Kennedy's death, I could not fight the feeling of **elation** that stirred in my chest. Today was the day I was to visit Eugene in his house. He had asked me to come over after school to study for an American history test with him. We had also planned to walk to the public library together. I looked down into his yard. The oak tree was bare of leaves and the ground looked gray with ice. The light through the large kitchen window of his house told me that El Building blocked the sun to such an extent that they had to turn lights on in the middle of the day. I felt ashamed about it. But the white kitchen table with the lamp hanging just above it looked cozy and inviting. I would soon sit there, across from Eugene, and I would tell him about my perch just above his house. Maybe I should.

22 In the next thirty minutes I changed clothes, put on a little pink lipstick, and got my books together. Then I went in to tell my mother that I was going to a friend's house to study. I did not expect her reaction.

23 "You are going out *today*?" The way she said "today" sounded as if a storm warning had been issued. It was said in utter disbelief.

**elation** (ee LAY shuhn) *n.* great happiness and excitement

---

5. **Dios mío** (DEE ohs MEE oh) Spanish for "My God!"

Before I could answer, she came toward me and held my elbows as I clutched my books.

24    "*Hija*,[6] the President has been killed. We must show respect. He was a great man. Come to church with me tonight."

25    She tried to embrace me, but my books were in the way. My first **impulse** was to comfort her, she seemed so distraught, but I had to meet Eugene in fifteen minutes.

26    "I have a test to study for, Mama. I will be home by eight."

27    "You are forgetting who you are, *Niña*[7]. I have seen you staring down at that boy's house. You are heading for humiliation and pain." My mother said this in Spanish and in a resigned tone that surprised me, as if she had no intention of stopping me from "heading for humiliation and pain." I started for the door. She sat in front of the TV holding a white handkerchief to her face.

28    I walked out to the street and around the chainlink fence that separated El Building from Eugene's house. The yard was neatly edged around the little walk that led to the door. It always amazed me how Paterson, the inner core of the city, had no apparent logic to its architecture. Small, neat, single residences like this one could be found right next to huge, dilapidated apartment buildings like El Building. My guess was that the little houses had been there first, then the immigrants had come in droves, and the monstrosities had been raised for them—the Italians, the Irish, the Jews, and now us, the Puerto Ricans and the blacks. The door was painted a deep green: *verde*, the color of hope, I had heard my mother say it: *Verde-Esperanza*.[8]

29    I knocked softly. A few suspenseful moments later the door opened just a crack. The red, swollen face of a woman appeared. She had a halo of red hair floating over a delicate ivory face—the face of a doll—with freckles on the nose. Her smudged eye make-up made her look unreal to me, like a mannequin seen through a warped store window.

30    "What do you want?" Her voice was tiny and sweet-sounding, like a little girl's, but her tone was not friendly.

31    "I'm Eugene's friend. He asked me over. To study." I thrust out my books, a silly gesture that embarrassed me almost immediately.

32    "You live there?" She pointed up to El Building, which looked particularly ugly, like a gray prison with its many dirty windows and rusty fire escapes. The woman had stepped halfway out and I could see that she wore a white nurse's uniform with St. Joseph's Hospital on the name tag.

33    "Yes. I do."

34    She looked intently at me for a couple of heartbeats, then said as if to herself, "I don't know how you people do it." Then directly to me: "Listen. Honey. Eugene doesn't want to study with you. He is a smart

NOTES

**impulse** (IHM puls) *n.* sudden urge to act or do something

**CLOSE READ**

**ANNOTATE:** In paragraphs 29 and 30, mark details that describe Eugene's mother's appearance and behavior.

**QUESTION:** Which details suggest softness or sweetness, and which suggest hardness or harshness?

**CONCLUDE:** What is the effect of these contrasting details?

---

6. **Hija** (EE hah) Spanish for "daughter."
7. **Niña** (NEE nyah) Spanish for "child," used here as an endearment.
8. **Verde-Esperanza** (vehr day ehs pay RAHN sah) Spanish for "green-hope."

boy. Doesn't need help. You understand me. I am truly sorry if he told you you could come over. He cannot study with you. It's nothing personal. You understand? We won't be in this place much longer, no need for him to get close to people—it'll just make it harder for him later. Run back home now."

35     I couldn't move. I just stood there in shock at hearing these things said to me in such a honey-drenched voice. I had never heard an accent like hers, except for Eugene's softer version. It was as if she were singing me a little song.

36     "What's wrong? Didn't you hear what I said?" She seemed very angry, and I finally snapped out of my trance. I turned away from the green door, and heard her close it gently.

37     Our apartment was empty when I got home. My mother was in someone else's kitchen, seeking the solace she needed. Father would come in from his late shift at midnight. I would hear them talking softly in the kitchen for hours that night. They would not discuss their dreams for the future, or life in Puerto Rico, as they often did; that night they would talk sadly about the young widow and her two children, as if they were family. For the next few days, we would observe *luto*[9] in our apartment; that is, we would practice restraint and silence—no loud music or laughter. Some of the women of El Building would wear black for weeks.

38     That night, I lay in my bed trying to feel the right thing for our dead President. But the tears that came up from a deep source inside me were strictly for me. When my mother came to the door, I pretended to be sleeping. Sometime during the night, I saw from my bed the streetlight come on. It had a pink halo around it. I went to my window and pressed my face to the cool glass. Looking up at the light I could see the white snow falling like a lace veil over its face. I did not look down to see it turning gray as it touched the ground below. ❧

---

9. **luto** (LOO toh) Spanish for "mourning."

# Comprehension Check

Complete the following items after you finish your first read.

**1.** On what memorable day in history does this story take place?

**2.** How does the narrator first become aware of Eugene?

**3.** Why does the narrator like Eugene even before she meets him?

**4.** According to her mother, how does Elena seem to feel about Eugene?

**5.** How does Eugene's mother react to Elena's visit?

**6.** ⊟ **Notebook** Write a summary of "American History."

- - - - - - - - - - - - - - - - - - - - - - - - - - - - - - - - - - - - - - - - - - - - - - -

## RESEARCH

**Research to Clarify** Choose at least one unfamiliar detail from the text. Briefly research that detail. In what way does the information you learned shed light on an aspect of the story?

**Research to Explore** Choose something from the text that interested you, and formulate a research question.

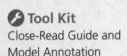

AMERICAN HISTORY

## Close Read the Text

1. The model, from paragraph 1 of the story, shows two sample annotations, along with questions and conclusions. Close read the passage and find another detail to annotate. Then, write a question and your conclusion.

**Close Read**
ANNOTATE · QUESTION · CONCLUDE

ANNOTATE: This clause includes strong, emotionally charged language.

QUESTION: What do these words suggest about the nature of life in El Building?

CONCLUDE: *Whatever* and *currently* suggest that the people had many different problems, while the word *enduring* suggests that they faced long-term struggles with no easy solutions.

At almost any hour of the day, El Building was like a monstrous jukebox, blasting out *salsas* from open windows as the residents, mostly new immigrants just up from the island, tried to drown out whatever they were currently enduring with loud music.

ANNOTATE: These two words are especially colorful.

QUESTION: What picture of El Building is the narrator painting with these word choices?

CONCLUDE: *Monstrous* suggests El Building is large, strange, and dangerous. *Blasting* suggests loudness and aggression. It is a big, fierce place.

🔧 **Tool Kit**
Close-Read Guide and Model Annotation

2. For more practice, go back into the selection, and complete the close-read notes.

3. Revisit a section of the text you found important during your first read. Read this section closely, and **annotate** what you notice. Ask yourself **questions** such as "Why did the author make this choice?" What can you **conclude**?

## Analyze the Text

**CITE TEXTUAL EVIDENCE**
to support your answers.

📓 **Notebook** Respond to these questions.

1. **Compare and Contrast** Explain the contrast in Elena's feelings toward her own home and Eugene's house. Cite descriptive details that reflect these feelings.

2. **Analyze** In what ways does this story reflect social issues facing America in the 1960s? Consider descriptions of Elena's school and neighborhood, as well as Eugene's mother's reaction to Elena.

3. **(a)** What subject is Elena planning to study with Eugene?
**(b) Interpret** What other reasons might Ortiz Cofer have for calling this story "American History"?

4. **Essential Question:** *What does it mean to be "American"?* What have you learned about American identity from reading this selection?

📑 **STANDARDS**
**RL.9–10.3** Analyze how complex characters develop over the course of a text, interact with other characters, and advance the plot or develop the theme.

# Analyze Craft and Structure

**Narrative Structure** Every story is driven by a **conflict**, or struggle between opposing forces. Characters in stories may face two different types of conflict—internal and external.

- In an **internal conflict**, a character grapples with his or her own beliefs, values, needs, or desires. For example, a character may know something is wrong but still be pulled to do it.

- In an **external conflict**, a character struggles against an outside force. This force may be another character, nature, or society. For example, a character trying to survive a hurricane at sea is experiencing an external conflict.

A character's efforts to resolve, or fix, a conflict form the basis for the plot of a story. In "American History," the main character, Elena, experiences both internal and external conflicts.

## Practice

**CITE TEXTUAL EVIDENCE** to support your answers.

📓 **Notebook** Respond to these questions.

1. (a) What is the main conflict in this story? (b) Is that main conflict primarily external or internal? Explain.

2. Use the chart to identify conflicts Elena faces in addition to the main conflict. For each conflict you note, identify at least one story detail that supports your answer.

| ELENA VS. AN OUTSIDE FORCE | ELENA VS. HERSELF |
|---|---|
|  |  |
|  |  |
|  |  |
|  |  |

3. (a) In the last scene of the story, why does Elena say that her tears are just for herself? (b) In what ways does the assassination of the president both add to and minimize the importance of Elena's suffering? Explain.

AMERICAN HISTORY

# Concept Vocabulary

| | | |
|---|---|---|
| anticipated | enthralled | elation |
| infatuated | devoted | impulse |

**Why These Words?** The six concept vocabulary words from the text all involve having a fascination with or an attraction to something. For example, Elena is *enthralled* by the book *Gone With the Wind*. She is captivated by the story, which is set in a romantic and tragic place.

1. How do the vocabulary words help the writer describe characters' emotions?

2. Find two other words in the selection that describe a strong emotion.

## Practice

📄 **Notebook** The concept vocabulary words appear in "American History."

1. Use each concept vocabulary word in a sentence that demonstrates its meaning.

2. Rewrite each sentence using a synonym for the concept vocabulary word. How does the replacement change the meaning of the sentence?

# Word Study

**Cognates** When two words in different languages share a common origin, they are called **cognates**. Often, they are spelled and pronounced similarly in the two languages and still share a common meaning. Recognizing when two words are cognates can help you determine an unfamiliar word's meaning. If you know Spanish, for example, you can quickly guess the meanings of the English words *bicycle* and *paradise* from knowing their Spanish cognates: *bicicleta* and *paraíso*.

1. For each Spanish word in the chart, write its English cognate. Then, write the meaning the pair of cognates shares.

| SPANISH WORD | ENGLISH COGNATE | MEANING |
|---|---|---|
| *anticipación* | | |
| *pasión* | | |

2. Look back at paragraph 11 of "American History." What English word is a cognate of the Spanish word *enamorada*? Write the word and its definition. Consult a bilingual dictionary if necessary.

## 🔗 WORD NETWORK

Add interesting words related to American identity from the text to your Word Network.

## ▤ STANDARDS

**L.9–10.1.b** Use various types of phrases and clauses to convey specific meanings and add variety and interest to writing or presentations.

**L.9–10.4.c** Consult general and specialized reference materials, both print and digital, to find the pronunciation of a word or determine or clarify its precise meaning, its part of speech, or its etymology.

**L.9–10.5** Demonstrate understanding of figurative language, word relationships, and nuances in word meanings.

## Conventions

**Types of Phrases** A **preposition** is a word such as *of, in, to, for* or *with* that relates a noun or a pronoun to another word in the sentence. A **prepositional phrase** is a group of words that begins with a preposition and ends with a noun or pronoun, called the **object of the preposition**.

When a prepositional phrase modifies a noun or a pronoun, by telling *what kind* or *which one*, it is an **adjective phrase.** When it modifies a verb, an adjective, or an adverb, by pointing out *where, why, when, in what way*, or *to what extent*, it is an **adverb phrase.** In the chart, the prepositional phrases are italicized, and the words they modify are underlined.

CLARIFICATION
Refer to the Grammar Handbook to learn more about these terms.

| SENTENCE | TYPE OF PHRASE | HOW PHRASE FUNCTIONS |
|---|---|---|
| Let's take a picture *of the Eiffel Tower*. | adjective phrase | tells *what kind* |
| The snowball *on the table* melted. | adjective phrase | tells *which one* |
| I left my wallet *in the car*. | adverb phrase | tells *where* |
| The other team played *with more skill*. | adverb phrase | tells *in what way* |

### Read It

1. Mark every prepositional phrase in each of these sentences. Then, indicate whether each phrase is an adjective phrase or an adverb phrase.

   a. Elena's mother was unhappy in Paterson.

   b. When Elena sat on the fire escape, she was above Eugene's backyard.

   c. The boys tossed basketballs through a hoop in the yard.

2. Reread paragraph 29 of "American History." Mark one adjective phrase and one adverb phrase. Then, note which word each phrase modifies.

### Write It

🗒 **Notebook** Add either an adjective phrase or an adverb phrase to each sentence. Label each phrase you add.

> Example
> We drove.
> We drove *to the suburbs*. (adverb phrase)
> We drove to the suburbs *of Paterson and Clifton*. (adjective phrase)

1. Elena observed Eugene.

2. I could see the snow falling like a lace veil.

AMERICAN HISTORY

# Writing to Sources

A story can be a way of exploring and even of explaining a topic. The conflicts a writer chooses to address in a work of fiction often reflect issues people encounter in real life. The resolutions to those conflicts may suggest authentic solutions.

### Assignment

Consider the conflicts Elena faces in "American History" and the choices she makes as she faces them. Ask yourself whether she could have made different choices and whether those other options might have had a better or, perhaps, a worse result. Then, write an **alternative ending** to the story. Start your ending after Elena knocks on Eugene's door. Consider how you will either resolve or leave open the main conflicts Elena faces in the story.

- Your new ending should flow logically from the story's earlier events.
- Your new ending should be consistent with your understanding of the characters.
- Your new ending should either provide a resolution to the conflict or demonstrate a realization Elena experiences.

**Vocabulary and Conventions Connection** Consider including several concept vocabulary words in your alternative ending. Also, consider using prepositional phrases to make your writing more precise.

| anticipated | enthralled | elation |
| infatuated | devoted | impulse |

## Reflect on Your Writing

After you have written your alternative ending, answer these questions.

1. How did you make your portrayal of the characters consistent with the earlier part of the story? Explain.

2. Did you include any prepositional phrases in your writing? If so, how did they help you be more descriptive or precise?

3. **Why These Words?** Which words in your writing do you feel are especially effective in portraying characters' thoughts or feelings? List a few of these words.

4. **Essential Question:** *What does it mean to be "American"?* What have you learned about American identity from reading this selection?

© Pearson Education, Inc., or its affiliates. All rights reserved.

### STANDARDS

**W.9–10.3** Write narratives to develop real or imagined experiences or events using effective technique, well-chosen details, and well-structured event sequences.

**W.9–10.3.e** Provide a conclusion that follows from and reflects on what is experienced, observed, or resolved over the course of the narrative.

# Speaking and Listening

## Assignment

Write and present a **monologue** from the point of view of a character in "American History" other than Elena. A monologue is an uninterrupted speech often used in drama. It is delivered by one character to an audience of silent listeners and allows the character to present his or her version of events. For example, your monologue may present Eugene's thoughts and feelings after his mother sends Elena away.

1. **Choose a Character** Other than Elena, which character in the story would have something interesting and important to say? When choosing your character, consider the following elements:

   - the character's knowledge, attitude, and feelings about the story's events

   - the character's relationship to Elena and connection to the main events of the story

2. **Plan and Write** Brainstorm for ideas, perceptions, experiences, and thoughts your chosen character would have and might want to explain to others. Then, write your monologue.

   - Adopt the character's point of view and write using first-person pronouns—*I, me, us,* and *we.*

   - Create an authentic voice by working to "hear" the character's voice in your head as you write. Include details that show how he or she sees the setting, events, and other characters.

   - Remember that your character's knowledge is limited. Include only what he or she actually knows about the events of the story.

3. **Prepare and Deliver** Practice your delivery before you present to the class.

   - Speak clearly without rushing.

   - Employ body language and gestures to add drama or create emphasis. Try to be true to the type of movements or speech patterns your character would use.

   - Vary your speech cadence and emphasis to express your character's ideas.

4. **Evaluate** Use the evaluation guide to evaluate your classmates' monologues.

### MONOLOGUE EVALUATION GUIDE

Rate each item on a scale of 1 (not demonstrated) to 5 (demonstrated) for each speaker.

☐ The speaker spoke clearly and effectively.

☐ The monologue sounded authentic and accurately reflected the story's setting and events.

☐ The speaker varied tone and cadence to enhance meaning.

☐ The speaker's body language helped express ideas.

### ☑ EVIDENCE LOG

Before moving on to a new selection, go to your Evidence Log and record what you learned from "American History."

WRITING TO SOURCES

- A QUILT OF A COUNTRY
- THE IMMIGRANT CONTRIBUTION
- AMERICAN HISTORY

**🔧 Tool Kit**
Student Model of a
Narrative

# Write a Nonfiction Narrative

You've read an essay, an excerpt from a nonfiction book, and a short story that deal with issues of American identity. In "A Quilt of a Country," written shortly after September 11, 2001, author Anna Quindlen explores how well the United States holds "the many" together as one. In the "The Immigrant Contribution," published in 1958, then-Senator John F. Kennedy explains how immigrants have contributed to the country. Finally, in "American History," the narrator describes how a personal experience of discrimination overshadowed her grief on the day in 1963, when President Kennedy was assassinated.

### Assignment

Think about how the authors of "A Quilt of a Country," "The Immigrant Contribution," and "American History" explore American identity. Consider how the idea of American identity has changed over time. Then, use your own experience, or that of someone you know or have studied, to write a brief narrative that explores this question:

> How does your generation define what it means to be an American today?

## Elements of a Nonfiction Narrative

A **nonfiction narrative** is a true story, a series of events that occurred in real life rather than in an author's imagination. A nonfiction narrative describes real experiences or events along with reflections on those experiences. An effective nonfiction narrative includes these elements:

- a clearly described situation or problem
- a well-structured, logical sequence of events
- details that show time and place
- effective story elements such as dialogue, description, and reflection
- a reflective conclusion
- your thoughts, feelings, or views about the significance of events
- correct grammar

## ACADEMIC VOCABULARY

As you craft your narrative, consider using some of the academic vocabulary you learned in the beginning of the unit.

**conflict**
**description**
**dialogue**
**exposition**
**sequence**

**Model Narrative** For a model of a well-crafted narrative, see the Launch Text, "Music for My Mother."

Challenge yourself to find all of the elements of an effective narrative in the text. You will have the opportunity to review these elements as you start to write your own narrative.

As you consider how to capture an aspect of today's American identity in a story, it can help to imagine your narrative being included in a time capsule. Ask yourself: What would you want a future American to know about Americans today?

## STANDARDS

**W.9–10.3** Write narratives to develop real or imagined experiences or events using effective technique, well-chosen details, and well-structured event sequences.

**W.9–10.10** Write routinely over extended time frames and shorter time frames for a range of tasks, purposes, and audiences.

# Prewriting / Planning

**Choose an Event to Explore** Now that you have read the selections and thought about American identity, think of a true story that captures something unique about American identity today. It could have happened to you or someone you know—or to someone you have only heard or read about. Write a sentence describing the experience.

Experience: _____

_____ .

**Structure the Sequence** Create a detailed record of the **sequence of events**, or the events in the order that they happened, by filling out the chart below. Each event should be a part of an overall narrative that captures what it means to be an American today.

Event 1: _____ .

Event 2: _____ .

Event 3: _____ .

Event 4: _____ .

**Gather Details** Before you draft, gather details about people, places, and actions that will bring them to life for readers. Include the following:

- **descriptive words and phrases** that show how different people look and speak

- **precise language** about how people behave

- **sensory details**—words that appeal to the senses of sight, smell, taste, touch, and hearing—about key places

Using strong details adds interest and depth to your writing. For example, in the Launch Text, the writer uses lyrics of a specific song her brother sang for their mother. This detail helps readers understand the characters' feelings better.

> *I remember washing dishes while Pedrito sang: "And seeing myself so lonely and sad like a leaf in the wind, I want to cry . . . from this feeling."*
>
> —"Music for My Mother"

**Develop Situation and Point of View** Use remaining time to figure out how to describe the central situation or problem memorably. Sharpen your description by emphasizing key conflicts or describing how an important moment felt. Your narrative will be even more memorable if it conveys strong points of view. For added depth, you can take a step back and consider how other people might have perceived the same events as well.

**◢ EVIDENCE LOG**

Review your Evidence Log and identify key details you may want to cite in your narrative.

**☰ STANDARDS**

**W.9–10.3.a** Engage and orient the reader by setting out a problem, situation, or observation, establishing multiple point(s) of view, and introducing a narrator and/or characters; create a smooth progression of experiences or events.

**W.9–10.3.d** Use precise words and phrases, telling details, and sensory language to convey a vivid picture of the experiences, events, setting, and/ or characters.

# Drafting

**Organize Your Narrative** Most narratives describe events in *chronological* order, or the sequence in which they occurred. They also center on a *conflict,* or problem, that is somehow resolved. As the conflict develops, the tension should increase until it reaches its *climax,* or point of greatest intensity. After that, the tension should decrease as you move toward the ending, or *resolution.* Use a basic narrative structure like the one shown here.

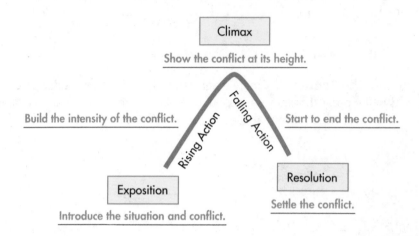

**Use Narrative Techniques** Once you have established the basic narrative structure, you can consider using narrative techniques to add interest. For example, you might jump back in time with a *flashback* to add a memory that will give readers insight into a person's thinking. Alternatively, you could jump forward in time and add a *flash-forward.* Finally, you could add a subplot, a minor narrative that sheds light on the main story.

Whatever you choose to do, make sure that the events you describe are true and tie together into a story that makes sense as whole, so readers will be able to follow along. Notice that the Launch Text actually starts *in medias res*—in the middle of the story, chronologically—and then goes backward then forward in time. Readers are still able to follow the sequence of events.

**First event described ("middle" of story):** The author's brother Pedrito is singing a traditional Spanish song because his mother misses life in her native country.

**Second event described ("beginning" of story):** The family arrives in the United States, and the parents have a more difficult time adjusting than the children have.

**Third event described ("end" of story):** Everyone has fully adjusted to life in the United States. Both children have successful careers, and the parents live with Pedrito.

**Write a First Draft** Consider the narrative techniques you plan to include in your story, and write a first draft. Remember to introduce a clear situation in the exposition and use descriptive details as you write about characters and places. Also be sure to include your own thoughts and feelings as you describe events and what they show about this generation of Americans.

**STANDARDS**

**W.9–10.3.b** Use narrative techniques, such as dialogue, pacing, description, reflection, and multiple plot lines, to develop experiences, events, and/or characters.

**W.9–10.3.c** Use a variety of techniques to sequence events so that they build on one another to create a coherent whole.

## LANGUAGE DEVELOPMENT: AUTHOR'S STYLE

# Exposition and Dialogue

**Exposition** In every narrative, certain elements need to be established, including the setting, the characters, and the situation. As you begin your narrative, think about showing the reader your story, instead of just telling it. Give clues instead of always stating information. When readers have to figure small things out, they become more involved in the story.

> TELL IT
>
> I was in the desert and it was morning. My brother and sister were with me. We had our bikes and we were going to ride. We were being careful because riding in the desert can be dangerous.
>
> SHOW IT
>
> The sun was just rising, throwing golden light over the miles of sand in front of us. My brother Gio checked our bikes one last time for any problems. My sister Lisa was on her cell phone, giving our parents our exact location. Just in case.

**Dialogue** It's not always necessary to include dialogue in a narrative, but it can often bring a story to life. What happens if we add dialogue to the exposition above?

> The sun was rising, throwing golden light over the miles of sand in front of us.
>
> "Bikes are ready," said my brother Gio. "I checked everything. Twice."
>
> "Cool," I said. "Don't want a breakdown."
>
> "Mom and Dad have our coordinates," said my sister Lisa, putting her cell phone back into her pack.

If you want your dialogue to sound real, you need to write the way people actually talk. Try listening to people talking in the lunchroom or after school. These are some of the things you may notice:

- short, incomplete sentences
- slang and other informal word choices
- repetition

**Pacing** Both description and dialogue can dramatically affect the *pacing*, or speed, of a story. For example, a large amount of description can slow down the pace, while short bursts of clipped dialogue can speed it up. Good writers read over their narratives, deciding when they want a reader to slow down and enjoy a description or deciding when to speed up and allow readers to get caught up in an exciting event.

**Write It** As you write your narrative, use these techniques: tell instead of show, use realistic dialogue, and vary your pacing.

TIP

STYLE
Make sure to use precise language in your narrative as you describe events.

- Use a dictionary if you are not sure you are using a word correctly.
- Use a thesaurus to find synonyms for words you know.

▦ STANDARDS
**W.9-10.3.b** Use narrative techniques, such as dialogue, pacing, description, reflection, and multiple plot lines, to develop experiences, events, and/or characters.

# Revising

## Evaluating Your Draft

Use the following checklist to evaluate the effectiveness of your first draft. Then, use your evaluation and the instruction on this page to guide your revision.

| FOCUS AND ORGANIZATION | EVIDENCE AND ELABORATION | CONVENTIONS |
|---|---|---|
| ☐ Provides an introduction to a real situation and develops a narrative. | ☐ Includes interesting exposition that shows as well as tells the reader. | ☐ Follows the norms and conventions of a nonfiction narrative, especially in structure and in the punctuation of dialogue. |
| ☐ Introduces the key people involved in the narrative. | ☐ Uses various techniques to create natural-sounding dialogue. | |
| ☐ Relates a problem or conflict. | | |
| ☐ Provides a smooth progression of events. | | |
| ☐ Concludes with a reflection on the significance of events. | | |

## WORD NETWORK

Include interesting words from your Word Network in your narrative.

## Revising for Focus and Organization

**Conclusion** Reread your narrative, paying attention to how the conclusion works with the rest of the piece. Do you include reflections on the significance of events? Do you consider whether Americans from different time periods see American identity differently? When you are finished considering these questions, revise your conclusion to make it more meaningful to readers. End your narrative with a reflection, an observation, or an insight that ties the story to the theme of American identity today.

## Revising for Evidence and Elaboration

**Exposition** Go to the beginning of your narrative, where you establish the setting, key people, and situation. Have you done all you can to make the exposition interesting to the reader by showing these elements and leaving details for the reader to infer? Put a star next to passages that feel insubstantial or do not give readers enough of a feel for what an experience was like. Then, go back into these passages, and find precise words or phrases that describe thoughts or physical sensations.

**Dialogue** Look over the dialogue you have included in your narrative. Does it sound like real people talking? Can you improve it by shortening sentences or using more casual language? Look for other places in your narrative where dialogue might bring your story to life.

## STANDARDS

**W 9–10.3.d** Use precise words and phrases, telling details, and sensory language to convey a vivid picture of the experiences, events, setting, and/or characters.

**W.9–10.3.e** Provide a conclusion that follows from and reflects on what is experienced, observed, or resolved over the course of the narrative.

**PEER REVIEW**

Exchange narratives with a classmate. Use the checklist to evaluate your classmate's narrative and provide supportive feedback.

**1.** Is the exposition clear?

☐ yes ☐ no If no, explain what confused you.

**2.** Are the events sequenced logically?

☐ yes ☐ no If no, what about the sequence did not work?

**3.** Does the author include thoughts, feelings, and reflections?

☐ yes ☐ no If no, write a brief note explaining what you thought was missing.

**4.** What is the strongest part of your classmate's narrative? Why?

_____

_____

_____

_____

## Editing and Proofreading

**Edit for Conventions** Reread your draft for accuracy and consistency. Correct errors in grammar and word usage. Check your narrative to make sure you have used commas correctly in compound and complex sentences.

**Proofread for Accuracy** Read your draft carefully, looking for errors in spelling and punctuation. Double-check the capitalization of names and places. Common nouns name general categories and are lowercase. Proper nouns name specific people, places, or things and are capitalized.

## Publishing and Presenting

Create a final version of your narrative. Share it with a small group so that your classmates can read it and make comments. In turn, review and comment on your classmates' work. Together, determine what your different narratives convey about Americans today. Listen and respond respectfully to comments about your work.

## Reflecting

Think about what you learned while writing your narrative. What techniques did you learn that you could use when writing another nonfiction narrative? How might you make your main point clearer? For example, you might write more reflections on why the events of the narrative were important.

ESSENTIAL QUESTION:

# What does it mean to be "American"?

What is it like to build a new life in America? And what happens when newcomers are greeted with confusion or suspicion rather than welcome? The selections you will read present different perspectives on the experience of becoming American. You will work in a group to continue your exploration of American identity.

## Small-Group Learning Strategies

Throughout your life, in school, in your community, and in your career, you will continue to learn and work with others.

Review these strategies and the actions you can take to practice them as you work in teams. Add ideas of your own for each step. Use these strategies during Small-Group Learning.

| STRATEGY | ACTION PLAN |
| --- | --- |
| Prepare | • Complete your assignments so that you are prepared for group work.<br>• Organize your thinking so that you can contribute to your group's discussion.<br>• |
| Participate fully | • Make eye contact to signal that you are listening and taking in what is being said.<br>• Use text evidence when making a point.<br>• |
| Support others | • Build off ideas from others in your group.<br>• Invite others who have not yet spoken to join the discussion.<br>• |
| Clarify | • Paraphrase the ideas of others to ensure that your understanding is correct.<br>• Ask follow-up questions.<br>• |

SCAN FOR MULTIMEDIA

# CONTENTS

### PERFORMANCE TASK

SPEAKING AND LISTENING FOCUS
## Present a Nonfiction Narrative

The Small-Group readings explore issues relating to cultural diversity and citizenship in the United States. After reading, your group will produce a podcast that includes a narrative on the topic of American identity.

## Working as a Team

**1. Take a Position** In your group, discuss the following question:

> Which do you think would be easier, immigrating to America from another country, or emigrating from America to another country?

As you take turns sharing your positions, be sure to provide reasons for your choice. After all group members have shared, discuss some of the political and social realities that could make such transitions challenging.

**2. List Your Rules** As a group, decide on the rules that you will follow as you work together. Samples are provided; add two more of your own. As you work together, you may add or revise rules based on your experience together.

- Everyone should participate in group discussions.
- Build upon each other's ideas.

- _____

- _____

**3. Apply the Rules** Share what you have learned about American identity. Make sure each person in the group contributes. Take notes and be prepared to share with the class one thing that you heard from another member of your group.

**4. Name Your Group** Choose a name that reflects the unit topic.

Our group's name: _____

**5. Create a Communication Plan** Decide how you want to communicate with one another. For example, you might use online collaboration tools, email, or instant messaging.

Our group's decision: _____

_____

## Making a Schedule

First, find out the due dates for the Small-Group activities. Then, preview the texts and activities with your group and make a schedule for completing the tasks.

| SELECTION | ACTIVITIES | DUE DATE |
|---|---|---|
| Rules of the Game | | |
| The Writing on the Wall | | |
| With a Little Help From My Friends | | |
| Morning Talk<br>Immigrant Picnic | | |

## Working on Group Projects

As your group works together, you'll find it more effective if each person has a specific role. Different projects require different roles. Before beginning a project, discuss the necessary roles, and choose one for each group member. Some possible roles are listed here. Add your own ideas to the list.

**Project Manager:** monitors the schedule and keeps everyone on task

**Researcher:** organizes information-gathering activities

**Recorder:** takes notes during group meetings

_____

_____

_____

_____

_____

_____

 SCAN FOR MULTIMEDIA

## About the Author

**Amy Tan** (b. 1952) grew up in Oakland, California, across the bay from where "Rules of the Game" takes place. Tan first published "Rules of the Game" in a magazine and then expanded the story into the novel *The Joy Luck Club*. *The Joy Luck Club* was praised for how it depicted the complicated relationships between Chinese mothers and their Chinese American daughters. It was hugely successful, receiving critical acclaim, and was a *New York Times* bestseller. Tan has received numerous awards, and her books have been translated into 25 languages.

# Rules of the Game

## Concept Vocabulary

As you perform your first read of "Rules of the Game," you will encounter these words.

| deftly | relented | plotted | concessions |

**Context Clues** To infer the meaning of an unfamiliar word, look to its context—the words and sentences that surround it.

**Example:** The emergency exit doors were clearly marked to allow for rapid and safe **evacuation** from the building.

**Explanation:** The underlined context clues provide hints that an *evacuation* is a fast exit from a dangerous situation.

**Example:** The **simulation** of the crash seemed so life-like, it was a relief to discover that it was not real.

**Explanation:** The underlined context clues help you infer that the word *simulation* refers to something that is not real, but is an enactment of events.

Apply your knowledge of context clues and other vocabulary strategies to determine the meanings of unfamiliar words you encounter during your first read. Confirm your definitions using a print or online dictionary.

## First Read FICTION

Apply these strategies as you conduct your first read. You will have an opportunity to complete a close read after your first read.

**NOTICE** *whom* the story is about, *what* happens, *where* and *when* it happens, and *why* those involved react as they do.

**ANNOTATE** by marking vocabulary and key passages you want to revisit.

**First Read**

NOTICE   ANNOTATE
CONNECT   RESPOND

**CONNECT** ideas within the selection to what you already know and what you have already read.

**RESPOND** by completing the Comprehension Check and by writing a brief summary of the selection.

:::: **STANDARDS**

**RL.9–10.10** By the end of grade 9, read and comprehend literature, including stories, dramas, and poems, in the grades 9–10 text complexity band proficiently, with scaffolding as needed at the high end of the range.

**L.9–10.4.a** Use context as a clue to the meaning of a word or phrase.

# Rules
## of the
# Game

*from*
## The Joy Luck Club

## Amy Tan

## BACKGROUND

Chess is a game of strategy that has gained world-wide popularity. Winning a game of chess requires capturing the opposing king piece, using your own pieces. Chess organizations record the rankings of players. The most successful players are called *grand masters*.

SCAN FOR MULTIMEDIA

NOTES

1    I was six when my mother taught me the art of invisible strength. It was a strategy for winning arguments, respect from others, and eventually, though neither of us knew it at the time, chess games.

2    "Bite back your tongue," scolded my mother when I cried loudly, yanking her hand toward the store that sold bags of salted plums. At home, she said, "Wise guy, he not go against wind. In Chinese we say, Come from South, blow with wind—poom!—North will follow. Strongest wind cannot be seen."

3    The next week I bit back my tongue as we entered the store with the forbidden candies. When my mother finished her shopping, she quietly plucked a small bag of plums from the rack and put it on the counter with the rest of the items.

\* \* \*

4    My mother imparted her daily truths so she could help my older brothers and me rise above our circumstances. We lived in San Francisco's Chinatown. Like most of the other Chinese children who played in the back alleys of restaurants and curio shops, I didn't think we were poor. My bowl was always full, three five-course meals every day, beginning with a soup full of mysterious things I didn't want to know the names of.

5    We lived on Waverly Place, in a warm, clean, two-bedroom flat that sat above a small Chinese bakery specializing in steamed pastries and dim sum.[1] In the early morning, when the alley was still quiet, I could smell fragrant red beans as they were cooked down to a pasty sweetness. By daybreak, our flat was heavy with the odor of fried sesame balls and sweet curried chicken crescents. From my bed, I would listen as my father got ready for work, then locked the door behind him, one-two-three clicks.

6    At the end of our two-block alley was a small sandlot playground with swings and slides well-shined down the middle with use. The play area was bordered by wood-slat benches where old-country people sat cracking roasted watermelon seeds with their golden teeth and scattering the husks to an impatient gathering of gurgling pigeons. The best playground, however, was the dark alley itself. It was crammed with daily mysteries and adventures. My brothers and I would peer into the medicinal herb shop, watching old Li dole out onto a stiff sheet of white paper the right amount of insect shells, saffron-colored seeds, and pungent leaves for his ailing customers. It was said that he once cured a woman dying of an ancestral curse that had eluded the best of American doctors. Next to the pharmacy was a printer who specialized in gold-embossed wedding invitations and festive red banners.

7    Farther down the street was Ping Yuen Fish Market. The front window displayed a tank crowded with doomed fish and turtles struggling to gain footing on the slimy green-tiled sides. A hand-written sign informed tourists, "Within this store, is all for food, not for pet." Inside, the butchers with their bloodstained white smocks **deftly** gutted the fish while customers cried out their orders and shouted, "Give me your freshest," to which the butchers always protested, "All are freshest." On less crowded market days, we would inspect the crates of live frogs and crabs which we were warned not to poke, boxes of dried cuttlefish, and row upon row of iced prawns, squid, and slippery fish. The sanddabs made me shiver each time; their eyes lay on one flattened side and reminded me of my mother's story of a careless girl who ran into a crowded street and was crushed by a cab. "Was smash flat," reported my mother.

8    At the corner of the alley was Hong Sing's, a four-table café with a recessed stairwell in front that led to a door marked "Tradesmen." My brothers and I believed the bad people emerged from this door

Mark context clues or indicate another strategy you used that helped you determine meaning.

**deftly** (DEHFT lee) *adv.*

MEANING:

---

1. **dim sum** small dishes of traditional Chinese foods meant to be shared.

at night. Tourists never went to Hong Sing's, since the menu was printed only in Chinese. A Caucasian man with a big camera once posed me and my playmates in front of the restaurant. He had us move to the side of the picture window so the photo would capture the roasted duck with its head dangling from a juice-covered rope. After he took the picture, I told him he should go into Hong Sing's and eat dinner. When he smiled and asked me what they served, I shouted, "Guts and duck's feet and octopus gizzards!" Then I ran off with my friends, shrieking with laughter as we scampered across the alley and hid in the entryway grotto of the China Gem Company, my heart pounding with hope that he would chase us.

9    My mother named me after the street that we lived on: Waverly Place Jong, my official name for important American documents. But my family called me Meimei, "Little Sister." I was the youngest, the only daughter. Each morning before school, my mother would twist and yank on my thick black hair until she had formed two tightly wound pigtails. One day, as she struggled to weave a hard-toothed comb through my disobedient hair, I had a sly thought.

10   I asked her, "Ma, what is Chinese torture?" My mother shook her head. A bobby pin was wedged between her lips. She wetted her palm and smoothed the hair above my ear, then pushed the pin in so that it nicked sharply against my scalp.

11   "Who say this word?" she asked without a trace of knowing how wicked I was being. I shrugged my shoulders and said, "Some boy in my class said Chinese people do Chinese torture."

12   "Chinese people do many things," she said simply. "Chinese people do business, do medicine, do painting. Not lazy like American people. We do torture. Best torture."

※  ※  ※

13   My older brother Vincent was the one who actually got the chess set. We had gone to the annual Christmas party held at the First Chinese Baptist Church at the end of the alley. The missionary ladies had put together a Santa bag of gifts donated by members of another church. None of the gifts had names on them. There were separate sacks for boys and girls of different ages.

14   One of the Chinese parishioners had donned a Santa Claus costume and a stiff paper beard with cotton balls glued to it. I think the only children who thought he was the real thing were too young to know that Santa Claus was not Chinese. When my turn came up, the Santa man asked me how old I was. I thought it was a trick question; I was seven according to the American formula and eight by the Chinese calendar. I said I was born on March 17, 1951. That seemed to satisfy him. He then solemnly asked if I had been a very, very good girl this year and did I believe in Jesus Christ and obey my parents. I knew the only answer to that. I nodded back with equal solemnity.

15    Having watched the other children opening their gifts, I already knew that the big gifts were not necessarily the nicest ones. One girl my age got a large coloring book of biblical characters, while a less greedy girl who selected a smaller box received a glass vial of lavender toilet water. The sound of the box was also important. A ten-year-old boy had chosen a box that jangled when he shook it. It was a tin globe of the world with a slit for inserting money. He must have thought it was full of dimes and nickels, because when he saw that it had just ten pennies, his face fell with such undisguised disappointment that his mother slapped the side of his head and led him out of the church hall, apologizing to the crowd for her son who had such bad manners he couldn't appreciate such a fine gift.

16    As I peered into the sack, I quickly fingered the remaining presents, testing their weight, imagining what they contained. I chose a heavy, compact one that was wrapped in shiny silver foil and a red satin ribbon. It was a twelve-pack of Life Savers and I spent the rest of the party arranging and rearranging the candy tubes in the order of my favorites. My brother Winston chose wisely as well. His present turned out to be a box of intricate plastic parts; the instructions on the box proclaimed that when they were properly assembled he would have an authentic miniature replica of a World War II submarine.

> As I peered into the sack, I quickly fingered the remaining presents, testing their weight, imagining what they contained.

Vincent got the chess set, which would have been a very decent present to get at a church Christmas party, except it was obviously used and, as we discovered later, it was missing a black pawn and a white knight. My mother graciously thanked the unknown benefactor, saying, "Too good. Cost too much." At which point, an old lady with fine white, wispy hair nodded toward our family and said with a whistling whisper, "Merry, merry Christmas."

18    When we got home, my mother told Vincent to throw the chess set away. "She not want it. We not want it," she said, tossing her head stiffly to the side with a tight, proud smile. My brothers had deaf ears. They were already lining up the chess pieces and reading from the dog-eared instruction book.

❋    ❋    ❋

19    I watched Vincent and Winston play during Christmas week. The chess board seemed to hold elaborate secrets waiting to be untangled. The chessmen were more powerful than Old Li's magic herbs that cured ancestral curses. And my brothers wore such serious faces that I was sure something was at stake that was greater than avoiding the tradesmen's door to Hong Sing's.

20    "Let me! Let me!" I begged between games when one brother or the other would sit back with a deep sigh of relief and victory,

the other annoyed, unable to let go of the outcome. Vincent at first refused to let me play, but when I offered my Life Savers as replacements for the buttons that filled in for the missing pieces, he **relented**. He chose the flavors: wild cherry for the black pawn and peppermint for the white knight. Winner could eat both.

NOTES

Mark context clues or indicate another strategy you used that helped you determine meaning.

**relented** (rih LEHNT ihd) *v.*

MEANING:

21     As our mother sprinkled flour and rolled out small doughy circles for the steamed dumplings that would be our dinner that night, Vincent explained the rules, pointing to each piece. "You have sixteen pieces and so do I. One king and queen, two bishops, two knights, two castles, and eight pawns. The pawns can only move forward one step, except on the first move. Then they can move two. But they can only take men by moving crossways like this, except in the beginning, when you can move ahead and take another pawn."

22     "Why?" I asked as I moved my pawn. "Why can't they move more steps?"

23     "Because they're pawns," he said.

24     "But why do they go crossways to take other men. Why aren't there any women and children?"

25     "Why is the sky blue? Why must you always ask stupid questions?" asked Vincent. "This is a game. These are the rules. I didn't make them up. See. Here. In the book." He jabbed a page with a pawn in his hand. "Pawn. P-A-W-N. Pawn. Read it yourself."

26     My mother patted the flour off her hands. "Let me see book," she said quietly. She scanned the pages quickly, not reading the foreign English symbols, seeming to search deliberately for nothing in particular.

27     "This American rules," she concluded at last. "Every time people come out from foreign country, must know rules. You not know, judge say, Too bad, go back. They not telling you why so you can use their way go forward. They say, Don't know why, you find out yourself. But they knowing all the time. Better you take it, find out why yourself." She tossed her head back with a satisfied smile.

28     I found out about all the whys later. I read the rules and looked up all the big words in a dictionary. I borrowed books from the Chinatown library. I studied each chess piece, trying to absorb the power each contained.

29     I learned about opening moves and why it's important to control the center early on; the shortest distance between two points is straight down the middle. I learned about the middle game and why tactics between two adversaries are like clashing ideas; the one who plays better has the clearest plans for both attacking and getting out of traps. I learned why it is essential in the endgame[2] to have foresight, a mathematical understanding of all possible moves, and patience; all weaknesses and advantages become evident to a strong adversary and are obscured to a tiring opponent. I discovered that

---

2. **endgame** final stage of a chess game, when few pieces remain.

for the whole game one must gather invisible strengths and see the endgame before the game begins.

30   I also found out why I should never reveal "why" to others. A little knowledge withheld is a great advantage one should store for future use. That is the power of chess. It is a game of secrets in which one must show and never tell.

31   I loved the secrets I found within the sixty-four black and white squares. I carefully drew a handmade chessboard and pinned it to the wall next to my bed, where at night I would stare for hours at imaginary battles. Soon I no longer lost any games or Life Savers, but I lost my adversaries. Winston and Vincent decided they were more interested in roaming the streets after school in their Hopalong Cassidy cowboy hats.

32   On a cold spring afternoon, while walking home from school, I detoured through the playground at the end of our alley. I saw a group of old men, two seated across a folding table playing a game of chess, others smoking pipes, eating peanuts, and watching. I ran home and grabbed Vincent's chess set, which was bound in a cardboard box with rubber bands. I also carefully selected two prized rolls of Life Savers. I came back to the park and approached a man who was observing the game.

33   "Want to play?" I asked him. His face widened with surprise and he grinned as he looked at the box under my arm. "Little sister, been a long time since I play with dolls," he said, smiling benevolently. I quickly put the box down next to him on the bench and displayed my retort.

34   Lau Po, as he allowed me to call him, turned out to be a much better player than my brothers. I lost many games and many Life Savers. But over the weeks, with each diminishing roll of candies, I added new secrets. Lau Po gave me the names. The Double Attack from the East and West Shores. Throwing Stones on the Drowning Man. The Sudden Meeting of the Clan. The Surprise from the Sleeping Guard. The Humble Servant Who Kills the King. Sand in the Eyes of Advancing Forces. A Double Killing Without Blood.

35   There were also the fine points of chess etiquette. Keep captured men in neat rows, as well-tended prisoners. Never announce "Check" with vanity, lest someone with an unseen sword slit your throat. Never hurl pieces into the sandbox after you have lost a game, because then you must find them again, by yourself, after apologizing to all around you. By the end of the summer, Lau Po had taught me all he knew, and I had become a better chess player.

36   A small weekend crowd of Chinese people and tourists would gather as I played and defeated my opponents one by one. My mother would join the crowds during these outdoor exhibition games. She sat proudly on the bench, telling my admirers with proper Chinese humility, "Is luck."

37     A man who watched me play in the park suggested that my mother allow me to play in local chess tournaments. My mother smiled graciously, an answer that meant nothing. I desperately wanted to go, but I bit back my tongue. I knew she would not let me play among strangers. So as we walked home I said in a small voice that I didn't want to play in the local tournament. They would have American rules. If I lost, I would bring shame on my family.

38     "Is shame you fall down nobody push you," said my mother.

39     During my first tournament, my mother sat with me in the front row as I waited for my turn. I frequently bounced my legs to unstick them from the cold metal seat of the folding chair. When my name was called, I leapt up. My mother unwrapped something in her lap. It was her *chang,* a small tablet of red jade which held the sun's fire. "Is luck," she whispered, and tucked it into my dress pocket. I turned to my opponent, a fifteen-year-old boy from Oakland. He looked at me, wrinkling his nose.

40     As I began to play, the boy disappeared, the color ran out of the room, and I saw only my white pieces and his black ones waiting on the other side. A light wind began blowing past my ears. It whispered secrets only I could hear.

41     "Blow from the South," it murmured. "The wind leaves no trail." I saw a clear path, the traps to avoid. The crowd rustled. "Shhh! Shhh!" said the corners of the room. The wind blew stronger. "Throw sand from the East to distract him." The knight came forward ready for the sacrifice. The wind hissed, louder and louder. "Blow, blow, blow. He cannot see. He is blind now. Make him lean away from the wind so he is easier to knock down."

42  "Check,"[3] I said, as the wind roared with laughter. The wind died down to little puffs, my own breath.

✳  ✳  ✳

43  My mother placed my first trophy next to a new plastic chess set that the neighborhood Tao society had given to me. As she wiped each piece with a soft cloth, she said, "Next time win more, lose less."

44  "Ma, it's not how many pieces you lose," I said. "Sometimes you need to lose pieces to get ahead."

45  "Better to lose less, see if you really need."

46  At the next tournament, I won again, but it was my mother who wore the triumphant grin.

47  "Lost eight piece this time. Last time was eleven. What I tell you? Better off lose less!" I was annoyed, but I couldn't say anything.

48  I attended more tournaments, each one farther away from home. I won all games, in all divisions. The Chinese bakery downstairs from our flat displayed my growing collection of trophies in its window, amidst the dust-covered cakes that were never picked up. The day after I won an important regional tournament, the window encased a fresh sheet cake with whipped-cream frosting and red script saying, "Congratulations, Waverly Jong, Chinatown Chess Champion." Soon after that, a flower shop, headstone engraver, and funeral parlor offered to sponsor me in national tournaments. That's when my mother decided I no longer had to do the dishes. Winston and Vincent had to do my chores.

49  "Why does she get to play and we do all the work," complained Vincent.

50  "Is new American rules," said my mother. "Meimei play, squeeze all her brains out for win chess. You play, worth squeeze towel."

51  By my ninth birthday, I was a national chess champion. I was still some 429 points away from grand-master status, but I was touted as the Great American Hope, a child prodigy and a girl to boot. They ran a photo of me in *Life* magazine next to a quote in which Bobby Fischer[4] said, "There will never be a woman grand master." "Your move, Bobby," said the caption.

52  The day they took the magazine picture I wore neatly plaited braids clipped with plastic barrettes trimmed with rhinestones. I was playing in a large high school auditorium that echoed with phlegmy coughs and the squeaky rubber knobs of chair legs sliding across freshly waxed wooden floors. Seated across from me was an American man, about the same age as Lau Po, maybe fifty. I remember that his sweaty brow seemed to weep at my every move. He wore a dark, malodorous suit. One of his pockets was stuffed with

---

3. **Check** term in chess meaning a player's king is in danger.
4. **Bobby Fischer** (1943–2008) American chess prodigy who attained the top rank of grand master in 1958.

a great white kerchief on which he wiped his palm before sweeping his hand over the chosen chess piece with great flourish.

53    In my crisp pink-and-white dress with scratchy lace at the neck, one of two my mother had sewn for these special occasions, I would clasp my hands under my chin, the delicate points of my elbows poised lightly on the table in the manner my mother had shown me for posing for the press. I would swing my patent leather shoes back and forth like an impatient child riding on a school bus. Then I would pause, suck in my lips, twirl my chosen piece in midair as if undecided, and then firmly plant it in its new threatening place, with a triumphant smile thrown back at my opponent for good measure.

✳ ✳ ✳

54    I no longer played in the alley of Waverly Place. I never visited the playground where the pigeons and old men gathered. I went to school, then directly home to learn new chess secrets, cleverly concealed advantages, more escape routes.

55    But I found it difficult to concentrate at home. My mother had a habit of standing over me while I plotted out my games. I think she thought of herself as my protective ally. Her lips would be sealed tight, and after each move I made, a soft "Hmmmmph" would escape from her nose.

56    "Ma, I can't practice when you stand there like that," I said one day. She retreated to the kitchen and made loud noises with the pots and pans. When the crashing stopped, I could see out of the corner of my eye that she was standing in the doorway. "Hmmmph!" Only this one came out of her tight throat.

57    My parents made many concessions to allow me to practice. One time I complained that the bedroom I shared was so noisy that I couldn't think. Thereafter, my brothers slept in a bed in the living room facing the street. I said I couldn't finish my rice; my head didn't work right when my stomach was too full. I left the table with half-finished bowls and nobody complained. But there was one duty I couldn't avoid. I had to accompany my mother on Saturday market days when I had no tournament to play. My mother would proudly walk with me, visiting many shops, buying very little. "This my daughter Wave-ly Jong," she said to whoever looked her way.

58    One day, after we left a shop I said under my breath, "I wish you wouldn't do that, telling everybody I'm your daughter." My mother stopped walking. Crowds of people with heavy bags pushed past us on the sidewalk, bumping into first one shoulder, then another.

Mark context clues or indicate another strategy you used that helped you determine meaning.

**plotted** (PLOT ihd) *v.*

MEANING:

**concessions** (kuhn SEHSH uhnz) *n.*

MEANING:

> My mother had a habit of standing over me while I plotted out my games. I think she thought of herself as my protective ally.

59    "Aiii-ya. So shame be with mother?" She grasped my hand even tighter as she glared at me.

60    I looked down. "It's not that, it's just so obvious. It's just so embarrassing."

61    "Embarrass you be my daughter?" Her voice was cracking with anger.

62    "That's not what I meant. That's not what I said."

63    "What you say?"

64    I knew it was a mistake to say anything more, but I heard my voice speaking. "Why do you have to use me to show off? If you want to show off, then why don't you learn to play chess."

65    My mother's eyes turned into dangerous black slits. She had no words for me, just sharp silence.

66    I felt the wind rushing around my hot ears. I jerked my hand out of my mother's tight grasp and spun around, knocking into an old woman. Her bag of groceries spilled to the ground.

67    "Aii-ya! Stupid girl!" my mother and the woman cried. Oranges and tin cans careened down the sidewalk. As my mother stooped to help the old woman pick up the escaping food, I took off.

68    I raced down the street, dashing between people, not looking back as my mother screamed shrilly, "Meimei! Meimei!" I fled down an alley, past dark curtained shops and merchants washing the grime off their windows. I sped into the sunlight, into a large street crowded with tourists examining trinkets and souvenirs. I ducked into another dark alley, down another street, up another alley. I ran until it hurt and I realized I had nowhere to go, that I was not running from anything. The alleys contained no escape routes.

69    My breath came out like angry smoke. It was cold. I sat down on an upturned plastic pail next to a stack of empty boxes, cupping my chin with my hands, thinking hard. I imagined my mother, first walking briskly down one street or another looking for me, then giving up and returning home to await my arrival. After two hours, I stood up on creaking legs and slowly walked home.

70    The alley was quiet and I could see the yellow lights shining from our flat like two tiger's eyes in the night. I climbed the sixteen steps to the door, advancing quietly up each so as not to make any warning sounds. I turned the knob; the door was locked. I heard a chair moving, quick steps, the locks turning—click! click! click!—and then the door opened.

71    "About time you got home," said Vincent. "Boy, are you in trouble."

72    He slid back to the dinner table. On a platter were the remains of a large fish, its fleshy head still connected to bones swimming upstream in vain escape. Standing there waiting for my punishment, I heard my mother speak in a dry voice.

73    "We not concerning this girl. This girl not have concerning for us."

74    Nobody looked at me. Bone chopsticks clinked against the insides of bowls being emptied into hungry mouths.

75    I walked into my room, closed the door, and lay down on my bed. The room was dark, the ceiling filled with shadows from the dinnertime lights of neighboring flats.

76    In my head, I saw a chessboard with sixty-four black and white squares. Opposite me was my opponent, two angry black slits. She wore a triumphant smile. "Strongest wind cannot be seen," she said.

77    Her black men advanced across the plane, slowly marching to each successive level as a single unit. My white pieces screamed as they scurried and fell off the board one by one. As her men drew closer to my edge, I felt myself growing light. I rose up into the air and flew out the window. Higher and higher, above the alley, over the tops of tiled roofs, where I was gathered up by the wind and pushed up toward the night sky until everything below me disappeared and I was alone.

78    I closed my eyes and pondered my next move. ❧

"Rules of the Game", from The Joy Luck Club by Amy Tan, copyright © 1989 by Amy Tan. Used by permission of G. P. Putnam's Sons, an imprint of Penguin Publishing Group, a division of Penguin Random House LLC.

NOTES

# Comprehension Check

Complete the following items after you finish your first read. Review and clarify details with your group.

**1.** How does Waverly first obtain a chess set?

**2.** What advice does Waverly's mother give her about finding out "why" important things are done?

**3.** Why does Waverly become angry with her mother at the market?

**4.** 📓 **Notebook** Write a summary of the story to check your understanding.

## RESEARCH

**Research to Explore** Choose an aspect of the story to research. For example, you may want to learn more about chess or San Francisco's Chinatown.

---

© Pearson Education, Inc., or its affiliates. All rights reserved.

## Close Read the Text

With your group, revisit sections of the text you marked during your first read. **Annotate** details that you notice. What **questions** do you have? What can you **conclude**?

---

## Analyze the Text

**CITE TEXTUAL EVIDENCE**
to support your answers.

☐ **Notebook** Complete the activities.

1. **Review and Clarify** With your group, reread paragraphs 1–3 and 76–77 of "Rules of the Game." What does the image of the "strongest wind" represent to you? Why does Tan return to the "strongest wind" image at the end of the story? Explain.

2. **Present and Discuss** Now, work with your group to share other key passages from the story. Discuss parts of the text that you found to be most meaningful, as well as questions you asked and the conclusions you reached as a result of reading those passages.

3. **Essential Question:** *What does it mean to be "American"?* What has this selection taught you about American identity? Discuss this idea with your group.

---

## LANGUAGE DEVELOPMENT

## Concept Vocabulary

| deftly | relented | plotted | concessions |
|--------|----------|---------|-------------|

**Why These Words?** The four concept vocabulary words are related. With your group, determine what the words have in common. Write your ideas, and add another word that fits the category.

### Practice

☐ **Notebook** Use a dictionary to confirm the definitions for the concept vocabulary words. Then, write a sentence using each of the words. How did the concept vocabulary words make your sentences more vivid?

## Word Study

**Connotation and Denotation** The **denotation** of a word is its literal dictionary definition. The same word may also have a **connotation**, a suggested meaning that evokes either positive or negative feelings. In "Rules of the Game," for example, Waverly is described as *plotting* out her games. The word *plotting* has overtones of a dark conspiracy. Its connotation is more negative than the neutral word *planning*. Find two other words in the text, and describe their connotative meanings.

---

# Analyze Craft and Structure

**Complex Characters** In the best stories, the main characters are interesting and **complex**, or well-rounded. You can identify complex characters in the following ways:

- They show multiple or even contradictory **traits**, or qualities.
- They struggle with conflicting **motivations**, or reasons for acting as they do.
- They change or learn something important by the end of the story.

**Characters Advance Plot** As characters interact with one another and struggle to overcome problems, their choices move the story along. A character's action—or decision *not* to take action—can lead to new plot developments and may intensify the conflict, heightening tension or suspense in the story.

**Characters Develop Theme** A character's struggles with a conflict can teach a general lesson. In this way, characters help develop a story's **theme**—the central insight that it conveys. As you read a short story, pay close attention to the ways that characters change and to the lessons that they learn. These details will point you toward the story's theme.

Find your own examples in "Rules of the Game" where the author builds characters. Identify each character's traits, motivations, and actions, and interpret how these details help to establish theme.

## Practice

**CITE TEXTUAL EVIDENCE** to support your answers.

📓 **Notebook** Work with your group to complete the following activities.

1. Use the chart to identify at least two conflicts Waverly and her mother face. For each conflict, explain how the character responds and the reasons for her responses.

| CHARACTER | CONFLICTS | CHARACTER'S RESPONSE | CHARACTER'S MOTIVATIONS |
|---|---|---|---|
| Waverly | | | |
| Mrs. Jong | | | |

2. **(a)** Cite at least two ways in which Waverly's actions or reactions change the situation and move the plot forward. **(b)** Do the same for Mrs. Jong.

3. Do Waverly and Mrs. Jong change or grow as a result of their experiences? If so, in what ways? If not, why?

4. **(a)** What central ideas do Waverly and her mother's conflict emphasize? **(b)** What insights about life or the human condition does the story express?

RULES OF THE GAME

# Conventions

**Participles and Participial Phrases** A **participle** is a verb form that acts as an adjective. The **present participle** of a verb ends in *-ing (frightening, entertaining).* The **past participle** of a regular verb ends in *-ed (frightened, entertained).* The past participle of an irregular verb may have any of a variety of endings, such as *-t (burnt)* or *-en (written).*

A **participial phrase** consists of a participle and its objects, complements, or modifiers, all acting together as an adjective. A participial phrase may either precede or follow the word it modifies.

In the chart, participles are italicized, participial phrases are highlighted, and the nouns or pronouns they modify are underlined.

| SENTENCE | HOW PHRASE FUNCTIONS |
|---|---|
| *Exhausted* by the arduous climb, we rested by the side of the trail. | modifies the subject |
| The movers carefully unloaded the van *packed* with antiques. | modifies the direct object |
| Rosa handed the woman *wearing* the gray suit her application. | modifies the indirect object |
| The hallways were clogged with students *going* to class. | modifies the object of the preposition |
| Ann Pace is a scientist *known* for her work in aeronautics. | modifies the subject complement |

## Read It

Work individually. Mark the participial phrase in each of these sentences from "Rules of the Game," and write the word it modifies. When you have finished, compare your responses with those of your team.

1. We lived on Waverly Place, in a warm, clean, two-bedroom flat that sat above a small Chinese bakery specializing in steamed pastries and dim sum.

2. "Little sister, been a long time since I play with dolls," he said, smiling benevolently.

3. I felt the wind rushing around my hot ears.

4. Her black men advanced across the plane, slowly marching to each successive level as a single unit.

## Write It

🖉 **Notebook** Work individually. Write a short paragraph about "Rules of the Game," using two participial phrases. Mark the participial phrases, and identify the words they are modifying.

🎓 **STANDARDS**

**L.9–10.1** Demonstrate command of the conventions of standard English grammar and usage when writing or speaking.

**L.9–10.1.b** Use various types of phrases and clauses to convey specific meanings and add variety and interest to writing or presentations.

# Speaking and Listening

## Assignment

With your group, present a **scene** that further develops characters and events Amy Tan describes in "Rules of the Game." Assign roles to members of your group, rehearse, and then perform your scene in front of the class. You may develop one of the following options or pick an alternative your group prefers.

☐ Waverly confronts her mother about what happened on the street.

☐ Waverly meets Bobby Fischer after he says there will never be a female grand master.

☐ Waverly and Lau Po have a phone conversation in which she thanks him for influencing her and tells him about an achievement that he inspired.

**Project Plan** Make a list of tasks that your group will need to carry out. Write a script for your scene, and obtain any props you may need.

**Practice** Practice your scene before you present it to your class. Include the following performance techniques to achieve the desired effect.

- Speak clearly and comfortably without rushing.
- Use your voice in a way that reflects your character's emotions and situation. Vary your tone and pitch and avoid speaking in a flat, monotonous style.
- Make sure your body language is appropriate for the character and is neither too limited nor too exaggerated.

**Evaluate Scenes** Use a presentation evaluation guide like the one shown to analyze your classmates' scenes.

### PRESENTATION EVALUATION GUIDE

**Rate each statement on a scale of 1 (not demonstrated) to 5 (demonstrated).**

☐ The speakers communicated events that fit well with the story.

☐ The speakers included details from the story to demonstrate shifts in feeling.

☐ The speakers used their voices effectively to reflect the characters and situations.

☐ The speakers used gestures and other body language effectively.

☐ The dialogue was clear and easy to follow.

### EVIDENCE LOG

Before moving on to a new selection, go to your Evidence Log and record what you learned from "Rules of the Game."

### STANDARDS

**SL.9–10.4.b** Plan, memorize, and present a recitation that: conveys the meaning of the selection and includes appropriate performance techniques to achieve the desired aesthetic effect.

## About the Author

**Camille Dungy** (b. 1972) often moved during her childhood because her father taught medicine at different schools around the country. Dungy studied English at Stanford University and became a poet and professor. Her poems have been published widely and have won several awards. Her interest in social issues and nature led her to edit a collection of African American poets and their writings on nature.

# The Writing on the Wall

## Concept Vocabulary

As you perform your first read of "The Writing on the Wall," you will encounter these words.

| memento | composed | inscribed |
|---|---|---|

**Context Clues** If these words are unfamiliar to you, try using context clues. There are various types of context clues that you may encounter.

**Similarity of Ideas:** The ineffective laws revealed the **futility** of the fight against oppression.

**Restatement of Ideas:** Once the rations were **apportioned**, the men had to live on their share of the food.

**Contrast of Ideas:** Once the refugees **emigrated** from their war-torn country, they settled in a new home in a peaceful land.

Apply your knowledge of context clues and other vocabulary strategies to determine the meanings of unfamiliar words you encounter during your first read.

## First Review NONFICTION

Apply these strategies as you conduct your first read. You will have an opportunity to complete a close read after your first read.

**NOTICE** the general ideas of the text. *What* is it about? *Who* is involved?

**ANNOTATE** by marking vocabulary and key passages you want to revisit.

**First Read**

**CONNECT** ideas within the selection to what you already know and what you have already read.

**RESPOND** by completing the Comprehension Check and by writing a brief summary of the selection.

:::icon::: STANDARDS

**RI.9–10.10** By the end of grade 9, read and comprehend literary nonfiction in the grades 9–10 text complexity band proficiently, with scaffolding as needed at the high end of the range.

**L.9–10.4.a** Use context as a clue to the meaning of a word or a phrase.

# The Writing on the Wall

Camille Dungy

## BACKGROUND

Between 1882 and 1943, the United States severely restricted the number of immigrants from Asia who were allowed to enter the country. Many people wanted to move from Asia to America, and many whose families had come to the United States before 1882 wanted to visit China and then return to the United States. As a result of the restrictions, many travelers between Asia and the United States encountered delays and difficulties.

SCAN FOR MULTIMEDIA

1   "Over a hundred poems are on the walls.
Looking at them, they are all pining[1] at the delayed progress.
What can one sad person say to another?
Unfortunate travelers everywhere wish to commiserate . . ."

*(Island: Poetry and History of Chinese Immigrants on Angel Island, 1910–1940, Eds Him Mark Lai, Genny Lim, and Judy Yung)*

NOTES

2   Imagine you have traveled on a ship from China to America. Imagine it is sometime between 1910 and 1940, and you may or may not know the man who you will call your father when you arrive in the new country whose language you likely do not know. Imagine that when you arrive you are not admitted to the country you've traveled so far and paid so dearly to reach, but instead you are taken to an island in the middle of one of the world's 10 largest bays. It's called Angel Island, but you may not know that. All you might know is that you have been ushered into a room filled with perhaps

1. **pining** *v.* wasting away, as if in ill health.

250 other men. You will not know that men from as many as 80 other countries have suffered the same fate as you, but you will know that the women and small children are kept in another building, that the Asian men are separated from the European men, that the European men received comparably better treatment than the Asian men, and that though you can see Oakland through the window of the wooden building you do not know if you will ever walk its streets. The air on the island is by turns foggy and cool and salty and warm. There are moss roses and fragrant stands of eucalyptus. You might call it beautiful, but you are a detainee, not a vacationer, and you are very far from any place that you could call home. Imagine if, in these circumstances, lying in bunks stacked three high and 6 deep, you glanced at the wooden walls around you and saw poems.

3       "On a long voyage I traveled across the sea.
Feeding on wind and sleeping on dew, I tasted hardships.
Even though Su Wu was detained among the barbarians,
he would one day return home.
When he encountered a snow storm, Wengong sighed,
thinking of bygone years.
In days of old, heroes underwent many ordeals.
I am, in the end, a man whose goal is unfulfilled.
Let this be an expression of the torment which fills my belly.
Leave this as a **memento** to encourage fellow souls."

Mark context clues or indicate another strategy you used that helped you determine meaning.

**memento** (muh MEHN toh) *n.*

MEANING:

4       Imagine you saw not just one poem written on or etched into the walls, but hundreds. Imagine nearly every inch of available wall space was taken up by a poem, and there was only a little space left. Imagine you were one of the most educated men in your village, the man on whom several families had penned their hopes. Imagine you had little but a knife or a pen and your calligraphy was beautiful. Would you take the opportunity to add a new poem to that wall?

5       ". . . Do not treat these words as idle words.
Why not let them deport you back to China?
You will find some work and endure to earn a couple of meals."

6       What I am describing is not fantasy. What I am describing was the reality for hundreds of Chinese immigrants who sought entry into America through the immigration station in the San Francisco Bay. If an immigrant's papers were in order, they could go straight away into their new lives in America. But if there were health concerns or irregularities with papers, if the would-be immigrant suffered the fate of so many as a result of the Chinese Exclusion Act of 1882, they were sent to a detention center on Angel Island, in the middle of the Bay. Held there for 2 days, 2 weeks, 2 months, and in one case as long as 2 years, many of these would-be immigrants took to writing on the walls.

7    These were not just idle scribbles. The Chinese immigrants, in particular, raised with a tradition of public poetry, **composed** carefully crafted verses that drew on Classical traditions, forms, and allusions. There is often little way to know whether a poem was written in 1910 or 1935, the poems these men wrote would stand the test of time.

8    "The insects chirp outside the four walls.
     The inmates often sigh.
     Thinking of affairs back home,
     Unconscious tears wet my lapel."[2]

9    The poem above may well reference a poem written in the 6th century AD. The first poem I copied references a poet who wrote in the 8th century AD. The poets held at the Angel Island Immigration Station were partaking of a centuries-old tradition, creating a camaraderie[3] far beyond the confines of the walls they found themselves isolated inside. Likely separated from friends and family by thousands of miles and piles of bureaucracy,[4] these writers turned to the ancient tradition of public poetry to reconstruct their sense of self.

10   "The west wind ruffles my thin gauze clothing.
     On the hill sits a tall building with a room of wooden planks.
     I wish I could travel on a cloud far away, reunite my wife and son.
     When the moonlight shines on me alone, the night seems even
        longer.
     At the head of the bed there is wine and my heart is constantly
        drunk.
     There is no flower beneath my pillow and my dreams are not
        sweet.
     To whom can I confide my innermost feelings?
     I rely solely on close friends to relieve my loneliness."

11   Here is a picture of San Francisco State University Professor Charles Egan pointing at the poem quoted above. Here we are, at least 60 years after this poem was penned, with a man from a different country, reading this lonely man's words and sharing them with people who have come to read them.

San Francisco State University Professor Charles Egan

12   In the early 1940s the administration building of the Angel Island Immigration burned, and the facilities were turned over to the Army for the war

---

2. **lapel** (luh PEHL) *n.* fold of the front of a coat underneath the collar.
3. **camaraderie** (kom uh ROD uh ree) *n.* friendship or fellowship
4. **bureaucracy** (byu ROK ruh see) *n.* inflexible routines related to government.

effort. The buildings were painted again, and after the war the barracks were deserted for years. Eventually derelict, there was talk of selling the whole island off as Army surplus. There was talk of letting local fire departments use all the island's buildings for practice. (This was the fate of several of the Julia Morgan designed employee cottages), but for the male detainee's barracks, poetry once again came to save the day.

13    Look at this picture and notice how difficult it might be to spot the poetry.

Park superintendent Roy McNamee shines a light on a poem written on a wall of the barracks.

14    If you didn't know what you were looking for, you might miss it entirely. I'm reminded of a Lucille Clifton poem, "mulberry fields," in which she talks about a similar problem.

> ". . . they say that the rocks were shaped
> some of them scratched with triangles and other forms   they
> must have been trying to invent some new language they say"

15    In the case of the Angel Island Detention Center, as in the case of the Clifton poem, the language, actually "marked an old tongue." But it was years before many people recognized what was being said and why it mattered.

16    Or, I should say in the case of the detention center that it was years before anyone who was not being directly addressed recognized the language and understood why it mattered. Because so many of the poets actually spoke to each other in their "posts," we know that the poems mattered to the people to whom they were addressed at the time. Eventually someone else saw the value as well. Someone walked through the detention center and recognized the language, recognized the poems on the wall, the hundreds of poems that documented the lives of nearly 175,000 people. Once the need **inscribed** on those walls was translated, efforts began to preserve the detention center and to give the Angel Island Detention Center a place of honor in a newly created State Park. Now this world

Mark context clues or indicate another strategy you used that helped you determine meaning.

**inscribed** (ihn SKRYBD) *adj.*

MEANING:

history record is preserved and available for viewing. Scholars are researching the poems, and people and poets like me, who need to believe in the power of poetry to speak beyond the here and now, can stand in front of those walls and understand the power of poetry: to calm, to communicate, to commiserate, and to conserve. 🙟

# Comprehension Check

Complete the following items after you finish your first read. Review and clarify details with your group.

1. Who was sent to Angel Island and under what circumstances?

2. Why were the poems inscribed on the walls at Angel Island so hard to see?

3. According to the writer, how will preservation of the Angel Island Detention Center poetry benefit her as a poet?

4. 📔 **Notebook** Write a summary of the text to confirm your understanding.

## RESEARCH

**Research to Clarify** Choose at least one unfamiliar detail from the text. Briefly research that detail. In what way does the information you learned shed light on an aspect of the blog post?

**Research to Explore** Further explore an aspect of the text that you find interesting. For example, you might want to learn more about the Chinese Exclusion Act of 1882.

THE WRITING ON THE WALL

## Close Read the Text

With your group, revisit sections of the text you marked during your first read. **Annotate** details that you notice. What **questions** do you have? What can you **conclude**?

---

## Analyze the Text

**CITE TEXTUAL EVIDENCE** to support your answers.

Notebook  Complete the activities.

1. **Review and Clarify** With your group, reread the poem in paragraph 3 of the selection. How do you interpret this poem? How does the speaker compare with the heroes of the past?

2. **Present and Discuss** Now, work with your group to share the passages from the text that you found especially important. Take turns presenting your passages. Discuss what you notice in the text, the questions you asked, and the conclusions you reached.

3. **Essential Question:** *What does it mean to be "American"?* What have you learned about American identity from reading this text? Discuss with your group.

LANGUAGE DEVELOPMENT

## Concept Vocabulary

| memento | composed | inscribed |
| --- | --- | --- |

**Why These Words?** The three concept vocabulary words are related. With your group, determine what the words have in common. Write your ideas, and add another word that fits the category.

### Practice

Notebook  Use a print or online dictionary to confirm the definitions of the three concept vocabulary words. Write a sentence using each of the words. How did the concept vocabulary words make your sentences more vivid? Discuss.

## Word Study

**Latin Root: -mem-** The word *memento* comes from Latin and contains the root -*mem*-, which means "to remember." In fact, the word *remember* itself was also formed from this root. Identify two other words that were formed from the root -*mem*-. Write the words and their definitions.

© Pearson Education, Inc., or its affiliates. All rights reserved.

---

### TIP

**GROUP DISCUSSION**
Take notes on your group members' comments so that you can refer to them later or ask for clarification.

### WORD NETWORK

Add interesting words related to American identity from the text to your Word Network.

### STANDARDS

**RI.9–10.2** Determine a central idea of a text and analyze its development over the course of the text, including how it emerges and is shaped and refined by specific details; provide an objective summary of the text.

**L.9–10.4.b** Identify and correctly use patterns of word changes that indicate different meanings or parts of speech and continue to apply knowledge of Greek and Latin roots and affixes.

# Analyze Craft and Structure

**Informative Text** Many blog posts, including "The Writing on the Wall," are essentially essays that are posted online. Like all effective essays, this blog post expresses a **central idea**, the main idea the author wants readers to understand. The author **develops and refines** the central idea by explaining it and making connections to other, related ideas. Pieces of information that illustrate, expand on, or prove an author's ideas are called **supporting details.** These are some types of supporting details:

- **Facts:** information that can be proved true
- **Statistics:** numbers used to compare groups of people or things
- **Examples:** specific cases of a general concept
- **Descriptions:** details that tell what something looks like, feels like, and so on
- **Reasons:** logical claims that justify a belief
- **Expert opinions:** comments of people with special knowledge

An essay may not include every type of supporting detail, but most writers try to include a variety. Doing so makes a text more interesting and convincing.

## Practice

**CITE TEXTUAL EVIDENCE** to support your answers.

Work individually to complete the activities. Then, discuss your responses with your group.

**1. (a)** At what point in "The Writing on the Wall" does Dungy state her central idea?

**(b)** In your own words, restate that idea.

**2.** Use the chart to identify one or more examples from the text of each type of detail listed. Explain how the detail develops or refines the central idea.

| SUPPORTING DETAIL | HOW IT DEVELOPS OR REFINES CENTRAL IDEA |
|---|---|
| Description | |
| Example | |
| Fact | |
| Reasons | |

THE WRITING ON THE WALL

**TIP**

**GROUP DISCUSSION**
If you feel confused during the discussion, don't be afraid to ask questions. Other members of the group may be thankful that you asked for clarification.

## Author's Style

**Word Choice** Both poems and prose are enhanced by the use of sound devices, such as **alliteration, assonance,** and **consonance**. The use of sound devices may emphasize meaning, create a particular mood, or express **tone**—the author's attitude toward the subject or audience.

| SOUND DEVICES IN POETRY AND PROSE | | |
|---|---|---|
| SOUND DEVICE | DEFINITION | EXAMPLE |
| **alliteration** | repetition of first consonant sound in stressed syllables of consecutive or nearby words | • *The snake sneaked past the snail.* |
| **assonance** | repetition of vowel sounds within consecutive or nearby words | • *The green leaves fluttered in the breeze.* |
| **consonance** | repetition of internal or ending consonant sounds within consecutive or nearby words | • *The king sang a rousing song.* |

## Read It

Work individually. Find examples of alliteration, assonance, and consonance in "The Writing on the Wall." You may consider both Dungy's prose and the poetry examples she cites. Then, discuss with your group how each example emphasizes meaning or helps to convey a specific tone.

| SOUND DEVICE | EXAMPLE FROM "THE WRITING ON THE WALL" |
|---|---|
| alliteration | |
| assonance | |
| consonance | |

## Write It

📓 **Notebook** Write a paragraph in which you use one example each of alliteration, assonance, and consonance.

**STANDARDS**

**RL.9–10.4** Determine the meaning of words and phrases as they are used in a text, including figurative, connotative, and technical meanings; analyze the cumulative impact of specific word choices on meaning and tone.

**W.9–10.7** Conduct short as well as more sustained research projects to answer a question or solve a problem; narrow or broaden the inquiry when appropriate; synthesize multiple sources on the subject, demonstrating understanding of the subject under investigation.

**SL.9–10.5** Make strategic use of digital media in presentations to enhance understanding of findings, reasoning, and evidence and to add interest.

# Research

## Assignment

With your group, conduct research using a variety of sources and prepare a **digital presentation**. Gather relevant visual evidence to strengthen your presentation. Choose from the following topics:

☐ **Angel Island** Research the Angel Island Immigration Station. Find maps, photos, records, blueprints, and other items to give your audience an understanding of exactly where the station was and what it was like. Make sure your presentation addresses questions such as: Who exactly was brought to Angel Island? Were all inmates immigrants? Where were the groups (Europeans, women and children, Asians) each housed and under what conditions did they live?

☐ **Poetry** The poems of Angel Island are said to follow the classic style of well-known Chinese poets. Research one or two of these poets and compare their work with that of one of the poets on Angel Island. Classic poets to investigate include Li Bai, Tu Fu, and Wang Wei.

☐ **Chinese Immigration** Research Chinese immigration to the United States from 1910 to 1940. How many Chinese immigrants arrived? What were the common reasons that most of these immigrants came to San Francisco? How did their motivations and expectations influence the poetry at Angel Island?

**Finding Materials** Your presentation may include photos, video, and audio as well as text. Use the Internet and other sources to obtain these materials.

**Presentation Plan** Work with your group to plan your presentation. Try out different approaches and ideas. Take notes to mark down which ideas work best. Use the chart to plan your presentation.

| VISUALS | NOTES |
|---|---|
| VISUAL 1: | |
| VISUAL 2: | |
| VISUAL 3: | |
| VISUAL 4: | |

**EVIDENCE LOG**

Before moving on to a new selection, go to your Evidence Log and record what you learned from "The Writing on the Wall."

## About the Author

**Firoozeh Dumas** (b. 1966) split her childhood between Iran, the country of her birth, and California. Her father loved to tell stories of his life, and she decided to tell stories, too. She originally wrote her first book, *Funny in Farsi*, for her children. It was published in 2003 and became a bestseller. Today, Dumas travels throughout the world spreading a message of humor and shared humanity.

# With a Little Help From My Friends

## Concept Vocabulary

As you perform your first read of "With a Little Help From My Friends," you will encounter these words.

| | | |
|---|---|---|
| proximity | correspondents | interpreter |

**Base Words** If these words are unfamilar to you, see whether they contain a base word you know. Use your knowledge of the "inside" word, along with context, to determine the meaning. Here is an example of how to apply the strategy.

> **Unfamiliar Word:** *translation*
>
> **Familiar "Inside" Word:** *translate*, with meanings including "convert words from one language to another language"
>
> **Context:** The *translation* of the German author's novel sold very well throughout the United States.
>
> **Conclusion:** *Translation* is being used as a noun. It must mean "a work which has been translated, or converted from one language to another."

Apply your knowledge of base words and other vocabulary strategies to determine the meanings of unfamiliar words you encounter during your first read.

## First Read NONFICTION

Apply these strategies as you conduct your first read. You will have an opportunity to complete a close read after your first read.

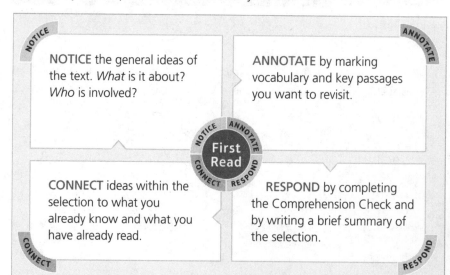

**NOTICE** the general ideas of the text. *What* is it about? *Who* is involved?

**ANNOTATE** by marking vocabulary and key passages you want to revisit.

**CONNECT** ideas within the selection to what you already know and what you have already read.

**RESPOND** by completing the Comprehension Check and by writing a brief summary of the selection.

### STANDARDS

**RI.9–10.10** By the end of grade 9, read and comprehend literary nonfiction in the grades 9–10 text complexity band proficiently, with scaffolding as needed at the high end of the range.

**L.9–10.4.a** Use context as a clue to the meaning of a word or phrase.

# With a
# Little Help
# From My
# Friends

*from* Funny in Farsi

Firoozeh Dumas

## BACKGROUND

Once known as Persia, Iran is an oil-rich country in the Middle East. In 1953, the United States had helped to remove Iran's government and to place a Shah, or king, in power. In 1972, when this excerpt begins, the Iranian government was still a monarchy led by the Shah. However, seven years later, during the Iranian Revolution of 1979, the country would undergo the political upheaval the author refers to in her first sentence. The Shah would be overthrown and replaced with a government that was unfriendly to the United States. Many Americans returned the hostility.

SCAN FOR
MULTIMEDIA

1  I was lucky to have come to America years before the political upheaval in Iran. The Americans we encountered were kind and curious, unafraid to ask questions and willing to listen. As soon as I spoke enough English to communicate, I found myself being interviewed nonstop by children and adults alike. My life became one long-running *Oprah* show, minus the free luxury accommodations in Chicago, and Oprah.

2  On the topic of Iran, American minds were tabulae rasae.[1] Judging from the questions asked, it was clear that most Americans in 1972 had never heard of Iran. We did our best to educate. "You know Asia? Well, you go south at the Soviet Union and there we are." Or we'd try

NOTES

---

1. **tabulae rasae** (TAB yuh lee RAY see) *n.* blank slates, or minds free from preconceived ideas.

to be more bucolic, mentioning being south of the beautiful Caspian Sea, "where the famous caviar comes from." Most people in Whittier did not know about the famous caviar and once we explained what it was, they'd scrunch up their faces. "Fish eggs?" they would say. "Gross." We tried mentioning our proximity to Afghanistan or Iraq, but it was no use. Having exhausted our geographical clues, we would say, "You've heard of India, Japan, or China? We're on the same continent."

3   We had always known that ours is a small country and that America is very big. But even as a seven-year-old, I was surprised that so many Americans had never noticed us on the map. Perhaps it's like driving a Yugo[2] and realizing that the eighteen-wheeler can't see you.

4   In Iran, geography is a requirement in every grade. Since the government issues textbooks, every student studies the same material in the same grade. In first-grade geography, I had to learn the shape of Iran and the location of its capital, Tehran. I had to memorize that we shared borders with Turkey, Afghanistan, Pakistan, Iraq, and the USSR.[3] I also knew that I lived on the continent of Asia.

5   None of the kids in Whittier, a city an hour outside of Los Angeles, ever asked me about geography. They wanted to know about more important things, such as camels. How many did we own back home? What did we feed them? Was it a bumpy ride? I always disappointed them by admitting that I had never seen a camel in my entire life. And as far as a ride goes, our Chevrolet was rather smooth. They reacted as if I had told them that there really was a person in the Mickey Mouse costume.

6   We were also asked about electricity, tents, and the Sahara. Once again, we disappointed, admitting that we had electricity, that we did not own a tent, and that the Sahara was on another continent. Intent to remedy the image of our homeland as backward, my father took it upon himself to enlighten Americans whenever possible. Any unsuspecting American who asked my father a question received, as a bonus, a lecture on the successful history of the petroleum industry in Iran. As my father droned on, I watched the faces of these kind Americans, who were undoubtedly making mental notes never to talk to a foreigner again.

7   My family and I wondered why Americans had such a mistaken image of Iran. We were offered a clue one day by a neighbor, who told us that he knew about Iran because he had seen *Lawrence of Arabia*.[4] Whoever Lawrence was, we had never heard of him, we said. My father then explained that Iranians are an Indo-European people; we are not Arabs. We do, however, have two things in common with Saudi Arabia, he continued: "Islam and petroleum." "Now, I

---

2. **Yugo** (YOO goh) small car manufactured in Yugoslavia.
3. **USSR** Union of Soviet Socialist Republics, name for a former country composed of 15 states, including Russia, that disbanded in 1991.
4. *Lawrence of Arabia* movie made in 1962 about a military officer in the Arabian Peninsula during World War I.

won't bore you with religion," he said, "but let me tell you about the petroleum industry."

8  Another neighbor, a kindly old lady who taught me how to take care of indoor plants, asked whether we had many cats back home. My father, with his uncanny ability to forge friendships, said, "We don't keep pets in our homes. They are dirty." "But your cats are so beautiful!" our neighbor said. We had no idea what she was talking about. Seeing our puzzled expressions, she showed us a picture of a beautiful, longhaired cat. "It's a Persian cat," she said. That was news to us; the only cats we had ever seen back home were the mangy strays that ate scraps behind people's houses. From that day, when I told people I was from Iran, I added "where Persian cats come from." That impressed them.

9  I tried my best to be a worthy representative of my homeland, but, like a Hollywood celebrity relentlessly pursued by paparazzi, I sometimes got tired of the questions. I, however, never punched anybody with my fists; I used words. One boy at school had a habit of asking me particularly stupid questions. One day he inquired about camels, again. This time, perhaps foreshadowing a vocation in storytelling, I told him that, yes, we had camels, a one-hump and a two-hump. The one-hump belonged to my parents and the two-hump was our family station wagon. His eyes widened.

10  "Where do you keep them?" he asked.

11  "In the garage, of course," I told him.

12  Having heard what he wanted to hear, he ran off to share his knowledge with the rest of the kids on the playground. He was very angry once he realized that I had fooled him, but at least he never asked me another question.

13  Often kids tried to be funny by chanting, "I ran to I-ran, I ran to I-ran." The correct pronunciation, I always informed them, is "Ee-rahn." "I ran" is a sentence, I told them, as in "I ran away from my geography lesson."

14  Older boys often asked me to teach them "some bad words in your language." At first, I politely refused. My refusal merely increased their determination, so I solved the problem by teaching them phrases like *man kharam*, which means "I'm an idiot." I told them that what I was teaching them was so nasty that they would have to promise never to repeat it to anyone. They would then spend all of recess running around yelling, "I'm an idiot! I'm an idiot!" I never told them the truth. I figured that someday, somebody would.

15  But almost every person who asked us a question asked with kindness. Questions were often followed by suggestions of places to visit in California. At school, the same children who inquired about camels also shared their food with me. "I bet you've never tried an Oreo! Have one," or "My mom just baked these peanut butter cookies and she sent you one." Kids invited me to their houses to show me what their rooms looked like. On Halloween, one family brought over a costume, knowing that I would surely be the only

kid in the Halloween parade without one. If someone had been able to encapsulate the kindness of these second-graders in pill form, the pills would undoubtedly put many war **correspondents** out of business.

16      After almost two years in Whittier, my father's assignment was completed and we had to return home. The last month of our stay, I attended one slumber party after another, all thrown in my honor. This avalanche of kindness did not make our impending departure any easier. Everyone wanted to know when we would come back to America. We had no answer, but we invited them all to visit us in Iran. I knew no one would ever take us up on our offer, because Iran was off the radar screen for most people. My friends considered visiting their grandmothers in Oregon to be a long trip, so visiting me in Iran was like taking a left turn at the next moon. It wasn't going to happen. I didn't know then that I would indeed be returning to America about two years later.

17      Between frenzied shopping trips to Sears to buy presents for our relatives back home, my mother spent her last few weeks giving gifts to our American friends. I had wondered why my mother had brought so many Persian handicrafts with her; now I knew. Everyone, from my teachers to the crossing guard to the Brownie leader to the neighbors, received something. "Dees eez from my countay-ree. Es-pay-shay-ley for you," she would explain. These handicrafts, which probably turned up in garage sales the following year, were received with tears and promises to write.

18      My mother was particularly sad to return to Iran. I had always assumed that she would be relieved to return to her family and to a land where she spoke the language and didn't need me to act as her **interpreter**. But I realized later that even though my mother could not understand anything the crossing guard, Mrs. Popkin, said, she understood that this woman looked out for me. And she understood her smiles. Even though my mother never attended a Brownie meeting, she knew that the leader, Carrie's mom, opened up her home to us every week and led us through all kinds of projects. No one paid her for this. And my mother knew that when it had been my turn to bring snacks for the class, one of the moms had stepped in and baked cupcakes. My best friend Connie's older sister, Michele, had tried to teach me to ride a bike, and Heather's mom, although single with two daughters, had hosted me overnight more times than I can remember. Even though I had been the beneficiary of all the attention, my mother, watching silently from a distance, had also felt the warmth of generosity and kindness. It was hard to leave.

19      When my parents and I get together today, we often talk about our first year in America. Even though thirty years have passed, our memories have not faded. We remember the kindness more than ever, knowing that our relatives who immigrated to this country after the Iranian Revolution did not encounter the same America. They saw

Americans who had bumper stickers on their cars that read "Iranians: Go Home" or "We Play Cowboys and Iranians." The Americans they met rarely invited them to their houses. These Americans felt that they knew all about Iran and its people, and they had no questions, just opinions. My relatives did not think Americans were very kind. ⁊

NOTES

# Comprehension Check

Complete the following items after you finish your first read. Review and clarify details with your group.

1. How did most Americans treat Dumas and her family during their first year in the United States?

2. What surprised the young Dumas about Americans' knowledge of geography?

3. What joke did Dumas play on boys who pestered her to teach them bad words in her native language?

4. According to Dumas, how did things change for Iranian immigrants to the United States after the Iranian Revolution?

5. 📓 **Notebook** Write a summary of the selection.

- - - - - - - - - - - - - - - - - - - - - - - - - - - - - - - - - - - - - - - - - - - -

## RESEARCH

**Research to Clarify** Choose at least one unfamiliar detail from the text. Briefly research that detail. In what way does the information you learned shed light on an aspect of the memoir?

**Research to Explore** Choose something from the text that interested you, and formulate a research question.

WITH A LITTLE HELP
FROM MY FRIENDS

---

TIP

**GROUP DISCUSSION**
If you do not fully
understand a classmate's
comment, don't hesitate to
ask for clarification. Use a
friendly and respectful tone
when you ask.

---

**WORD NETWORK**

Add interesting words
related to American identity
from the text to your Word
Network.

---

**STANDARDS**

**RI.9–10.3** Analyze how the author
unfolds an analysis or series of
ideas or events, including the order
in which the points are made, how
they are introduced and developed,
and the connections that are drawn
between them.

**L.9–10.4.b** Identify and correctly
use patterns of word changes that
indicate different meanings or parts
of speech and continue to apply
knowledge of Greek and Latin roots
and affixes.

---

## Close Read the Text

With your group, revisit sections of the text you marked
during your first read. **Annotate** details that you notice.
What **questions** do you have? What can you **conclude**?

---

## Analyze the Text

**CITE TEXTUAL EVIDENCE**
to support your answers.

📓 **Notebook** Complete the activities.

1. **Review and Clarify** With your group, reread paragraphs 18–19 of "With
   a Little Help From My Friends." What change in the attitude of Americans
   toward Iran did Dumas see in a few short years? How did Dumas feel
   about the change, and were her feelings justified?

2. **Present and Discuss** Now, work with your group to share the passages
   from the text that you found especially important. Take turns presenting
   your passages. Discuss what you notice in the text, the questions you
   asked, and the conclusions you reached.

3. **Essential Question:** *What does it mean to be "American"?* What
   has this selection taught you about American identity? Discuss with your
   group.

---

**LANGUAGE DEVELOPMENT**

## Concept Vocabulary

| proximity | correspondents | interpreter |

**Why These Words?** The three concept vocabulary words are related. With
your group, determine what the words have in common. Write your ideas,
and add another word that fits the category.

### Practice

📓 **Notebook** Use a print or online dictionary to confirm the definitions
of the three concept vocabulary words. Write a sentence using each of the
words. How did they make your sentences more vivid? Discuss.

## Word Study

**Latin Prefix: *inter-*** The Latin prefix *inter-*, which begins the word
*interpreter*, means "between" or "among." For instance, an *international*
agreement is an agreement between or among different nations.

Reread paragraph 1 of "With a Little Help From My Friends." Mark the word
that begins with the prefix *inter-*. Write the word here, and explain how the
prefix *inter-* contributes to its meaning.

# Analyze Craft and Structure

**Literary Nonfiction** **Autobiographical writing** is any type of nonfiction in which an author tells his or her own story. A full autobiography usually covers the author's entire life or a large span of time. A **memoir**, by contrast, is a limited kind of autobiographical writing that focuses on one period or aspect of the writer's life. Memoirs share these elements:

- written in first person, using the pronouns *I*, *me*, *we*, and *us*
- written in story form; may read like a work of fiction
- expresses the writer's attitude and insights

Memoirs often show how the writer's personal life intersects the **social and historical context**, or the circumstances of the time and place in which the story occurs. Aspects of the context include politics, language, values, beliefs, foods, customs, and traditions. In this memoir, Dumas expresses insights about the social and historical context of her childhood.

## Practice

**CITE TEXTUAL EVIDENCE**
to support your answers.

Work independently. Use the chart to identify details from the memoir that show each aspect of the social and historical context. Add a fifth category of your own. Then, discuss with your group how Dumas uses each detail to support an insight.

| ASPECT OF THE CONTEXT | TEXTUAL DETAIL(S) | DUMAS'S INSIGHT |
|---|---|---|
| Politics | | |
| Traditions | | |
| Foods | | |
| Values or Beliefs | | |
| Other | | |

WITH A LITTLE HELP
FROM MY FRIENDS

## Author's Style

**Humor** Language that is used imaginatively rather than literally is called **figurative language**. Writers often use figurative language to make their ideas more vivid and rich. As figurative language involves surprising contrasts, writers also use it to make their writing funny. In this memoir, Dumas uses three types of figurative language—metaphor, simile, and hyperbole—to add zest and humor to her story.

A **metaphor** compares by describing one thing as if it were another.
**Example:** My chores were a mountain waiting to be climbed.

A **simile** uses the word *like* or *as* to compare two unlike items.
**Example:** Gerald is like a pesky housefly that keeps coming around again and again.

**Hyperbole** is a deliberate, extreme exaggeration.
**Example:** The cake was ten stories tall.

### Read It

On your own, identify each type of figurative language from "With a Little Help From My Friends." Then, share your work with your group.

| EXAMPLE FROM THE TEXT | TYPE OF FIGURATIVE LANGUAGE | EFFECT |
|---|---|---|
| *My life became one long-running Oprah show, minus the free luxury accommodations in Chicago, and Oprah.* (paragraph 1) | | |
| *I tried my best to be a worthy representative of my homeland, but, like a Hollywood celebrity relentlessly pursued by paparazzi, I sometimes got tired of the questions.* (paragraph 9) | | |
| *This avalanche of kindness did not make our impending departure any easier.* (paragraph 16) | | |
| *If someone had been able to encapsulate the kindness of these second-graders in pill form, the pills would undoubtedly put many war correspondents out of business.* (paragraph 15) | | |

### Write It

⊟ **Notebook** Write a paragraph describing daily events in your school. Use at least one metaphor, simile, and hyperbole.

⊞ **STANDARDS**
**L.9–10.5.a** Interpret figures of speech in context and analyze their role in the text.

## Writing to Sources

### Assignment

Write an **essay** in which you interpret an important detail or quotation from the selection. Explain what the quote you chose means and how it adds to the portrait Dumas paints of herself as a child, her family, and their relationship to their community in California.

With your group, choose one of the following quotations:

- ☐ "After almost two years in Whittier, my father's assignment was completed and we had to return home. The last month of our stay, I attended one slumber party after another, all thrown in my honor."

- ☐ "They wanted to know about more important things, such as camels. How many did we own back home? What did we feed them? Was it a bumpy ride?"

- ☐ "We remember the kindness more than ever, knowing that our relatives who immigrated to this country after the Iranian Revolution did not encounter the same America."

**Writing Plan** Consider the steps of the writing process—planning/ prewriting, drafting, revising, and editing. Discuss options for organizing the work of group writing. For example, you may plan and prewrite as a group, but then have one person draft the essay, another revise it, and another edit. Alternatively, you may choose to have all group members write first drafts and then organize the various versions into a single, finished piece. Find the best way to make sure that all group members contribute equally and that you create a polished essay.

As a group, choose the quote you will write about. Then, brainstorm for ideas you will include in your essay. Use the chart to record your notes.

### Brainstorming and Discussion Notes

Chosen Quote: _____

| WHAT THE QUOTE SHOWS ABOUT... | EXPLANATION |
| --- | --- |
| Dumas as a child: | |
| Dumas's parents: | |
| The relationship of Dumas and her family to their community in California: | |

📝 EVIDENCE LOG

Before moving on to a new selection, go to your Evidence Log and record what you learned from "With a Little Help From My Friends."

**STANDARDS**

**W.9–10.2** Write informative/ explanatory texts to examine a topic and convey ideas, concepts, and information through the selection, organization, and analysis of relevant content.

**W.9–10.2b** Develop the topic with relevant facts, definitions, concrete details, quotations, or other information and examples.

POETRY COLLECTION

# Morning Talk
# Immigrant Picnic

## Concept Vocabulary

As you perform your first read, you will encounter these words.

| chirruped | teased | pipes |
|-----------|--------|-------|

**Context Clues** To find the meaning of unfamiliar words, look for **context clues**, or other words and phrases in nearby text. There are several different types of context clues.

> **Definition:** The word is clearly defined in the text.
>
> **Example:** Rick was surprised that he liked **ornithology** so much. He did not expect the study of birds to be so interesting.
>
> **Contrast:** A word or phrase signaling a contrast appears near the word.
>
> **Example:** Simone's room is **pristine**, but Olivia's room is disorganized and messy.
>
> **Synonym:** A word with a similar meaning appears nearby.
>
> **Example:** It is a pleasure to teach these students because they are so insightful and **perceptive**.

Apply your knowledge of context clues and other vocabulary strategies to determine the meanings of unfamiliar words you encounter during your first read.

## First Read POETRY

Apply these strategies as you conduct your first read. You will have an opportunity to complete a close read after your first read.

STANDARDS

**RL.9–10.10** By the end of grade 9, read and comprehend literature, including stories, dramas, and poems, in the grades 9–10 text complexity band proficiently, with scaffolding as needed at the high end of the range.

**L.9–10.4** Determine or clarify the meaning of unknown and multiple-meaning words and phrases based on grades 9–10 reading and content, choosing flexibly from a range of strategies.

**NOTICE** who or what is "speaking" the poem and whether the poem tells a story or describes a single moment.

**ANNOTATE** by marking vocabulary and key passages you want to revisit.

**CONNECT** ideas within the selection to what you already know and what you have already read.

**RESPOND** by completing the Comprehension Check.

## About the Poets

**Roberta Hill Whiteman** (b. 1947) is a nationally recognized poet, scholar, and member of the Oneida Nation of Wisconsin. Born in Baraboo, Wisconsin, Hill holds an MFA in Creative Writing and a PhD in American Studies. Her doctoral dissertation centered on her grandmother, and inspiration, Dr. Lillie Rose Minoka, one of the first Native American physicians. Hill's work draws on her experience as a Native American woman and on Oneida history. In addition to two critically acclaimed poetry collections, she has written a biography of her grandmother.

**Gregory Djanikian** (b. 1949) moved from his birthplace of Alexandria, Egypt, to Williamsport, Pennsylvania, when he was eight years old. He became interested in writing poetry while studying English at the University of Pennsylvania, and is now Director of Creative Writing at his alma mater. He has published six volumes of poetry, which often deal with family, culture, and the ways immigrants to America enrich the English language. He believes that "poetry is a communication between people on the most intense level, even if it's only between two people—writer and reader."

## Backgrounds

### Morning Talk

The songbird commonly referred to as the North American "robin" is actually a thrush. It was named "robin" by the Europeans who settled the Americas because it looks like the European robin. The two birds are not actually related. These facts play a key role in this poem.

### Immigrant Picnic

This poem is full of wordplay, including puns and malapropisms, that is both funny and pointed. *Puns* are jokes that play on differences in the meanings of words with similar sounds. *Malapropisms* involve the mistaken use of a wrong word that shares similar pronunciation with the right word— for example, "a hypodermic question," rather than "a hypothetical question."

# Morning
# Talk

Roberta Hill Whiteman

*for Melissa L Whiteman*

"Hi, guy," said I to a robin
perched on a pole in the middle
of the garden. Pink and yellow
firecracker zinnias, rough green
5   leaves of broccoli,
and deep red tomatoes on dying stems
frame his still presence.

"I've heard you're not
THE REAL ROBIN. Bird watchers have
10  agreed," I said. "THE REAL ROBIN
lives in England. They claim
you are misnamed and that we ought
to call you 'a red-breasted thrush'
because you are
15  indigenous."

He fluffed up. "Am I not
*Jis ko ko?*"* he cried, "that persistent
warrior who carries warmth
northward every spring?"
20  He seemed so young, his red belly
a bit light and his wings, still
faded brown. He watched me
untangling the hose to water squash.

"Look who's talking!" he **chirruped**.
25  "Your people didn't come
from Europe or even India.
The turtles say you're a relative
to red clay on this great island."
Drops of crystal water
30  sparkled on the squash.

"Indigenous!" he **teased**
as he flew by.

---
*   ***Jis ko ko*** (jihs koh koh) Iroquoian name for "robin."

Mark context clues or indicate another strategy you used that helped you determine meaning.
---
**chirruped** (CHIHR uhpt) *v.*

MEANING:

Mark context clues or indicate another strategy you used that helped you determine meaning.
---
**teased** (TEEZD) *v.*

MEANING:

# Immigrant Picnic

Gregory Djanikian

NOTES

It's the Fourth of July, the flags
are painting the town,
the plastic forks and knives
are laid out like a parade.

5 And I'm grilling, I've got my apron,
I've got potato salad, macaroni, relish,
I've got a hat shaped
like the state of Pennsylvania.

I ask my father what's his pleasure
10 and he says, "Hot dog, medium rare,"
and then, "Hamburger, sure,
what's the big difference,"
as if he's really asking.

I put on hamburgers and hot dogs,
15 slice up the sour pickles and Bermudas,[1]
uncap the condiments. The paper napkins
are fluttering away like lost messages.

"You're running around," my mother says,
"like a chicken with its head loose."

20 "Ma," I say, "you mean cut off,
loose and cut off being as far apart
as, say, son and daughter."

She gives me a quizzical look as though
I've been caught in some impropriety.
25 "I love you and your sister just the same," she says,
"Sure," my grandmother **pipes** in,
"you're both our children, so why worry?"

That's not the point I begin telling them,
and I'm comparing words to fish now,
30 like the ones in the sea at Port Said,[2]
or like birds among the date palms by the Nile,[3]
unrepentantly elusive, wild

Mark context clues or indicate
another strategy you used that
helped you determine meaning.

**pipes** (pyps) *v.*

MEANING:

---

1. **Bermudas** sweet onions grown on the island of Bermuda.
2. **Port Said** (sah EED) city in northeast Egypt.
3. **Nile** river in northeast Africa, considered the longest in the world.

"Sonia," my father says to my mother,
"what the hell is he talking about?"
35  "He's on a ball," my mother says.

"That's roll!" I say, throwing up my hands,
"as in hot dog, hamburger, dinner roll. . . ."

"And what about roll out the barrels?" my mother asks,
and my father claps his hands, "Why sure," he says,
40  "let's have some fun," and launches
into a polka, twirling my mother
around and around like the happiest top,

and my uncle is shaking his head, saying
"You could grow nuts listening to us,"

45  and I'm thinking of pistachios in the Sinai[4]
burgeoning without end,
pecans in the South, the jumbled
flavor of them suddenly in my mouth,
wordless, confusing,
50  crowding out everything else.

---

4. **Sinai** (SY ny) triangular peninsula in Egypt.

# Comprehension Check

Complete the following items after you finish your first read. Review and clarify details with your group.

## MORNING TALK

**1.** According to the speaker, what have bird watchers agreed?

**2.** According to the robin, where did the speaker's people come from?

## IMMIGRANT PICNIC

**1.** On what day does the picnic take place?

**2.** What type of food is the speaker thinking of at the end of the poem?

## RESEARCH

**Research to Clarify** Choose at least one unfamiliar detail from one of the poems. Briefly research that detail. In what way does the information you found shed light on an aspect of the poem?

**Research to Explore** These poems may spark your curiosity to learn more. Briefly research a topic that interests you. You may want to share what you discover with your group.

POETRY COLLECTION

# Close Read the Text

With your group, revisit sections of the text you marked during your first read. **Annotate** details that you notice. What **questions** do you have? What can you **conclude**?

---

# Analyze the Text

> **CITE TEXTUAL EVIDENCE**
> to support your answers.

📓 **Notebook** Complete the activities.

1. **Review and Clarify** With your group, reread lines 45–50 of "Immigrant Picnic." What recognition is the poet making when he compares words to nuts? Explain.

2. **Present and Discuss** Share with your group the passages from the texts that you found important. Take turns presenting your passages. Discuss what you noticed in the text, the questions you asked, and the conclusions you reached.

3. **Essential Question: *What does it mean to be "American"?*** What have these poems taught you about American identity? Discuss this question with your group.

## LANGUAGE DEVELOPMENT

# Concept Vocabulary

| chirruped | teased | pipes |
|---|---|---|

**Why These Words?** The three concept vocabulary words are related. With your group, determine what the words have in common. Write your ideas, and add another word that fits the category.

## Practice

📓 **Notebook** Use a dictionary to confirm the definitions of the three concept vocabulary words. Write a sentence using each of the words. Be sure to use context clues that hint at each word's meaning.

# Word Study

**Multiple-Meaning Words** Some words in English have multiple meanings, or more than one distinct definition. For example, the word *pipes*, which appears in "Immigrant Picnic," has several different meanings. Write the meaning of *pipes* as the poet uses it. Then, write another definition of the word. Finally, find two other multiple-meaning words. Write down the words and two of their definitions.

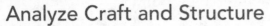

# Analyze Craft and Structure

**Poetic Structures** The basic structures of poetry are lines and stanzas. A **line** is a group of words arranged in a row. A line of poetry may break, or end, in different ways.

- An **end-stopped line** is one in which both the grammatical structure and sense are complete at the end of the line. It may include punctuation, such as a comma or period. Example: *How do I love thee?/ Let me count the ways.*

- A **run-on, or enjambed, line** is one in which both the grammatical structure and sense continue past the end of the line. Example: *I love thee to the depth and breadth and height / My soul can reach, when feeling out of sight / For the ends of Being and ideal Grace.*

A **stanza** is a group of lines, usually separated from other stanzas by space. Like a paragraph in prose, a stanza often expresses a single idea. The ways in which a poet organizes a poem into lines and stanzas affects how a poem looks and sounds and even what it means.

## Practice

**CITE TEXTUAL EVIDENCE** to support your answers.

Working on your own, use the chart to analyze the stanzas and line breaks in these poems. Record and share your observations.

| MORNING TALK | IMMIGRANT PICNIC |
|---|---|
| Summarize the action of each stanza. | Which stanzas set the scene? Explain. |
| What type of line breaks appear in stanzas 1, 2, 3, and 5? Explain. | In which stanza does the first incorrect use of an English expression appear? How does the stanza length change? Why? |
| How do the line breaks in stanza 4 differ from those in the rest of the poem? Why? | How do the last lines of stanzas 11 and 12 break? How do the line breaks reinforce the actions and feelings that are expressed? |

POETRY COLLECTION

# Author's Style

**Word Choice** Poets may draw on informal types of language to make scenes, settings, and characters come alive. **Idioms** are informal expressions in which the literal meanings of the words do not add up to the actual meaning. For example, the idiom "raining cats and dogs" does not mean cats and dogs are falling from the sky. It means it is raining very hard. In "Immigrant Picnic," the speaker's family members attempt to use idioms in their new language. Their mistakes create humor and are an important part of the poem.

### Examples of Common English Idioms

| SENTENCE | MEANING OF THE IDIOM |
|---|---|
| Grilling hot dogs and hamburgers is not **rocket science**. | Grilling is not very difficult. |
| First they told him he wasn't born here; then to **add insult to injury**, they told him he wasn't really a robin. | They made the situation worse. |
| When it comes to understanding what *indigenous* means, they completely **missed the boat**. | They failed to understand. |

## Read It

Work individually. Use this chart to define idioms that are either used or referred to in the poems. If the idiom is not used correctly, correct it. Then, rewrite the idiom in formal language that means the same thing.

| IDIOM | CORRECTION IF NEEDED | REWRITE IN FORMAL LANGUAGE |
|---|---|---|
| Look who's talking! (from "Morning Talk') | | |
| the flags / are painting the town (from "Immigrant Picnic") | | |
| like a chicken with its head loose (from "Immigrant Picnic") | | |
| He's on a ball. (from "Immigrant Picnic") | | |

## Write It

🗒 **Notebook** Write at least three idioms with which you are familiar. Explain what each one means. Then, use each idiom in a sentence.

© Pearson Education, Inc., or its affiliates. All rights reserved.

**STANDARDS**

**L.9–10.5.a** Interpret figures of speech in context and analyze their role in the text.

# Speaking and Listening

### Assignment

With your group, organize a **panel discussion** to discuss the poems. Panel members should ask and answer questions to clarify and politely challenge one another's ideas. Choose one of the following topics:

☐ **Poetry Comparison** Compare and contrast the two poems. Discuss the attitudes of the speakers, each poet's use of language, and the message or insight each poem conveys. Which poem is more positive in its message?

☐ **Poetry Ranking** Rate the two poems on a scale of 1 to 5, with 1 being ineffective and 5 being extremely effective. Then, share your ratings, and discuss your reasons for making them.

☐ **Poetry Definition** What is a poem? Is it simply a string of words set up in lines and stanzas, or is there more to it? Propose and discuss various definitions of poetry, using the two poems as examples.

**Discussion Plan** Once the group has chosen the focus for the panel discussion, work individually to gather ideas about the topic and the poems that you would like to work into the conversation. Jot down your ideas in the chart.

| POEM | INSIGHTS TO SHARE | SPECIFIC PASSAGES TO CITE |
|------|-------------------|---------------------------|
| Morning Talk | | |
| Immigrant Picnic | | |

**Participation Plan** As you participate in the panel discussion, do not read your notes aloud, but use them to remind yourself of insights you had earlier. Speak clearly, using language that is appropriate for an academic setting. Make sure you understand one another's points by summarizing them before contributing your own ideas. Ask follow-up questions respectfully.

### EVIDENCE LOG

Before moving on to a new selection, go to your Evidence Log and record what you learned from "Morning Talk" and "Immigrant Picnic."

### ▤ STANDARDS

**SL.9–10.1.c** Propel conversations by posing and responding to questions that relate the current discussion to broader themes or larger ideas; actively incorporate others into the discussion; and clarify, verify, or challenge ideas and conclusions.

**SL.9–10.1.d** Respond thoughtfully to diverse perspectives, summarize points of agreement and disagreement, and, when warranted, qualify or justify their own views and understanding and make new connections in light of the evidence and reasoning presented.

# Produce a Podcast

**Assignment**

You have read about immigrants' experiences as they strove to adjust to the United States. Work with your group to develop a podcast that addresses this question:

> How do the realities of immigrants' experiences reflect or fail to reflect American ideals?

## Plan With Your Group

**Analyze the Text** With your group, discuss the types of experiences that new immigrants to the United States have. Consider new immigrants' social interactions, their efforts to acquire a new language, and the economic challenges they face. Use the chart to list your ideas. First, discuss how you would define American ideals. Then, for each selection, identify key immigrant experiences and whether or not they reflect American ideals, such as fairness and equality of opportunity.

| TITLE | KEY EXPERIENCES / AMERICAN IDEALS |
|---|---|
| The Rules of the Game | |
| The Writing on the Wall | |
| With a Little Help From My Friends | |
| Morning Talk | |
| Immigrant Picnic | |

**Gather Evidence and Media Examples** Identify specific examples from the selections to support your group's claims. Then, brainstorm ideas for types of media you can use to illustrate or elaborate on each example. Consider having group members research various aspects of the immigrant experience and integrate their findings into the podcast. Group members could also conduct interviews with former or current immigrants about American ideals and their experiences, then select clips to include in the podcast.

**STANDARDS**

**SL.9–10.4** Present information, findings, and supporting evidence clearly, concisely, and logically such that listeners can follow the line of reasoning and the organization, development, substance, and style are appropriate to purpose audience, and task.

**SL.9–10.5** Make strategic use of digital media in presentations to enhance understanding of findings, reasoning, and evidence and to add interest.

**SL.9–10.6** Adapt speech to a variety of contexts and tasks, demonstrating command of formal English when indicated or appropriate.

**W.9–10.6** Use technology, including the Internet, to produce, publish, and update individual or shared writing products, taking advantage of technology's capacity to link to other information and to display information flexibly and dynamically.

**Organize Your Ideas** Use the **Podcast Script** chart to organize the script for your podcast presentation. Assign roles for each part of the podcast that you plan to present. Note when each segment will begin, and record what the speaker will say. Plan where audio clips and music will be used.

| PODCAST SCRIPT | | |
|---|---|---|
| | Audio | Script |
| Speaker 1 | | |
| Speaker 2 | | |
| Speaker 3 | | |

## Rehearse With Your Group

**Practice With Your Group** As you run through rehearsals, use this checklist to evaluate the effectiveness of your podcast.

| CONTENT | USE OF MEDIA | PRESENTATION TECHNIQUES |
|---|---|---|
| ☐ The podcast has a clear introduction, explaining the focus of the story. | ☐ The media support the main points. | ☐ Media are audible. |
| ☐ The podcast presents a clear story and point of view. | ☐ The media communicate key ideas. | ☐ Transitions between speakers' segments and other audio clips are smooth. |
| ☐ Main ideas are supported with evidence from the texts. | ☐ Media are used evenly throughout the podcast. | ☐ Each speaker speaks clearly. |
| | ☐ Equipment functions properly. | |

**Fine-Tune the Content** To make your podcast stronger, review each speaker's segment to make sure it supports the group's response to the question about American ideals and the immigrant experience. Be sure that group members touch on aspects of the immigrant experience they encountered in the literature they read in this unit, as well as in their research and interviews. Check with your group to identify key points that are not clear. Find another way to word these ideas.

**Improve Your Use of Media** Review all audio clips and sound effects to make sure they communicate key ideas and help create a cohesive story. Ensure that the equipment is working properly.

## Present and Evaluate

When you present as a group, be sure that each member has taken into account each of the checklist items. As you listen to other groups, evaluate how well they meet the checklist.

ESSENTIAL QUESTION:

# What does it mean to be "American"?

Being an American is different for everyone. In this section, you will complete your study of American identity by exploring an additional selection related to the topic. You'll then share what you learn with classmates. To choose a text, follow these steps.

**Look Back** Think about the selections you have already studied. What more do you want to know about the topic of American identity?

**Look Ahead** Preview the selections by reading the descriptions. Which one seems most interesting and appealing to you?

**Look Inside** Take a few minutes to scan the text you chose. Choose a different one if this text doesn't meet your needs.

## Independent Learning Strategies

Throughout your life, in school, in your community, and in your career, you will need to rely on yourself to learn and work on your own. Review these strategies and the actions you can take to practice them during Independent Learning. Add ideas of your own for each category.

| STRATEGY | ACTION PLAN |
|---|---|
| Create a schedule | • Understand your goals and deadlines.<br>• Make a plan for what to do each day.<br>• |
| Practice what you have learned | • Use first-read and close-read strategies to deepen your understanding.<br>• Evaluate the usefulness of the evidence to help you understand the topic.<br>• Consider the quality and reliability of the source.<br>• |
| Take notes | • Record important ideas and information.<br>• Review your notes before preparing to share with a group.<br>• |

SCAN FOR
MULTIMEDIA

# CONTENTS

Choose one selection. Selections are available online only.

SCAN FOR MULTIMEDIA

# First-Read Guide

Use this page to record your first-read ideas.

Selection Title: _____

🔧 **Tool Kit**
First-Read Guide and
Model Annotation

**NOTICE** new information or ideas you learn about the unit topic as you first read this text.

**ANNOTATE** by marking vocabulary and key passages you want to revisit.

**First Read**
NOTICE · ANNOTATE · CONNECT · RESPOND

**CONNECT** ideas within the selection to other knowledge and the selections you have read.

**RESPOND** by writing a brief summary of the selection.

**STANDARD**

**Anchor Reading Standard 10** Read and comprehend complex literary and informational texts independently and proficiently.

# Close-Read Guide

Use this page to record your close-read ideas.

Selection Title: _____

## Close Read the Text

Revisit sections of the text you marked during your first read. Read these sections closely and **annotate** what you notice. Ask yourself **questions** about the text. What can you **conclude?** Write down your ideas.

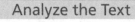

## Analyze the Text

Think about the author's choices of patterns, structure, techniques, and ideas included in the text. Select one, and record your thoughts about what this choice conveys.

## QuickWrite

Pick a paragraph from the text that grabbed your interest. Explain the power of this passage.

:≡ STANDARD
**Anchor Reading Standard 10** Read and comprehend complex literary and informational texts independently and proficiently.

☑ EVIDENCE LOG

Go to your Evidence Log
and record what you
learned from the text
you read.

# Share Your Independent Learning

## Prepare to Share

**What does it mean to be "American"?**

Even when you read something independently, your understanding continues
to grow when you share what you have learned with others. Reflect on the
text you explored independently, and write notes about its connection to the
unit. In your notes, consider why this text belongs in this unit.

## Learn From Your Classmates

💬 **Discuss It** Share your ideas about the text you explored on your own.
As you talk with your classmates, jot down ideas that you learn from them.

## Reflect

Review your notes, and mark the most important insight you gained from
these writing and discussion activities. Explain how this idea adds to your
understanding of American identity.

☰ STANDARDS

**SL.9–10.1** Initiate and participate
effectively in a range of collaborative
discussions with diverse partners
on *grades 9–10 topics, texts, and
issues*, building on others' ideas
and expressing their own clearly
and persuasively.

# Review Evidence for a Nonfiction Narrative

At the beginning of the unit, you expressed a point of view about the following question:

How is an "American" identity created?

### ✎ EVIDENCE LOG

Review your Evidence Log and your QuickWrite from the beginning of the unit. What have you learned?

| NOTES | NOTES |
| --- | --- |
| Identify at least three pieces of evidence that interested you about the experiences of immigrants, both past and present. | Identify at least three pieces of evidence that reinforced your initial point of view. |
| 1. | 1. |
| 2. | 2. |
| 3. | 3. |

Identify a real-life experience that illustrates one of your revised ideas about

American identity: _____

_____

_____

Develop your thoughts into a topic sentence for a nonfiction narrative. Complete this sentence starter:

*I learned a great deal about the experience of immigrant life in America*

*when* _____

_____

_____

**Evaluate the Strength of Your Evidence** Consider your point of view. How did the texts you read impact your point of view?

SOURCES

- WHOLE-CLASS SELECTIONS
- SMALL-GROUP SELECTIONS
- INDEPENDENT LEARNING

# PART 1
# Writing to Sources: Nonfiction Narrative

In this unit, you read about various characters, both real and fictional, who moved from other countries and had to work to build an American identity. It was easier for some than for others.

## Assignment

Write a **nonfiction narrative** on the following topic:

### How is an "American" identity created?

Use your own experience or the experience of someone you know to write a narrative answering this question. Consider geographical, social, legal, and emotional aspects of this question. What is the connection between a sense of one's personal identity and one's national identity? Do those aspects of identity ever come into conflict? As you write your narrative, draw comparisons to the real or imagined experiences described in the selections in this unit. Ensure that the ideas you want to express are fully developed by meaningful details, and that you establish a clear sequence of events.

**Reread the Assignment** Review the assignment to be sure you fully understand it. The assignment may reference some of the academic words presented at the beginning of the unit. Be sure you understand each of the words in order to complete the assignment correctly.

**Academic Vocabulary**

| conflict | dialogue | sequence |
| --- | --- | --- |
| description | exposition | |

**Review the Elements of Effective Nonfiction Narrative** Before you begin writing, read the Nonfiction Narrative Rubric. Once you have completed your first draft, check it against the rubric. If one or more of the elements is missing or is not as strong as it could be, revise your narrative to add or strengthen that component.

---

**WORD NETWORK**

As you write and revise your narrative, use your Word Network to help vary your word choices.

---

**STANDARDS**

**W.9–10.3.a–e** Write narratives to develop real or imagined experiences or events using effective technique, well-chosen details, and well-structured event sequences.

**W.9–10.9** Draw evidence from literary or informational texts to support analysis, reflection, and research.

# Nonfiction Narrative Rubric

| | Focus and Organization | Evidence and Elaboration | Language Conventions |
|---|---|---|---|
| **4** | The narrative engages and orients the reader by setting out a clear problem, situation, or observation. | The specific details and descriptions create a vivid picture of events and characters. | The narrative intentionally follows standard English conventions of usage and mechanics. |
| | The narrative includes a variety of narrative techniques. | The narrative includes story elements such as dialogue, pacing, and reflection. | |
| | The narrative includes a smooth sequence of events or ideas. | The language in the narrative is always precise and appropriate for the audience and purpose. | |
| | The conclusion follows from the events in the narrative and provides insightful reflection on the experiences related in the narrative. | The tone of the narrative is always engaging. | |
| **3** | The narrative orients the reader by setting out a problem, situation, or observation. | The details and descriptions create a picture of events and characters. | The narrative demonstrates accuracy in standard English conventions of usage and mechanics. |
| | The narrative includes narrative techniques. | The narrative includes some story elements, such as dialogue, pacing, and reflection. | |
| | The narrative includes a sequence of events or ideas. | The language in the narrative is precise and appropriate for the audience and purpose. | |
| | The conclusion follows from the events in the narrative and restates important ideas. | The tone of the narrative is mostly narrative engaging. | |
| **2** | The narrative sets out a problem, situation, or observation. | Some details and descriptions are included to create a picture of events and characters. | The narrative demonstrates some accuracy in standard English conventions of usage and mechanics. |
| | The narrative includes at least one narrative technique. | The narrative includes at least one story element. | |
| | The narrative includes a somewhat logical sequence of events or ideas. | The language in the narrative is sometimes precise and appropriate for the audience and purpose. | |
| | The conclusion follows from the events in the narrative. | The tone of the narrative is occasionally engaging. | |
| **1** | The narrative does not clearly set out a problem, situation, or observation. | Details and descriptions are not included to create a picture of events and characters. | The narrative contains mistakes in standard English conventions of usage and mechanics. |
| | The narrative does not include narrative techniques. | The narrative does not include story elements. | |
| | The sequence of events or ideas is not presented smoothly or logically. | The language in the narrative is not precise or appropriate for the audience and purpose. | |
| | The conclusion does not follow from the events in the narrative, or the narrative has no conclusion. | The tone of the narrative is not engaging. | |

## PART 2
# Speaking and Listening: Interpretive Reading

**Assignment**
After completing the final draft of your nonfiction narrative, plan and present a brief **interpretive reading.**

Do not simply read your narrative aloud. Take the following steps to make your presentation lively and engaging.

- Go back to your narrative, and annotate the ideas that provide reflection on your experiences and events.
- Refer to your annotations to guide your presentation.
- Use appropriate eye contact, adequate volume, and clear pronunciation.

**Review the Rubric** The criteria by which your narrative will be evaluated appear in the rubric below. Review these criteria before presenting to ensure that you are prepared.

**STANDARDS**

**SL.9–10.4.b** Plan, memorize, and present a recitation that: conveys the meaning of the selection and includes appropriate performance techniques to achieve the desired aesthetic effect.

| | Content | Organization | Presentation Technique |
|---|---|---|---|
| 3 | The narrative engages and orients listeners by setting out a clear problem, situation, or observation. The presentation includes a variety of story elements and narrative techniques. The conclusion follows from and reflects on what is in the rest of the presentation. | The speaker uses time very effectively by spending the right amount of time on each part. The narrative includes a smooth sequence of events or ideas. Listeners can always follow the presentation. | The speaker makes occasional eye contact and speaks clearly with adequate volume. The speaker varies tone and emphasis to create an engaging presentation. |
| 2 | The narrative sets out a problem, situation, or observation. The presentation includes some story elements and narrative techniques. The conclusion follows from what is in the rest of the presentation. | The speaker uses time effectively by spending the right amount of time on each part. The narrative includes a sequence of events or ideas. Listeners can mostly follow the presentation. | The speaker makes minimal eye contact and speaks clearly with adequate volume. The speaker sometimes varies tone and emphasis to create an engaging presentation. |
| 1 | The narrative does not set out a problem, situation, or observation. The presentation does not include story elements or narrative techniques. The conclusion does not follow from what is in the rest of the presentation. | The speaker does not use time effectively by spending the right amount of time on each part. The narrative does not include a sequence of events or ideas. Listeners cannot follow the presentation. | The speaker does not maintain effective eye contact or speak clearly with adequate volume. The speaker does not vary tone and emphasis to create an engaging presentation. |

# Reflect on the Unit

Now that you've completed the unit, take a few moments to reflect on your learning.

## Reflect on the Unit Goals

Look back at the goals at the beginning of the unit. Use a different-colored pen to rate yourself again. Think about readings and activities that contributed the most to the growth of your understanding. Record your thoughts.

## Reflect on the Learning Strategies

**Discuss It** Write a reflection on whether you were able to improve your learning based on your Action Plans. Think about what worked, what didn't, and what you might do to keep working on these strategies. Record your ideas before a class discussion.

## Reflect on the Text

Choose a selection that you found challenging and explain what made it difficult.

Explain something that surprised you about a text in the unit.

Which activity taught you the most about what it means to be "American"? What did you learn?

 SCAN FOR MULTIMEDIA

# Survival

The quest for survival is a powerful human instinct. What determines who lives and who dies?

**Amazing Stories of Rescues and Survival in Nepal**

**💬 Discuss It** What are the circumstances for victims and rescuers after an earthquake hits Nepal?

**Write your response before sharing your ideas.**

SCAN FOR
MULTIMEDIA

## UNIT INTRODUCTION

ESSENTIAL QUESTION:

# What does it take to survive?

LAUNCH TEXT
ARGUMENT MODEL
The Cost of Survival

---

### WHOLE-CLASS LEARNING

ANCHOR TEXT: SHORT STORY

**The Seventh Man**
*Haruki Murakami*

ANCHOR TEXT: EDITORIAL

**The Moral Logic of Survivor Guilt**
*Nancy Sherman*

MEDIA: RADIO BROADCAST

**The Key to Disaster Survival? Friends and Neighbors**
*Shankar Vedantam*

---

### SMALL-GROUP LEARNING

COMPARE

NARRATIVE NONFICTION

**The Voyage of the James Caird**
*from* The Endurance
*Caroline Alexander*

MEDIA: PHOTO GALLERY

**The *Endurance* and the *James Caird* in Images**
*Frank Hurley*

NOVEL EXCERPT

*from* **Life of Pi**
*Yann Martel*

ARGUMENT

**The Value of a Sherpa Life**
*Grayson Schaffer*

POETRY COLLECTION

**I Am Offering This Poem**
*Jimmy Santiago Baca*

**The Writer**
*Richard Wilbur*

**Hugging the Jukebox**
*Naomi Shihab Nye*

---

### INDEPENDENT LEARNING

SHORT STORY

**To Build a Fire**
*Jack London*

SHORT STORY

**The Most Dangerous Game**
*Richard Connell*

BIOGRAPHY

*from* **Unbroken**
*Laura Hillenbrand*

EXPOSITORY NONFICTION

**Seven Steps to Surviving a Disaster**
*Jim Y. Kim*

MAGAZINE ARTICLE

***Titanic* vs. *Lusitania*: How People Behave in a Disaster**
*Jeffrey Kluger*

PUBLIC LETTER

**Survival is Your Own Responsibility**
*Daryl R. Miller*

---

PERFORMANCE TASK

WRITING FOCUS:
**Write an Argument**

PERFORMANCE TASK

SPEAKING AND LISTENING FOCUS:
**Present an Argument**

PERFORMANCE-BASED ASSESSMENT PREP

**Review Evidence for an Argument**

---

## PERFORMANCE-BASED ASSESSMENT

Argument: Essay and Oral Presentation

PROMPT:

# Should people in life-or-death situations be held accountable for their actions?

# Unit Goals

Throughout this unit you will deepen your perspective of survival by reading, writing, speaking, listening, and presenting. These goals will help you succeed on the Unit Performance-Based Assessment.

Rate how well you meet these goals right now. You will revisit your ratings later when you reflect on your growth during this unit.

| SCALE | 1 | 2 | 3 | 4 | 5 |
|---|---|---|---|---|---|
| | NOT AT ALL WELL | NOT VERY WELL | SOMEWHAT WELL | VERY WELL | EXTREMELY WELL |

## READING GOALS

|  | 1 | 2 | 3 | 4 | 5 |
|---|---|---|---|---|---|
| • Evaluate written arguments by analyzing how authors state and support their claims. | ○ | ○ | ○ | ○ | ○ |
| • Expand your knowledge and use of academic and concept vocabulary. | ○ | ○ | ○ | ○ | ○ |

## WRITING AND RESEARCH GOALS

|  | 1 | 2 | 3 | 4 | 5 |
|---|---|---|---|---|---|
| • Write an argumentative essay in which you effectively incorporate the key elements of an argument. | ○ | ○ | ○ | ○ | ○ |
| • Conduct research projects of various lengths to explore a topic and clarify meaning. | ○ | ○ | ○ | ○ | ○ |

## LANGUAGE GOAL

|  | 1 | 2 | 3 | 4 | 5 |
|---|---|---|---|---|---|
| • Correctly use transitions to create cohesion in your writing and presentations. | ○ | ○ | ○ | ○ | ○ |

## SPEAKING AND LISTENING GOALS

|  | 1 | 2 | 3 | 4 | 5 |
|---|---|---|---|---|---|
| • Collaborate with your team to build on the ideas of others, develop consensus, and communicate. | ○ | ○ | ○ | ○ | ○ |
| • Integrate audio, visuals, and text in presentations. | ○ | ○ | ○ | ○ | ○ |

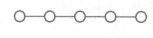
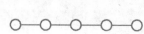

## ⊞ STANDARDS

**L.9–10.6** Acquire and use accurately general academic and domain-specific words and phrases, sufficient for reading, writing, speaking, and listening at the college and career readiness level; demonstrate independence in gathering vocabulary knowledge when considering a word or phrase important to comprehension or expression.

SCAN FOR MULTIMEDIA

# Academic Vocabulary: Argument

Academic terms appear in all subjects and can help you read, write, and discuss with more precision. Here are five academic words that will be useful to you in this unit as you analyze and write arguments.

**Complete the chart.**

1. Review each word, its root, and the mentor sentences.

2. Use the information and your own knowledge to predict the meaning of each word.

3. For each word, list at least two related words.

4. Refer to a dictionary or other resources if needed.

**TIP**

**FOLLOW THROUGH**

Study the words in this chart, and highlight them or their forms wherever they appear in the unit.

| WORD | MENTOR SENTENCES | PREDICT MEANING | RELATED WORDS |
|------|------------------|-----------------|---------------|
| **evidence**<br><br>ROOT:<br>**-vid-**<br>"to see" | 1. The receipt from the cashier was *evidence* that she had paid the bill.<br><br>2. The students' outstanding short film is *evidence* of their creativity. | | evident; evidently |
| **credible**<br><br>ROOT:<br>**-cred-**<br>"to believe" | 1. Marco is a *credible* witness because he pays attention and tells the truth.<br><br>2. Even if a story seems *credible*, confirm the details before you accept it as fact. | | |
| **valid**<br><br>ROOT:<br>**-val-**<br>"worth" | 1. An answer is *valid* if it can be proved true.<br><br>2. Jon's license is *valid* for another three years, and then he will renew it. | | |
| **formulate**<br><br>ROOT:<br>**-form-**<br>"shape" | 1. A researcher has to carefully *formulate* a topic that will be worth studying.<br><br>2. It took time for Erika to *formulate* a response to the complex question. | | |
| **logical**<br><br>ROOT:<br>**-log-**<br>"word"; "reason" | 1. If your reasoning is *logical*, you will be able to show the connections between your ideas.<br><br>2. Mathematics is *logical* because it is based on rules and patterns. | | |

This selection is an example of an **argumentative text,** a type of writing in which an author states and defends a position on a topic. This is the type of writing you will develop in the Performance-Based Assessment at the end of the unit.

**As you read,** look at the way the writer builds a case. Mark the text to help you answer this question: What is the writer's position and what evidence supports it?

# The **Cost** of **Survival**

NOTES

1   **S**ome people willingly put themselves in life-and-death situations. Mountain climbers and base jumpers knowingly face danger, and they usually walk away safely. However, when things don't turn out well, a lost climber or an injured base jumper may need help. The police, fire department, rescue workers, and medical teams do their best to save an adventurer's life. These efforts can cost a lot of money. The adventurer should be the one to foot the bill.

2   Two big news stories of 2014 involved rescue missions. In one, a family of four called for help when their child became ill. They were on a sailboat 900 miles off the coast of Mexico. Their rescue involved the U.S. Navy, the Coast Guard, and the California Air National Guard. In another news story, a caver in Germany was nearly 4,000 feet underground when he was hit by a falling rock. It took rescue teams 11 days to get him safely back to the surface.

SCAN FOR
MULTIMEDIA

NOTES

3    It is easy to argue that people should be stopped from putting themselves in danger. However, this would be impossible to enforce. Usually, when people need to be rescued, it is because something unexpected happened. In 2012, millions of people hiked, climbed, and boated in national parks, but only 2,876 needed help. More than 1,600 of those emergencies may have been caused by risky decisions. Someone has to pay for those rescues. The rescue of the family stranded at sea cost $663,000. That figure does not include pay for the rescue workers. Getting the caver safely to the surface involved 728 people.

4    Some people wind up in trouble because of bad luck, but others make dangerous choices. We need to treat these two groups differently. People who take extreme risks should pay for their rescue operation. Some states have passed laws to reflect this belief. In New Hampshire, for example, hikers who get lost or injured because of reckless behavior can be billed for rescue services.

5    Not everyone agrees that people should be responsible for the costs of their rescue. Howard Paul, a spokesman for the National Association for Search and Rescue, says, "We know that when people believe that they are going to receive a large bill for an SAR mission, they delay a call for help or they refuse to call for help." He can list many examples of people making their problems worse by not calling for help because they are worried about the cost. And a second lieutenant in the California Air National Guard who helped rescue the family at sea put it this way: "We're out there to save lives. You can't put a price on that."

6    However, arguments against charging for rescue miss an important point. Many rescue workers have lost their own lives saving others. In addition, the idea of holding people responsible is not to stop rescuing them. It's to discourage them from behaving in foolish and dangerous ways. That can only be a good thing!

7    In the end, taxpayers cover the cost of rescue for those who put themselves at risk. Maybe there are better uses for our money. ❧

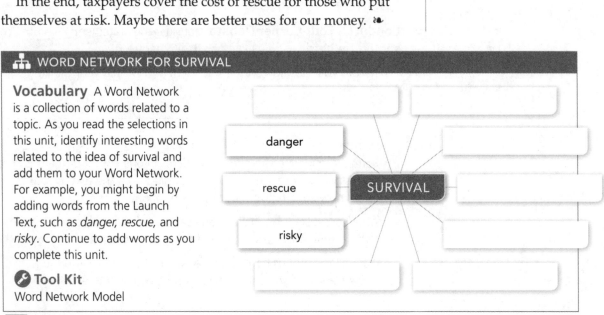

### 🔗 WORD NETWORK FOR SURVIVAL

**Vocabulary** A Word Network is a collection of words related to a topic. As you read the selections in this unit, identify interesting words related to the idea of survival and add them to your Word Network. For example, you might begin by adding words from the Launch Text, such as *danger, rescue,* and *risky.* Continue to add words as you complete this unit.

danger

rescue

risky

SURVIVAL

### 🔧 Tool Kit
Word Network Model

 SCAN FOR MULTIMEDIA

## Summary

Write a summary of "The Cost of Survival." A **summary** is a concise, complete, and accurate overview of a text. It should not include a statement of your opinion or an analysis.

## Launch Activity

**Conduct a Four-Corner Debate** Consider this statement: Adventurers should be held responsible for their rescue.

- Record your position on the statement and explain your thinking.

  ☐ Strongly Agree   ☐ Agree   ☐ Disagree   ☐ Strongly Disagree

  _____

  _____

- Form a group with like-minded students in one corner of the classroom. Discuss questions such as "What examples from the text or your own prior knowledge led you to take this position?"

- After your discussion, have a representative from each group present a two- to three-minute summary of the group's position.

- After all the groups have presented their views, move into the four corners again. If you change your corner, be ready to explain why.

# QuickWrite

Consider class discussions, presentations, the video, and the Launch Text as you think about the prompt. Record your initial position here.

PROMPT: **Should people in life-or-death situations be held accountable for their actions?**

## EVIDENCE LOG FOR SURVIVAL

Review your QuickWrite. Summarize your thoughts in one sentence to record in your Evidence Log. Then, record textual details or evidence from "The Cost of Survival" that support your thinking.

Prepare for the Performance-Based Assessment at the end of the unit by completing the Evidence Log after each selection.

🔧 **Tool Kit**
Evidence Log Model

Title of Text: _____ Date: _____

| CONNECTION TO PROMPT | TEXT EVIDENCE/DETAILS | ADDITIONAL NOTES/IDEAS |
|---|---|---|
| | | |

How does this text change or add to my thinking? Date: _____

ESSENTIAL QUESTION:

# What does it take to survive?

Everyone knows what it feels like to be ashamed to have done something—but why do people sometimes feel guilty for things they *didn't* do? Survivors' feelings can be complicated. You will work with your whole class to explore the concept of survival. The selections you are going to read present insights into some less-examined costs of survival.

## Whole-Class Learning Strategies

Throughout your life, in school, in your community, and in your career, you will continue to learn and work in large-group environments.

Review these strategies and the actions you can take to practice them as you work with your whole class. Add ideas of your own for each step. Get ready to use these strategies during Whole-Class Learning.

| STRATEGY | ACTION PLAN |
|---|---|
| Listen actively | • Eliminate distractions. For example, put your cell phone away.<br>• Keep your eyes on the speaker.<br>• |
| Clarify by asking questions | • If you're confused, other people probably are, too. Ask a question to help your whole class.<br>• If you see that you are guessing, ask a question instead.<br>• |
| Monitor understanding | • Notice what information you already know and be ready to build on it.<br>• Ask for help if you are struggling.<br>• |
| Interact and share ideas | • Share your ideas and answer questions, even if you are unsure.<br>• Build on the ideas of others by adding details or making a connection.<br>• |

SCAN FOR
MULTIMEDIA

# CONTENTS

PERFORMANCE TASK

WRITING FOCUS

## Write an Argument

Both Whole-Class readings deal with the guilt that haunts people who have
survived when others have died. The radio broadcast deals with finding help to
survive a disaster. After reading and listening, you will write an argument on the
topic of survivor guilt.

### About the Author

In 1978, **Haruki Murakami** (b. 1949) was attending a baseball game in Japan where the American player Dave Hilton hit a double. In that moment, Murakami had a flash of inspiration during which he decided he could write a novel. He began writing that evening. Since then, his numerous novels and short stories have been translated more than the works of any other Japanese writer of his generation.

**Tool Kit**
First-Read Guide and Model Annotation

# The Seventh Man

## Concept Vocabulary

You will encounter the following words as you read "The Seventh Man." Before reading, note how familiar you are with each word. Then, rank the words in order from most familiar (1) to least familiar (6).

| WORD | YOUR RANKING |
|------|--------------|
| desperate | |
| entranced | |
| hallucination | |
| premonition | |
| profound | |
| meditative | |

After completing the first read, come back to the concept vocabulary and review your rankings. Mark changes to your original rankings as needed.

## First Read FICTION

Apply these strategies as you conduct your first read. You will have an opportunity to complete the close-read notes after your first read.

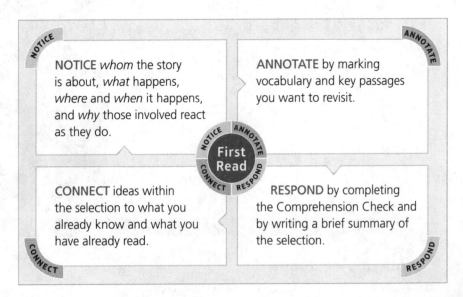

**NOTICE** whom the story is about, what happens, where and when it happens, and why those involved react as they do.

**ANNOTATE** by marking vocabulary and key passages you want to revisit.

**CONNECT** ideas within the selection to what you already know and what you have already read.

**RESPOND** by completing the Comprehension Check and by writing a brief summary of the selection.

**First Read**

**STANDARDS**

**RL.9–10.10** By the end of grade 9, read and comprehend literature, including stories, dramas, and poems in the grades 9–10 text complexity band proficiently, with scaffolding as needed at the end of the range.

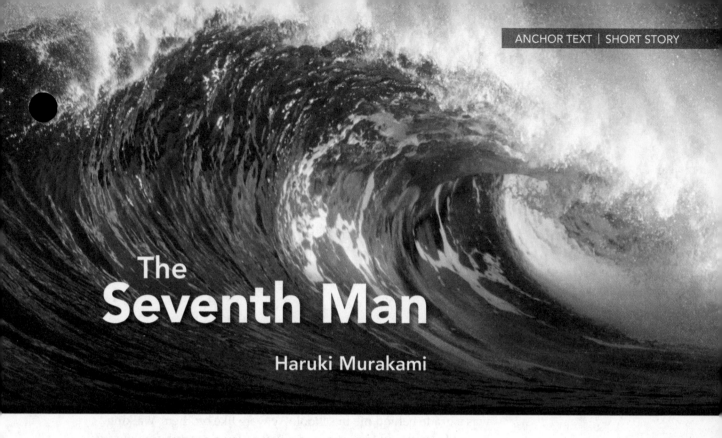

# The
# Seventh Man

## Haruki Murakami

## BACKGROUND

Hurricanes that originate in the northwest Pacific Ocean are called typhoons. They can stretch up to 500 miles in diameter and produce high winds, heavy rains, enormous waves, and severe flooding. On average, Japan is hit by three severe typhoons each year due to its location and climatic conditions.

SCAN FOR MULTIMEDIA

1   "A huge wave nearly swept me away," said the seventh man, almost whispering. "It happened one September afternoon when I was ten years old."

2   The man was the last one to tell his story that night. The hands of the clock had moved past ten. The small group that huddled in a circle could hear the wind tearing through the darkness outside, heading west. It shook the trees, set the windows to rattling, and moved past the house with one final whistle.

3   "It was the biggest wave I had ever seen in my life," he said. "A strange wave. An absolute giant."

4   He paused.

5   "It just barely missed me, but in my place it swallowed everything that mattered most to me and swept it off to another world. I took years to find it again and to recover from the experience—precious years that can never be replaced."

6   The seventh man appeared to be in his mid-fifties. He was a thin man, tall, with a moustache, and next to his right eye he had a short but deep-looking scar that could have been made by the stab of a small blade. Stiff, bristly patches of white marked his short hair. His face had the look you see on people when they can't quite find the words they need. In his case, though, the expression seemed to have

NOTES

**CLOSE READ**

**ANNOTATE:** Mark details in paragraph 2 that describe where the action takes place.

**QUESTION:** What can you tell about the story's setting?

What details about the setting are left unclear?

**CONCLUDE:** Describe the **mood**, or feeling, that the annotated details create.

been there from long before, as though it were part of him. The man wore a simple blue shirt under a gray tweed coat, and every now and then he would bring his hand to his collar. None of those assembled there knew his name or what he did for a living.

7    He cleared his throat, and for a moment or two his words were lost in silence. The others waited for him to go on.

8    "In my case, it was a wave," he said. "There's no way for me to tell, of course, what it will be for each of you. But in my case it just happened to take the form of a gigantic wave. It presented itself to me all of a sudden one day, without warning. And it was devastating."

\* \* \*

9    I grew up in a seaside town in the Province of S. It was such a small town, I doubt that any of you would recognize the name if I were to mention it. My father was the local doctor, and so I led a rather comfortable childhood. Ever since I could remember, my best friend was a boy I'll call K. His house was close to ours, and he was a grade behind me in school. We were like brothers, walking to and from school together, and always playing together when we got home. We never once fought during our long friendship. I did have a brother, six years older, but what with the age difference and differences in our personalities, we were never very close. My real brotherly affection went to my friend K.

10   K. was a frail, skinny little thing, with a pale complexion and a face almost pretty enough to be a girl's. He had some kind of speech impediment,[1] though, which might have made him seem retarded to anyone who didn't know him. And because he was so frail, I always played his protector, whether at school or at home. I was kind of big and athletic, and the other kids all looked up to me. But the main reason I enjoyed spending time with K. was that he was such a sweet, pure-hearted boy. He was not the least bit retarded, but because of his impediment, he didn't do too well at school. In most subjects, he could barely keep up. In art class, though, he was great. Just give him a pencil or paints and he would make pictures that were so full of life that even the teacher was amazed. He won prizes in one contest after another, and I'm sure he would have become a famous painter if he had continued with his art into adulthood. He liked to do seascapes. He'd go out to the shore for hours, painting. I would often sit beside him, watching the swift, precise movements of his brush, wondering how, in a few seconds, he could possibly create such lively shapes and colors where, until then, there had been only blank white paper. I realize now that it was a matter of pure talent.

11   One year, in September, a huge typhoon hit our area. The radio said it was going to be the worst in ten years. The schools were closed, and all

---

1. **speech impediment** (ihm PEHD uh muhnt) obstacle to speaking clearly, such as a lisp or stammer.

the shops in town lowered their shutters in preparation for the storm. Starting early in the morning, my father and brother went around the house nailing shut all the storm-doors, while my mother spent the day in the kitchen cooking emergency provisions. We filled bottles and canteens with water, and packed our most important possessions in rucksacks[2] for possible evacuation. To the adults, typhoons were an annoyance and a threat they had to face almost annually, but to the kids, removed as we were from such practical concerns, it was just a great big circus, a wonderful source of excitement.

12     Just after noon the color of the sky began to change all of a sudden. There was something strange and unreal about it. I stayed outside on the porch, watching the sky, until the wind began to howl and the rain began to beat against the house with a weird dry sound, like handfuls of sand. Then we closed the last storm-door and gathered together in one room of the darkened house, listening to the radio. This particular storm did not have a great deal of rain, it said, but the winds were doing a lot of damage, blowing roofs off houses and capsizing ships. Many people had been killed or injured by flying debris. Over and over again, they warned people against leaving their homes. Every once in a while, the house would creak and shudder as if a huge hand were shaking it, and sometimes there would be a great crash of some heavy-sounding object against a storm-door. My father guessed that these were tiles blowing off the neighbors' houses. For lunch we ate the rice and omelettes my mother had cooked, waiting for the typhoon to blow past.

13     But the typhoon gave no sign of blowing past. The radio said it had lost momentum[3] almost as soon as it came ashore at S. Province, and now it was moving north-east at the pace of a slow runner. The wind kept up its savage howling as it tried to uproot everything that stood on land.

14     Perhaps an hour had gone by with the wind at its worst like this when a hush fell over everything. All of a sudden it was so quiet, we could hear a bird crying in the distance. My father opened the storm-door a crack and looked outside. The wind had stopped, and the rain had ceased to fall. Thick, gray clouds edged across the sky, and patches of blue showed here and there. The trees in the yard were still dripping their heavy burden of rainwater.

15     "We're in the eye of the storm," my father told me. "It'll stay quiet like this for a while, maybe fifteen, twenty minutes, kind of like an intermission. Then the wind'll come back the way it was before."

16     I asked him if I could go outside. He said I could walk around a little if I didn't go far. "But I want you to come right back here at the first sign of wind."

17     I went out and started to explore. It was hard to believe that a wild storm had been blowing there until a few minutes before. I looked

---

2. **rucksacks** *n.* knapsacks.
3. **momentum** *n.* force or speed of movement.

NOTES

**CLOSE READ**
ANNOTATE: In paragraph 12, annotate at least four vivid details about the storm. Underline those that compare one thing to another.

QUESTION: What is being compared? What picture does each detail create in the reader's mind?

CONCLUDE: How do these descriptions help you visualize the typhoon?

up at the sky. The storm's great "eye" seemed to be up there, fixing its cold stare on all of us below. No such "eye" existed, of course: we were just in that momentary quiet spot at the center of the pool of whirling air.

18     While the grown-ups checked for damage to the house, I went down to the beach. The road was littered with broken tree branches, some of them thick pine boughs that would have been too heavy for an adult to lift alone. There were shattered roof tiles everywhere, cars with cracked windshields, and even a doghouse that had tumbled into the middle of the street. A big hand might have swung down from the sky and flattened everything in its path.

19     K. saw me walking down the road and came outside.

20     "Where are you going?" he asked.

21     "Just down to look at the beach," I said.

22     Without a word, he came along with me. He had a little white dog that followed after us.

23     "The minute we get any wind, though, we're going straight back home," I said, and K. gave me a silent nod.

24     The shore was a 200-yard walk from my house. It was lined with a concrete breakwater—a big dyke[4] that stood as high as I was tall in those days. We had to climb a short flight of steps to reach the water's edge. This was where we came to play almost every day, so there was no part of it we didn't know well. In the eye of the typhoon, though, it all looked different: the color of the sky and of the sea, the sound of the waves, the smell of the tide, the whole expanse of the shore. We sat atop the breakwater for a time, taking in the view without a word to each other. We were supposedly in the middle of a great typhoon, and yet the waves were strangely hushed. And the point where they washed against the beach was much farther away than usual, even at low tide. The white sand stretched out before us as far as we could see. The whole, huge space felt like a room without furniture, except for the band of flotsam[5] that lined the beach.

25     We stepped down to the other side of the breakwater and walked along the broad beach, examining the things that had come to rest there. Plastic toys, sandals, chunks of wood that had probably once been parts of furniture, pieces of clothing, unusual bottles, broken crates with foreign writing on them, and other, less recognizable items: it was like a big candy store. The storm must have carried these things from very far away. Whenever something unusual caught our attention, we would pick it up and look at it every which way, and when we were done, K.'s dog would come over and give it a good sniff.

26     We couldn't have been doing this more than five minutes when I realized that the waves had come up right next to me. Without any sound or other warning, the sea had suddenly stretched its long,

---

4. **dyke** (dyk) *n.* barrier built along the edge of a body of water to prevent flooding.
5. **flotsam** (FLOT suhm) *n.* refuse or debris from a ship.

smooth tongue out to where I stood on the beach. I had never seen anything like it before. Child though I was, I had grown up on the shore and knew how frightening the ocean could be—the savagery with which it could strike unannounced.

27     And so I had taken care to keep well back from the waterline. In spite of that, the waves had slid up to within inches of where I stood. And then, just as soundlessly, the water drew back—and stayed back. The waves that had approached me were as unthreatening as waves can be—a gentle washing of the sandy beach. But something ominous about them—something like the touch of a reptile's skin—had sent a chill down my spine. My fear was totally groundless—and totally real. I knew instinctively that they were alive. The waves were alive. They knew I was here and they were planning to grab me. I felt as if some huge, man-eating beast were lying somewhere on a grassy plain, dreaming of the moment it would pounce and tear me to pieces with its sharp teeth. I had to run away.

28     "I'm getting out of here!" I yelled to K. He was maybe ten yards down the beach, squatting with his back to me, and looking at something. I was sure I had yelled loud enough, but my voice did not seem to have reached him. He might have been so absorbed in whatever it was he had found that my call made no impression on him. K. was like that. He would get involved with things to the point of forgetting everything else. Or possibly I had not yelled as loudly as I had thought. I do recall that my voice sounded strange to me, as though it belonged to someone else.

29     Then I heard a deep rumbling sound. It seemed to shake the earth. Actually, before I heard the rumble I heard another sound, a weird gurgling as though a lot of water was surging up through a hole

NOTES

**CLOSE READ**

**ANNOTATE:** In paragraph 27, mark how the author divides sentences 3, 4, 5, and 6 into parts.

**QUESTION:** Why do you think the author uses dashes? What patterns does this punctuation create?

**CONCLUDE:** What is the effect of dividing these sentences in this way?

in the ground. It continued for a while, then stopped, after which I heard the strange rumbling. Even that was not enough to make K. look up. He was still squatting, looking down at something at his feet, in deep concentration. He probably did not hear the rumbling. How he could have missed such an earth-shaking sound, I don't know. This may seem odd, but it might have been a sound that only I could hear—some special kind of sound. Not even K.'s dog seemed to notice it, and you know how sensitive dogs are to sound.

30    I told myself to run over to K., grab hold of him, and get out of there. It was the only thing to do. I *knew* that the wave was coming, and K. didn't know. As clearly as I knew what I ought to be doing, I found myself running the other way—running full speed towards the dyke, alone. What made me do this, I'm sure, was fear, a fear so overpowering it took my voice away and set my legs to running on their own. I ran stumbling along the soft sand beach to the breakwater, where I turned and shouted to K.

31    "Hurry, K.! Get out of there! The wave is coming!" This time my voice worked fine. The rumbling had stopped, I realized, and now, finally, K. heard my shouting and looked up. But it was too late. A wave like a huge snake with its head held high, poised to strike, was racing towards the shore. I had never seen anything like it in my life. It had to be as tall as a three-story building. Soundlessly (in my memory, at least, the image is soundless), it rose up behind K. to block out the sky. K. looked at me for a few seconds, uncomprehending. Then, as if sensing something, he turned towards the wave. He tried to run, but now there was no time to run. In the next instant, the wave had swallowed him.

32    The wave crashed on to the beach, shattering into a million leaping waves that flew through the air and plunged over the dyke where I stood. I was able to dodge its impact by ducking behind the breakwater. The spray wet my clothes, nothing more. I scrambled back up on to the wall and scanned the shore. By then the wave had turned and, with a wild cry, it was rushing back out to sea. It looked like part of a gigantic rug that had been yanked by someone at the other end of the earth. Nowhere on the shore could I find any trace of K., or of his dog. There was only the empty beach. The receding wave had now pulled so much water out from the shore that it seemed to expose the entire ocean bottom. I stood alone on the breakwater, frozen in place.

33    The silence came over everything again—a **desperate** silence, as though sound itself had been ripped from the earth. The wave had swallowed K. and disappeared into the far distance. I stood there, wondering what to do. Should I go down to the beach? K. might be down there somewhere, buried in the sand . . . But I decided not to leave the dyke. I knew from experience that big waves often came in twos and threes.

34    I'm not sure how much time went by–maybe ten or twenty seconds of eerie emptiness–when, just as I had guessed, the next wave came. Another gigantic roar shook the beach, and again, after

**CLOSE READ**

**ANNOTATE:** In paragraph 30, mark thoughts the narrator had. Then, mark actions the narrator actually took.

**QUESTION:** What do you notice about the thoughts and the actions?

**CONCLUSION:** What do these details reveal about the narrator's character?

**desperate** (DEHS puhr iht) *adj.* involving extreme danger or disaster

the sound had faded, another huge wave raised its head to strike. It towered before me, blocking out the sky, like a deadly cliff. This time, though, I didn't run. I stood rooted to the sea wall, **entranced**, waiting for it to attack. What good would it do to run, I thought, now that K. had been taken? Or perhaps I simply froze, overcome with fear. I can't be sure what it was that kept me standing there.

© Pearson Education, Inc., or its affiliates. All rights reserved.

35     The second wave was just as big as the first—maybe even bigger. From far above my head it began to fall, losing its shape, like a brick wall slowly crumbling. It was so huge that it no longer looked like a real wave. It was like something from another, far-off world, that just happened to assume the shape of a wave. I readied myself for the moment the darkness would take me. I didn't even close my eyes. I remember hearing my heart pound with incredible clarity.

36     The moment the wave came before me, however, it stopped. All at once it seemed to run out of energy, to lose its forward motion and simply hover there, in space, crumbling in stillness. And in its crest,[6] inside its cruel, transparent tongue, what I saw was K.

37     Some of you may find this impossible to believe, and if so, I don't blame you. I myself have trouble accepting it even now. I can't explain what I saw any better than you can, but I know it was no illusion, no **hallucination**. I am telling you as honestly as I can what happened at that moment—what really happened. In the tip of the wave, as if enclosed in some kind of transparent capsule, floated K.'s body, reclining on its side. But that is not all. K. was looking straight at me, smiling. There, right in front of me, so close that I could have reached out and touched him, was my friend, my friend K. who, only moments before, had been swallowed by the wave. And he was smiling at me. Not with an ordinary smile—it was a big, wide-open grin that literally stretched from ear to ear. His cold, frozen eyes were locked on mine. He was no longer the K. I knew. And his right arm was stretched out in my direction, as if he were trying to grab my hand and pull me into that other world where he was now. A little closer, and his hand would have caught mine. But, having missed, K. then smiled at me one more time, his grin wider than ever.

38     I seem to have lost consciousness at that point. The next thing I knew, I was in bed in my father's clinic. As soon as I awoke the nurse went to call my father, who came running. He took my pulse, studied my pupils, and put his hand on my forehead. I tried to move my arm, but I couldn't lift it. I was burning with fever, and my mind was clouded. I had been wrestling with a high fever for some time, apparently. "You've been asleep for three days," my father said to me. A neighbor who had seen the whole thing had picked me up and carried me home. They had not been able to find K. I wanted to say something to my father. I *had* to say something to him. But my numb and swollen tongue could not form words. I felt as if some kind of creature had taken up residence in my mouth. My father asked me

---

6. **crest** *n.* top of a wave.

**entranced** (ehn TRANST) *adj.* in a state of wonder or amazement

**hallucination** (huh loo suh NAY shuhn) *n.* something perceived that has no reality

to tell him my name, but before I could remember what it was, I lost consciousness again, sinking into darkness.

39    Altogether, I stayed in bed for a week on a liquid diet. I vomited several times, and had bouts of delirium. My father told me afterwards that I was so bad that he had been afraid I might suffer permanent neurological[7] damage from the shock and high fever. One way or another, though, I managed to recover—physically, at least. But my life would never be the same again.

40    They never found K.'s body. They never found his dog, either. Usually when someone drowned in that area, the body would wash up a few days later on the shore of a small inlet to the east. K.'s body never did. The big waves probably carried it far out to sea—too far for it to reach the shore. It must have sunk to the ocean bottom to be eaten by the fish. The search went on for a very long time, thanks to the cooperation of the local fishermen, but eventually it petered out.[8] Without a body, there was never any funeral. Half crazed, K.'s parents would wander up and down the beach every day, or they would shut themselves up at home, chanting sutras.[9]

41    As great a blow as this had been for them, though, K.'s parents never chided me for having taken their son down to the shore in the midst of a typhoon. They knew how I had always loved and protected K. as if he had been my own little brother. My parents, too, made a point of never mentioning the incident in my presence. But I knew the truth. I knew that I could have saved K. if I had tried. I probably could have run over and dragged him out of the reach of the wave. It would have been close, but as I went over the timing of the events in memory, it always seemed to me that I could have made it. As I said before, though, overcome with fear, I abandoned him there and saved only myself. It pained me all the more that K.'s parents failed to blame me and that everyone else was so careful never to say anything to me about what had happened. It took me a long time to recover from the emotional shock. I stayed away from school for weeks. I hardly ate a thing, and spent each day in bed, staring at the ceiling.

42    K. was always there, lying in the wave tip, grinning at me, his hand outstretched, beckoning. I couldn't get that picture out of my mind. And when I managed to sleep, it was there in my dreams— except that, in my dreams, K. would hop out of his capsule in the wave and grab my wrist to drag me back inside with him.

43    And then there was another dream I had. I'm swimming in the ocean. It's a beautiful summer afternoon, and I'm doing an easy breaststroke far from shore. The sun is beating down on my back, and the water feels good. Then, all of a sudden, someone grabs my right leg. I feel an ice-cold grip on my ankle. It's strong, too strong to shake off. I'm being dragged down under the surface. I see K.'s face there.

---

7. **neurological** (nur uh LOJ uh kuhl) *adj.* relating to the nervous system.
8. **petered out** came to an end.
9. **sutras** (SOO truhz) *n.* short religious texts meant to be chanted.

He has the same huge grin, split from ear to ear, his eyes locked on mine. I try to scream, but my voice will not come. I swallow water, and my lungs start to fill.

44    I wake up in the darkness, screaming, breathless, drenched in sweat.

45    At the end of the year I pleaded with my parents to let me move to another town. I couldn't go on living in sight of the beach where K. had been swept away, and my nightmares wouldn't stop. If I didn't get out of there, I'd go crazy. My parents understood and made arrangements for me to live elsewhere. I moved to Nagano Province in January to live with my father's family in a mountain village near Komoro.[10] I finished elementary school in Nagano and stayed on through junior and senior high school there. I never went home, even for holidays. My parents came to visit me now and then.

46    I live in Nagano to this day. I graduated from a college of engineering in the City of Nagano and went to work for a precision toolmaker in the area. I still work for them. I live like anybody else. As you can see, there's nothing unusual about me. I'm not very sociable, but I have a few friends I go mountain climbing with. Once I got away from my home town, I stopped having nightmares all the time. They remained a part of my life, though. They would come to me now and then, like debt collectors at the door. It happened whenever I was on the verge of forgetting. And it was always the same dream, down to the smallest detail. I would wake up screaming, my sheets soaked with sweat.

47    That is probably why I never married. I didn't want to wake someone sleeping next to me with my screams in the middle of the night. I've been in love with several women over the years, but I never spent a night with any of them. The terror was in my bones. It was something I could never share with another person.

48    I stayed away from my home town for over forty years. I never went near that seashore—or any other. I was afraid that if I did, my dream might happen in reality. I had always enjoyed swimming, but after that day I never even went to swim in a pool. I wouldn't go near deep rivers or lakes. I avoided boats and wouldn't take a plane to go abroad. Despite all these precautions, I couldn't get rid of the image of myself drowning. Like K.'s cold hand, this dark **premonition** caught hold of my mind and refused to let go.

49    Then, last spring, I finally revisited the beach where K. had been taken by the wave.

50    My father had died of cancer the year before, and my brother had sold the old house. In going through the storage shed, he had found a cardboard carton crammed with childhood things of mine, which he sent to me in Nagano. Most of it was useless junk, but there was one bundle of pictures that K. had painted and given to me. My parents had probably put them away for me as a keepsake of K., but

NOTES

**CLOSE READ**
**ANNOTATE:** In paragraphs 45 and 46, mark verbs that reveal the time frame.

**QUESTION:** Why has the writer switched from past tense verbs in paragraph 45 to present tense verbs in paragraph 46?

**CONCLUDE:** What shift in the story's time frame is revealed through the use of verbs?

**premonition** (prehm uh NIHSH uhn) *n.* feeling that something bad will happen

10. **Nagano Province . . . village near Komoro** northwestern area of Japan and a town in that area.

the pictures did nothing but reawaken the old terror. They made me feel as if K.'s spirit would spring back to life from them, and so I quickly returned them to their paper wrapping, intending to throw them away. I couldn't make myself do it, though. After several days of indecision, I opened the bundle again and forced myself to take a long, hard look at K.'s watercolors.

51    Most of them were landscapes, pictures of the familiar stretch of ocean and sand beach and pine woods and the town, and all done with that special clarity and coloration I knew so well from K.'s hand. They were still amazingly vivid despite the years, and had been executed with even greater skill than I recalled. As I leafed through the bundle, I found myself steeped in warm memories. The deep feelings of the boy K. were there in his pictures—the way his eyes were opened on the world. The things we did together, the places we went together began to come back to me with great intensity. And I realized that his eyes were my eyes, that I myself had looked upon the world back then with the same lively, unclouded vision as the boy who had walked by my side.

52    I made a habit after that of studying one of K.'s pictures at my desk each day when I got home from work. I could sit there for hours with one painting. In each I found another of those soft landscapes of childhood that I had shut out of my memory for so long. I had a

sense, whenever I looked at one of K.'s works, that something was permeating my very flesh.

53  Perhaps a week had gone by like this when the thought suddenly struck me one evening: I might have been making a terrible mistake all those years. As he lay there in the tip of the wave, surely K. had not been looking at me with hatred or resentment; he had not been trying to take me away with him. And that terrible grin he had fixed me with: that, too, could have been an accident of angle or light and shadow, not a conscious act on K.'s part. He had probably already lost consciousness, or perhaps he had been giving me a gentle smile of eternal parting. The intense look of hatred I thought I saw on his face had been nothing but a reflection of the **profound** terror that had taken control of me for the moment.

54  The more I studied K.'s watercolor that evening, the greater the conviction with which I began to believe these new thoughts of mine. For no matter how long I continued to look at the picture, I could find nothing in it but a boy's gentle, innocent spirit.

55  I went on sitting at my desk for a very long time. There was nothing else I could do. The sun went down, and the pale darkness of evening began to envelop the room. Then came the deep silence of night, which seemed to go on for ever. At last, the scales tipped, and dark gave way to dawn. The new day's sun tinged the sky with pink.

56  It was then I knew I must go back.

57  I threw a few things in a bag, called the company to say I would not be in, and boarded a train for my old home town.

58  I did not find the same quiet, little seaside town that I remembered. An industrial city had sprung up nearby during the rapid development of the Sixties, bringing great changes to the landscape. The one little gift shop by the station had grown into a mall, and the town's only movie theatre had been turned into a supermarket. My house was no longer there. It had been demolished some months before, leaving only a scrape on the earth. The trees in the yard had all been cut down, and patches of weeds dotted the black stretch of ground. K.'s old house had disappeared as well, having been replaced by a concrete parking lot full of commuters' cars and vans. Not that I was overcome by sentiment. The town had ceased to be mine long before.

59  I walked down to the shore and climbed the steps of the breakwater. On the other side, as always, the ocean stretched off into the distance, unobstructed, huge, the horizon a single straight line. The shoreline, too, looked the same as it had before: the long beach, the lapping waves, people strolling at the water's edge. The time was after four o'clock, and the soft sun of late afternoon embraced everything below as it began its long, almost **meditative**, descent to the west. I lowered my bag to the sand and sat down next to it in silent appreciation of the gentle seascape. Looking at this scene, it was impossible to imagine that a great typhoon had once raged here, that a massive wave had swallowed my best friend in all the world. There was almost no one left now, surely, who remembered those

© Pearson Education, Inc., or its affiliates. All rights reserved.

NOTES

**profound** (pruh FOWND) *adj.* intense; deep

**CLOSE READ**
**ANNOTATE:** In paragraph 58, mark details that suggest harshness or hardness. Then, mark details in paragraph 59 that suggest softness and calm.

**QUESTION:** Why does the author use these particular details in this way?

**CONCLUDE:** What change in the narrator's perspective is revealed by the author's word choice?

**meditative** (MEHD uh tay tihv) *adj.* given to extended thought

terrible events. It began to seem as if the whole thing were an illusion that I had dreamed up in vivid detail.

60    And then I realized that the deep darkness inside me had vanished. Suddenly. As suddenly as it had come. I raised myself from the sand and, without bothering to take off my shoes or roll up my cuffs, walked into the surf to let the waves lap at my ankles.

61    Almost in reconciliation, it seemed, the same waves that had washed up on the beach when I was a boy were now fondly washing my feet, soaking black my shoes and pant cuffs. There would be one slow-moving wave, then a long pause, and then another wave would come and go. The people passing by gave me odd looks, but I didn't care.

62    I looked up at the sky. A few gray cotton chunks of cloud hung there, motionless. They seemed to be there for me, though I'm not sure why I felt that way. I remembered having looked up at the sky like this in search of the "eye" of the typhoon. And then, inside me, the axis of time gave one great heave. Forty long years collapsed like a dilapidated house, mixing old time and new time together in a single swirling mass. All sounds faded, and the light around me shuddered. I lost my balance and fell into the waves. My heart throbbed at the back of my throat, and my arms and legs lost all sensation. I lay that way for a long time, face in the water, unable to stand. But I was not afraid. No, not at all. There was no longer anything for me to fear. Those days were gone.

63    I stopped having my terrible nightmares. I no longer wake up screaming in the middle of the night. And I am trying now to start life over again. No, I know it's probably too late to start again. I may not have much time left to live. But even if it comes too late, I am grateful that, in the end, I was able to attain a kind of salvation, to effect some sort of recovery. Yes, grateful: I could have come to the end of my life unsaved, still screaming in the dark, afraid.

*  *  *

64    The seventh man fell silent and turned his gaze upon each of the others. No one spoke or moved or even seemed to breathe. All were waiting for the rest of his story. Outside, the wind had fallen, and nothing stirred. The seventh man brought his hand to his collar once again, as if in search of words.

65    "They tell us that the only thing we have to fear is fear itself; but I don't believe that," he said. Then, a moment later, he added: "Oh, the fear is there, all right. It comes to us in many different forms, at different times, and overwhelms us. But the most frightening thing we can do at such times is to turn our backs on it, to close our eyes. For then we take the most precious thing inside us and surrender it to something else. In my case, that something was the wave." ❧

## CLOSE READ

**ANNOTATE:** In paragraph 62, mark words or phrases that suggest dramatic motion and stillness.

**QUESTION:** How do these words and phrases show what is happening to the narrator physically?

**CONCLUDE:** What deeper idea is the author conveying through this word choice?

# Comprehension Check

Complete the following items after you finish your first read.

1. What traumatic event changes the seventh man's life?

2. Why does the seventh man's father allow him to go outside during the storm?

3. At the beach, why doesn't K. respond when his friend calls out to him?

4. What does the seventh man see inside the second wave?

5. What does the seventh man do when he returns to his hometown that shows he has finally recovered from his traumatic experience?

6. 🗂 **Notebook** To confirm your understanding, write a summary of "The Seventh Man."

- - - - - - - - - - - - - - - - - - - - - - - - - - - - - - - - - - - - - - - - - - - -

## RESEARCH

**Research to Clarify** Choose at least one unfamiliar detail from the text. Briefly research that detail. In what way does the information you learned shed light on an aspect of the story?

**Research to Explore** Choose something from the text that interested you and formulate a research question.

THE SEVENTH MAN

## Close Read the Text

1. The model, from paragraph 5 of the story, shows two sample annotations, along with questions and conclusions. Close read the passage, and find another detail to annotate. Then, write a question and your conclusion.

**Close Read**
ANNOTATE · QUESTION · CONCLUDE

> ANNOTATE: This phrase describes the wave in almost human terms.
>
> QUESTION: What effect does this word choice create?
>
> CONCLUDE: This description makes the wave seem alive and evil.

ANNOTATE: This word is repeated.

QUESTION: Why does the author repeat the word *years*?

CONCLUDE: The repetition emphasizes how long it takes the man to recover from the experience.

> "It just barely missed me, but in my place it swallowed everything that mattered most to me and swept it off to another world. I took years to find it again and to recover from the experience—precious years that can never be replaced."

**Tool Kit**
Close-Read Guide and Model Annotation

2. For more practice, go back into the story and complete the close-read notes.

3. Revisit a section of the text you found important during your first read. Read this section closely, and **annotate** what you notice. Ask yourself **questions** such as "Why did the author make this choice?" What can you **conclude**?

## Analyze the Text

**CITE TEXTUAL EVIDENCE** to support your answers.

**Notebook** Respond to these questions.

1. **Interpret** What does the wave **symbolize,** or represent, to the seventh man?

2. (a) After he rediscovers K.'s watercolors, what does the seventh man do with them? (b) **Interpret** What do K.'s watercolors symbolize to him?

3. (a) **Paraphrase** When you **paraphrase,** you restate a text in your own words. Paraphrase the seventh man's comments about fear in the story's final paragraph. (b) **Make a Judgment** Do you agree or disagree with the seventh man's comments? Explain.

4. **Evaluate** Although the seventh man did not die, did he truly escape the wave? Explain your position, citing story details.

5. **Essential Question:** *What does it take to survive?* What have you learned about the nature of survival by reading this story?

**STANDARDS**
**RL.9–10.5** Analyze how an author's choices concerning how to structure a text, order events within it, and manipulate time create such effects as mystery, tension, or surprise.

# Analyze Craft and Structure

**Author's Choices: Order of Events** A **frame story** is a story that brackets—or *frames*—another story or group of stories. This device creates a story-within-a-story narrative structure.

- Typically, the frame story is found at the beginning and again at the end of the work.

- Within this frame, the author shifts the narrative to a second, or interior, story.

- The interior story may be told by a different narrator or shift to a different point of view.

In "The Seventh Man," the frame story is told by a **third-person narrator**, who is an outside voice rather than a participant in the story. By contrast, the interior story is told in **first-person narration** by the seventh man himself.

## Practice

CITE TEXTUAL EVIDENCE to support your answers.

Reread paragraphs 1–8 and 63–65 of "The Seventh Man."

📓 **Notebook** **Respond to these questions.**

1. (a) At what points in "The Seventh Man" does the frame story begin and end? (b) What aspects of the text change to indicate these shifts?

2. (a) Record in the chart details from the frame story that describe the seventh man. (b) What do these details tell you about the seventh man's character?

| THE SEVENTH MAN: FRAME STORY DETAILS | |
|---|---|
| his appearance | |
| his speaking style | |
| his behavior | |

3. (a) Imagine that the frame story used first-person narration. Which details from your chart would most likely not appear in the story? (b) How does the use of third-person narration in the frame affect readers' understanding of the seventh man?

4. How does the use of first-person narration affect what readers learn and feel about the seventh man, K., and the events of the interior story?

5. Why do you think the author chose to use a frame structure to tell this story? What does the frame structure allow that a more basic story structure might not?

THE SEVENTH MAN

## Concept Vocabulary

| | | |
|---|---|---|
| desperate | hallucination | profound |
| entranced | premonition | meditative |

**Why These Words?** These concept words help to reveal the emotional state of the seventh man. For example, when the wave approaches, the seventh man is *entranced*, waiting for it to attack. After the wave hits, the seventh man believes he sees his friend K. in the wave and claims that this experience was no *hallucination*. Notice that both words relate to experiences that occur only in the mind of the seventh man.

1. How does the concept vocabulary sharpen the reader's understanding of the mental or emotional state of the seventh man?

2. What other words in the selection connect to this concept?

### Practice

🔲 **Notebook** The concept vocabulary words appear in "The Seventh Man."

1. Use each concept word in a sentence that demonstrates your understanding of the word's meaning.

2. Challenge yourself to replace the concept word with one or two synonyms. How does the word change affect the meaning of your sentence? For example, which sentence is stronger? Which has a more positive meaning?

## Word Study

**Latin Suffix: -tion** The Latin suffix *-tion* often indicates that a word is a noun. Sometimes this suffix is spelled *-ion* or *-ation.* In any of its forms, it means "act, state, or condition of." In "The Seventh Man," the word *premonition* means "the state of being forewarned."

1. Record a definition of *hallucination* based on your understanding of its root word and the meaning of the suffix *-tion*.

2. Look back at paragraphs 37–40 and find two other words that end with the suffix *-tion*. In each case, identify the root word that has been combined with the suffix. Record a definition for each word.

---

**🔀 WORD NETWORK**

Add interesting words related to survival from the text to your Word Network.

---

**⠿ STANDARDS**

**L.9–10.1.b** Use various types of phrases and clauses to convey specific meanings and add variety and interest to writing or presentations.

**L.9–10.4.b** Identify and correctly use patterns of word changes that indicate different meanings or parts of speech, and continue to apply knowledge of Greek and Latin roots and affixes.

**L.9–10.5.b** Analyze nuances in the meaning of words with similar denotations.

# Conventions

**Infinitives and Infinitive Phrases** An **infinitive** is a verb form that generally appears with the word *to* in front of it and acts as a noun, an adjective, or an adverb. An **infinitive phrase** consists of an infinitive and its objects, complements, or modifiers, all acting together as a single part of speech. Like an infinitive, an infinitive phrase acts as a noun, an adjective, or an adverb.

The examples in the chart show uses of infinitives and infinitive phrases.

**TIP**

**CLARIFICATION**
Don't confuse infinitives with prepositional phrases. A prepositional phrase always ends with a noun or a pronoun. An infinitive always ends with a verb.

| INFINITIVE | INFINITIVE PHRASE |
|---|---|
| **Used as a Noun** <br><br> *To succeed* requires dedication. <br><br> (functions as the subject of the sentence) | **Used as a Noun** <br><br> We chose *to take the old foot path*. <br><br> (functions as the direct object of the verb *chose*) |
| **Used as an Adjective** <br><br> I wish I had the <u>ability</u> *to fly*. <br><br> (tells *what kind* of ability) | **Used as an Adjective** <br><br> Dana's <u>desire</u> *to do well* made Mama proud. <br><br> (tells *which* desire) |
| **Used as an Adverb** <br><br> When Derrick <u>sat</u> down *to study,* he concentrated. <br><br> (tells *why* Derrick sat down) | **Used as an Adverb** <br><br> She <u>called</u> the editor *to voice her opinion*. <br><br> (tells *why* she called) |

## Read It

1. Mark the infinitive in each sentence from "The Seventh Man." Then, label each infinitive phrase as a noun, an adjective, or an adverb.

   a. I didn't want to wake someone sleeping next to me with my screams in the middle of the night.

   b. It took me a long time to recover from the emotional shock.

   c. This was where we came to play almost every day, so there was no part of it we didn't know well.

2. Reread paragraph 31 of "The Seventh Man." Mark each infinitive, and label each infinitive phrase as a noun, an adjective, or an adverb.

## Write It

📓 **Notebook** For each of these sentences, write a new sentence that expresses a similar idea but includes an infinitive or infinitive phrase. Mark each infinitive, and note whether each infinitive or infinitive phrase is a noun, an adjective, or an adverb.

1. K. was an unimaginably gifted artist for his age.

2. The seventh man was so filled with grief he never married.

THE SEVENTH MAN

# Writing to Sources

Critical writing is a type of argumentation in which you explain your insights about a literary work and persuade others to share your point of view. Like any argument, critical writing requires you to state a claim, or position, and to support it with strong evidence.

### Assignment

Write a **critical review** of "The Seventh Man" that could appear in your school paper or website. State specific reasons why you either recommend or do not recommend the story to other readers.

Your review should include:

- Title and author of the work being reviewed
- A brief summary of the work
- A clear statement of your claim, or position
- Valid reasoning that is supported by text evidence

**Vocabulary and Conventions Connection** In your review, consider including several of the concept vocabulary words. Also, consider using infinitive phrases to add variety to your sentences.

| desperate | hallucination | profound |
|-----------|---------------|----------|
| entranced | premonition | meditative |

- - - - - - - - - - - - - - - - - - - - - - - - - - - - - - - - - - - - - - - - - - - - -

## Reflect on Your Writing

After you have written your critical review, answer the following questions.

1. How do you think writing your critical review strengthened your understanding of the story?

2. What evidence and supporting details did you use in your writing? How did they help support your claim?

3. **Why These Words?** The words you choose make a difference in your writing. Which words did you specifically choose to add power to your critical review?

**STANDARDS**
**W.9–10.1.a** Introduce precise claim(s), distinguish the claim(s) from alternate or opposing claims, and create an organization that establishes clear relationships among the claim(s), counterclaims, reasons, and evidence.

**SL.9–10.4.b** Plan, memorize, and present a recitation that: conveys the meaning of the selection and includes appropriate performance techniques to achieve the desired aesthetic effect.

## Speaking and Listening

**Assignment**

With a partner, prepare a **retelling** of "The Seventh Man" from another point of view. For example, you may choose to retell the story from K.'s parents' point of view, or from that of a hidden onlooker. Refresh your memory by rereading the selection. Then, follow these steps to complete the assignment.

1. **Identify Your Character** Choose your character and determine how he or she fits into the original story. Decide what important information you will need to tell your audience to clarify the character's background and motivations.

2. **Plan Your Retelling** Once you've identified your character, think about his or her perspective on the events in the story. As you plan your retelling, keep the following in mind:

   • How does your character see the story differently from the seventh man? What fresh perspective does he or she offer?

   • Make a list of the story events, as experienced by your character. Then, weave those events into a coherent retelling.

   • Choose language that is appropriate to the character you chose. For example, a child would choose simple words and sentences and may not fully understand what is he or she is observing.

3. **Prepare Your Delivery** Practice your retelling with your partner. Include the following performance techniques to help you achieve the desired effect.

   • Vary your intonation to reflect the emotions of your character. Avoid speaking in a flat, monotone style.

   • As you speak, use facial expressions and gestures that help convey your character's personality.

   • Make eye contact with your audience to engage them in the story.

4. **Evaluate Retellings** As your classmates deliver their retellings, listen attentively. Use an evaluation guide like the one shown to analyze their delivery.

**EVALUATION GUIDE**

**Rate each statement on a scale of 1 (not demonstrated) to 4 (demonstrated).**

☐ The character was clearly identified.

☐ The speaker communicated clearly and expressively.

☐ The speaker used a variety of speaking tones and pitches.

☐ The speaker used effective gestures and other body language.

**EVIDENCE LOG**

Before moving on to a new selection, go to your Evidence Log and record what you learned from "The Seventh Man."

## About the Author

**Nancy Sherman**
(b. 1951) always wanted to understand more about what her father went through as a soldier during World War II. Her opportunity came when she served as the first Distinguished Chair in Ethics at the U.S. Naval Academy from 1997–99. Sherman is now a University Professor of Philosophy at Georgetown University, and her research includes military ethics, the history of moral philosophy, and moral psychology.

**Tool Kit**
First-Read Guide and Model Annotation

STANDARDS

**RI.9–10.10** By the end of grade 9, read and comprehend literary nonfiction in the grades 9–10 text complexity band proficiently, with scaffolding as needed at the high end of the range.

# The Moral Logic of Survivor Guilt

## Concept Vocabulary

You will encounter the following words as you read "The Moral Logic of Survivor Guilt." Before reading, note how familiar you are with each word. Then, rank the words in order from most familiar (1) to least familiar (6).

| WORD | YOUR RANKING |
|------|--------------|
| burden | |
| culpability | |
| conscience | |
| remorse | |
| entrusted | |
| empathic | |

After completing your first read, review your original rankings. Make any changes to your rankings as needed.

## First Read NONFICTION

Apply these strategies as you conduct your first read. You will have an opportunity to complete the close-read notes after your first read.

**NOTICE** the general ideas of the text. *What* is it about? *Who* is involved?

**ANNOTATE** by marking vocabulary and key passages you want to revisit.

**First Read**

**CONNECT** ideas within the selection to what you already know and what you have already read.

**RESPOND** by completing the Comprehension Check and by writing a brief summary of the selection.

# The Moral Logic of Survivor Guilt

Nancy Sherman

SCAN FOR
MULTIMEDIA

## BACKGROUND

Traumatic events take a toll on the physical and mental well-being of the individuals who must endure them. Survivors of the Holocaust, rescue workers, and war veterans, for example, might wonder how they were able to make it out alive when others did not. The term "survivor guilt" is used to describe these feelings.

1   If there is one thing we have learned from returning war veterans—especially those of the last decade—it's that the emotional reality of the soldier at home is often at odds with that of the civilian public they left behind. And while friends and families of returning service members may be experiencing gratefulness or relief this holiday,[1] many of those they've welcomed home are likely struggling with other emotions.

### Is the sense of responsibility soldiers feel toward each other irrational?

2   High on that list of emotions is guilt. Soldiers often carry this **burden** home—survivor guilt being perhaps the kind most familiar to us. In war, standing here rather than there can save your life but cost a buddy his. It's flukish luck, but you feel responsible. The guilt begins an endless loop of counterfactuals—thoughts that you could have or should have done otherwise, though in fact you did nothing wrong. The feelings are, of course, not restricted to the battlefield. But given the magnitude[2] of loss in war, they hang heavy there and are pervasive. And they raise the question of just how irrational those feelings are, and if they aren't, of what is the basis of their reasonableness.

NOTES

**CLOSE READ**
**ANNOTATE:** Mark words in paragraph 1 that show opposites.

**QUESTION:** What groups of people are being contrasted by using these opposites?

**CONCLUDE:** What does this contrast suggest about the two groups?

**burden** (BURD uhn) *n.* something that is carried with difficulty or obligation

---

1. **this holiday** This essay was originally published the day before the Fourth of July (Independence Day).
2. **magnitude** *n.* great size or extent.

3       Capt. Adrian Bonenberger, head of a unit in Afghanistan, pondered those questions recently as he thought about Specialist Jeremiah Pulaski, who was killed by police in the wake of a deadly bar fight shortly after he returned home. Back in Afghanistan, Pulaski had saved Bonenberger's life twice on one day, but when Pulaski needed help, Bonenberger couldn't be there for him: "When he was in trouble, he was alone," Captain Bonenberger said. "When we were in trouble, he was there for us. I know it's not rational or reasonable. There's nothing logical about it. But I feel responsible."

4       But how unreasonable is that feeling? Subjective guilt, associated with this sense of responsibility, is thought to be irrational because one feels guilty despite the fact that he knows he has done nothing wrong. Objective or rational guilt, by contrast—guilt that is "fitting" to one's actions—accurately tracks real wrongdoing or **culpability**: guilt is appropriate because one acted to deliberately harm someone, or could have prevented harm and did not. Blameworthiness, here, depends on the idea that a person could have done something other than he did. And so he is held responsible or accountable, by himself or others.

5       But as Bonenberger's remarks make clear, we often *take* responsibility in a way that goes beyond what we can reasonably be *held* responsible for. And we feel the guilt that comes with that sense of responsibility. Nietzsche is the modern philosopher who well understood this phenomenon: "Das schlechte Gewissen," (literally, "bad **conscience**")—his term for the consciousness of guilt where one has done no wrong, doesn't grow in the soil where we would most expect it, he argued, such as in prisons where there are actually "guilty" parties who should feel **remorse** for wrongdoing. In "The Genealogy of Morals," he appeals to an earlier philosopher, Spinoza, for support: "The bite of conscience," writes Spinoza in the "Ethics," has to do with an "offense" where "something has gone unexpectedly wrong." As Nietzsche adds, it is not really a case of "I ought not to have done that."

6       But what then is it a case of? Part of the reasonableness of survivor guilt (and in a sense, its "fittingness") is that it tracks a moral significance that is broader than moral *action*. Who I am, in terms of my character and relationships, and not just what I do, matters morally. Of course, character is expressed in action, and when we don't "walk the walk," we are lacking; but it is also expressed in emotions and attitudes. Aristotle[3] in his "Nicomachean Ethics" insists on the point: "virtue is concerned with emotions and actions;" to have good character is to "hit the mean"[4] with respect to both. Moreover, many of the feelings that express character are not about what one has done or should have done, but rather about what one cares deeply about. Though Aristotle doesn't himself talk about guilt, it is the emotion that best expresses that conflict—the desire or obligation to help frustrated by the inability, through no fault of one's

**culpability** (kuhl puh BIHL uh tee) *n.* guilt or blame that is deserved; blameworthiness

**conscience** (KON shuhns) *n.* inner sense of what is morally right or wrong in one's actions

**remorse** (rih MAWRS) *n.* deep sense of regret for having done wrong

**CLOSE READ**

**ANNOTATE:** In paragraph 6, mark the words or passages that describe what it means to be a good person.

**QUESTION:** Why does the writer focus on defining what it is to be "good"?

**CONCLUDE:** What purpose do these definitions and examples serve?

---

3. **Aristotle** (AR ihs tot uhl) (384–322 B.C.) ancient Greek philosopher and scientist.
4. **mean** *n.* middle point between two things.

own, to do so. To not feel the guilt is to be numb to those pulls. It is that vulnerability, those pulls, that Bonenberger feels when he says he wasn't there for Pulaski when he needed him.

## The sacred bond among soldiers originates not just in duty, but in love.

7    In many of the interviews I've conducted with soldiers over the years, feelings of guilt and responsibility tangle with feelings of having betrayed fellow soldiers. At stake is the duty to those soldiers, the imperative[5] to hold intact the bond that enables them to fight for and with each other in the kind of "sacred band" that the ancients memorialized and that the Marine motto *semper fidelis*[6] captures so well. But it is not just duty at work. It is love.

8    Service members, especially those higher in rank, routinely talk about unit members as "*my* soldiers," "*my* Marines," "*my* sailors." They are family members, their own children, of sorts, who have been **entrusted** to them. To fall short of unconditional care is experienced as a kind of perfidy, a failure to be faithful. Survivor guilt piles on the unconscious thought that luck is part of a zero-sum game. To have good luck is to deprive another of it. The anguish of guilt, its sheer pain, is a way of sharing some of the ill fate. It is a form of **empathic** distress.

9    Many philosophers have looked to other terms to define the feeling. What they have come up with is "agent-regret" (a term coined by the British philosopher Bernard Williams, but used by many others). The classic scenario is not so much one of good luck (as in survivor guilt), but of bad luck, typically having to do with accidents where again, there is little or no culpability for the harms caused. In these cases, people may be *causally* responsible for harm—they bring about the harm through their agency—but they are not morally responsible for what happened.

10    But to my ear, agent-regret is simply tone-deaf to how subjective guilt feels. Despite the insertion of "agent," it sounds as passive and flat as "regretting that the weather is bad." Or more tellingly, as removed from empathic distress as the message sent to the next of kin, after an official knock on the door: "The Secretary of Defense regrets to inform you that . . . ."[7]

11    Indeed, the soldiers I've talked to, involved in friendly fire accidents that took their comrades' lives, didn't feel regret for what happened, but raw, deep, unabashed guilt. And the guilt persisted long after they were formally investigated and ultimately exonerated. In one wrenching case in April 2003 in Iraq, the gun on a Bradley

---

**entrusted** (ehn TRUHST ihd) *v.* given the responsibility of doing something or caring for someone or something

**empathic** (ehm PATH ihk) *adj.* characterized by empathy, the ability to identify with the feelings or thoughts of others

---

5. **imperative**  *n.* act or duty that is very important or required.
6. **semper fidelis**  (SEHM puhr fih DAY lihs) Latin phrase that means "always faithful." It is the motto of the United States Marine Corps, a branch of the military.
7. **"The Secretary of Defense regrets to inform you that. . . ."**  first sentence of a scripted message spoken by United States military officers when they report the death of a soldier to that soldier's closest living relative.

fighting vehicle misfired, blowing off most of the face of Private Joseph Mayek who was standing guard near the vehicle. The accident was ultimately traced to a faulty replacement battery that the commander in charge had authorized. When the Bradley's ignition was turned on, the replacement battery in the turret (a Marine battery rather than an Army one) failed to shut off current to the gun. Mayek, who was 20, died.

12    The Army officer in charge, then Capt. John Prior, reconstructed the ghastly scene for me, and the failed attempts in the medic tent to save Mayek's life. He then turned to his feelings of responsibility: "I'm the one who placed the vehicles; I'm the one who set the security. As with most accidents, I'm not in jail right now. Clearly I wasn't egregiously responsible. But it is a comedy of errors. Any one of a dozen decisions made over the course of a two-month period and none of them really occurs to you at the time. Any one of those made differently may have saved his life. So I dealt with and still deal with the guilt of having cost him his life essentially. . . . There's probably not a day that doesn't go by that I don't think about it, at least fleetingly."

13    What Prior feels are feelings of guilt, and not simply regret that things didn't work out differently. He feels the awful weight of self-indictment,[8] the empathy with the victim and survivors, and the need to make moral repair. If he didn't feel that, we would probably think less of him as a commander.

14    In his case, moral repair came through an empathic, painful connection with Mayek's mother. After the fratricide, Prior and his first sergeant wrote a letter to Mayek's mother. And for some time after, she replied with care packages to the company and with letters. "Oh it was terrible," said Prior. "The letters weren't just very matter of fact—here's what we did today; it was more like a mother writing to her son." Prior had become the son who was no longer. "It was her way of dealing with the grief," said Prior. "And so I had a responsibility to try to give back."

15    In all this we might say guilt, subjective guilt, has a redemptive side. It is a way that soldiers impose moral order on the chaos and awful randomness of war's violence. It is a way they humanize war for themselves, for their buddies, and for us as civilians, too.

16    But if that's all that is involved, it sounds too moralistic. It makes guilt appropriate or fitting because it's good for society. It is the way we all can deal with war. Maybe, instead, we want to say it is fitting because it is evolutionarily adaptive in the way that fear is. But again, this doesn't do justice to the phenomenon. The guilt that soldiers feel isn't just morally expedient[9] or species-adaptive. It is fitting because it gets right certain moral (or evaluative) features of a soldier's world—that good soldiers depend on each other, come to

---

**CLOSE READ**

**ANNOTATE:** In paragraph 14, mark sentences in which the author states her own observations.

**QUESTION:** How does the quotation from Prior add to or support the author's observations?

**CONCLUDE:** What is the effect of the author's choice to quote Prior?

---

8. **self-indictment** (sehlf ihn DYT muhnt) *n.* expression of strong disapproval toward oneself; self-blame.
9. **expedient** (ehk SPEE dee uhnt) *adj.* providing an easy way to do something; quick.

love each other, and have duties to care and bring each other safely home. Philosophers, at least since the time of Kant,[10] have called these "imperfect duties": even in the best circumstances, we can't perfectly fulfill them. And so, what duties to others need to make room for, even in a soldier's life of service and sacrifice, are duties to self, of self-forgiveness and self-empathy. These are a part of full moral repair. ❧

___

10. **Kant** (1724–1804) Immanuel Kant, German philosopher who was a foremost thinker of the European Enlightenment.

# Comprehension Check

Complete the following items after you finish your first read.

1. What is survivor guilt?

2. According to the writer, what other emotions do soldiers describe when they talk about feeling guilt?

3. What happened to Private Joseph Mayek, and why does Captain John Prior feel responsible?

4. 🗒 **Notebook** Write a summary of "The Moral Logic of Survivor Guilt" to confirm your understanding of the text.

- - - - - - - - - - - - - - - - - - - - - - - - - - - - - - - - - - - - - - - - - -

## RESEARCH

**Research to Clarify** Choose at least one unfamiliar detail from the text. Briefly research that detail. In what way does the information you learned shed light on an aspect of the editorial?

**Research to Explore** Conduct research to learn about the history of the official Marine code, *semper fidelis*, and what it signifies.

THE MORAL LOGIC OF
SURVIVOR GUILT

## Close Read the Text

1. This model, from paragraph 4 of the text, shows two sample annotations, along with questions and conclusions. Close read the passage, and find another detail to annotate. Then, write a question and your conclusion.

Close
Read

ANNOTATE QUESTION CONCLUDE

ANNOTATE: This phrase signals that the writer is contrasting two ideas.

QUESTION: What two ideas are being contrasted here?

CONCLUDE: The writer contrasts subjective and objective guilt.

ANNOTATE: These details define subjective and objective guilt.

QUESTION: Why does the author add these details?

CONCLUDE: The writer is making sure to define key concepts so that readers are not confused and can follow her logic.

> Subjective guilt, associated with this sense of responsibility, is thought to be irrational because one feels guilty despite the fact that he knows he has done nothing wrong. Objective or rational guilt, by contrast—guilt that is "fitting" to one's actions—accurately tracks real wrongdoing or culpability: guilt is appropriate because one acted to deliberately harm someone, or could have prevented harm and did not.

2. For more practice, go back into the text and complete the close-read notes.

3. Revisit a section of the text you found important during your first read. Read this section closely, and **annotate** what you notice. Ask yourself **questions** such as "Why did the author make this choice?" What can you **conclude**?

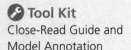

**Tool Kit**
Close-Read Guide and
Model Annotation

### STANDARDS

**RI.9–10.1** Cite strong and thorough textual evidence to support analysis of what the text says explicitly as well as inferences drawn from the text.

**RI.9–10.2** Determine a central idea of a text and analyze its development over the course of the text, including how it emerges and is shaped and refined by specific details; provide an objective summary of the text.

**RI.9–10.8** Delineate and evaluate the argument and specific claims in a text, assessing whether the reasoning is valid and the evidence is relevant and sufficient; identify false statements and fallacious reasoning.

## Analyze the Text

CITE TEXTUAL EVIDENCE
to support your answers.

**Notebook** Respond to these questions.

1. (a) **Make Inferences** Why do many people consider survivor guilt to be irrational, or unreasonable? (b) **Draw Conclusions** How does Sherman respond to this opinion? Explain.

2. **Interpret** What does Sherman mean when she refers to "moral logic" in the title of her essay?

3. (a) **Compare and Contrast** How are Captain Bonenberger's and Captain Prior's experiences similar and different? (b) **Connect** What idea do both of their stories support? Explain.

4. **Essential Question**: *What does it take to survive?* What have you learned about the nature of survival by reading this text?

# Analyze Craft and Structure

**Development of Ideas** "The Moral Logic of Survivor Guilt" is an editorial, a form of argumentative writing. As with all types of arguments, an effective editorial must include a clear claim, or central idea, and specific supporting details.

- The **claim** or **central idea** of a text is more than the topic—it is the key message that the writer wants to communicate about the topic.

- **Specific details** are the evidence a writer uses to support and develop the central idea. Facts, examples, numerical data, personal observations, and expert opinions are different types of supporting details.

In "The Moral Logic of Survivor Guilt," the writer unfolds an argument through careful reasoning. She supports her argument with examples, quotations from or references to the ideas of famous philosophers, and her own observations as a professional in her field.

## Practice

**CITE TEXTUAL EVIDENCE** to support your answers.

📖 **Notebook** Respond to these questions.

1. (a) What key question does Sherman ask early in this editorial? (b) In your own words, briefly state her answer, which is her central idea.

2. Use the chart to record examples of each type of supporting detail Sherman uses to develop her claim, or central idea.

| EXAMPLES FROM REAL LIFE | FAMOUS PHILOSOPHERS' IDEAS | AUTHOR'S IDEAS |
|---|---|---|
|  |  |  |
|  |  |  |
|  |  |  |

3. Choose one of the supporting details you identified in the chart. Explain how Sherman's use of that detail adds to the development of her central idea.

4. (a) In paragraph 8, Sherman compares survivor guilt to "a zero-sum game." Define *zero-sum game*. (b) How does Sherman's use of this mathematical term support her argument?

5. Is Sherman's claim and support well-reasoned and convincing? Explain, citing specific details to support your position.

THE MORAL LOGIC OF
SURVIVOR GUILT

## Concept Vocabulary

| burden | conscience | entrusted |
|---|---|---|
| culpability | remorse | empathic |

**Why These Words?** These concept words help us describe how people take care of others—or fail to do so. For example, Sherman explains that soldiers often carry the burden of guilt home with them. The word *burden* emphasizes that this guilt is both difficult to carry and an obligation. She later discusses *conscience* in order to emphasize the moral dimension of soldiers' emotional responses.

1. How does the concept vocabulary help readers understand the complex experience of survivor guilt?

2. What other words in the selection connect to the idea of taking care of others?

### Practice

🔲 **Notebook** The concept vocabulary words appear in "The Moral Logic of Survivor Guilt."

1. Use each concept word in a sentence that demonstrates your understanding of the word's meaning. Then, create fill-in puzzles by taking turns reading a sentence aloud, but leaving out the concept word. Invite listeners to guess the missing word.

2. Discuss each fill-in puzzle. Which sentences were easy for listeners to complete, and which were difficult? Why?

## Word Study

**Greek Root: -*path*-** The Greek root -*path*-, which appears in the concept vocabulary word *empathic*, means "feeling." It comes from the Greek word *pathos*, meaning "feeling" or "suffering."

1. Write a definition of *empathic* based on your understanding of its root.

2. Define these words that include the same root: *pathetic*, *empathize*, *sympathy*. Consult a college-level dictionary if necessary.

# Conventions

**Punctuation** Writers use punctuation to clarify the relationships among ideas, establish rhythm, and add sentence variety. This chart shows uses for three punctuation marks: **colons (:)**, **semicolons (;)**, and **dashes (—)**.

| USE COLONS TO . . . | EXAMPLES |
|---|---|
| • introduce a list | We bought the following: milk, eggs, and cheese. |
| • introduce a quotation, when it is formal or lengthy or when there is no introductory expression | Holmes wrote this about freedom: "It is only through free debate and free exchange of ideas that government remains responsive to the will of the people." |
| • introduce a sentence that summarizes or explains the sentence before it | His explanation for being late was believable: He had had a flat tire on the way. |

| USE SEMICOLONS TO . . . | EXAMPLES |
|---|---|
| • join closely related complete sentences, without a coordinating conjunction | We explored the attic together; we were amazed at all the useless junk we found there. |
| • join closely related complete sentences, with a transitional word or phrase | They visited shops in eight counties in only two days; consequently, they had no time to relax. |
| • avoid confusion when items in a list or series already contain commas | I sent letters to Alex, my friend from camp; Alana, my pen pal; and Hassan, my cousin. |

| USE DASHES TO . . . | EXAMPLES |
|---|---|
| • indicate an abrupt change of thought or a dramatic interrupting idea | The pagoda was built—you may find this hard to believe—in a single month. |
| • set off a summary statement at the end of a sentence | To see her jersey hanging from the rafters—this was Cherie's greatest dream. |
| • set off a nonessential appositive that is long or already punctuated | The cause of the damage—a rare South American termite—went undiscovered for years. |

## Read It

In these sentences from "The Moral Logic of Survivor Guilt," mark each colon, semicolon, or dash. Then, explain its function in the sentence.

1. The guilt begins an endless loop of counterfactuals—thoughts that you could have or should have done otherwise. . . .

2. Objective or rational guilt . . . tracks real wrongdoing or culpability: Guilt is appropriate because one acted to deliberately harm. . . .

3. "The letters weren't just very matter of fact—here's what we did today; it was more like a mother writing to her son."

## Write It

📓 **Notebook** Write three sentences about the editorial. Use at least one colon, one semicolon, and one dash.

THE MORAL LOGIC OF
SURVIVOR GUILT

# Writing to Sources

The ability to define concepts can be key to a successful argument. When you introduce an unfamiliar or academic idea, it is important to give your readers a clear and accurate definition so that they understand the concept. For example, if you are writing an essay about survivor guilt, you need to explain what is meant by this term before you continue your analysis.

### Assignment

Write an **encyclopedia entry** in which you define the idea of imperfect duty, discussed in paragraph 16 of "The Moral Logic of Survivor Guilt." Present a clear definition of the concept, and then clarify your definition with two types of information:

- key details from Sherman's essay that help you understand this concept (see paragraph 16).

- an anecdote, or brief story, that illustrates the concept. Use your own anecdote, not one provided by Sherman in her essay.

**Vocabulary and Conventions Connection** You might consider using some of the concept vocabulary in your definition, explanation, and anecdote. Use colons, semicolons, and dashes to clarify connections between ideas and add emphasis.

| | | |
|---|---|---|
| burden | conscience | entrusted |
| culpability | remorse | empathic |

- - - - - - - - - - - - - - - - - - - - - - - - - - - - - - - - - - - - - - - - - - - -

### Reflect on Your Writing

After you have written your encyclopedia entry, answer the following questions:

1. How did providing an anecdote help you clarify the concept of an imperfect duty?

2. What advice would you give to another student writing an encyclopedia entry?

3. **Why These Words?** The words you choose make a difference in your writing. Which words did you specifically choose to add power or clarity to your entry?

STANDARDS

**W.9–10.2.a** Introduce a topic or thesis statement; organize complex ideas, concepts, and information to make important connections and distinctions; include formatting, graphics, and multimedia when useful to aiding comprehension.

**SL.9–10.4.a** Plan and deliver an informative/explanatory presentation that: presents evidence in support of a thesis, conveys information from primary and secondary sources coherently, uses domain specific vocabulary, and provides a conclusion that summarizes the main points.

# Speaking and Listening

## Assignment

Write and deliver a **pep talk** you might give to a group of firefighters, a Scout troop, or members of another service organization who have experienced a failure. Explain why it is important that they strive to fulfill their vows, but also forgive themselves when they fail. Include ideas from Sherman's essay, explaining or simplifying them as needed.

1. **Organize Your Talk** Use an outline to gather ideas for your pep talk. Once you have gathered details, organize them logically and delete unneeded information.

| | |
|---|---|
| Introduction | Describe the reasons for your speech, including your knowledge of the recent failure. State your central idea clearly and in inspiring language. |
| Body | Provide details that explain your ideas. Arrange the details logically, in an order that makes sense. Note the ideas from Sherman's essay that you will include. For example, you might point out that your listeners' vows are "imperfect duties." |
| Conclusion | Summarize your main points. |

2. **Prepare Your Delivery** Using the notes in your outline, practice giving your pep talk. Record yourself rehearsing, or ask a partner to listen and respond. While rehearsing, keep these techniques in mind:
   - Maintain eye contact with your audience.
   - Use body language to emphasize important ideas.
   - Speak clearly without rushing, taking care to pronounce unfamiliar terms slowly.

3. **Evaluate Presentations** As your classmates deliver their pep talks, listen attentively. Use a presentation evaluation guide like the one shown to analyze their presentations.

### PRESENTATION EVALUATION GUIDE

Rate each statement on a scale of 1 (not demonstrated) to 6 (demonstrated).

☐ The speaker communicated a positive message clearly and effectively.

☐ The speaker used examples from Sherman's essay effectively.

☐ The speaker maintained eye contact with the audience.

☐ The speaker used effective gestures and other body language.

☐ The information was presented logically and effectively.

☐ The pep talk concluded with a restatement of the speaker's main points.

### ☑ EVIDENCE LOG

Before moving on to a new selection, go to your Evidence Log and record what you learned from "The Moral Logic of Survivor Guilt."

## About the Narrator

**Shankar Vedantam**
(b. 1969) worked as a reporter for the *Washington Post* for ten years before joining National Public Radio as a science correspondent in 2011. Inspired by a story he had done about hidden biases, Vedantam wrote *The Hidden Brain*, a book that examines the complexities of the unconscious. His reporting ties together his interests in both human behavior and the social sciences, giving readers and listeners unique insight into daily news.

# The Key to Disaster Survival? Friends and Neighbors

## Media Vocabulary

The following words or concepts will be useful to you as you analyze, discuss, and write about media.

| | |
|---|---|
| **Introduction:** context and background information about the topic of a radio broadcast, provided at its beginning | • The introduction is meant to grab listeners' attention so they'll want to keep listening and learn more about the story.<br>• The introduction is usually brief and functions to "set the stage" for the full story. |
| **Expert Commentary:** information delivered by a person who has special knowledge of the subject | • Expert commentary is often used to support a specific point of view.<br>• Although expert commentary may be used to validate a story, it is still up to listeners to decide whether it is credible. |
| **Interpreter:** person who changes the words of one language into another for the benefit of listeners | • Listeners will often hear a response in the speaker's language before the interpreter restates the words in the listeners' language. |

## First Review MEDIA: AUDIO

Apply these strategies as you listen to the radio broadcast.

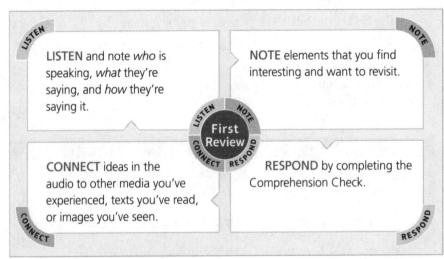

LISTEN and note *who* is speaking, *what* they're saying, and *how* they're saying it.

NOTE elements that you find interesting and want to revisit.

CONNECT ideas in the audio to other media you've experienced, texts you've read, or images you've seen.

RESPOND by completing the Comprehension Check.

## Listening Strategy: Take Notes

**Notebook** As you listen, write down your observations and questions, making sure to note time codes so you can easily revisit sections later.

## ☷ STANDARDS

**L.9–10.6** Acquire and use accurately grade-appropriate general academic and domain-specific words and phrases, sufficient for reading, writing, speaking, and listening at the college and career readiness level; demonstrate independence in gathering vocabulary knowledge when considering a word or phrase important to comprehension or expression.

# The Key to Disaster Survival? Friends and Neighbors

Shankar Vedantam

## BACKGROUND

Since the beginning of the twenty-first century, there have been numerous large-scale natural disasters. The earthquake and tsunami that hit the east coast of Japan in 2011 killed more than 15,000 people and caused an estimated 300 billion dollars' worth of damage. The tragic, catastrophic 2004 Indian Ocean tsunami killed more than 230,000 people. In the wake of natural disaster, governments and NGOs—nongovernment organizations—try to rebuild the affected regions. In areas at risk of disaster, people are encouraged to make preparations such as drafting a survival plan, stockpiling resources, and designating a storm shelter in their home.

SCAN FOR MULTIMEDIA

NOTES

# Comprehension Check

Complete the following items after you finish your first review.

1. What information does the show's host give the listener during the introduction of the broadcast?

2. What event causes Daniel Aldridge's neighbor to knock on Aldridge's door late at night?

3. What event does Aldridge use to study the effect of neighbors' helping one another in Japan?

4. Who helped Michinori Watanabe save his father?

**MEDIA VOCABULARY**

Use these words as you discuss and write about the broadcast.

**introduction**
**expert commentary**
**interpreter**

⬢ WORD NETWORK

Add interesting survival words from the broadcast to your Word Network.

≣ STANDARDS

**SL.9–10.3** Evaluate a speaker's point of view, reasoning, and use of evidence and rhetoric, identifying any fallacious reasoning or exaggerated or distorted evidence.

**SL.9–10.4.a** Plan and deliver an informative/explanatory presentation that: presents information in support of a thesis, conveys information from primary and secondary sources coherently, uses domain specific vocabulary, and provides a conclusion that summarizes the main points.

## Close Review

Listen to the broadcast again. Write down any new observations that seem important. What **questions** do you have? What can you **conclude**?

## Analyze the Media

**CITE TEXTUAL EVIDENCE**
to support your answers.

▣ **Notebook** Respond to these questions.

1. **(a)** What does Michinori Watanabe's story add to the broadcast? **(b) Evaluate** Is it important to hear Watanabe's firsthand account translated for an English audience? Explain.

2. **(a)** What information does Emily Chamlee-Wright provide? **(b) Draw a Conclusion** Why do you think Shankar Vedantam includes the economist's thoughts after the stories of people in disaster situations?

3. The central idea is reiterated at the end of the broadcast. How does the story of the fishing villages contribute to the central idea?

4. **Essential Question: *What does it take to survive?*** What have you learned about the nature of survival by listening to this broadcast?

THE KEY TO DISASTER SURVIVAL?
FRIENDS AND NEIGHBORS

# Writing to Sources

Many radio-show websites include a comments section and invite listeners to share their thoughts about the shows.

### Assignment

Write a **listener comment** about this radio broadcast. In one to three paragraphs, explain how the show affected you and evaluate the points of view of the people documented in the broadcast, their reasoning, and their explanations.

- Use a friendly but formal tone.
- Develop your ideas by jotting down answers to these questions:
  - Does the broadcast convince you that neighbors can be more effective at helping than authorities? Explain your thinking.
  - Are there other questions you think Shankar Vedantam should have asked? If so, what are they?
  - How do you think professional rescue workers might respond to this broadcast? What do you think a government official would say?

# Speaking and Listening

This broadcast summarizes the circumstances of a few individuals who faced disaster scenarios.

### Assignment

Consider this question: *Does the radio broadcast present the full picture?* With a partner, research disaster relief efforts. Consult primary and secondary sources: newspapers, broadcast media, and accounts written by disaster survivors. Plan, write, and present your findings in an informal **oral presentation**.

- Organize your information into talking points—a list of brief statements you can refer to while sharing your findings.
- Include a statement that answers the research question.
- Using your talking points, present your findings to the class.

### ✒ EVIDENCE LOG

Before moving on to a new selection, go to your Evidence Log and record what you learned from "The Key to Disaster Survival? Friends and Neighbors."

WRITING TO SOURCES

- THE SEVENTH MAN

- THE MORAL LOGIC OF SURVIVOR GUILT

- THE KEY TO DISASTER SURVIVAL? FRIENDS AND NEIGHBORS

# Write an Argument

You've read a short story and a newspaper opinion piece that deal with the issue of survivor guilt. You've also listened to a radio broadcast about the ways in which friends can help one another in survival situations. In "The Seventh Man," the narrator describes the loss of his closest friend. In "The Moral Logic of Survivor Guilt," the author makes an argument about the guilt that surviving soldiers often feel for their fallen comrades. In the radio broadcast, neighbors and friends come to one another's aid.

**Assignment**

Use your knowledge of "The Seventh Man," "The Moral Logic of Survivor Guilt," and "The Key to Disaster Survival…" to take and defend a position on the topic. Write a brief **argument** in which you state and support your position on this question:

> Should the narrator of "The Seventh Man" forgive himself for his failure to save K.?

## Elements of an Argument

An **argument** is a logical way of presenting a viewpoint, belief, or stand on an issue. A well-written argument may convince the reader, change the reader's mind, or motivate the reader to take a certain action.

An effective argument contains these elements:

- a precise claim
- consideration of counterclaims, or opposing positions, and a discussion of their strengths and weaknesses
- logical organization that makes clear connections among claim, counterclaim, reasons, and evidence
- valid reasoning and relevant and sufficient evidence
- a concluding statement or section that logically completes the argument
- formal and objective language and tone
- error-free grammar, including accurate use of transitions

**ACADEMIC VOCABULARY**

As you craft your argument, consider using some of the academic vocabulary you learned in the beginning of the unit.

evidence
credible
valid
formulate
logical

**Model Argument** For a model of a well-crafted argument, see the Launch Text, "The Cost of Survival."

Challenge yourself to find all of the elements of an effective argument in the text. You will have an opportunity to review these elements as you prepare to write your own argument.

LAUNCH TEXT

The Cost of Survival

**STANDARDS**
**W.9–10.1.a–e** Write arguments to support claims in an analysis of substantive topics or texts, using valid reasoning and relevant and sufficient evidence.

**W.9–10.10** Write routinely over extended time frames and shorter time frames for a range of tasks, purposes, and audiences.

# Prewriting / Planning

**Write a Claim** Now that you have thought about how the authors of the selections in this unit make their arguments, write a sentence in which you state your **claim**, or position on the question posed in this assignment. As you continue to write, you may revise your claim or even change it entirely. For now, it will help you choose reasons and supporting evidence.

Claim: _____

_____ .

**Consider Possible Counterclaims** Remember that part of your job is to address **counterclaims**, or opposing positions. Complete these sentences to address a counterclaim.

Another reader might say that _____ .

The reason he or she might think this is because _____ .

The evidence that supports this is _____ .

However, my position is stronger because _____ .

**Gather Evidence From Sources** There are many different types of evidence you can use to support your argument:

- **facts:** statements that can be proved true

- **statistics:** facts presented in the form of numbers

- **anecdotes:** brief stories that illustrate a point

- **quotations from authorities:** statements from experts

- **examples:** facts, ideas, or events that support a general idea

The use of varied evidence can make your argument stronger. For example, you could use the following quotation from the Launch Text to support the point that even professionals sometimes fail in rescue attempts.

*However, arguments against charging for rescue miss an important point. Many rescue workers have lost their own lives saving others.*

—"The Cost of Survival"

**Connect Across Texts** As you write your argument, you will be using evidence from one text to support your analysis of another. Incorporate that evidence in different ways. If the precise words are important, use **exact quotations**. To clarify a complex idea, **paraphrase**, or restate it in your own words. Make sure that your paraphrases accurately reflect the original text.

### ✍ EVIDENCE LOG

Review your Evidence Log and identify key details you may want to cite in your argument.

### ☰ STANDARDS

**W.9–10.1.a** Introduce precise claim(s), distinguish the claim(s) from alternate or opposing claims, and create an organization that establishes clear relationships among claim(s), counterclaims, reasons, and evidence.

**W.9–10.1.b** Develop claim(s) and counterclaims fairly, supplying evidence for each while pointing out the strengths and limitations of both in a manner that anticipates the audience's knowledge level and concerns.

# Drafting

**Organize Your Argument** Most arguments are composed of three parts:

- the **introduction**, in which you state your claim
- the **body**, in which you provide analysis, supporting reasons, and evidence
- the **conclusion**, in which you summarize or restate your claim

Each part of your argument should build on the part that came before, and every point should connect directly to your main claim. This outline shows the key sections of the Launch Text. Notice that each paragraph fulfills a specific purpose.

## Model: "The Cost of Survival" Outline

**INTRODUCTION**
Paragraph 1 states claim: *The adventurer should be the one to foot the bill.*

**BODY**
Paragraph 2 establishes importance: *Two big news stories of 2014 involved rescue missions.*

Paragraph 3 presents/refutes counterclaim: *It is easy to argue that people should be stopped from putting themselves in danger. However, this would be impossible to enforce.*

Paragraph 4 presents support for main claim: *People who take extreme risks should pay for their rescue operation.*

Paragraph 5 presents counterclaim: *Not everyone agrees that people should be responsible for the costs of their rescue.*

Paragraph 6 refutes counterclaim: *However, arguments against charging for rescue miss an important point. Many rescue workers have lost their own lives saving others.*

**CONCLUSION**
Paragraph 7 restates claim: *In the end, taxpayers cover the cost of rescue for those who put themselves at risk. Maybe there are better places for our money.*

## Argument Outline

INTRODUCTION

_____

BODY

_____

CONCLUSION

**Write a First Draft** Use your outline to write your first draft. Remember to include a precise claim and to address possible counterclaims. Use a variety of evidence and make clear connections to your claim and counterclaims. Keep your audience in mind as you craft your argument. Begin with an interesting point to engage them, and conclude by logically completing your argument. Keep in mind what your audience might already know and what might be unfamiliar to them.

**:≡ STANDARDS**
**W.9–10.1.e** Provide a concluding statement or section that follows from and supports the argument presented.

# Create Cohesion: Transitions

**Transitions** are words and phrases that connect and show relationships between ideas. Transitional words and phrases perform an essential function in an argument. They help the writer guide the reader through a line of reasoning.

## Read It

These sentences from the Launch Text use transitions to show specific connections between ideas.

- However, *when things don't turn out well, a lost climber or an injured base jumper may need help.* (shows contrast)
- Even so, *someone has to pay for those rescues.* (shows emphasis)
- *In New Hampshire,* for example, *hikers who get lost or injured because of reckless behavior can be billed for rescue services.* (illustrates or shows)
- In addition, *the idea of holding people responsible is not to stop rescuing them.* (adds idea)

## Write It

As you draft your argument, choose transitions that accurately show specific relationships between your ideas. Transitions are especially important when connecting one paragraph to the next.

| If you want to . . . | consider using one of these transitions |
|---|---|
| **list or add ideas** | *first of all, secondly, next, lastly, in addition* |
| **compare** | *also, equally, likewise* |
| **contrast** | *although, however, on the other hand* |
| **emphasize** | *most of all, immediately, in fact* |
| **show effect** | *therefore, as a result, so, consequently* |
| **illustrate or show** | *for example, for instance, specifically* |

**PUNCTUATION**

Make sure to punctuate transitional expressions correctly.

- Use a comma after a transitional expression at the beginning of a sentence.
- Use a comma before and after a transitional expression in the middle of a clause or sentence unless the transition follows a semicolon. In that case, add a comma only *after* the transition.

**STANDARDS**

**W.9–10.1.c** Use words, phrases, and clauses to link the major sections of the text, create cohesion, and clarify the relationships between claim(s) and reasons, between reasons and evidence, and between claim(s) and counterclaims.

# Revising

## Evaluating Your Draft

Use the following checklist to evaluate the effectiveness of your first draft. Then, use your evaluation and the instruction on this page to guide your revision.

| FOCUS AND ORGANIZATION | EVIDENCE AND ELABORATION | CONVENTIONS |
|---|---|---|
| ☐ Provides an introduction that leads to the argument. | ☐ Develops the claim and opposing claims fairly, supplying evidence for each, while pointing out the strengths and limitations of both. | ☐ Attends to the norms and conventions of the discipline, especially the correct use and punctuation of transitions. |
| ☐ Introduces a precise claim. | | |
| ☐ Distinguishes the claim from opposing claims. | | |
| ☐ Provides a conclusion that follows from the argument. | ☐ Provides adequate examples for each major idea. | |
| ☐ Establishes a logical organization and develops a progression throughout the argument. | ☐ Uses vocabulary and word choice that are appropriate for the audience and purpose. | |
| ☐ Uses words, phrases, and clauses to clarify the relationships between and among ideas. | ☐ Establishes and maintains a formal style and an objective tone. | |

## 🖧 WORD NETWORK

Include interesting words from your Word Network in your argument.

## ☷ STANDARDS

**W.9–10.1.d** Establish and maintain a formal style and objective tone while attending to the norms and conventions of the discipline in which they are writing.

**W.9–10.4** Produce clear and coherent writing in which the development, organization, and style are appropriate to task, purpose, and audience.

**W.9–10.5** Develop and strengthen writing as needed by planning, revising, editing, rewriting, or trying a new approach, focusing on addressing what is most significant for a specific purpose and audience.

## Revising for Focus and Organization

**Internal Logic** Reread your argument, paying attention to the flow of ideas. Are they presented in a logical order? Have you made the connections between your ideas clear?

## Revising for Evidence and Elaboration

**Word Choice** Review your draft. Identify and replace words that are vague, or imprecise. Then, look for words that are repeated throughout your draft. Consider replacing overused words with synonyms. Refer to your Word Network for help varying your word choice.

**Tone** A writer's **tone** is his or her attitude toward the audience or subject. Because the purpose of an argument is to convince readers of the accuracy of your claim, the tone you use should convey a sense of seriousness and authority.

Apply the following steps to create and maintain a formal tone:

- Avoid slang and abbreviations, and limit the use of contractions.
- Make use of academic vocabulary whenever possible.
- Generally, avoid the use of idioms, which tend to be less formal in tone.
- Refer to places, people, or formal concepts by their proper names.
- A pure argument does not generally use "I" statements. For example, instead of writing, "I think that survivors owe a debt to society," shorten and strengthen the thought: "Survivors owe a debt to society."

## PEER REVIEW

Exchange papers with a classmate. Use the checklist to evaluate your classmate's argument and provide supportive feedback.

**1.** Is the claim clear?

[ ] yes    [ ] no    If no, explain what confused you.

**2.** Is the counterclaim clearly stated? Is there sufficient evidence to counter it?

[ ] yes    [ ] no    If no, point out what is missing.

**3.** Did you find the argument convincing?

[ ] yes    [ ] no    If no, write a brief note explaining what you thought was missing.

**4.** What is the strongest part of your classmate's paper? Why?

_____

_____

_____

# Editing and Proofreading

**Edit for Conventions** Reread your draft for accuracy and consistency. Correct errors in grammar and word usage. Consult a grammar handbook or use online tools if you need help.

**Proofread for Accuracy** Read your draft carefully, correcting for errors in spelling and punctuation. Check the spelling of plurals. You can make most words plural by simply adding -*s*, but there are some words, such as *libraries*, *arches*, and *echoes*, that don't follow this rule. If you are unsure, use a resource to help you.

# Publishing and Presenting

Create a final version of your essay. Share it with your class so that your classmates can read it and make comments. In turn, review and comment on your classmates' work. Consider the ways in which other students' arguments are both similar to and different from your own. Always maintain a polite and respectful tone when commenting.

# Reflecting

Think about what you learned by writing your argument. What could you do differently the next time you need to write an argument to make the writing experience easier and to make your argument stronger?

OVERVIEW: SMALL-GROUP LEARNING

ESSENTIAL QUESTION:
# What does it take to survive?

Survival is not always straightforward. What is required for survival in one situation may be a detriment in another. You will read selections that examine characteristics that helped people survive life-and-death situations. You will work in a group to continue your exploration of the concept of survival.

## Small-Group Learning Strategies

Throughout your life, in school, in your community, in college, and in your career, you will continue to learn and work with others.

Look at these strategies and the actions you can take to practice them as you work in teams. Add ideas of your own for each step. Use these strategies during Small-Group Learning.

| STRATEGY | ACTION PLAN |
|---|---|
| Prepare | • Complete your assignments so that you are prepared for group work.<br>• Organize your thinking so you can contribute to your group's discussions.<br><br>• |
| Participate fully | • Make eye contact to signal that you are listening and taking in what is being said.<br>• Use text evidence when making a point.<br><br>• |
| Support others | • Build off ideas from others in your group.<br>• Invite others who have not yet spoken to do so.<br><br>• |
| Clarify | • Paraphrase the ideas of others to ensure that your understanding is correct.<br>• Ask follow-up questions.<br><br>• |

© Pearson Education, Inc., or its affiliates. All rights reserved.

**174** UNIT 2 • SURVIVAL

SCAN FOR
MULTIMEDIA

# CONTENTS

## Working as a Team

1. **Take a Position** In your group, discuss the following question:

   Would you rather be stranded at the top of a mountain, on a deserted island, or in the middle of the ocean?

   As you take turns sharing your positions, be sure to provide reasons for your choice. After all group members have shared, discuss some of the personal attributes that might be required to survive each of these situations.

2. **List Your Rules** As a group, decide on the rules that you will follow as you work together. Samples are provided; add two more of your own. You may add or revise rules based on your experience together.

   - Everyone should participate in group discussions.
   - People should not interrupt.

   - _____

   _____

   - _____

   _____

3. **Apply the Rules** Share what you have learned about survival. Make sure each person in the group contributes. Take notes and be prepared to share with the class one thing that you heard from another member of your group.

4. **Name Your Group** Choose a name that reflects the unit topic.

   Our group's name: _____

5. **Create a Communication Plan** Decide how you want to communicate with one another. For example, you might use online collaboration tools, email, or instant messaging.

   Our group's decision: _____

   _____

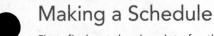

## Making a Schedule

First, find out the due date for the Small-Group activities. Then, preview the texts and activities with your group, and make a schedule for completing the tasks.

| SELECTION | ACTIVITIES | DUE DATE |
|---|---|---|
| The Voyage of the *James Caird*<br>The *Endurance* and the *James Caird* in Images | | |
| *from* Life of Pi | | |
| The Value of a Sherpa Life | | |
| I Am Offering This Poem<br>The Writer<br>Hugging the Jukebox | | |

## Working on Group Projects

As your group works together, you'll find it more effective if each person has a specific role. Different projects require different roles. Before beginning a project, discuss the necessary roles and choose one for each group member. Here are some possible roles; add your own ideas.

**Project Manager:** monitors the schedule and keeps everyone on task

**Researcher:** organizes research activities

**Recorder:** takes notes during group meetings

_____

_____

_____

_____

_____

SCAN FOR
MULTIMEDIA

THE VOYAGE OF THE
JAMES CAIRD

## Comparing Texts

In this lesson, you will read and compare the narrative nonfiction "The Voyage of the *James Caird*" and review the photo gallery "The *Endurance* and the *James Caird* in Images." First, you will complete the first-read and close-read activities for "The Voyage of the *James Caird*." The work you do with your group on this title will help prepare you for the comparing task.

THE *ENDURANCE* AND THE
*JAMES CAIRD* IN IMAGES

### About the Author

**Caroline Alexander**
(b. 1956) was born in Florida and has lived in Europe, Africa, and the Caribbean. In her writing, Alexander often combines literary detective work with travel writing. She is also drawn to the reinterpretation of legendary figures, including Achilles, the hero of Homer's *Iliad*, and Ernest Shackleton, the true-life adventurer whose spectacular failed expedition serves as the subject of Alexander's critically acclaimed book, *The Endurance*.

## STANDARDS

**RI.9–10.10** By the end of grade 9, read and comprehend literary nonfiction in the grades 9–10 text complexity band proficiently, with scaffolding as needed at the high end of the range.

**L.9–10.4.a** Use context as a clue to the meaning of a word or phrase.

# The Voyage of the *James Caird*

## Concept Vocabulary

As you perform your first read of "The Voyage of the *James Caird*," you will encounter these words.

> pitched    reeling    upheaval

**Context Clues** If these words are unfamiliar to you, try using context clues to help you determine their meanings. There are various types of context clues that you may encounter as you read.

> **Restatement, or Synonyms:** The recent **dearth** of milk has resulted in a shortage of other dairy products.
>
> **Elaborating details:** Singing protest songs and waving placards, the demonstrators were clearly **ardent** about their cause.
>
> **Contrast of ideas:** After the coach **derided** the team during the whole game, it was strange that she praised them afterward.

Apply your knowledge of context clues and other vocabulary strategies to determine the meanings of unfamiliar words you encounter during your first read.

## First Read NONFICTION

Apply these strategies as you conduct your first read. You will have an opportunity to complete a close read after your first read.

**NOTICE** the general ideas of the text. What is it about? Who is involved?

**ANNOTATE** by marking vocabulary and key passages you want to revisit.

**First Read**

**CONNECT** ideas within the selection to what you already know and what you have already read.

**RESPOND** by completing the Comprehension Check and by writing a brief summary of the selection.

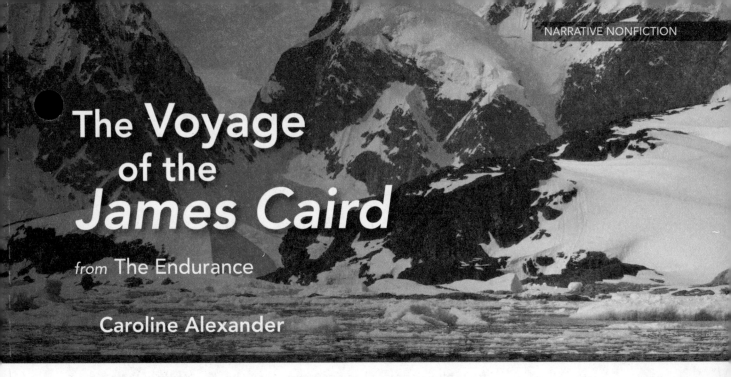

# The Voyage of the James Caird

*from* The Endurance

## Caroline Alexander

## BACKGROUND

Ernest Shackleton was a British explorer famous for his failed attempt to cross Antarctica. His ship, *Endurance*, sailed from London in August of 1914 and crossed the Antarctic Circle in December. Icebound, the ship drifted for months and finally sank. Encamped on Elephant Island, Shackleton decided that he and five others would sail in one of the lifeboats—the *James Caird*—800 miles to South Georgia Island, where there was a whaling station.

SCAN FOR
MULTIMEDIA

NOTES

> Tues 25th  Fine WSW breeze running all day sky overcast.
>
> Wed 26th  W.SW gale squally & cloudy run 105 mile
>
> Thurs 27th  Northerly gale overcast & heavy squalls hove too.
>
> Friday 28th  Light N.W to W winds misty high NW swell
>
> Sat 29th  Fresh W to SW breeze sqaly running high seas
>
> Sunday 30th  hove too at 8 AM & put out sea anchor at 3 PM heavy sprays breaking over the boat & freezing solid.
>
> Mon May 1st  SSW gale laying to sea anchor & mizzen
>
> Tues May 2nd —
>
> —Henry McNish, *diary*

1   "The tale of the next sixteen days is one of supreme strife amid heaving waters," wrote Shackleton. The crew of the *Caird* had departed on a day of rare sunshine that made the water sparkle and dance, and the peaks and glacial slopes of Elephant Island glittered with deceptive beauty as they slowly fell away behind the boat. An hour and a half after taking leave of the line of dark figures on the lonely beach, the *Caird*'s crew ran into their old enemy, the pack. Once again, they entered the eerie landscape of fantastically shaped ancient, wrecked bergs. A channel they had spotted before departure

from the beach led them through the heaving, strangely rustling pack to open water by nightfall. Even on this first, relatively easy day the *Caird* shipped water, soaked by spray and soused by breaking waves. The crew wore woolen underwear under ordinary cloth trousers, Jaeger sweaters, woolen socks, mitts, and balaclavas.[1] Over these, each man had his Burberry overalls and helmet.

2    "These, although windproof, were unfortunately not waterproof," Worsley observed.

3    Shackleton hoped to run north for a few days, away from the ice and towards warmer weather, before bearing east and setting a course for South Georgia Island. This was not the nearest landfall—Cape Horn was closer—but the prevailing westerly gales made it the only one feasible.

4    The men took their first meal under the low canvas deck in a heavy swell, fighting to steady the little Primus stove on which hot food depended. Unable to sit upright, they ate with great difficulty, their chests almost pressed against their stomachs. The staple of their diet was "hoosh," a brick of beef protein, lard, oatmeal, sugar, and salt originally intended as sledging rations[2] for the transcontinental trek that now lay on the fringe of memory. Mixed with water, hoosh made a thick stew over which the coveted Nut Food could be crumbled. All but Worsley and McCarthy were seasick. After the meal, McNish, Crean, McCarthy, and Vincent crawled into their wet bags and lay down on the hard, shifting ballast of stones, while Worsley and Shackleton shared the first watch. With the Southern Cross shining from the clear, cold sky overhead, they sailed north by the stars.

5    "Do you know I know nothing about boat-sailing?" Worsley reports Shackleton as saying with a laugh, on this first night watch. He continues: "'Alright, Boss,' I replied, 'I do, this is my third boat-journey.'"

6    Worsley's report of the conversation was intended as a tribute to Shackleton's courage in undertaking such a dangerous voyage as a land explorer whose seafaring days were behind him. But in fact, it is striking how many of the British polar explorers were experienced sailors. Not only had Shackleton served twenty years in the Merchant Service, but each member of the *James Caird*'s small crew had so many years of experience at sea that expertise was taken for granted. Each man had the assurance that when he went "below deck" to crawl into his bag, his companions above who worked the sails and tiller knew, even under the unprecedented conditions, exactly what they were doing.

7    By dawn, when Crean emerged to light the Primus, the *Caird* had made forty-five miles from Elephant Island. Breakfast was prepared below deck, with the sea breaking over the canvas covering and running down the men's necks. In the afternoon, the wind rose to

---

1. **balaclavas** (bol uh KLOV uhz) *n*. hats that cover all but part of the head and face, usually leaving the eyes, mouth, and nose open.
2. **sledging rations** food to be eaten while sledging, or sledding.

a gale from the west-southwest, with a dangerous high cross sea that racked the heavily ballasted boat with a hard, jerky motion. Shackleton divided the crew into two watches, with himself, Crean, and McNish taking one, and Worsley, McCarthy, and Vincent the other, rotating four-hour shifts.

8    "The routine," wrote Worsley, "was, three men in bags deluding themselves that they were sleeping, and three men 'on deck'; that is one man steering for an hour, while the other two when not pumping, baling or handling sails were sitting in our 'saloon' (the biggest part of the boat, where we generally had grub)." Going "below" was a dreaded ordeal: The space amid the increasingly waterlogged ballast was only five by seven feet. The men had to line up one behind the other and crawl, in heavy, wet clothes, over the stones and under a low thwart to reach their bags. With the boat rolling and shipping water, entrapment in this narrow space held all the horror of being buried alive, and many times men who had nodded off awoke to the sickening sensation that they were drowning.

9    "Real rest we had none," wrote Shackleton. The worn-out reindeer-skin bags were shedding badly, and their bristly hairs appeared everywhere—in the men's clothes, in their food, in their mouths. There was nothing to relieve the long hours of darkness, from six at night until seven in the morning; the boat carried only a makeshift oil lamp and two candles, which provided meager, carefully hoarded light. On the first night out, the cries of penguins coming from the dark sea reminded the men of lost souls.

10    On the third day, despite snowy, stormy weather, Worsley snatched the journey's first observation of the sun between patches of racing cloud. Kneeling on a thwart while Vincent and McCarthy strained to brace him in the pitching boat, Worsley managed to fix his sextant[3] and take his "snap." The precious almanac and logarithm charts, against which the observations were calculated, had become dangerously pulpy, the pages sticking together and the numbers blurred. Nonetheless, Worsley's calculations revealed that they had come 128 miles from Elephant Island.

11    They were, however, widely off the position he had previously reckoned. Worsley wrote,

12        Navigation is an art, but words fail to give my efforts a correct name. Dead reckoning or DR—the seaman's calculation of courses and distance—had become a merry jest of guesswork. . . . The procedure was: I peered out from our burrow—precious sextant cuddled under my chest to prevent seas falling on it. Sir Ernest stood by under the canvas with chronometer pencil and book. I shouted "Stand by," and knelt on the thwart—two men holding me up on either side. I brought the sun down to where the horizon ought to be and as the boat

---

3. **sextant** *n.* instrument used by navigators to measure the position of the stars and the sun to determine location.

leaped frantically upward on the crest of a wave, snapped a good guess at the altitude and yelled, "Stop," Sir Ernest took the time, and I worked out the result. . . . My navigation books had to be half opened page by page till the right one was reached, then opened carefully to prevent utter destruction.

13    Steering at night was especially difficult. Under dense skies that allowed no light from moon or stars, the boat charged headlong into the darkness, the men steering by the "feel" of the wind, or the direction of a small pennant attached to the mast. Once or twice each night, the wind direction was verified by compass, lit by a single precious match. And yet navigation was every bit as critical as keeping the boat upright; the men knew that even a mile off course could result in a missed landfall, and the *Caird* would be swept into 3,000 miles of ocean.

14    In the afternoon of the third day, the gale backed to the north, and then blew continuously the next twenty-four hours. The heaving waves were gray, the sky and lowering clouds were gray, and all was obscured with mist. Heavy seas poured over the *Caird*'s port quarter. The canvas decking, sagging under the weight of so much water, threatened to pull loose the short nails McNish had extracted from packing cases. As if to underscore their own vulnerability, a flotsam of ship wreckage drove past them.

15    "We were getting soaked on an average every three or four minutes," wrote Worsley. "This went on day and night. The cold was intense." Particularly hateful was the task of working the pump, which one man had to hold hard against the bottom of the boat with bare hands—a position that could not be endured beyond five or six minutes at a time.

16    In the afternoon of April 28, the fifth day, the wind died and the seas settled into the towering swells characteristic of the latitude; "The highest, broadest and longest swells in the world," as Worsley wrote. So high were the waves that the *Caird*'s sails slackened in the artificial calm between wave crests; then the little craft was lifted onto the next hill of water, and hurled down an ever-steepening slope. On the following day, a west-southwest gale **pitched** and rolled the *Caird* in a high lumpy sea, but gave an excellent run of ninety-two miles on the desired northeast course. They had now come 238 miles from Elephant Island, "but not in a straight line," as Worsley observed ruefully.

17    On April 30, the gale strengthened and shifted from the south, blowing off the ice fields behind them, as they knew by the increasing cold. Shackleton wanted to run before the wind, but realizing that the *Caird* was in danger of being swung broadside to the surging waves, or driven headlong into the sea, he reluctantly gave the order to head into the wind and stand by.

18    "We put out a sea anchor to keep the *James Caird*'s head up into the sea," Shackleton wrote. "This anchor consisted of a triangular canvas

Mark context clues or indicate another strategy you used that helped you determine meaning.

**pitched** (PIHCHT) *v.*

MEANING:

bag fastened to the end of the painter[4] and allowed to stream out from the bows." The drag of the sea anchor counteracted the boat's drift to the lee, and held her head into the wind so that she met the sea head-on. Up until now, however much the *Caird* was battered, however much icy water she shipped, she had moved forward, slowly, perceptibly closing the distance that lay between them and South Georgia. Now, soaked by bitter spray, the men waited anxiously in the pitching darkness and knew their suffering brought little progress.

19   "Looking out abeam," wrote Shackleton, "we would see a hollow like a tunnel formed as the crest of a big wave toppled over on to the swelling body of water." The spray that broke upon the **reeling** boat froze almost on impact, and towards the end of the eighth day, the *Caird*'s motion had changed alarmingly. No longer rising with the swell of the sea, she hung leaden in the water. Every soaking inch of wood, canvas, and line had frozen solid. Encased in icy armor fifteen inches thick, she was sinking like a dead weight.

20   Immediate action had to be taken. While the wind howled and the sea shattered over them, the men took turns crawling across the precariously glassy deck to chip away the ice. Worsley tried to evoke the unimaginable "difficulty and the peril of that climb in the darkness up that fragile slippery bit of decking. . . . Once, as the boat gave a tremendous lurch, I saw Vincent slide right across the

Mark context clues or indicate another strategy you used that helped you determine meaning.

**reeling** (REEL ihng) *adj.*

MEANING:

4. **painter** *n.* rope used for towing or tying a boat.

icy sheathing of the canvas. . . . Fortunately he managed to grasp the mast just as he was going overboard."

21    Three times the boat had to be chipped clear. Whether using an axe or a knife, the task required strength, but also delicacy as the canvas decking had to be protected from damage at all cost. Flimsy though it was, it was their only shelter, and without it they could not survive. Two of the hated sleeping bags were now discarded; they had frozen solid in the night and had previously begun to putrefy—Shackleton estimated that they weighed as much as forty pounds apiece. By these painstaking efforts, the *Caird* rose incrementally in the water and began to rise and fall again with the movement of the swell.

22    The next morning, the *Caird* gave a sudden, sickening roll leeward; the painter carrying the sea anchor had been severed by a block of ice that had formed on it, out of reach. Beating the ice off the canvas, the men scrambled to unfurl the frozen sails, and once they succeeded in raising them, headed the *Caird* into the wind. It was on this day, May 2, that McNish abruptly gave up any attempt to keep a diary.

23    "We held the boat up to the gale during that day, enduring as best we could discomforts that amounted to pain," wrote Shackleton, in an uncharacteristically direct reference to their physical suffering. The men were soaked to the bone and frostbitten. They were badly chafed by wet clothes that had not been removed for seven months, and afflicted with saltwater boils. Their wet feet and legs were a sickly white color and swollen. Their hands were black—with grime, blubber, burns from the Primus and frostbite. The least movement was excruciating.

24    "We sat as still as possible," wrote Worsley. "[I]f we moved a quarter of an inch one way or the other we felt cold, wet garments on our flanks and sides. Sitting very still for a while, life was worth living." Hot meals afforded the only relief. Shackleton ensured that the men had hot food every four hours during the day and scalding powdered milk every four hours of the long night watches.

25    "Two of the party at least were very close to death," Worsley wrote. "Indeed, it might be said that [Shackleton] kept a finger on each man's pulse. Whenever he noticed that a man seemed extra cold and shivered, he would immediately order another hot drink of milk to be prepared and served to all. He never let the man know that it was on his account, lest he became nervous about himself." To stave off cold, they also drank the blubber oil that had been intended to calm the troubled seas. As Worsley noted, the oil would have sufficed for only one gale; there were ten days of gales on the journey.

26    Their ordeal had already taken a heavy toll on Vincent, who from late April, to use Shackleton's enigmatic words, had "ceased to be an active member of the crew." Worsley attributed the trouble to rheumatism,[5] but the collapse appears to have been mental as much

---

5. **rheumatism** (ROO muh tihz uhm) *n.* disease characterized by pain in the joints.

as physical, for later in the journey he does not appear to have been entirely incapacitated. Physically, he had been the strongest member of the entire *Endurance* company.

27 McCarthy shamed them all.

28 "[He] is the most irrepressable optimist I've ever met," Worsley wrote in his navigating book. "When I relieve him at the helm, boat iced & seas pourg: down yr neck, he informs me with a happy grin 'It's a grand day, sir.'"

29 Between Shackleton and Crean was a special rapport. As Worsley wrote,

30 Tom Crean had been so long and done so much with Sir E that he had become a priviledged retainer. As they turned in, a kind of wordless rumbling, muttering, growling noise could be heard issuing from the dark & gloomy lair in the bows sometimes directed at one another, sometimes at things in general, & sometimes at nothing at all. At times they were so full of quaint conceits & Crean's remarks were so Irish that I ran risk of explosion by suppressed laughter. "Go to sleep Crean & don't be clucking like an old hen." "Boss I can't eat those reindeer hairs. I'll have an inside on me like a billygoats neck. Let's give 'em to the Skipper & McCarthy. They never know what they're eating" & so on.

31 Worsley, despite the rank discomfort, was in his element. He was conscious of being in the midst of a great adventure—which had been his life's ambition. The fact that he was able to continue taking bemused stock of his shipmates is proof that he retained his sense of humor. Of McNish, there is little record. Shackleton stated only, "The carpenter was suffering particularly, but he showed grit and spirit." McNish appears to have endured each day's developments with his customary dour, matter-of-fact forbearance; he had not been born to a life that had promised things to be easy. Shackleton himself was in extreme discomfort; on top of everything else, his sciatica[6] had returned.

32 At midnight on May 2, Shackleton relieved Worsley at the helm just as he was being struck full in the face by a torrent of water. The gale had been gaining strength for eight hours, and a heavy cross sea was running under snow squalls. Alone at the helm, Shackleton noticed a line of clear sky behind them, and called out to the men below that it was at last clearing.

33 "Then a moment later I realized that what I had seen was not a rift in the clouds but the white crest of an enormous wave," wrote Shackleton. "During twenty-six years' experience of the ocean in all its moods I had not encountered a wave so gigantic. It was a mighty **upheaval** of the ocean, a thing quite apart from the big white-capped

© Pearson Education, Inc., or its affiliates. All rights reserved.

---

6. **sciatica** (sy AT uh kuh) *n.* pain in the lower back, hip, or leg caused by damage to the sciatic nerve.

NOTES

Mark context clues or indicate another strategy you used that helped you determine meaning.

**upheaval** (uhp HEE vuhl) *n.*

MEANING:

seas that had been our tireless enemies for so many days. I shouted, 'For God's sake, hold on! It's got us!'"

34    After an unnatural lull, a torrent of thundering foam broke over them. Staggering under the flood, the boat nonetheless rose, emerging, to use Shackleton's words, "half-full of water, sagging to the dead weight and shuddering under the blow." The men bailed with all their energy until they felt the *Caird* float true beneath them. Then it took a full hour of bailing to clear her.

35    On the morning of May 3, after blowing for forty-eight hours at its height, this fierce, bitter gale at last subsided, and the sun appeared amid great, clean cumulus clouds. The sails were unreefed, and the wet sleeping bags and clothing were hung from the mast and the deck, as they set course for South Georgia Island. It was still clear and bright at noon, enabling Worsley to take a sighting for their latitude; they had been six days without taking an observation. His calculations revealed that despite the monstrous difficulties, they had covered 444 miles since leaving Elephant Island—more than half the required distance. Suddenly, success seemed possible.

36    The good weather held, affording them "a day's grace," as Worsley said. On May 5, the twelfth day at sea, the *Caird* made an excellent run of ninety-six miles—the best of the journey—in lumpy swell that raked the boat. Willis Island, off the western tip of South Georgia, was 155 miles away. On May 6, a return of heavy seas and a northwest gale caused them to lay to again, with a reefed jib sail. The next day, the gale moderated, and they set course once more.

37    Worsley was now increasingly worried about getting his observational sights for their position. Since leaving Elephant Island fourteen days earlier, he had been able to sight the sun only four times. "Two of these," he noted, were "mere snaps or guesses through slight rifts in the clouds." He continued:

38        It was misty, the boat was jumping like a flea, shipping seas fore and aft and there was no "limb" to the sun so I had to observe the center by guesswork. Astronomically, the limb is the edge of sun or moon. If blurred by cloud or fog it cannot be accurately "brought down" to the horizon. The center is the spot required, so when the limb is too blurred you bring the center of the bright spot behind the clouds down to the horizon. By practice and taking a series of "sights" you can obtain an average that has no bigger error than one minute of arc.

39    When Worsley informed Shackleton that he "could not be sure of our position to ten miles," it was decided that they would aim for the west coast of South Georgia, which was uninhabited, rather than the east coast where the whaling stations—and rescue—lay. This ensured that if they missed their landfall, the prevailing westerlies would carry them towards the other side of the island. Were they to fail to make an eastern landfall directly, the westerlies would carry them out

to sea. If Worsley's calculations were correct, the *James Caird* was now a little more than eighty miles from South Georgia Island.

40     Before darkness fell on May 7, a piece of kelp floated by. With mounting excitement the crew sailed east-northeast through the night, and at dawn on the fifteenth day, they spotted seaweed. The thrill of anticipation made them momentarily forget the most recent setback: One of the kegs of water was discovered to have become brackish from seawater that evidently had got in when the *Caird* had almost capsized shortly before leaving Elephant Island. They were now plagued with mounting thirst.

41     Cape pigeons such as they had admired so many months before at Grytviken made frequent appearances, along with mollyhawks and other birds whose presence hinted at land. Worsley continued anxiously to monitor the sky, but heavy fog obscured the sun, and all else that might lie ahead. Two cormorants were spotted, birds known not to venture much beyond fifteen miles from land. There were heavy, lumpy cross swells, and when the fog cleared around noon low, hard-driving clouds bore in from the west-northwest, with misty squalls. Then at half past noon, McCarthy cried out that he saw land.

42     "There, right ahead through a rift in the flying scud our glad but salt-rimmed eyes saw a towering black crag with a lacework of snow around its flank," wrote Worsley. "One glimpse, and it was hidden again. We looked at each other with cheerful foolish grins. The thoughts uppermost were 'We've done it.'" The land, Cape Demidov, was only ten miles distant, and it was on course with Worsley's calculations.

43     By three in the afternoon, the men were staring at patches of green tussock grass that showed through the snow on the land ahead—the first living vegetation they had beheld since December 5, 1914, seventeen months before. It was impossible to make for the whaling stations: The nearest lay 150 miles away—a formidable distance given the conditions and changing winds. Also, they had been without fresh water for forty-eight hours. Two alternative landing sites were considered: Wilson Harbor, which lay north, but to windward, and was thus impossible to reach; and King Haakon Sound, which opened to the West, and where a westerly swell shattered on jagged reefs, spouting surf up to forty feet in the air.

44     "Our need of water and rest was wellnigh desperate," wrote Shackleton, "but to have attempted a landing at that time would have been suicidal. There was nothing for it but to haul off till the following morning." As he well knew, making landfall could be the most dangerous part of sailing.

45     A stormy sunset closed the day, and the men prepared to wait out the hours of darkness. Although they were weak in the extreme, their swollen mouths and burning thirst made eating almost impossible. The small crew tacked through the darkness until midnight, when they stood to, eighteen miles offshore. Then, in the bleak, early hours of the morning, the wind strengthened and, as the *Caird* rose and fell, increased to a gale that showered sleet and hail upon the men. Although they hove to with only a reefed jib, they were shipping water and forced to bail continuously. By break of day, the *Caird* was trapped in a perilously heavy cross sea and enormous swell that was driving them towards the coast.

46     Rain, hail, sleet, and snow hammered down, and by noon the gale had become a full-fledged hurricane whipping a mountainous sea into foam and obscuring every trace of land.

47     "None of us had ever seen anything like it before," wrote Worsley. The storm, he continued, "Was driving us, harder than ever, straight for that ironbound coast. We thought but did not say those words, so fateful to the seaman, 'a lee shore.'"

48     At one in the afternoon, the clouds rent, suddenly exposing a precipitous front to their lee. The roar of breakers told them they were heading dead for unseen cliffs. In desperation, Shackleton ordered the double-reefed sails set for an attempt to beat into wind and pull away from the deadly course.

49     "The mainsail, reefed to a rag, was already set," wrote Worsley, "and in spite of the smallness of the reefed jib and mizzen it was the devil's own job to set them. Usually such work is completed inside of ten minutes. It took us an hour."

50     As the *James Caird* clawed her way against the wind, she struck each heaving swell with a brutal thud. With each blow, her bow planks opened, and water squirted in; caulked with oil paints and seal blood, the *Caird* was straining every joint. Five men pumped and

bailed, while the sixth held her on her fearful course. She was not so much inching forward as being squeezed sideways.

51    "At intervals we lied, saying 'I think she'll clear it,'" Worsley wrote. After three hours of this battle, the land had safely receded, when suddenly the snow-covered mountains of Annenkov Island loomed out of the dusk to their lee. They had fought their way past one danger only to be blown into the path of another.

52    "I remember my thoughts clearly," wrote Worsley. "Regret for having brought my diary and annoyance that no one would ever know we had got so far."

53    "I think most of us had a feeling that the end was very near," wrote Shackleton. It was growing dark as the *Caird* floundered into the backwash of waves breaking against the island's precipitous coastline. Suddenly the wind veered round to the southwest. Coming about in the foaming, confused current, the *Caird* sheered away from the cliffs, and from destruction. Darkness fell, and the hurricane they had fought for nine hours abated.

54    "We stood offshore again, tired almost to the point of apathy," wrote Shackleton. "The night wore on. We were very tired. We longed for day."

55    When the morning of May 10 dawned, there was virtually no wind at all, but a heavy cross sea. After breakfast, chewed with great difficulty through parched lips, the men steered the *Caird* towards King Haakon Bay. The few charts at their disposal had been discovered to be incomplete or faulty, and they were guided in part by Worsley's instinct for the lay of the land.

56    Setting course for the bay, they approached a jagged reef line, which, in Shackleton's words, seemed "like blackened teeth" to bar entrance to the inlet. As they steered towards what appeared to be a propitious gap, the wind shifted once again, blowing right out of the bay, against them. Unable to approach directly, they backed off and tried to tack in, angling for entry. Five times they bore up and tacked, and on the last attempt the *Caird* sailed through the gap and into the mouth of the bay.

57    It was nearly dusk. A small cove guarded by a reef appeared to the south. Standing in the bows, Shackleton directed the boat through a narrow entrance in the reef.

58    "In a minute or two we were inside," wrote Shackleton, "and in the gathering darkness the *James Caird* ran in on a swell and touched the beach."

59    Jumping out, he held the frayed painter and pulled against the backward surge; and when the boat rolled in again with the surf, the other men stumbled ashore and loosely secured her. The sound of running water drew them to a small stream nearly at their feet. They fell upon their knees and drank their fill.

60    "It was," wrote Shackleton, "a splendid moment."

61    McNish's handiwork had stood up to all that the elements had flung at it. Throughout their seventeen-day ordeal, Worsley had

never allowed his mind to relax and cease its calculations. Together, the six men had maintained a ship routine, a structure of command, a schedule of watches. They had been mindful of their seamanship under the most severe circumstances a sailor would ever face. They had not merely endured; they had exhibited the grace of expertise under ungodly pressure.

62      Undoubtedly they were conscious of having achieved a great journey. They would later learn that a 500-ton steamer had foundered with all hands in the same hurricane they had just weathered. But at the moment they could hardly have known—or cared—that in the carefully weighed judgment of authorities yet to come, the voyage of the *James Caird* would be ranked as one of the greatest boat journeys ever accomplished.  ❧

# Comprehension Check

Complete the following items after you finish your first read. Review and clarify details with your group.

**1.** Whose points of view are represented in this piece?

**2.** What is the purpose of the voyage of the *James Caird*?

**3.** How does the author know what happened during the voyage of the *James Caird*?

**4.** 🗐 **Notebook** Confirm your understanding of the text by listing the obstacles the crew of the *James Caird* faced during their voyage and explaining how they overcame those obstacles.

- - - - - - - - - - - - - - - - - - - - - - - - - - - - - - - - - - - - - - - - - - - -

## RESEARCH

**Research to Clarify**  Choose at least one unfamiliar detail from the text. Briefly research that detail. In what way does the information you learned shed light on an aspect of the story?

## Close Read the Text

With your group, revisit sections of the text you marked during your first read. **Annotate** details that you notice. What **questions** do you have? What can you **conclude**?

THE VOYAGE OF THE *JAMES CAIRD*

## Analyze the Text

**CITE TEXTUAL EVIDENCE**
to support your answers.

**Notebook** Complete the activities.

1. **Review and Clarify** With your group, reread paragraph 29 of the selection. Why do you think the author describes Worsley's character at this point in the selection? What is the author trying to say about Worsley?

2. **Present and Discuss** Now work with your group to share passages from the selection that you found especially important. Take turns presenting your passages. Discuss what you notice in the selection, the questions you asked, and the conclusions you reached.

3. **Essential Question:** *What does it take to survive?* What has this narrative taught you about survival? Discuss with your group.

**LANGUAGE DEVELOPMENT**

## Concept Vocabulary

| pitched | reeling | upheaval |

**Why These Words?** The three concept vocabulary words from the text are related. With your group, determine what the words have in common. How do these word choices enhance the impact of the text?

### Practice

**Notebook** Confirm your understanding of these words from the text by using them in a paragraph. Be sure to use context clues that hint at each word's meaning.

## Word Study

**Notebook** **Multiple-Meaning Words** Many words in English have multiple meanings, or more than one distinct definition. For example, the word *pitched*, which appears in "The Voyage of the *James Caird*," has several different meanings. Write the meaning of *pitched* as Caroline Alexander uses it. Then, write two more definitions of the word. Finally, find two other multiple-meaning words in the text. Record the words, and list two definitions for each.

**WORD NETWORK**

Add interesting words related to survival from the text to your Word Network.

**STANDARDS**

**L.9–10.4** Determine or clarify the meaning of unknown and multiple-meaning words and phrases based on *grades 9–10 reading and content*, choosing flexibly from a range of strategies.

THE VOYAGE OF THE *JAMES CAIRD*

## Analyze Craft and Structure

**Series of Events** Writing that tells a real-life story is called **narrative nonfiction**. Even though the events of a nonfiction narrative are true, the story is still shaped by the **author's perspective**—his or her interpretations of the events and the people involved. To be believable, that interpretation needs to be supported with evidence. In this account, the author uses **primary sources** in the form of sailors' journals as evidence that supports her interpretation. Her use of the journals also allows her to incorporate the sailors' voices to make their personalities and experiences more vivid.

**TIP**

**GROUP DISCUSSION**
Keep in mind that members of your group might have different impressions of Shackleton and the other sailors than you do. There's no right impression or conclusion, but talking out differing opinions and the reasons for them will help you clarify your thoughts and learn from one another.

**Practice**

**CITE TEXTUAL EVIDENCE** to support your answers.

In your own words, describe the people who appear in this narrative. Cite details from the text that support your descriptions. Work on your own to gather your ideas in the chart. Then, share with your group.

| PERSON | DESCRIPTION | TEXTUAL EVIDENCE |
|--------|-------------|------------------|
| Shackleton | | |
| McNish | | |
| Worsley | | |
| McCarthy | | |
| Crean | | |
| Vincent | | |

📓 **Notebook** Respond to these questions.

1. Which member of the expedition do you think Alexander admires most? Why?

2. The story of the *Endurance* was famous even before Alexander wrote her book. Why do you think she felt the story was worth retelling? Explain, citing evidence from this excerpt.

**STANDARDS**

**RI.9–10.3** Analyze how the author unfolds an analysis or series of ideas or events, including the order in which the points are made, how they are introduced and developed, and the connections that are drawn between them.

**RI.9–10.4** Determine the meaning of words and phrases as they are used in a text, including figurative, connotative, and technical meanings; analyze the cumulative impact of specific word choices on meaning and tone.

**L.9–10.1.b** Use various types of phrases and clauses to convey specific meanings and add variety and interest to writing or presentations.

## Author's Style

**Word Choice**  A **description** is a portrait in words of a person, place, or thing. Descriptions include details that appeal to the senses: sight, hearing, taste, smell, and touch. The effectiveness of a description depends upon **vivid word choice**, or the language a writer uses to create a specific impression.

In "The Voyage of the *James Caird*," the author makes extensive use of participles and participial phrases. A **participle** is a verb form that acts as an adjective. A **participial phrase** consists of a participle and its objects, complements, or modifiers, all acting together as an adjective. Because they are formed from verbs, participles and participial phrases often add energy to sentences by conveying to the reader a vivid sense of motion or action.

> **Example / Participle:**  On the third day, despite snowy, stormy weather, Worsley snatched the journey's first observation of the sun between patches of **racing** cloud.
>
> **Example / Participial Phrase:**  The canvas decking, **sagging under the weight of so much water**, threatened to pull loose the short nails McNish had extracted from packing cases.

### Read It

Working individually, use this chart to identify each participle in these sentences from "The Voyage of the *James Caird*." Then, discuss with your group how each participial affects what you picture as you read the sentence.

| PASSAGE | PARTICIPLE(S) | EFFECT |
|---|---|---|
| "The tale of the next sixteen days is one of supreme strife amid heaving waters," wrote Shackleton. (paragraph 1) | | |
| . . . in the foaming, confused current, the Caird sheered away from the cliffs, and from destruction. (paragraph 53) | | |
| After the meal, McNish, Crean, McCarthy, and Vincent crawled into their wet bags and lay down on the hard, shifting ballast of stones. . . . (paragraph 4) | | |

### Write It

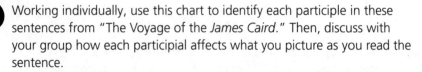 **Notebook**  Write a paragraph in which you explain what you learned about navigating uncharted waters from "The Voyage of the *James Caird*." Use participles and participial phrases to make your language more vivid and precise or to create a sense of motion.

THE VOYAGE OF THE
JAMES CAIRD

## Comparing Text to Media

The photographs on the following pages were taken by the *Endurance* expedition photographer Frank Hurley. While looking at this selection, you will compare the differences between how written text and photographs can tell a story.

THE *ENDURANCE* AND THE
*JAMES CAIRD* IN IMAGES

### About the Photographer

**Frank Hurley** (1885–1962) was an Australian photographer known for the stunning photos he took during Shackleton's *Endurance* expedition. In the words of one of the crew members, "Hurley [was] a warrior with his camera and would go anywhere or do anything to get a picture." Remarkably, Hurley was able to save many plate glass negatives from the *Endurance* as well as an album of photos he had already printed. After the ship sank, Hurley had to leave his photographic equipment behind. From that point on, he used a small hand-held camera to take an additional 38 photos, all of which survived.

# The *Endurance* and the *James Caird* in Images

## Media Vocabulary

These words will be useful to you as you analyze, discuss, and write about photographs.

| | |
|---|---|
| **Composition:** arrangement of the parts of a picture; the *foreground* is closest to the camera lens, while the *background* is farther away | • The composition may stress one part of an image more than another.<br>• The composition may show what the photographer thinks is important in the subject. |
| **Perspective or Angle:** vantage point from which a photo is taken | • The camera may be looking down, looking up, or looking head on at the subject.<br>• The subject may seem very far away, at a middle distance, or very close. |
| **Lighting and Color:** use of light, shadow, and color in a picture | • Some images are full color, while others are black and white. There are countless variations of color options.<br>• Some parts of an image are brighter or darker than others. |

## First Review MEDIA: ART AND PHOTOGRAPHY

Study each photograph and its caption using these strategies.

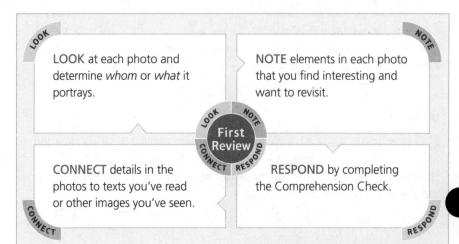

**LOOK** at each photo and determine *whom* or *what* it portrays.

**NOTE** elements in each photo that you find interesting and want to revisit.

First Review

**CONNECT** details in the photos to texts you've read or other images you've seen.

**RESPOND** by completing the Comprehension Check.

# The *Endurance* and the *James Caird* in Images

### Frank Hurley

## BACKGROUND

Sir Ernest Shackleton's trans-Antarctica expedition of 1914–1917 was a true-life adventure that rivals any work of fiction for drama, bravery, and daring. Shackleton's goal was to cross the Antarctic continent from one coast to the other. The expedition never made it. Instead, Shackleton and his men were forced to abandon their ship, the *Endurance*, when it became stuck in Antarctic pack ice in 1915. The crew set up camp on an ice floe and eventually reached Elephant Island in April 1916. From there, Shackleton and five crewmen sailed the *James Caird*—a small lifeboat—800 miles to South Georgia Island to seek help at a whaling station. That August, using a boat on loan from Chile, Shackleton finally rescued the rest of the crew from Elephant Island.

SCAN FOR MULTIMEDIA

**PHOTO 1: *Endurance* in the ice** To photographer Frank Hurley, the pack ice often looked like ocean waves.

NOTES

**PHOTO 2: The port side of the ship, October 19, 1915** Shackleton is the man leaning over the side of the ship in the foreground. He called this photo "The Beginning of the End."

NOTES

**PHOTO 3: The end** The expedition's sled dogs are shown in the foreground looking at the trapped and ruined ship.

NOTES

**PHOTO 4: Hauling the *James Caird*** After the *Endurance* sank, the men dragged the *James Caird* three quarters of a mile to a new camp. The boat weighed approximately 2,000 pounds.

NOTES

**PHOTO 5: Launching the *Caird*** As they attempted to launch the boat in heavy surf, two of the men were thrown overboard.

NOTES

**PHOTO 6: The rescue** The crew members who were left on Elephant Island welcome the rescue ship.

NOTES

# Comprehension Check

Complete the following items after you finish your first review.

1. Which details help explain why Shackleton would call Photo 2 "The Beginning of the End"?

2. What is happening to the *Endurance* in Photo 3?

3. In Photo 5, which details show the conditions of the surf when the *James Caird* was launched?

4. ⊟ **Notebook** Confirm your understanding of the *Endurance* and the *James Caird* photo gallery by writing a description of the setting, people, and events the images portray.

## Close Review

With your group, revisit the photographs and your first-review notes. Record any new observations that seem important. What **questions** do you have? What can you **conclude**?

THE *ENDURANCE* AND THE *JAMES CAIRD* IN IMAGES

## Analyze the Media

:::notebook: **Notebook** Complete the activities.

1. **Present and Discuss** Choose the photo you find most interesting or powerful. Share your choice with the group and discuss why you chose it. Explain what you notice in the photo, the questions it raises for you, and the conclusions you reach about it.

2. **Review and Synthesize** With your group, review all the photos. Do they do more than simply document the expedition? Are they examples of journalism, of art, or of both? Explain.

3. :::notebook: **Notebook** **Essential Question:** *What does it take to survive?* What challenges did the men face when they lost the *Endurance*? What qualities do you think their survival required? Support your response with evidence from the photographs.

## Media Vocabulary

| composition | perspective or angle | lighting and color |
|---|---|---|

Use the vocabulary words in your responses to the questions.

1. **(a)** In Photo 1, what is the position of the ship in relation to the ice around it? **(b)** What might Hurley have wanted to convey in this photograph?

2. In Photo 2, which aspects help to emphasize the condition of the *Endurance*?

3. In Photo 4, what effect does the contrast between the background and the subjects create?

**STANDARDS**

**RI.9–10.1** Cite strong and thorough textual evidence to support analysis of what the text says explicitly as well as inferences drawn from the text.

THE VOYAGE OF THE *JAMES CAIRD*

THE *ENDURANCE* AND THE
*JAMES CAIRD* IN IMAGES

# Writing to Compare

Both "The Voyage of the *James Caird*" by Caroline Alexander and the photographs taken by Frank Hurley provide information about the legendary Antarctic expedition led by Sir Ernest Shackleton. Now, analyze the texts and consider how the medium in which information is provided—visual or verbal—affects what you learn about the subject.

> ### Assignment
>
> Create a **multimedia presentation** about the Shackleton expedition in which you weave together Alexander's text, Hurley's photographs, and your own commentary. In your presentation, explain how verbal accounts and photographs provide information that is valuable in different ways. Choose from these options:
>
> ☐ a **museum exhibit guide** for a show about the Shackleton expedition
>
> ☐ a page plan and content for a **website** about the Shackleton expedition
>
> ☐ the script for a **slide show** about the Shackleton expedition

## Analyze the Texts

**Compare the Text and Photographs** With your group, identify ways in which the verbal text and the photographs convey information. Use the chart to capture your observations.

| INFORMATION ABOUT THE EXPEDITION | WHAT I LEARNED FROM "THE VOYAGE OF THE *JAMES CAIRD*" | WHAT I LEARNED FROM THE EXPEDITION PHOTOGRAPHS | HOW TEXT COMPARES TO PHOTOGRAPHS |
|---|---|---|---|
| hardships the crew faced | | | |
| actions they took to survive | | | |
| details about the crew | | | |

⊟ **Notebook** Respond to these questions.

1. Do the photographs reveal aspects of the story that the text does not? Explain.

2. Does the text communicate aspects of the men's experience that the photographs do not? Explain.

## Planning and Prewriting

**Organize Tasks** Make a list of tasks you will have to accomplish in order to get your presentation done. Assign the tasks to individual group members. You may add to or modify this list as needed.

---

**TASK LIST**

**Research and Choose Photographs:** Decide whether you need additional photos of the expedition or its members. If you do, research and choose those images.

*Assigned To:* _____

**Research and Choose Texts:** Decide whether you need additional writings about the expedition or by its members. If you do, research and choose those texts.

*Assigned To:* _____

**Locate Other Media:** Find additional media—audio, video, or other visuals—to add interest and information. For example, you may want to include maps that show the routes Shackleton had planned and the ones the expedition actually took.

*Assigned To:* _____

**Make a Rough Outline:** Set a sequence for your content as well as any special sections of information you may want to include. You may always revise the sequence later as your project takes shape.

*Assigned To:* _____

---

**EVIDENCE LOG**

Before moving on to a new selection, go to your Evidence Log and record what you've learned from "The Voyage of the *James Caird*" and "The *Endurance* and the *James Caird* in Images."

## Drafting

**Provide Thorough Information** As you organize photos and texts and write content, work to answer five basic questions:

- What happened?
- Who was involved?
- Where did the events happen?
- Why did the events happen?
- What were the results or consequences of the events?

**Include Comparisons of Texts to Photographs** Use your notes from the analysis you did earlier to explain how images and texts contribute to readers' and viewers' understanding of the Shackleton expedition in similar and different ways.

## Revising

Make sure all the images or other media you have chosen add value to the presentation. If necessary, cut content to make your presentation more focused and effective.

**STANDARDS**

**RI.9–10.7** Analyze various accounts of a subject told in different mediums, determining which details are emphasized in each account.

**SL.9–10.5** Make strategic use of digital media in presentations to enhance understanding of findings, reasoning, and evidence and to add interest.

## About the Author

**Yann Martel** (b. 1963) was born in Spain to Canadian parents and lived in many different places, including Costa Rica, Mexico, Alaska, and Canada. After graduating from college, he worked various jobs, such as dishwasher and security guard. Unsure about what he wanted to pursue as a career, he started to write. Though he found critical success, sales of his stories did not follow. Eventually, Martel traveled to India, where he found the inspiration for his most successful work, *Life of Pi*.

## STANDARDS

**RL.9–10.10** By the end of grade 9, read and comprehend literature, including stories, dramas, and poems, in the grades 9–10 text complexity band proficiently, with scaffolding as needed at the high end of the range.

**L.9–10.4** Determine or clarify the meaning of unknown and multiple-meaning words and phrases based on *grades 9–10 reading and content*, choosing flexibly from a range of strategies.

# *from* Life of Pi

## Concept Vocabulary

As you perform your first read of the excerpt from *Life of Pi*, you will encounter the following words.

> irresolvable    predatory    adversary

**Base Words** If these words are unfamiliar to you, analyze each one to see whether it contains a base word you know. Then, use your knowledge of the "inside" word, along with context, to determine the meaning of the concept word. Here is an example of how to apply the strategy.

> **Unfamiliar Word:** *willful*
>
> **Familiar "Inside" Word:** *will*, with meanings including "choose," "intention," "determination"
>
> **Context:** A lifetime of peaceful vegetarianism stood between me and the **willful** beheading of a fish.
>
> **Conclusion:** The narrator is a vegetarian, and would not want to behead a fish, at least not on purpose. *Willful* might mean "with will," or "intentionally."

Apply your knowledge of base words and other vocabulary strategies to determine the meanings of unfamiliar words you encounter during your first read.

## First Read FICTION

Apply these strategies as you conduct your first read. You will have an opportunity to complete a close read after your first read.

**NOTICE** whom the story is about, *what* happens, *where* and *when* it happens, and *why* the main characters react as they do.

**ANNOTATE** by marking vocabulary and key passages you want to revisit.

**First Read**

**CONNECT** ideas within the selection to what you already know and what you have already read.

**RESPOND** by completing the Comprehension Check and by writing a brief summary of the selection.

*from*
# Life of Pi

**Yann Martel**

## BACKGROUND

In the novel *Life of Pi* by Yann Martel, the main character is a teenager whose family owns a zoo in India. The family decides to leave India with their animals and sail to Canada, but while traveling, their ship is struck by a violent storm and sinks. Pi escapes on a lifeboat with four of the family's animals: a hyena, a zebra, an orangutan—and a Bengal tiger named Richard Parker. The hyena kills the zebra and the orangutan but is in turn killed by the tiger. Pi constructs a raft for himself, where he can retreat to safety from the tiger, and sets about taming Richard Parker.

SCAN FOR
MULTIMEDIA

## Chapter 61

NOTES

1   The next morning I was not too wet and I was feeling strong. I thought this was remarkable considering the strain I was under and how little I had eaten in the last several days.

2   It was a fine day. I decided to try my hand at fishing, for the first time in my life. After a breakfast of three biscuits and one can of water, I read what the survival manual had to say on the subject. The first problem arose: bait. I thought about it. There were the

dead animals, but stealing food from under a tiger's nose was a proposition I was not up to. He would not realize that it was an investment that would bring him an excellent return. I decided to use my leather shoe. I had only one left. The other I had lost when the ship sank.

3    I crept up to the lifeboat and I gathered from the locker one of the fishing kits, the knife and a bucket for my catch. Richard Parker was lying on his side. His tail jumped to life when I was at the bow[1] but his head did not lift. I let the raft out.

4    I attached a hook to a wire leader, which I tied to a line. I added some lead weights. I picked three that had an intriguing torpedo shape. I removed my shoe and cut it into pieces. It was hard work; the leather was tough. I carefully worked the hook into a flat piece of hide, not through it but into it, so that the point of the hook was hidden. I let the line down deep. There had been so many fish the previous evening that I expected easy success.

5    I had none. The whole shoe disappeared bit by bit, slight tug on the line by slight tug on the line, happy freeloading fish by happy freeloading fish, bare hook by bare hook, until I was left with only the rubber sole and the shoelace. When the shoelace proved an unconvincing earthworm, out of sheer exasperation I tried the sole, all of it. It was not a good idea. I felt a slight, promising tug and then the line was unexpectedly light. All I pulled in was line. I had lost the whole tackle.

6    This loss did not strike me as a terrible blow. There were other hooks, leader wires and weights in the kit, besides a whole other kit. And I wasn't even fishing for myself. I had plenty of food in store.

7    Still, a part of my mind—the one that says what we don't want to hear—rebuked me. "Stupidity has a price. You should show more care and wisdom next time."

8    Later that morning a second turtle appeared. It came right up to the raft. It could have reached up and bit my bottom if it had wanted to. When it turned I reached for its hind flipper, but as soon as I touched it I recoiled in horror. The turtle swam away.

9    The same part of my mind that had rebuked me over my fishing fiasco scolded me again. "What exactly do you intend to feed that tiger of yours? How much longer do you think he'll last on three dead animals? Do I need to remind you that tigers are not carrion eaters?[2] Granted, when he's on his last legs he probably won't lift his nose at much. But don't you think that before he submits to eating puffy, putrefied zebra he'll try the fresh, juicy Indian boy just a short dip away? And how are we doing with the water situation? You know how tigers get impatient with thirst. Have you smelled his breath recently? It's pretty awful. That's a bad sign. Perhaps you're hoping that he'll lap up the Pacific and in quenching his thirst

---

1. **bow (bow)** *n.* forward part of the ship.
2. **carrion eaters** animals that eat the flesh of other, dead animals.

allow you to walk to America? Quite amazing, this limited capacity to excrete salt that Sundarbans tigers have developed. Comes from living in a tidal mangrove forest, I suppose. But it *is* a limited capacity. Don't they say that drinking too much saline water makes a man-eater of a tiger? Oh, look. Speak of the devil. There he is. He's yawning. My, my, what an enormous pink cave. Look at those long yellow stalactites[3] and stalagmites.[4] Maybe today you'll get a chance to visit."

10    Richard Parker's tongue, the size and color of a rubber hot-water bottle, retreated and his mouth closed. He swallowed.

11    I spent the rest of the day worrying myself sick. I stayed away from the lifeboat. Despite my own dire predictions, Richard Parker passed the time calmly enough. He still had water from the rainfall and he didn't seem too concerned with hunger. But he did make various tiger noises—growls and moans and the like—that did nothing to put me at ease. The riddle seemed irresolvable: to fish I needed bait, but I would have bait only once I had fish. What was I supposed to do? Use one of my toes? Cut off one of my ears?

12    A solution appeared in the late afternoon in a most unexpected way. I had pulled myself up to the lifeboat. More than that: I had climbed aboard and was rummaging through the locker, feverishly looking for an idea that would save my life. I had tied the raft so that it was about six feet from the boat. I fancied that with a jump and a pull at a loose knot I could save myself from Richard Parker. Desperation had pushed me to take such a risk.

13    Finding nothing, no bait and no new idea, I sat up—only to discover that I was dead center in the focus of his stare. He was at the other end of the lifeboat, where the zebra used to be, turned my way and sitting up, looking as if he'd been patiently waiting for me to notice him. How was it that I hadn't heard him stir? What delusion was I under that I thought I could outwit him? Suddenly I was hit hard across the face. I cried out and closed my eyes. With feline speed he had leapt across the lifeboat and struck me. I was to have my face clawed off—this was the gruesome way I was to die. The pain was so severe I felt nothing. Blessed be shock. Blessed be that part of us that protects us from too much pain and sorrow. At the heart of life is a fuse box. I whimpered, "Go ahead, Richard Parker, finish me off. But please, what you must do, do it quickly. A blown fuse should not be over-tested."

14    He was taking his time. He was at my feet, making noises. No doubt he had discovered the locker and its riches. I fearfully opened an eye.

15    It was a fish. There was a fish in the locker. It was flopping about like a fish out of water. It was about fifteen inches long and it had wings. A flying fish. Slim and dark gray-blue, with dry, featherless wings and round, unblinking, yellowish eyes. It was this flying fish

NOTES

Mark base words or indicate another strategy you used to help you determine meaning.

**irresolvable** (ihr ih ZOL vuh buhl) *adj.*

MEANING:

---

3. **stalactites** (stuh LAK tyts) *n.* pointed pieces of rock that hang from a cave ceiling.
4. **stalagmites** (stuh LAG myts) *n.* pointed pieces of rock formed on the floor of a cave.

that had struck me across the face, not Richard Parker. He was still fifteen feet away, no doubt wondering what I was going on about. But he had seen the fish. I could read a keen curiosity on his face. He seemed about ready to investigate.

16    I bent down, picked up the fish and threw it towards him. This was the way to tame him! Where a rat had gone, a flying fish would follow. Unfortunately, the flying fish flew. In mid-air, just ahead of Richard Parker's open mouth, the fish swerved and dropped into the water. It happened with lightning speed. Richard Parker turned his head and snapped his mouth, jowls flapping, but the fish was too quick for him. He looked astonished and displeased. He turned to me again. "Where's my treat?" his face seemed to inquire. Fear and sadness gripped me. I turned with the half-hearted, half-abandoned hope that I could jump onto the raft before he could jump onto me.

17    At that precise instant there was a vibration in the air and we were struck by a school of flying fish. They came like a swarm of locusts. It was not only their numbers; there was also something insect-like about the clicking, whirring sound of their wings. They burst out of the water, dozens of them at a time, some of them flick-flacking over a hundred yards through the air. Many dived into the water just before the boat. A number sailed clear over it. Some crashed into its side, sounding like firecrackers going off. Several lucky ones returned to the water after a bounce on the tarpaulin. Others, less fortunate, fell directly into the boat, where they started a racket of flapping and flailing and splashing. And still others flew right into us. Standing unprotected as I was, I felt I was living the martyrdom of Saint Sebastian. Every fish that hit me was like an arrow entering my flesh. I clutched at a blanket to protect myself while also trying to catch some of the fish. I received cuts and bruises all over my body.

18    The reason for this onslaught became evident immediately: dorados were leaping out of the water in hot pursuit of them. The much larger dorados couldn't match their flying, but they were faster swimmers and their short lunges were very powerful. They could overtake flying fish if they were just behind them and lunging from the water at the same time and in the same direction. There were sharks too; they also leapt out of the water, not so cleanly but with devastating consequence for some dorados. This aquatic mayhem didn't last long, but while it did, the sea bubbled and boiled, fish jumped and jaws worked hard.

19    Richard Parker was tougher than I was in the face of these fish, and far more efficient. He raised himself and went about blocking, swiping and biting all the fish he could. Many were eaten live and whole, struggling wings beating in his mouth. It was a dazzling display of might and speed. Actually, it was not so much the speed that was impressive as the pure animal confidence, the total absorption in the moment. Such a mix of ease and concentration, such a being-in-the-present, would be the envy of the highest yogis.

20    When it was over, the result, besides a very sore body for me, was six flying fish in the locker and a much greater number in the lifeboat. I hurriedly wrapped a fish in a blanket, gathered a hatchet and made for the raft.

21    I proceeded with great deliberation. The loss of my tackle that morning had had a sobering effect on me. I couldn't allow myself another mistake. I unwrapped the fish carefully, keeping a hand pressed down on it, fully aware that it would try to jump away to save itself. The closer the fish was to appearing, the more afraid and disgusted I became. Its head came into sight. The way I was holding it, it looked like a scoop of loathsome fish ice cream sticking out of a wool blanket cone. The thing was gasping for water, its mouth and gills opening and closing slowly. I could feel it pushing with its wings against my hand. I turned the bucket over and brought its head against the bottom. I took hold of the hatchet. I raised it in the air.

22    Several times I started bringing the hatchet down, but I couldn't complete the action. Such sentimentalism may seem ridiculous considering what I had witnessed in the last days, but those were the deeds of others, of **predatory** animals. I suppose I was partly responsible for the rat's death, but I'd only thrown it; it was Richard Parker who had killed it. A lifetime of peaceful vegetarianism stood between me and the willful beheading of a fish.

Mark base words or indicate another strategy you used to help you determine meaning.

**predatory** (PREHD uh tawr ee) *adj.*

MEANING:

23     I covered the fish's head with the blanket and turned the hatchet around. Again my hand wavered in the air. The idea of beating a soft, living head with a hammer was simply too much.

24     I put the hatchet down. I would break its neck, sight unseen, I decided. I wrapped the fish tightly in the blanket. With both hands I started bending it. The more I pressed, the more the fish struggled. I imagined what it would feel like if I were wrapped in a blanket and someone were trying to break my neck. I was appalled. I gave up a number of times. Yet I knew it had to be done, and the longer I waited, the longer the fish's suffering would go on.

25     Tears flowing down my cheeks, I egged myself on until I heard a cracking sound and I no longer felt any life fighting in my hands. I pulled back the folds of the blanket. The flying fish was dead. It was split open and bloody on one side of its head, at the level of the gills.

26     I wept heartily over this poor little deceased soul. It was the first sentient[5] being I had ever killed. I was now a killer. I was now as guilty as Cain. I was sixteen years old, a harmless boy, bookish and religious, and now I had blood on my hands. It's a terrible burden to carry. All sentient life is sacred. I never forget to include this fish in my prayers.

27     After that it was easier. Now that it was dead, the flying fish looked like fish I had seen in the markets of Pondicherry. It was something else, something outside the essential scheme of creation. I chopped it up into pieces with the hatchet and put it in the bucket.

28     In the dying hours of the day I tried fishing again. At first I had no better luck than I'd had in the morning. But success seemed less elusive. The fish nibbled at the hook with fervor. Their interest was evident. I realized that these were small fish, too small for the hook. So I cast my line further out and let it sink deeper, beyond the reach of the small fish that concentrated around the raft and lifeboat.

29     It was when I used the flying fish's head as bait, and with only one sinker, casting my line out and pulling it in quickly, making the head skim over the surface of the water, that I finally had my first strike. A dorado surged forth and lunged for the fish head. I let out a little slack, to make sure it had properly swallowed the bait, before giving the line a good yank. The dorado exploded out of the water, tugging on the line so hard I thought it was going to pull me off the raft. I braced myself. The line became very taut. It was good line; it would not break. I started bringing the dorado in. It struggled with all its might, jumping and diving and splashing. The line cut into my hands. I wrapped my hands in the blanket. My heart was pounding. The fish was as strong as an ox. I was not sure I would be able to pull it in.

30     I noticed all the other fish had vanished from around the raft and boat. No doubt they had sensed the dorado's distress. I hurried. Its struggling would attract sharks. But it fought like a devil. My arms

5. **sentient** (SEHN shuhnt) *adj.* living and capable of feeling.

were aching. Every time I got it close to the raft, it beat about with such frenzy that I was cowed into letting out some line.

31    At last I managed to haul it aboard. It was over three feet long. The bucket was useless. It would fit the dorado like a hat. I held the fish down by kneeling on it and using my hands. It was a writhing mass of pure muscle, so big its tail stuck out from beneath me, pounding hard against the raft. It was giving me a ride like I imagine a bucking bronco would give a cowboy. I was in a wild and triumphant mood. A dorado is a magnificent-looking fish, large, fleshy and sleek, with a bulging forehead that speaks of a forceful personality, a very long dorsal fin as proud as a rooster's comb, and a coat of scales that is smooth and bright. I felt I was dealing fate a serious blow by engaging such a handsome **adversary**. With this fish I was retaliating against the sea, against the wind, against the sinking of ships, against all circumstances that were working against me. "Thank you, Lord Vishnu, thank you!" I shouted. "Once you saved the world by taking the form of a fish. Now you have saved *me* by taking the form of a fish. Thank you, thank you!"

32    Killing it was no problem. I would have spared myself the trouble—after all, it was for Richard Parker and he would have dispatched it with expert ease—but for the hook that was embedded in its mouth. I exulted at having a dorado at the end of my line—I would be less keen if it were a tiger. I went about the job in a direct way. I took the hatchet in both my hands and vigorously beat the fish on the head with the hammerhead (l still didn't have the stomach to use the sharp edge). The dorado did a most extraordinary thing as it died: it began to flash all kinds of colors in rapid succession. Blue, green, red, gold and violet flickered and shimmered neon-like on its surface as it struggled. I felt I was beating a rainbow to death. (I found out later that the dorado is famed for its death-knell iridescence.) At last it lay still and dull-colored, and I could remove the hook. I even managed to retrieve a part of my bait.

33    You may be astonished that in such a short period of time I could go from weeping over the muffled killing of a flying fish to gleefully bludgeoning to death a dorado. I could explain it by arguing that profiting from a pitiful flying fish's navigational mistake made me shy and sorrowful, while the excitement of actively capturing a great dorado made me sanguinary and self-assured. But in point of fact the explanation lies elsewhere. It is simple and brutal: a person can get used to anything, even to killing.

34    It was with a hunter's pride that I pulled the raft up to the lifeboat. I brought it along the side, keeping very low. I swung my arm and dropped the dorado into the boat. It landed with a heavy thud and provoked a gruff expression of surprise from Richard Parker. After a sniff or two, I heard the wet mashing sound of a mouth at work. I pushed myself off, not forgetting to blow the whistle hard several times, to remind Richard Parker of who had so graciously provided him with fresh food. I stopped to pick up some biscuits and a can of

Mark base words or indicate another strategy you used to help you determine meaning.

**adversary** (AD vuhr sehr ee) *n.*

MEANING:

water. The five remaining flying fish in the locker were dead. I pulled their wings off, throwing them away and wrapped the fish in the now-consecrated fish blanket.

35    By the time I had rinsed myself of blood, cleaned up my fishing gear, put things away and had my supper, night had come on. A thin layer of clouds masked the stars and the moon, and it was very dark. I was tired, but still excited by the events of the last hours. The feeling of busyness was profoundly satisfying; I hadn't thought at all about my plight or myself. Fishing was surely a better way of passing the time than yarn-spinning or playing I Spy. I determined to start again the next day as soon as there was light.

36    I fell asleep, my mind lit up by the chameleon-like flickering of the dying dorado. ❧

# Comprehension Check

Complete these items after you finish your first read. Review and clarify details with your group.

1. Briefly describe the problem that Pi faces.

2. At the beginning of the selection, what does Pi plan to do to solve his problem?

3. (a) What main problem does Pi face in executing his plan? (b) What event provides him with a solution?

4. What fact about Pi explains why he has such difficulty in killing his first flying fish?

5. (a) Compare and contrast Pi's attitude toward killing the flying fish with his attitude toward killing the dorado. (b) What does Pi believe explains the difference?

6. 🗒 **Notebook** Write a summary of the excerpt from *Life of Pi*.

- - - - - - - - - - - - - - - - - - - - - - - - - - - - - - - - - - - - - - - - - - - - -

## RESEARCH

**Research to Clarify** Choose at least one unfamiliar detail from the text. Briefly research that detail. In what way does the information that you found shed light on an aspect of the story?

*from LIFE OF PI*

## Close Read the Text

With your group, revisit sections of the text you marked during your first read. **Annotate** details that you notice. What **questions** do you have? What can you **conclude**?

## Analyze the Text

> **CITE TEXTUAL EVIDENCE**
> to support your answers.

**Notebook** Complete the activities.

1. **Review and Clarify** Work with your group to review your responses to the Comprehension Check questions. If there is any confusion or disagreement, review the text as a group to clarify and gain consensus.

2. **Present and Discuss** Share with your group the passages from the text that you found especially significant, taking turns with others. Discuss what you notice in the text, what questions you asked, and what conclusions you reached.

3. **Vote and Post** Vote on the passage your group would like to share with the whole class. Invite comments from the class.

4. **Essential Question:** *What does it take to survive?* What has this text taught you about survival? Discuss with your group.

## Concept Vocabulary

> irresolvable    predatory    adversary

**Why These Words?** The three concept vocabulary words from the excerpt are related. With your group, discuss the words and identify a concept they have in common. How do these word choices enhance the text?

### Practice

**Notebook** Confirm your understanding of these words from the text by using them in sentences. In each sentence, provide context clues that hint at the word's meaning.

## Word Study

**Notebook** **Latin suffixes: *-ory* and *-ary*** In *Life of Pi*, the narrator uses the words *predatory,* which ends with the Latin suffix *-ory*, and *sanguinary*, which ends with the Latin suffix *-ary*. These two suffixes are related and often mean "having to do with," "characterized by," or "tending to." Find four other words that feature either of these suffixes. Record the words and their meanings. Explain how the meaning of the suffix contributes to the meaning of each word.

---

**TIP**

**GROUP DISCUSSION**
If you do not fully understand a classmate's contribution to the discussion, don't hesitate to ask for clarification. To ensure an effective exchange, use a respectful and friendly tone. State exactly what it is you don't understand. In some cases, it might be helpful to pose alternatives: "When you said . . . , did you mean . . . or . . . ?"

---

**WORD NETWORK**

Identify words related to the idea of survival in *Life of Pi*. Add these words to your Word Network.

---

**STANDARDS**

**RL.9–10.3** Analyze how complex characters develop over the course of a text, interact with other characters, and advance the plot or develop the theme.

**L.9–10.4.b** Identify and correctly use patterns of word changes that indicate different meanings or parts of speech and continue to apply knowledge of Greek and Latin roots and affixes.

# Analyze Craft and Structure

**Characters** In the best fiction, the main characters are interesting and well-rounded, or complex. **Complex characters** are those that show both strengths and weaknesses and experience a mix of emotions. They have a variety of reasons, or multiple motivations, for behaving and reacting as they do. As the story progresses, they change. They are **dynamic**, rather than **static**, or unchanging.

**Characterization** is the way a writer develops a character's traits and personality. Writers may include the following elements as clues to a character's nature:

- descriptions of the character's appearance and actions
- descriptions of the character's emotions
- the character's spoken words, or **dialogue,** and thoughts

*Life of Pi* is narrated by the title character himself. To show Pi's thoughts with more dimension, the author uses **internal monologue**, a kind of "conversation" or dialogue Pi has with himself.

To better understand how Yann Martel develops Pi as a complex character, consider both *what* you learn about Pi and *how* you learn that information.

## Practice

Working independently, use the chart to identify details from the excerpt that reveal Pi's character. Note that each set of paragraphs may not include every type of detail. Then, gather your notes and share them with your group.

| PARAGRAPHS | PI'S ACTIONS | PI'S FEELINGS | PI'S WORDS OR THOUGHTS | WHAT IS PI LIKE? |
|---|---|---|---|---|
| paragraphs 4–5 | | | | |
| paragraphs 7–9 | | | | |
| paragraphs 23–27 | | | | |
| paragraphs 28–35 | | | | |

*from* LIFE OF PI

# Conventions

**Participial versus Absolute Phrases** A **participle** is a form of a verb used as an adjective. Participles often end with -*ed* or -*ing*. A **participial phrase** is a participle and its modifiers, objects, or complements.

| **catching** | the ball | quickly |
|---|---|---|
| PARTICIPLE | OBJECT | MODIFIER |

| **having seemed** | obvious |
|---|---|
| PARTICIPLE | COMPLEMENT |

The entire participial phrase functions as an adjective. It modifies a noun or pronoun in the sentence.

**Catching the ball quickly,** Sam helped make a double play.

An **absolute phrase** features a noun or pronoun and its modifiers. Often, the modifiers include a participle or participial phrase. Sometimes, the participle *being* or *having been* is omitted as understood.

| everyone's | **pencils** | [having been] sharpened |
|---|---|---|
| MODIFIER | NOUN | PARTICIPLE |

Rather than modifying an individual word, an absolute phrase modifies an entire clause or sentence. It may comment upon the clause or sentence, or it may place it in context.

**Everyone's pencils sharpened,** we were ready to take our test.

## Read It

Work individually. Mark the participle in each of these sentences from *Life of Pi*. Then, identify each phrase as a participial phrase or an absolute phrase. When you have finished, compare your responses with those of your team. Resolve any differences you see in your responses.

1. Tears flowing down my cheeks, I egged myself on. . . .

2. I brought it along the side, keeping very low.

3. Finding nothing, no bait and no new idea, I sat up—only to discover that I was dead center in the focus of his stare.

4. Richard Parker turned his head and snapped his mouth, jowls flapping, but the fish was too quick for him.

## Write It

🗐 **Notebook** Write a paragraph summarizing a scene from the excerpt from *Life of Pi*. In your paragraph, use at least two participial phrases and one absolute phrase.

# Writing to Sources

### Assignment

Write an **argument** that includes **claims**, or statements that express a position, and evidence that supports these claims. In your argument, also address and refute opposing opinions, called **counterclaims.** Once you have completed the writing, present your work to the class. Choose from the following topics:

☐ Take a position about the following statement: *Pi becomes a different person after he kills the flying fish.* Write a brief **essay** in which you state and support your position. Include a paragraph in which you discuss an opposing position.

☐ A **pitch** is a concise description of an idea for a movie. Write a pitch to persuade studio executives to make a movie version of *Life of Pi.* Anticipate and address objections executives might have to the project. Be sure to include passages from the text in your pitch.

☐ Pi is a vegetarian who abandons his principles by fishing. Is he right to do so? Take a position and write either a **defense** or a **criticism** of Pi. Include a paragraph in which you consider the opposing view.

**Project Plan** Before you begin, make a list of the tasks you will need to complete to fulfill the assignment. Decide how you will organize the work. Then, appoint individual group members to each task.

**Clarifying Ideas and Evidence** Write a sentence in which you clearly state your claim. Then, brainstorm for at least two reasons that support it. Identify evidence from *Life of Pi* that supports each reason. Use the chart to organize your reasons and supporting textual evidence.

Claim: _____

_____

| REASONS | TEXT EVIDENCE |
|---------|---------------|
|         |               |
|         |               |
|         |               |
|         |               |

**Present** After you have completed your argument, present the finished work to the class. Make sure all group members have a role to play in the presentation.

📝 EVIDENCE LOG

Before moving on to a new selection, go to your Evidence Log and record what you learned from *Life of Pi.*

## About the Author
**Grayson Schaffer** is a senior editor and writer at *Outside* magazine. As a climber himself, he became disturbed by the media attention that was paid to Westerners who died while climbing Mount Everest, while the deaths of Sherpas were largely ignored. He has written extensively about the working conditions of Sherpas on Everest.

# The Value of a Sherpa Life

## Concept Vocabulary

As you perform your first read of "The Value of a Sherpa Life" you will encounter these words.

| physiology | mortality | reincarnation |
|---|---|---|

**Context Clues**  If these words are unfamiliar to you, try using **context clues**—other words and phrases that appear in a text—to help you determine their meanings. There are various types of context clues that you may encounter as you read.

> **Restatement:** The major wreck on the highway was a **calamity**, or terrible misfortune.
>
> **Definition:** There are millions of **illiterate** people in the world—those who cannot read or write.
>
> **Contrast of ideas and topics:** Abandoning his usual **veracity**, Greg decided to lie about why he missed practice.

Apply your knowledge of context clues or other vocabulary strategies to determine the meanings of unfamiliar words you encounter during your first read of "The Value of a Sherpa Life." For example, you may look for familiar word parts or use a dictionary to unlock meaning.

## First Read NONFICTION

Apply these strategies as you conduct your first read. You will have an opportunity to complete a close read after your first read.

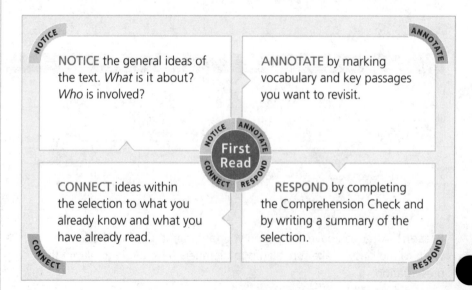

**NOTICE** the general ideas of the text. *What* is it about? *Who* is involved?

**ANNOTATE** by marking vocabulary and key passages you want to revisit.

**CONNECT** ideas within the selection to what you already know and what you have already read.

**RESPOND** by completing the Comprehension Check and by writing a summary of the selection.

**STANDARDS**
**RI.9–10.10** By the end of grade 9, read and comprehend literary nonfiction in the grades 9–10 text complexity band proficiently, with scaffolding as needed at the high end of the range.

**L.9–10.4.a** Use context as a clue to the meaning of a word or phrase.

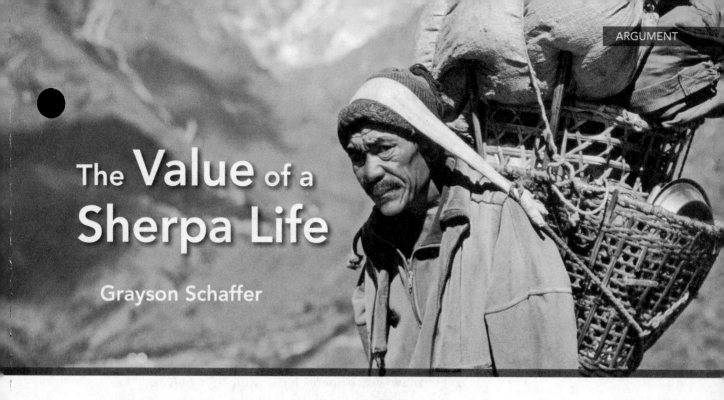

# The Value of a Sherpa Life

## Grayson Schaffer

## BACKGROUND

Located between Tibet and Nepal in southern Asia, Mount Everest is the tallest mountain in the world and one of the most dangerous to climb. More than 200 people have died attempting to reach the summit, including 17 Sherpa porters in 2014. Sherpas are a Nepalese ethnic group famous for their superior mountaineering skills. Companies that run expeditions up the mountain often employ Sherpas to guide climbers.

SCAN FOR
MULTIMEDIA

1   On April 18, at about 6:30 a.m. local time, an avalanche swept down off the west shoulder of Everest and killed 16 climbers. To anybody who's familiar with Everest climbing, it should come as no surprise that all of the men were Sherpa porters. Sherpas are Everest's workforce—the literal backbone of the climbing industry there. The men who were struck were either carrying 80-pound loads to Camps I and II,[1] or they were on their way back to Base Camp.[2] Without the hard work of the Sherpa porters, it would be largely impossible for Americans and Europeans with slightly above-average **physiology**, and well above-average disposable income, to scale the world's tallest mountain.

2   Increasingly, the pinnacle of adventure tourism—the summit of Everest—comes at too steep a cost. In the August 2013 issue, I wrote a story titled "Disposable Man," about the routinization of Sherpa deaths on Everest. Today's avalanche was the worst accident in the history of the mountain. Add to this the April 2 death of Sherpa Mingma Tenzing, who was working for the Peak Freaks expedition, as well as at least a dozen serious injuries from the avalanche, and 2014 stands out as the bloodiest year in Everest history—all before most teams have even set foot on the mountain.

NOTES

Mark context clues or indicate another strategy you used that helped you determine meaning.

**physiology** (fihz ee OL uh jee) *n.*

MEANING:

---

1. **Camps I and II** campsites located at 19,500 feet and 21,000 feet, respectively.
2. **Base Camp** campsite located at 17,500 feet, on the south side of Everest, in Nepal; where the true climb up the mountain begins.

Mark context clues or indicate another strategy you used that helped you determine meaning.

**mortality** (mawr TAL uh tee) *n.*

MEANING:

3    Yes, something needs to be done.

4    There's no question that guiding on Everest is ethically fraught. But shutting the industry down would anger the outfitters, clients, and, most of all, the Sherpas. That last group would lose jobs that pay between $2,000 and $6,000 per season, in a country where the median income is $540 per year. If, say, 1 percent of American college-aged raft guides or ski instructors were dying on the job—the **mortality** rate of Everest Sherpas—the guiding industry would vanish. But Himalayan climbing is understood to be extremely dangerous, and people who play the game still cling to its romantic roots in exploration rather than its current status as recreational tourism.

5    The answer isn't decreasing, or ending, the climbing business on Everest; the solution is increasing the value of a Sherpa life. Because right now—despite what anybody may feel in their heart—the industry clearly values life on a two-tiered basis: Westerners at the top, Sherpas at the bottom.

6    Want to know what a Sherpa life is worth? You only need to review the numbers that I reported last year: lower pay, lower standards for rescue insurance, lower payouts on accidental-death coverage in general. And, perhaps most significantly, the amount of time that Sherpas spend making laps through the deadly Khumbu Icefall[3] and up the Lhotse Face,[4] ferrying loads for predominantly Western expeditions so that clients can arrive fresh and minimize their exposure to the hazards of the mountain. Several organizations, including the Juniper Fund and Alex Lowe Charitable Foundation, have made valiant efforts to teach Sherpas the latest climbing, rescue, and first-aid skills via projects like the Khumbu Climbing School, but the hazards of the mountain remain.

7    Last June, after I'd finished reporting "Disposable Man," the Nepalese government announced that it would double the amount of insurance that high-altitude porters were required to carry, to $11,000. But for about $200 per policy, at least one Kathmandu[5]-based insurance company will cover Sherpas for $23,000. Even that is clearly insufficient to cover the loss. What's left instead is a patchwork of charity, in which some families find help from climbers to send their kids to school and others don't.

8    The change I'd most like to see would start at the very beginning of the tragedy, when outfitters describe what has happened to these men, in words that, at this point, sound rote. A typical blog post on an expedition website follows a predictable pattern, like this one from earlier this month: "Our team is overwhelmed with sadness. Our prayers go out to his family at this extremely difficult time. Tea lights have been lit, we hang our heads in sorrow." But after sorrow should come an acknowledgement of the deep sense of responsibility that is

---

3. **Khumbu** (KUHM boo) **Icefall**  dangerous area between Base Camp and Camp I where ice often shifts and snaps off over the heads of climbers.
4. **Lhotse** (loht SEE) **Face**  3,700-foot wall of glacial ice on the southern face of Lhotse, the fourth-highest mountain in the world; connected to Everest and in the path of climbers.
5. **Kathmandu** (kot mon DOO)  capital of Nepal.

tied in to hiring somebody to do such a dangerous job—for an end result that's ultimately meaningless.

9    In the press, largely as a result of a faulty translation to English, the deceased are always referred to as Sherpa "guides." It's generally a misleading job title for the men—and one or two women—who, each day, lean into their pack straps and haul supplies up the mountain for paying clientele.

10   As guides and Sherpas begin to wake up today in Nepal, they'll commit themselves to finding the remaining bodies. They'll loiter for hours, shovels in hand, under the same serac[6] that killed their friends. The Buddhist tradition is strict about needing a body to cremate if the deceased is to find a speedy **reincarnation**.

11   In the days to come, there will be 16 different puja[7] funeral ceremonies, most of them in the small villages of the Khumbu Valley.[8] In every village, there are already houses with missing men. Their photos, usually faded, smiling, and standing on the summit of the world, are still hung for visitors to see. Now there are 16 more. ❧

Mark context clues or indicate another strategy you used that helped you determine meaning.

**reincarnation** (ree ihn kahr NAY shuhn) *n.*

MEANING:

---

6. **serac** (suh RAK) *n.* pinnacle, sharp ridge, or block of ice among the large cracks in glaciers.
7. **puja** (POO jah) *n.* (in Buddhism) expressions of honor, worship, and devotion.
8. **Khumbu Valley** valley below Everest on the Nepalese side.

# Comprehension Check

Complete the following items after you finish your first read. Review and clarify details with your group.

**1.** What event prompted the author to write this argumentative essay?

**2.** According to the author, why would Sherpa porters likely object to scaling back or shutting down the climbing business on Everest?

**3.** What is the author saying about the value of a Sherpa life?

**4.** 📓 **Notebook** Confirm your understanding of the text by writing a summary.

- - - - - - - - - - - - - - - - - - - - - - - - - - - - - - - - - - - - - - - - - - - - -

## RESEARCH

**Research to Explore** This essay may spark your curiosity to learn more. Briefly research a topic that interests you. You may want to share what you discover with your group.

THE VALUE OF A SHERPA LIFE

## Close Read the Text

With your group, revisit sections of the text you marked during your first read. **Annotate** details that you notice. What **questions** do you have? What can you **conclude**?

Close Read
ANNOTATE QUESTION CONCLUDE

## Analyze the Text

**CITE TEXTUAL EVIDENCE** to support your answers.

⊕ **Notebook** Complete the activities.

1. **Review and Clarify** With your group, reread paragraph 4 of the selection. Discuss the author's counterargument to shutting down the Everest industry. Do you think that he would prefer the climbing industry to stop, or is there another alternative?

2. **Present and Discuss** Now, work with your group to share the passages from the selection that you found especially important. Take turns presenting your passages. Discuss what you notice in the selection, what questions you asked, and what conclusions you reached.

3. **Essential Question:** *What does it take to survive?* What has this essay taught you about survival? Discuss with your group.

---

**TIP**

**GROUP DISCUSSION**
Keep in mind that group members will have different interpretations of the text. These different perspectives enable group members to learn from one another and to clarify their own thoughts. Very often there is no single interpretation or conclusion.

---

⊞ **WORD NETWORK**

Add interesting words related to survival from the text to your Word Network.

## LANGUAGE DEVELOPMENT

## Concept Vocabulary

| physiology | mortality | reincarnation |

**Why These Words?** The concept vocabulary words from the text are related. With your group, determine what the words have in common. How do these word choices enhance the impact of the text?

### Practice

⊟ **Notebook** Confirm your understanding of these words from the text by using them in sentences. Be sure to use context clues that hint at each word's meaning.

## Word Study

**Latin root: -mort-** In "The Value of a Sherpa Life," the author draws attention to the *mortality* rate of Everest Sherpas. The word *mortality* was formed from the Latin root -mort-, which means "death." Find several other words that contain this root. Record the words and their meanings.

**STANDARDS**

**RI.9–10.5** Analyze in detail how an author's ideas or claims are developed and refined by particular sentences, paragraphs, or larger portions of a text.

**L.9–10.4.b** Identify and correctly use patterns of word changes that indicate different meanings or parts of speech and continue to apply knowledge of Greek and Latin roots and affixes.

# Analyze Craft and Structure

**Author's Claims and Ideas** An **argumentative essay** is a brief nonfiction work in which an author attempts to persuade readers to accept his or her point of view. The writer presents a position, or **claim**, and develops it through a sequence of logically linked ideas and evidence. Most essays follow a standard structure:

- **Introduction:** The writer introduces the topic, engages the reader, and states the main claim.

- **Body:** The writer develops the main claim with explanations, evidence, and reasons. The author may introduce additional claims that relate to the main claim. The author may also refine the main claim by making it narrower or more specific.

- **Conclusion:** The writer ends the essay in a memorable way. He or she may restate or summarize the main claim.

**TIP**

**CLARIFICATION**
An introduction or a conclusion may consist of multiple paragraphs, not just one.

## Practice

**CITE TEXTUAL EVIDENCE**
to support your answers.

Working with your group, analyze how the author of "The Value of a Sherpa Life" introduces, develops, and refines his argument.

1. Identify the paragraphs that make up the separate sections of the essay. (Use paragraph numbers or ranges, such as "paragraph 1," or "paragraphs 7-9.")

   **Introduction:** *paragraph(s)* _____

   **Body:** *paragraph(s)* _____

   **Conclusion:** *paragraph(s)* _____

📓 Notebook

2. Create a "reverse" outline of the essay. Using outline format, state the topic or main idea of each paragraph. Then, for each paragraph, list the evidence or reasons the author uses to support or develop that idea.

3. (a) What is the main claim of the essay? (b) Cite two pieces of evidence or reasons that develop or support that idea.

4. (a) At what point in the essay does the author refine the main claim by making it more specific? Cite the paragraph or sentence. (b) What specifically does the author want readers to think or to do?

5. (a) What is noteworthy or memorable about the essay's conclusion? (b) Is this conclusion persuasive? Explain.

THE VALUE OF A SHERPA LIFE

## Author's Style

**Use of Rhetoric  Rhetorical devices** are patterns of words that an author uses to support and emphasize ideas, create rhythm, and make a work memorable. Review the common rhetorical devices described here. Then, discuss the examples of each device with your group.

> **Parallelism:** the use of similar grammatical structures to express related ideas
> **Example:** We shall pay any price, bear any burden, oppose any foe . . .
>
> **Rhetorical Question:** a question to which no response is expected because the answer is obvious or is the point the writer intends to prove
> **Example:** If winter comes, can spring be far behind?
>
> **Charged Language:** strong words that appeal to the emotions and create a powerful impression on readers
> **Example:** Only a fool or a cheat would oppose these new rules.

**STANDARDS**

**RI.9–10.6** Determine an author's point of view or purpose in a text and analyze how an author uses rhetoric to advance that point of view or purpose.

**SL.9–10.5** Make strategic use of digital media in presentations to enhance understanding of findings, reasoning, and evidence and to add interest.

### Read It

Work individually. Use this chart to identify each passage from "The Value of a Sherpa Life" as an example of parallelism, rhetorical question, or charged language. Then, explain how each example helps to convey the author's point of view. When you finish, reconvene as a group to discuss your responses.

| SELECTION PASSAGE | RHETORICAL DEVICE | HOW IT CONVEYS POINT OF VIEW |
|---|---|---|
| *slightly above-average physiology, and well above-average disposable income* (paragraph 1) | | |
| *people who play the game still cling to its romantic roots* (paragraph 4) | | |
| *Want to know what a Sherpa life is worth?* (paragraph 6) | | |

### Write It

📓 **Notebook** Write a paragraph in which you explain what you learned about Everest expeditions from this essay. Use an example of parallelism, a rhetorical question, or charged language.

# Speaking and Listening

**Assignment**

Create a **digital presentation** in which you incorporate text and images to explain a subject. Choose from the following topics:

☐ a set of **illustrated maps** showing the route taken by most Everest expeditions conducted for tourists, including base camp locations and key topographical points

☐ a **profile** of the Sherpa people, including information about Sherpa history and culture

☐ a **report** about a historic expedition to the summit of Everest, including information about Westerners and Sherpas who participated and descriptions of key events

**Project Plan** Before you begin, make a list of the tasks you will need to accomplish in order to complete your digital presentation. Then, assign individual group members to each task. Finally, determine how you will make decisions about choices of images, text, and the overall design of your project.

**Finding Visuals** Make sure the visuals you choose accurately illustrate and enhance the text. Use this chart to collect your ideas. Consult a variety of research sources to gather information and images you will need. Remember to include appropriate citations.

| TEXT IMAGE ILLUSTRATES | DESCRIPTION OF IMAGE | SOURCE INFORMATION FOR CITATION |
|---|---|---|
| | | |
| | | |
| | | |
| | | |

📝 EVIDENCE LOG

Before moving on to a new selection, go to your Evidence Log and record what you learned from "The Value of a Sherpa Life."

# I Am Offering This Poem
# The Writer
# Hugging the Jukebox

## Concept Vocabulary

As you perform your first read of these three poems, you will encounter the following words.

| | | |
|---|---|---|
| treasure | iridescent | luminous |

**Familiar Word Parts** When determining the meaning of an unfamiliar word, look for word parts, such as roots or suffixes, that you know. Doing so may help you unlock word meanings.

**Root:** The words *thermos* and *thermometer* are built on the same root, *-therm-*, which refers to heat. If you know the root *-therm-*, you could guess that the word *thermal* has something to do with heat.

**Suffix:** The suffix *-ence* appears at the ends of words such as *dependence* and *residence*. It means "state or quality of being." If you know the suffix *-ence*, you can conclude that the word *emergence* means "state or quality of emerging"—arising or coming to be.

Apply your knowledge of familiar word parts and other vocabulary strategies to determine the meanings of unfamiliar words you encounter during your first read.

## First Read POETRY

Apply these strategies as you conduct your first read. You will have an opportunity to complete a close read after your first read.

**NOTICE** who or what is "speaking" the poem and whether the poem tells a story or describes a single moment.

**ANNOTATE** by marking vocabulary and key passages you want to revisit.

**First Read**

**CONNECT** ideas within the selection to what you already know and what you have already read.

**RESPOND** by completing the Comprehension Check.

**STANDARDS**

**RL.9–10.10** By the end of grade 9, read and comprehend literature, including stories, dramas, and poems, in the grades 9–10 text complexity band proficiently, with scaffolding as needed at the high end of the range.

**L.9–10.4** Determine or clarify the meaning of unknown and multiple-meaning words and phrases based on *grades 9–10 reading and content*, choosing flexibly from a range of strategies.

**L.9–10.4.b** Identify and correctly use patterns of word changes that indicate different meanings or parts of speech and continue to apply knowledge of Greek and Latin roots and affixes.

## About the Poets

**Jimmy Santiago Baca** (b. 1952) was born in New Mexico. He initially lived with his grandmother but was later sent to an orphanage. Baca ran away at age 13, and circumstances led him to illegal activities and prison. During his time in prison, he learned to read and write. Some of his poems were sent to a publisher, who included them in a book published the year Baca left prison. He continues to write and teach those who are experiencing hardship.

**Richard Wilbur** (b. 1921) earned his first dollar as a poet when he was eight years old. At the time, he did not think that he would pursue a literary career because he was more interested in painting and journalism. As a soldier during World War II, he wrote poems to calm his nerves. After the war, a college friend read the poems and asked Wilbur to write for his literary magazine. Wilbur went on to win two Pulitzer Prizes for Poetry and to serve as the second Poet Laureate of the United States.

**Naomi Shihab Nye**'s (b. 1952) experiences as a woman of mixed Palestinian and American heritage give her a unique perspective. Before attending college in Texas, she lived in Palestine and Jerusalem. In her writing, she often celebrates the extraordinary nature of everyday, ordinary life. After the terrorist attacks on the World Trade Center, Nye became an activist for Arab Americans, advocating for peace and tolerance.

## Backgrounds

### I Am Offering This Poem

Jimmy Santiago Baca's work draws on features of the American Southwest, including the imagery of the natural landscape and the indigenous ways of life. For example, in this poem, the speaker mentions the comforts of home by referencing the Navajo hogan, a traditional dwelling built out of logs and covered with mud. The entrance of a hogan typically faces east, toward the rising sun.

### The Writer

Before computers becam household items, anyone who did not want to write out a manuscript by hand used a typewriter. Typewriters could be noisy because the typists had to strike each key with enough force to push a typebar against an ink ribbon. In turn, the typebar made the impression on the ribbon to create each letter. In this poem, the speaker listens as a young writer uses a typewriter to work on a story.

### Hugging the Jukebox

A jukebox is a device that contains a number of vinyl records and a record player. The user typically inserts money and then selects which record to play. Jukeboxes were often found in dance halls and restaurants, and people could select the music for the crowd to hear. Jukeboxes were a major method of playing popular music for much of the twentieth century.

# I Am
## Offering This
# Poem

**Jimmy Santiago Baca**

I am offering this poem to you,
since I have nothing else to give.
Keep it like a warm coat
when winter comes to cover you,
5 or like a pair of thick socks
the cold cannot bite through,

       I love you,

I have nothing else to give you,
so it is a pot full of yellow corn
10 to warm your belly in winter,
it is a scarf for your head, to wear
over your hair, to tie up around your face,

       I love you,

Keep it, **treasure** this as you would
15 if you were lost, needing direction,
in the wilderness life becomes when mature;
and in the corner of your drawer,
tucked away like a cabin or hogan*
in dense trees, come knocking,
20 and I will answer, give you directions,
and let you warm yourself by this fire,
rest by this fire, and make you feel safe,

       I love you,

It's all I have to give,
25 and all anyone needs to live,
and to go on living inside,
when the world outside
no longer cares if you live or die;
remember,

30        I love you.

---

* **hogan** *n.* Navajo Indian dwelling made of logs and mud.

By Jimmy Santiago Baca, from *Immigrants in Our Own Land*, copyright ©1979 by Jimmy Santiago Baca. Reprinted by permission of New Directions Publishing Corp.

NOTES

Mark familiar word parts or
indicate another strategy you
used that helped you determine
meaning.

**treasure** (TREHZH uhr) *v.*

MEANING:

# The **Writer**

## Richard Wilbur

SCAN FOR
MULTIMEDIA

NOTES

In her room at the prow[1] of the house
Where light breaks, and the windows are tossed with linden,[2]
My daughter is writing a story.

I pause in the stairwell, hearing
5  From her shut door a commotion of typewriter-keys
Like a chain hauled over a gunwale.[3]

Young as she is, the stuff
Of her life is a great cargo, and some of it heavy:
I wish her a lucky passage.

---

1. **prow**  *n.* front of a ship.
2. **linden**  *n.* type of tree with yellowish-white flowers and heart-shaped leaves.
3. **gunwale**  (GUH nuhl) *n.* upper edge of a ship's side.

10 But now it is she who pauses,
   As if to reject my thought and its easy figure.
   A stillness greatens, in which

   The whole house seems to be thinking,
   And then she is at it again with a bunched clamor[4]
15 Of strokes, and again is silent.

   I remember the dazed starling[5]
   Which was trapped in that very room, two years ago;
   How we stole in, lifted a sash

   And retreated, not to affright it;
20 And how for a helpless hour, through the crack of the door,
   We watched the sleek, wild, dark

   And **iridescent** creature
   Batter against the brilliance, drop like a glove
   To the hard floor, or the desk-top,

25 And wait then, humped and bloody,
   For the wits to try it again; and how our spirits
   Rose when, suddenly sure,

   It lifted off from a chair-back,
   Beating a smooth course for the right window
30 And clearing the sill of the world.

   It is always a matter, my darling,
   Of life or death, as I had forgotten. I wish
   What I wished you before, but harder.

Mark familiar word parts or indicate another strategy you used that helped you determine meaning.

**iridescent** (ihr uh DEHS uhnt) *adj.*

MEANING:

---

4. **clamor** (KLAM uhr) *n.* loud, continuous noise.
5. **starling** *n.* dark brown or black bird that is common in Europe and the United States.

# Hugging the Jukebox

Naomi Shihab Nye

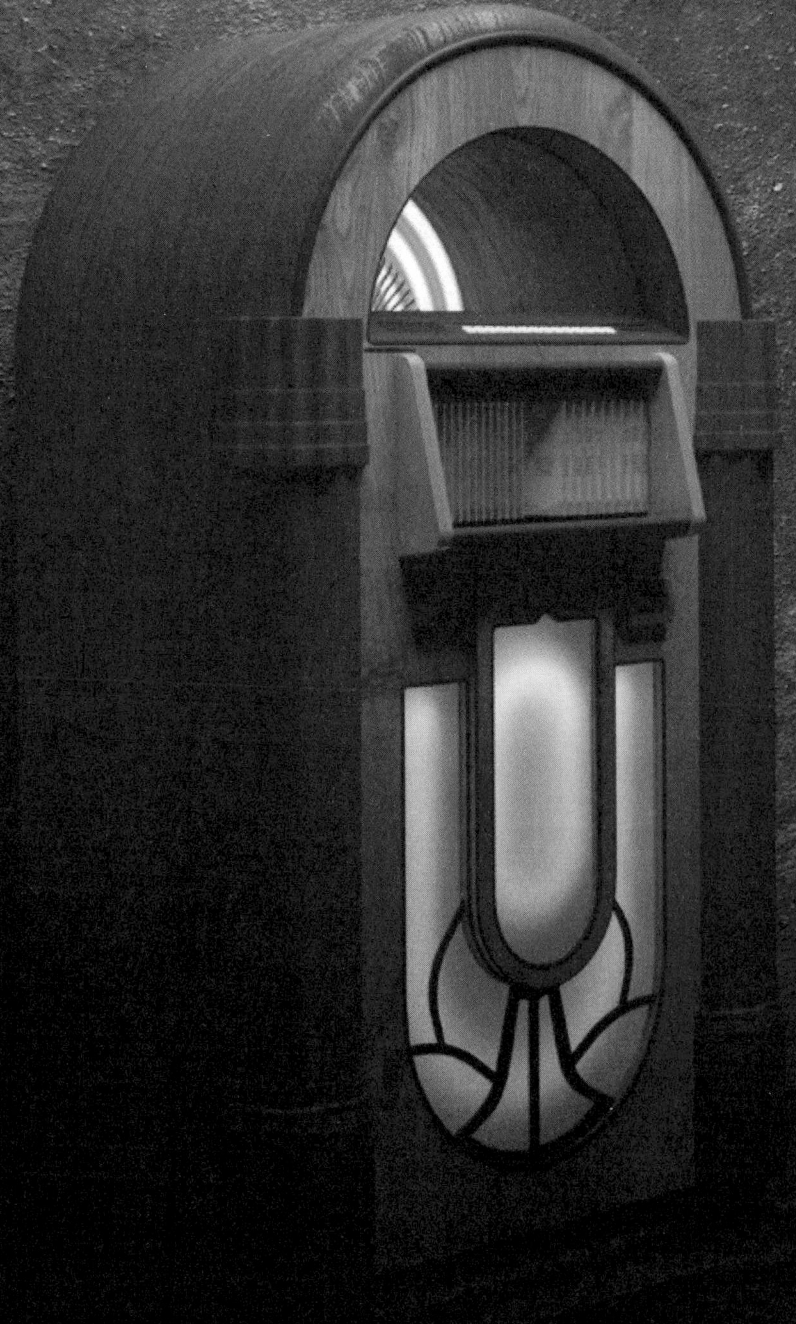

NOTES

On an island the soft hue of memory,
moss green, kerosene[1] yellow, drifting, mingling
in the Caribbean Sea,
a six-year-old named Alfred
5  learns all the words to all the songs
on his grandparents' jukebox, and sings them.
To learn the words is not so hard.
Many barmaids and teenagers have done as well.
But to sing as Alfred sings—
10 how can a giant whale live in the small pool of his chest?
How can there be breakers[2] this high, notes crashing
at the beach of the throat,
and a reef of coral so enormous only the fishes know its size?

The grandparents watch. They can't sing.
15 They don't know who this voice is, trapped in their grandson's body.
The boy whose parents sent him back to the island
to chatter mango-talk and scrap with chickens—
three years ago he didn't know the word "sad"!
Now he strings a hundred passionate sentences on a single line.
20 He bangs his fist so they will raise the volume.

What will they do together in their old age?
It is hard enough keeping yourself alive.
And this wild boy, loving nothing but music—
he'll sing all night, hugging the jukebox.
25 When a record pauses, that live second before dropping down,
Alfred hugs tighter, arms stretched wide
head pressed on the **luminous** belly. "Now!" he yells.
A half-smile when the needle breathes again.

They've tried putting him to bed, but he sings in bed.
30 Even in Spanish—and he doesn't speak Spanish!
Sings and screams, wants to go back to the jukebox.
*O mama I was born with a trumpet in my throat
    spent all these years tryin' to cough it up . . .*

He can't even read yet. He can't *tell time*.
35 But he sings, and the chairs in this old dance hall jerk to attention.
The grandparents lean on the counter, shaking their heads.
The customers stop talking and stare, goosey bumps[3] surfacing on
    their arms.

Mark familiar word parts or indicate another strategy you used that helped you determine meaning.

**luminous** (LOO muh nuhs) *adj.*

MEANING:

---

1. **kerosene** (KEHR uh seen) *n.* type of oil that is burned as fuel.
2. **breakers** *n.* waves that break into foam when they hit the shore.
3. **goosey bumps** variation of *goose bumps*, small bumps on the skin caused by cold, fear, or sudden excitement.

His voice carries out to the water where boats are tied
and sings for all of them, *a wave*.
40 For the hens, now roosting in trees,
for the mute boy next door, his second-best friend.
And for the hurricane, now brewing near Barbados[4]—
a week forward neighbors will be hammering boards over their
    windows,
rounding up dogs and fishing lines,
45 the generators will quit with solemn clicks in every yard.

But Alfred, hugging a sleeping jukebox, the names of the tunes gone
    dark,
will still be singing, doubly loud now, teasing his grandmother,
"Put a coin in my mouth!" and believing what she wants to believe;
this is not the end of the island, or the tablets this life has been
50 scribbled on, or the song.

*Utila,[5] Honduras*

---

4. **Barbados** (bahr BAY dohs) island nation in the southeastern Caribbean Sea.
5. **Utila** (OO tee lah) smallest of the Bay Islands of Honduras.

# Comprehension Check

Complete the following items after you finish your first read. Review and clarify
details with your group.

I AM OFFERING THIS POEM

**1.** Why does the speaker offer the poem to the reader rather than some other gift?

**2.** What are some of the benefits that the speaker hopes the poem will have for
the reader?

**3.** What phrase does the speaker repeat at the end of every stanza?

**1.** Early in the poem, what sound does the speaker hear?

**2.** What memory of a starling does the speaker describe?

**3.** What wish for the daughter does the speaker express twice?

**1.** What three things does the speaker say Alfred cannot do? What remarkable thing can Alfred do?

**2.** According to the speaker, what will Alfred continue to do during the upcoming hurricane?

## RESEARCH

**Research to Clarify** Choose at least one unfamiliar detail from one of the poems. Briefly research that detail. In what way does the information you learned shed light on an aspect of the poem?

POETRY COLLECTION

## Close Read the Text

With your group, revisit sections of the text you marked during your first read. **Annotate** details that you notice. What **questions** do you have? What can you **conclude**?

---

## Analyze the Text

> **CITE TEXTUAL EVIDENCE**
> to support your answers.

📓 **Notebook** Complete the activities.

1. **Review and Clarify** With your group, reread stanza 3 (lines 7–9) of "The Writer." Discuss the idea of the "cargo" of life. Where does a person carry his or her cargo? What does the speaker mean when saying some of the cargo can be heavy?

2. **Present and Discuss** Now work with your group to share key passages from "Hugging the Jukebox" and "I Am Offering This Poem." Why did you choose these passages? Take turns presenting your passages. Discuss what you notice in the text, what questions you asked, and what conclusions you reached.

3. **Essential Question:** *What does it take to survive?* What do these poems reveal about the idea of survival? Discuss with your group.

---

### LANGUAGE DEVELOPMENT

## Concept Vocabulary

| treasure | iridescent | luminous |
|----------|-----------|----------|

**Why These Words?** The concept vocabulary words from the poems are related. With your group, determine what the words have in common. Write your ideas and add another word that fits the category.

### Practice

📓 **Notebook** Confirm your understanding of each vocabulary word by answering this question: What are the qualities of something that is *iridescent* or *luminous*?

## Word Study

**Latin Root: -*lum*-** In "Hugging the Jukebox," the author refers to the jukebox as having a *luminous* belly. The word *luminous* was formed from the Latin root -*lum*-, which means "light." Find several other words that contain this root. Record the words and their meanings.

---

**TIP**

**GROUP DISCUSSION**
Keep in mind that personal experience can affect how a reader perceives a poem. Be aware and supportive of the impressions of others as your group discusses the poetry.

**WORD NETWORK**

Add interesting words related to survival from the text to your Word Network.

**STANDARDS**

**RL.9–10.2** Determine a theme or central idea of a text and analyze in detail its development over the course of the text, including how it emerges and is shaped and refined by specific details; provide an objective summary of the text.

**L.9–10.4.b** Identify and correctly use patterns of word changes that indicate different meanings or parts of speech and continue to apply knowledge of Greek and Latin roots and affixes.

# Analyze Craft and Structure

**Development of Theme** The **theme** of a poem is the central idea, message, or insight it expresses. In most poems, the theme is not stated directly. Instead, it is suggested through details and poetic elements. In some poems, the poet uses a central symbol to help develop a theme. A **symbol** is anything—an object, a person, an animal, a place, or an image—that has its own meaning, but also stands for something larger than itself, usually an abstract idea.

## Practice

CITE TEXTUAL EVIDENCE to support your answers.

Working independently, use the chart to analyze how the poets use symbols to develop the themes of these poems. Gather your notes and then share with your group.

| SYMBOL: The poem in "I Am Offering This Poem" |
| --- |
| What details does the speaker use to describe the poem? |
| What does the poem represent to the speaker? |
| What is the poem's theme? How does the symbol help develop that theme? |

| SYMBOL: The starling in "The Writer" |
| --- |
| What details describe the starling? |
| What does the starling represent to the speaker? |
| What is the poem's theme? How does the use of the symbol help develop the theme? |

| SYMBOL: Alfred's voice in "Hugging the Jukebox" |
| --- |
| What details describe Alfred's voice? |
| What does Alfred's voice represent to the speaker? |
| What is the poem's theme? How does the symbol help develop the theme? |

## Author's Style

**Figurative Language** Poets often use figurative language, or language that is not meant to be taken literally. Most figurative language points out a striking similarity between dissimilar things. Through these unexpected comparisons, poets help readers see familiar experiences or objects in a fresh new light. Metaphors and similes are two types of figurative language.

> **Metaphor:** A figure of speech in which one thing is spoken of as though it were something else.
> **Examples:** "The clouds are a thick blanket" or "My couch is a rock."
>
> **Simile:** A figure of speech in which the words *like* or *as* are used to compare two seemingly dissimilar things.
> **Examples:** "The clouds are as comforting as a thick blanket" or "My couch is like a rock."

### Read It

Work individually. Use this chart to identify and analyze metaphors and similes from the poems. Then gather as a group to discuss your responses.

| PASSAGE | METAPHOR OR SIMILE | WHAT IT COMPARES | HOW IT ADDS MEANING |
| --- | --- | --- | --- |
| Keep it . . . / . . . like a pair of thick socks / the cold cannot bite through. (I Am Offering This Poem, line 5) | | | |
| In her room at the prow of the house . . . (The Writer, line 1) | | | |
| . . . how can a giant whale live in the small pool of his chest? (Hugging the Jukebox, line 10) | | | |

### Write It

Complete each sentence. Write in words and phrases to create a metaphor or a simile. Be as imaginative as possible in your writing. Identify each comparison you write as a metaphor or a simile.

**1.** To Alfred, the jukebox is _____

_____.

**2.** In "The Writer," the sound of typewriter keys _____

_____.

**3.** In "I Am Offering This Poem," the individual words of a poem are

_____

_____

### STANDARDS

**RL.9–10.4** Determine the meaning of words and phrases as they are used in the text, including figurative and connotative meanings; analyze the cumulative impact of specific word choices on meaning and tone.

**L.9–10.5** Demonstrate understanding of figurative language, word relationships, and nuances in word meanings.

# Speaking and Listening

## Assignment

Create an **oral presentation** of the poem of your choice. When delivering your presentation, pay close attention to your eye contact, body language, pronunciation, tone, speaking rate, and voice modulation. Choose from the following options.

☐ **Theater Production** Perform one of the poems as a theater production that might include music, sound effects, costumes, stage props, and images. Dramatize the poem, using techniques such as alternating speakers and acting out the images in the poem. Aim to make your production convey the true meaning of the poem to the audience.

☐ **Video Presentation** Choose your favorite poem and create a brief, entertaining video in which your group performs the poem.

☐ **Discussion and Presentation** In "The Writer," the author says, "It is always a matter of life and death." With your group, discuss the following questions:

- What is the "it" to which the speaker of Wilbur's poem refers— what is "always a matter of life and death"?

- What might always be a matter of life and death for the speakers of the other two poems?

- Organize notes from the discussion into a brief presentation to share with the class.

**Discussion Plan** If you choose the discussion, make decisions about who the participants will be and which question each student will discuss. Write out a list of at least five discussion questions, including the ones provided.

**Presentation Plan** Before you begin the theater production or video presentation, make decisions about things such as the order of speakers, the music, props, images, costumes, and other items that might be needed. Create a written outline that provides that information for all members of the group. Then, gather the items and materials that you will need. Use this chart to organize your ideas.

| POEM STANZA | READER(S) | MUSIC/SOUND | PROPS, COSTUMES, IMAGES | PLAN |
|---|---|---|---|---|
| 1–2 | | | | |
| 3 | | | | |
| 4 | | | | |

© Pearson Education, Inc., or its affiliates. All rights reserved.

**EVIDENCE LOG**

Before moving on to a new selection, go to your Evidence Log and record what you learned from "I Am Offering This Poem," "The Writer," and "Hugging the Jukebox."

**STANDARDS**

**L.9–10.5.a** Interpret figures of speech in context and analyze their role in the text.

**SL.9–10.1.a** Come to discussions prepared, having read and researched material under study; explicitly draw on that preparation by referring to evidence from texts and other research on the topic or issue to stimulate a thoughtful, well-reasoned exchange of ideas.

**SL.9–10.6** Adapt speech to a variety of contexts and tasks, demonstrating command of formal English when indicated or appropriate.

**SL.9–10.1.b** Work with peers to set rules for collegial discussions and decision-making, clear goals and deadlines, and individual roles as needed.

# Present an Argument

## Assignment

You have read about people who showed different types of strength as they struggled to survive in life-or-death situations. Work with your group to develop and refine a multimedia presentation about emergency situations to present to a school or civic group. Your presentation should present an argument that addresses the following question:

> **What type of strength is most valuable in a survival situation?**

## Plan With Your Group

**Analyze the Text** With your group, discuss the various types of strength—such as physical and emotional strength—that factor into the survival stories you have read. Use the chart to list your ideas. For each selection, identify the type of strength that plays the most vital role. Then, come to a consensus about which type of strength your group believes is most valuable.

| TITLE | TYPES OF STRENGTH |
|---|---|
| The Voyage of the *James Caird* | |
| The *Endurance* and the *James Caird* in Images | |
| *from* Life of Pi | |
| The Value of a Sherpa Life | |
| I Am Offering This Poem<br>The Writer<br>Hugging the Jukebox | |
| Most Valuable Type of Strength: | |

**Gather Evidence and Media Examples** Scan the selections to record specific examples that support your group's claim. Then, brainstorm for types of media you can use to illustrate or elaborate on each example. Consider photographs, illustrations, music, charts, graphs, and video clips. Allow each group member to make suggestions. Keep your purpose and audience directly in mind while choosing media.

**Organize Your Ideas** Use a chart like this one to organize your script. Assign roles for each part of the presentation, note when each part begins, and record what the presenter will say.

| MULTIMEDIA PRESENTATION SCRIPT | | |
| --- | --- | --- |
| | Media Cues | Script |
| Presenter 1 | | |
| Presenter 2 | | |
| Presenter 3 | | |

## Rehearse With Your Group

**Practice With Your Group** Use this checklist to evaluate the effectiveness of your group's first run-through. Then, use your evaluation and the instructions here to guide your revision.

| CONTENT | USE OF MEDIA | PRESENTATION TECHNIQUES |
| --- | --- | --- |
| ☐ The presentation presents a clear thesis. <br> ☐ Main ideas are supported with evidence from the texts in Small-Group Learning. | ☐ The media support the thesis. <br> ☐ The media communicate key ideas. <br> ☐ Media are used evenly throughout the presentation. <br> ☐ Equipment functions properly. | ☐ Media are visible and audible. <br> ☐ Transitions between media segments are smooth. <br> ☐ The speaker uses eye contact and speaks clearly. |

**Fine-Tune the Content** To make your presentation stronger, you may need to go back into the texts to find more support for your ideas. Check with your group to identify key points that are not clear to listeners. Find another way to word these ideas. Remember to always keep your purpose and audience in mind.

- **Purpose:** Because your purpose is to inform your audience about how to behave in an emergency, make sure you address both mental and physical strength.
- **Audience:** If your audience is young children, keep your language and ideas simple and use plenty of visuals. If adults are your audience, don't "talk down" to them.

**Improve Your Use of Media** If media are not evenly distributed throughout the presentation, work to change the pacing.

## Present and Evaluate

When you present as a group, be sure that each member has taken into account each of the checklist items. As you watch other groups, evaluate how well they meet the criteria in the checklist.

**::** STANDARDS
**SL.9–10.5** Make strategic use of digital media in presentations to enhance understanding of findings, reasoning, and evidence and to add interest.

Performance Task: Present an Argument **239**

ESSENTIAL QUESTION:

# What does it take to survive?

The ways in which people survive life-or-death situations can be inspiring. In this section, you will complete your study of survival by exploring an additional selection related to the topic. You'll then share what you learn with classmates. To choose a text, follow these steps.

**Look Back** Think about the selections you have already studied. What more do you want to know about the topic of survival?

**Look Ahead** Preview the texts by reading the descriptions. Which one seems most interesting and appealing to you?

**Look Inside** Take a few minutes to scan the text you chose. Choose a different one if this text doesn't meet your needs.

## Independent Learning Strategies

Throughout your life, in school, in your community, and in your career, you will need to rely on yourself to learn and work on your own. Review these strategies and the actions you can take to practice them during Independent Learning. Add ideas of your own for each category.

| STRATEGY | ACTION PLAN |
|---|---|
| Create a schedule | • Understand your goals and deadlines.<br>• Make a plan for what to do each day.<br>• |
| Practice what you have learned | • Use first-read and close-read strategies to deepen your understanding.<br>• Evaluate the usefulness of the evidence to help you understand the topic.<br>• Consider the quality and reliability of the source.<br>• |
| Take notes | • Record important ideas and information.<br>• Review your notes before preparing to share with a group.<br>• |

SCAN FOR
MULTIMEDIA

# CONTENTS

**Choose one selection. Selections are available online only.**

**SCAN FOR MULTIMEDIA**

# First-Read Guide

Use this page to record your first-read ideas.

⚙ **Tool Kit**
First-Read Guide and
Model Annotation

Selection Title: _____

**NOTICE** new information or ideas you learn about the unit topic as you first read this text.

**ANNOTATE** by marking vocabulary and key passages you want to revisit.

**First Read**

NOTICE · ANNOTATE · CONNECT · RESPOND

**CONNECT** ideas within the selection to other knowledge and the selections you have read.

**RESPOND** by writing a brief summary of the selection.

▤ STANDARD

**Anchor Reading Standard 10** Read and comprehend complex literary and informational texts independently and proficiently.

# Close-Read Guide

Use this page to record your close-read ideas.

Selection Title: _____

## Close Read the Text

Revisit sections of the text you marked during your first read. Read these sections closely and **annotate** what you notice. Ask yourself **questions** about the text. What can you **conclude?** Write down your ideas.

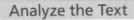

## Analyze the Text

Think about the author's choices of patterns, structure, techniques, and ideas included in the text. Select one, and record your thoughts about what this choice conveys.

## QuickWrite

Pick a paragraph from the text that grabbed your interest. Explain the power of this passage.

**:≡ STANDARD**
**Anchor Reading Standard 10** Read and comprehend complex literary and informational texts independently band proficiently.

# Share Your Independent Learning

## Prepare to Share

### What does it take to survive?

Even when you read something independently, your understanding continues to grow when you share what you have learned with others. Reflect on the text you explored independently and write notes about its connection to the unit. In your notes, consider why this text belongs in this unit.

## Learn From Your Classmates

💬 **Discuss It**  Share your ideas about the text you explored on your own. As you talk with your classmates, jot down ideas that you learn from them.

## Reflect

Review your notes, and underline the most important insight you gained from these writing and discussion activities. Explain how this idea adds to your understanding of the topic of survival.

**SL.9–10.1** Initiate and participate effectively in a range of collaborative discussions with diverse partners on grades 9–10 topics, texts, and issues, building on others' ideas and expressing their own clearly and persuasively.

# Review Evidence for an Argument

At the beginning of this unit, you took a position on the following question:

> Should people in life-or-death situations be held accountable for their actions?

## ✎ EVIDENCE LOG

Review your Evidence Log and your QuickWrite from the beginning of the unit. Has your position changed?

| ☐ YES | ☐ NO |
|---|---|
| Identify at least three pieces of evidence that convinced you to change your mind. | Identify at least three pieces of evidence that reinforced your initial position. |
| **1.** | **1.** |
| **2.** | **2.** |
| **3.** | **3.** |

State your position now: _____

_____

_____

Identify a possible counterclaim: _____

_____

_____

**Evaluate the Strength of Your Evidence** Consider your argument. Do you have enough evidence to support your claim? Do you have enough evidence to refute a counterclaim? If not, make a plan.

☐ Do more research            ☐ Talk with my classmates

☐ Reread a selection          ☐ Ask an expert

☐ Other: _____

**⊞ STANDARDS**
**W.9–10.1.a** Introduce precise claim(s), distinguish the claim(s) from alternate or opposing claims, and create an organization that establishes clear relationships among claim(s), counterclaims, reasons, and evidence.

## SOURCES

- WHOLE-CLASS SELECTIONS
- SMALL-GROUP SELECTIONS
- INDEPENDENT LEARNING

## PART 1
# Writing to Sources: Argument

In this unit, you read about various characters, both real and fictional, who found themselves in life-or-death situations. Some made choices of which they were most likely proud, while others did not.

### Assignment

Write an **argument** in which you state and defend a claim responding to the following question:

> Should people in life-or-death situations be held accountable for their actions?

Use credible evidence from at least three of the selections you read and researched in this unit to support your claim. Ensure that your claim is fully supported, that you use a formal tone, and that your organization is logical and easy to follow.

**Reread the Assignment** Review the assignment to be sure you fully understand it. The task may reference some of the academic words presented at the beginning of the unit. Be sure you understand each of the words given below in order to complete the assignment correctly.

### Academic Vocabulary

| | | |
|---|---|---|
| evidence | valid | logical |
| credible | formulate | |

**Review the Elements of Effective Argument** Before you begin writing, read the Argument Rubric. Once you have completed your first draft, check it against the rubric. If one or more of the elements is missing or not as strong as it could be, revise your essay to add or strengthen that component.

---

### ⬡ WORD NETWORK

As you write and revise your argument, use your Word Network to help vary your word choices.

---

### ▤ STANDARDS

**W.9–10.1.a–e** Write arguments to support claims in an analysis of substantive topics or texts, using valid reasoning and relevant and sufficient evidence.

**W.9–10.9** Draw evidence from literary or informational texts to support analysis, reflection, and research.

**W.9–10.10** Write routinely over extended time frames and shorter time frames for a range of tasks, purposes, and audiences.

**246** UNIT 2 • SURVIVAL

# Argument Rubric

| | Focus and Organization | Evidence and Elaboration | Language Conventions |
|---|---|---|---|
| **4** | The introduction is engaging and establishes the claim in a compelling way.<br><br>Includes valid reasons and evidence that address and support the claim while acknowledging counterclaims.<br><br>Ideas progress logically, and include a variety of sentence transitions.<br><br>The conclusion offers fresh insights into claim. | Sources of evidence are comprehensive and specific and contain relevant information.<br><br>The tone of the argument is formal and objective.<br><br>Uses vocabulary strategically and appropriately for the audience and purpose. | The argument intentionally uses standard English conventions of usage and mechanics.<br><br>Uses transitions to create cohesion. |
| **3** | The introduction is engaging and establishes the claim in a way that grabs readers' attention.<br><br>Includes reasons and evidence that address and support the claim while acknowledging counterclaims.<br><br>The ideas progress logically, and include sentence transitions that connect readers to the argument.<br><br>The conclusion restates information. | Sources of evidence contain relevant information.<br><br>The tone of the argument is mostly formal and objective.<br><br>Uses vocabulary that is generally appropriate for the audience and purpose. | The argument demonstrates accuracy in standard English conventions of usage and mechanics.<br><br>Sometime uses transitions to create cohesion. |
| **2** | The introduction establishes a claim.<br><br>Includes some reasons and evidence that address and support the claim while briefly acknowledging counterclaims.<br><br>Ideas progress somewhat logically. Includes a few sentence transitions that connect readers to the argument.<br><br>The conclusion offers some insight into the claim and restates information. | Sources of evidence contain some relevant information.<br><br>The tone of the argument is occasionally formal and objective.<br><br>Uses vocabulary that is somewhat appropriate for the audience and purpose. | The argument demonstrates some accuracy in standard English conventions of usage and mechanics.<br><br>Uses few transitions to create cohesion. |
| **1** | The claim is not clearly stated.<br><br>Does not include reasons or evidence to support the claim. Does not acknowledge counterclaims.<br><br>Ideas do not progress logically. The sentences are often short and choppy and do not connect readers to the argument.<br><br>The conclusion does not restate any information that is important. | Does not include reliable or relevant evidence.<br><br>The tone of the argument is informal.<br><br>The vocabulary is limited or ineffective. | The argument contains mistakes in standard English conventions of usage and mechanics.<br><br>Fails to use transitions to create cohesion. |

PART 2

# Speaking and Listening: Oral Presentation

**Assignment**

After completing the final draft of your argument, use it as the foundation for a three- to five-minute **oral presentation**.

Instead of simply reading your essay aloud, take the following steps to make your oral presentation lively and engaging.

- Go back to your essay and annotate the most important claims and supporting details from your introduction, body paragraphs, and conclusion.

- Refer to your annotated text to guide your presentation and keep it focused.

- Deliver your argument with conviction. Look up from your annotated text frequently, and make eye contact with listeners.

**Review the Oral Presentation Rubric** Before you deliver your presentation, check your plans against this rubric. If one or more of the elements is missing or not as strong as it could be, revise your presentation.

### STANDARDS

**SL.9–10.4** Present information, findings, and supporting evidence clearly, concisely, and logically such that listeners can follow the line of reasoning and the organization, development, substance, and style are appropriate to purpose, audience, and task.

| | Content | Organization | Presentation Technique |
|---|---|---|---|
| 3 | Introduction is engaging and establishes a claim in a compelling way.<br><br>Presentation has strong valid reasons and evidence that support the claim while clearly acknowledging counterclaims.<br><br>Conclusion offers fresh insight into the claim. | The speaker uses time very effectively by spending the right amount of time on each part.<br><br>Ideas progress logically, supported by a variety of sentence transitions. Listeners can follow the presentation. | The speaker maintains effective eye contact.<br><br>The speaker presents with strong conviction and energy. |
| 2 | Introduction establishes a claim.<br><br>Presentation has valid reasons and evidence that support the claim while acknowledging counterclaims. | The speaker uses time effectively by spending the right amount of time on most parts.<br><br>Ideas progress logically, supported by some sentence transitions. Listeners mostly follow the presentation. | The speaker mostly maintains effective eye contact.<br><br>The speaker presents with some level of conviction and energy. |
| 1 | Introduction does not clearly state a claim.<br><br>Presentation does not have reasons or evidence to support a claim or acknowledge counterclaims.<br><br>Conclusion does not restate important information about a claim. | The speaker does not use time effectively; some parts of the presentation are too long or too short.<br><br>Ideas do not progress logically. Listeners have difficulty following the presentation. | The speaker does not establish eye contact.<br><br>The speaker presents without conviction or energy. |

# Reflect on the Unit

Now that you've completed the unit, take a few moments to reflect on your learning.

## Reflect on the Unit Goals

Look back at the goals at the beginning of the unit. Use a different colored pen to rate yourself again. Then, think about readings and activities that contributed the most to the growth of your understanding. Record your thoughts.

## Reflect on the Learning Strategies

**Discuss It** Write a reflection on whether you were able to improve your learning based on your Action Plans. Think about what worked, what didn't, and what you might do to keep working on these strategies. Record your ideas before joining a class discussion.

## Reflect on the Text

Choose a selection that you found challenging, and explain what made it difficult.

Describe something that surprised you about a text in the unit.

Which activity taught you the most about survival? What did you learn?

SCAN FOR
MULTIMEDIA

# The Literature of Civil Rights

During the Civil Rights movement, writings and speeches inspired sweeping social change. What gave those words the power to change a nation?

Civil Rights Movement and Martin Luther King

💬 **Discuss It** How was Dr. Martin Luther King, Jr., important to the Civil Rights movement?

Write your response before sharing your ideas.

SCAN FOR MULTIMEDIA

## UNIT INTRODUCTION

**ESSENTIAL QUESTION:**

# How can words inspire change?

LAUNCH TEXT
INFORMATIVE MODEL
1963: The Year That
Changed Everything

---

### WHOLE-CLASS LEARNING

**COMPARE**

ANCHOR TEXT: SPEECH

"I Have a Dream"
*Dr. Martin Luther King, Jr.*

▶ MEDIA CONNECTION:
"I Have a Dream"

ANCHOR TEXT: LETTER

Letter From Birmingham Jail
*Dr. Martin Luther King, Jr.*

MEDIA: VIDEO

Remarks on the Assassination of Martin Luther King, Jr.
*Robert F. Kennedy*

PERFORMANCE TASK

WRITING FOCUS:
Write an Informative Essay

---

### SMALL-GROUP LEARNING

MEDIA: NEWSCAST

Remembering Civil Rights History, When "Words Meant Everything"
*PBS NewsHour*

POETRY COLLECTION

For My People
*Margaret Walker*

Incident
*Natasha Trethewey*

SPEECH

Lessons of Dr. Martin Luther King, Jr.
*Cesar Chavez*

MEMOIR

Traveling
*Grace Paley*

PERFORMANCE TASK

SPEAKING AND LISTENING FOCUS:
Multimedia Presentation

---

### INDEPENDENT LEARNING

MEDIA: NEWSCAST

Frank McCain Dies—Helped Start Sit-In Movement at Greensboro Lunch Counter
*Jeff Tiberii*

NEWS ARTICLE

How the Children of Birmingham Changed the Civil-Rights Movement
*Lottie L. Joiner*

NARRATIVE NONFICTION

Sheyann Webb
*from Selma, Lord, Selma*
*as told to Frank Sikora*

MAGAZINE ARTICLE

The Many Lives of Hazel Bryan
*David Margolick*

MEDIA: VIDEO

Fannie Lou Hamer
*BBC*

PERFORMANCE-BASED ASSESSMENT PREP

Review Evidence for an Informative Essay

---

## PERFORMANCE-BASED ASSESSMENT PREP

Informative Text: Essay and Multimedia Presentation

**PROMPT:**

Explain how words have the power to provoke, calm, or inspire.

## Unit Goals

Throughout the unit, you will deepen your perspective of the literature of civil rights by reading, writing, speaking, presenting, and listening. These goals will help you succeed on the Unit Performance-Based Assessment.

Rate how well you meet these goals right now. You will revisit your ratings later when you reflect on your growth during this unit.

| SCALE | 1 | 2 | 3 | 4 | 5 |
|---|---|---|---|---|---|
| | NOT AT ALL WELL | NOT VERY WELL | SOMEWHAT WELL | VERY WELL | EXTREMELY WELL |

### READING GOALS    1   2   3   4   5

- Evaluate written arguments and informative texts by analyzing how authors introduce and develop ideas. ○—○—○—○—○

- Expand your knowledge and use of academic and concept vocabulary. ○—○—○—○—○

### WRITING AND RESEARCH GOALS    1   2   3   4   5

- Write an informative essay in which you effectively convey complex ideas and information. ○—○—○—○—○

- Conduct research projects of various lengths to explore a topic and clarify meaning. ○—○—○—○—○

### LANGUAGE GOALS    1   2   3   4   5

- Smoothly integrate information from varied sources to create cohesion. ○—○—○—○—○

- Correctly use varied types of clauses as well as parallelism in writing and presentations. ○—○—○—○—○

### SPEAKING AND LISTENING GOALS    1   2   3   4   5

- Collaborate with your team to build on the ideas of others, develop consensus, and communicate. ○—○—○—○—○

- Integrate audio, visuals, and text in presentations. ○—○—○—○—○

## STANDARDS

**L.9–10.6** Acquire and use accurately general academic and domain-specific words and phrases, sufficient for reading, writing, speaking, and listening at the college and career readiness level; demonstrate independence in gathering vocabulary knowledge when considering a word or phrase important to comprehension or expression.

SCAN FOR MULTIMEDIA

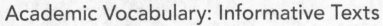
# Academic Vocabulary: Informative Texts

Academic terms appear in all subjects and can help you read, write, and discuss with more precision. Here are five academic words that will be useful to you in this unit as you analyze and write informative texts.

**Complete the chart.**

1. Review each word, its root, and the mentor sentences.

2. Use the information and your own knowledge to predict the meaning of each word.

3. For each word, list at least two related words.

4. Refer to a dictionary or other resources if needed.

**TIP**

**FOLLOW THROUGH**
Study the words in this chart, and highlight them or related word forms wherever they appear in the unit.

| WORD | MENTOR SENTENCES | PREDICT MEANING | RELATED WORDS |
|---|---|---|---|
| **disrupt**<br><br>ROOT:<br>**-rupt-**<br>"break"; "burst" | 1. We were worried a storm would *disrupt* the drive-in movie.<br>2. Golf fans are very quiet, so they do not *disrupt* the match. | | disruptive; disrupting |
| **coherent**<br><br>ROOT:<br>**-her-**<br>"stick"; "cling" | 1. It is important to organize academic writing in a logical and *coherent* manner.<br>2. Although the philosopher spoke well, his argument was not *coherent*. | | |
| **notation**<br><br>ROOT:<br>**-not-**<br>"mark"; "sign" | 1. The *notation* in the margin told more about the play.<br>2. The recipe contained a *notation* to substitute oil for butter. | | |
| **aggregate**<br><br>ROOT:<br>**-greg-**<br>"herd"; "flock" | 1. The pavers are an *aggregate* of three types of stone.<br>2. The collage was an *aggregate* of the artist's photographs. | | |
| **express**<br><br>ROOT:<br>**-press-**<br>"push"; "press down" | 1. *Express* your thoughts logically and clearly so that others can understand them.<br>2. We gave a gift because words alone could not fully *express* our gratitude. | | |

This selection is an example of an **informative text,** a type of writing in which the author examines concepts through the careful selection, organization, and analysis of information. This is the type of writing you will develop in the Performance-Based Assessment at the end of the unit.

**As you read,** think about how the writer describes events. Mark the text to help you answer this question: How does the writer help the reader understand the importance of these events?

# 1963:
## The Year That Changed Everything

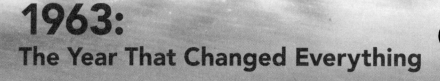

∧ During the Children's Crusade of May 1963, police turned fire hoses on young civil rights protesters, including this girl who was knocked to the ground by the force of the water.

NOTES

1  In 1865, the Thirteenth Amendment to the United States Constitution ended slavery. Nearly a century later, African Americans continued to struggle for equality under the law. A number of major events in this dramatic battle took place in 1963.

2  In April of that year—from behind the bars of a jail cell in Birmingham, Alabama—Dr. Martin Luther King, Jr., wrote a message that would inspire countless others. King had been arrested for breaking a law banning public protest. His message, the famous "Letter From Birmingham Jail," defends nonviolent resistance to injustice. "Injustice anywhere is a threat to justice everywhere," King wrote. He added, "Whatever affects one directly, affects all indirectly."

3  In early May, the young people of Birmingham took King's message to heart. Disobeying a court order, more than 1,000 African American students marched from the 16th Street Baptist Church. The next day, the students marched through Kelly Ingram Park. They were met by an angry white mob as well as police who blasted

SCAN FOR MULTIMEDIA

them with water from fire hoses and terrified them with dogs. The teenagers were jailed in temporary cells at the county fairgrounds. On the seventh day of the Children's Crusade, city officials agreed to negotiate with the African American community. A few days later, the two sides reached an agreement to end local segregation.

4      News of the Children's Crusade spread in the media, helping to transform the way Americans saw the civil rights movement. The *New York Times* ran more stories about civil rights in the two weeks after the Children's Crusade than it had in the previous two years combined. Scenes of children under attack were filmed and broadcast all over the world, setting off a global outcry. Polls showed that Americans across the land believed racial justice was the nation's biggest problem.

5      The struggle for civil rights continued to be marked by violence. On May 28, 1963, four African American college students in Jackson, Mississippi, were assaulted for sitting at a segregated lunch counter. Two weeks later, on June 12, an assassin killed civil rights activist Medgar Evers outside his home in Jackson.

6      That summer brought a landmark event in civil rights history. This was the March for Jobs and Freedom that took place in Washington, D.C., on August 28.  Under the shadow of the Lincoln Memorial, Dr. King delivered his famous "I Have a Dream" speech to a crowd of 200,000 people from all walks of life. The peace and hope of that event did not last long. On September 15, a bomb exploded inside Birmingham's 16th Street Baptist Church. The attack killed four little African American girls and injured twenty-two other people.

7      The struggle continued throughout 1963. The Southern Regional Council has records of protests that took place in more than 100 southern towns. Approximately 20,000 demonstrators were arrested. With words and actions, they delivered a demand for justice that could not be ignored.

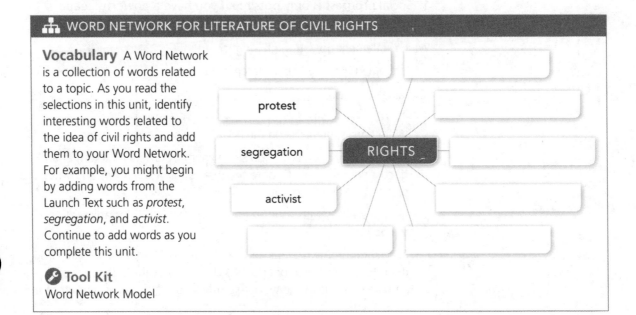

### WORD NETWORK FOR LITERATURE OF CIVIL RIGHTS

**Vocabulary** A Word Network is a collection of words related to a topic. As you read the selections in this unit, identify interesting words related to the idea of civil rights and add them to your Word Network. For example, you might begin by adding words from the Launch Text such as *protest*, *segregation*, and *activist*. Continue to add words as you complete this unit.

protest

segregation        RIGHTS

activist

**Tool Kit**
Word Network Model

## Summary

Write a summary of "1963: The Year That Changed Everything."
A **summary** is a concise, complete, and accurate overview of a text.
It should not include a statement of your opinion or an analysis.

## Launch Activity

**Group Discussion** Consider these statements:

1.  Social progress is only possible if you have a powerful leader.
2.  Social progress is only possible if it comes from the people.

Which statement do you think is right?

☐ statement 1          ☐ statement 2

Explain your reasons: _____

_____

- Write both statements on the board, leaving room for notes.

- Find two other students who share your response. Get together and discuss your reasons. Choose the three strongest reasons and write each one on a self-sticking note.

- Place the notes with your reasons under the relevant statement on the board.

- Read through the reasons and identify the ones that are similar. Group them together on the board. As a class, discuss the categories of reasons and evaluate their validity. Has your position changed as a result of the class discussion?

# QuickWrite

Consider class discussions, presentations, the video, and the Launch Text as you think about the prompt. Record your first thoughts here.

PROMPT: **Explain how words have the power to provoke, calm, or inspire.**

## ✎ EVIDENCE LOG FOR THE LITERATURE OF CIVIL RIGHTS

Review your QuickWrite. Summarize your thoughts in one sentence and record it in your Evidence Log. Then, record textual details or evidence from "1963: The Year That Changed Everything" that support your thinking.

Prepare for the Performance-Based Assessment at the end of the unit by completing the Evidence Log after each selection.

### 🔧 Tool Kit
Evidence Log Model

Title of Text: _____  Date: _____

| CONNECTION TO PROMPT | TEXT EVIDENCE/DETAILS | ADDITIONAL NOTES/IDEAS |
|---|---|---|
| | | |

How does this text change or add to my thinking?  Date: _____

SCAN FOR
MULTIMEDIA

ESSENTIAL QUESTION:
# How can words inspire change?

During the 1960s, the fight for racial equality in the United States gave rise to powerful literary statements. In speeches, essays, poetry, and fiction, writers rose to the challenge of documenting injustice and inspiring change. You will work with your whole class to explore the literature of the Civil Rights movement. The selections you are going to read capture the struggles and hopes of an important era in American history.

## Whole-Class Learning Strategies

Throughout your life, in school, in your community, and in your career, you will continue to learn and work in large-group environments.

Review these strategies and the actions you can take to practice them as you work with your whole class. Add ideas of your own for each step. Get ready to use these strategies during Whole-Class Learning.

| STRATEGY | ACTION PLAN |
|---|---|
| Listen actively | • Eliminate distractions. For example, put your cell phone away.<br>• Keep your eyes on the speaker.<br>• |
| Clarify by asking questions | • If you're confused, other people probably are, too. Ask a question to help your whole class.<br>• If you see that you are guessing, ask a question instead.<br>• |
| Monitor understanding | • Notice what information you already know and be ready to build on it.<br>• Ask for help if you are struggling.<br>• |
| Interact and share ideas | • Share your ideas and answer questions, even if you are unsure.<br>• Build on the ideas of others by adding details or making a connection.<br>• |

SCAN FOR
MULTIMEDIA

# CONTENTS

**PERFORMANCE TASK**

WRITING FOCUS

## Write an Informative Essay

Both Whole-Class readings and the two videos deal with the struggle for civil rights in the United States. After reading the selections and viewing the videos, you will conduct research and write your own informative essay about the power of the written and spoken word in the American Civil Rights movement.

COMPARE

"I HAVE A DREAM"

## Comparing Texts

In this lesson, you will read and compare two of Dr. Martin Luther King, Jr.'s most famous works. First, you will complete the first-read and close-read activities for the "I Have a Dream" speech. Then, you will compare the speech to the letter King wrote while a prisoner in a jail cell in Birmingham, Alabama.

LETTER FROM BIRMINGHAM JAIL

## About the Author

**Dr. Martin Luther King, Jr.** (1929–1968) was a prominent leader of the African American civil rights movement from 1955 until his assassination in 1968. His dedication to nonviolent resistance made him both a moral and a political leader. As a Baptist minister, he was a religious leader as well. Dr. King organized many of the largest and most effective civil rights protests of the era.

🔧 **Tool Kit**
First-Read Guide and Model Annotation

# "I Have a Dream"

## Concept Vocabulary

You will encounter the following words as you read King's speech. Before reading, note how familiar you are with each word. Then, rank the words in order from most familiar (1) to least familiar (6).

| WORD | YOUR RANKING |
|---|---|
| prosperity | |
| hallowed | |
| tribulations | |
| redemptive | |
| oppression | |
| exalted | |

After completing the first read, come back to the concept vocabulary and review your rankings. Mark any changes to your original rankings as needed.

## First Read NONFICTION

Apply these strategies as you conduct your first read. You will have an opportunity to complete the close-read notes after your first read.

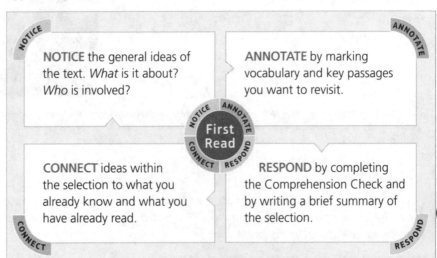

**NOTICE** the general ideas of the text. *What* is it about? *Who* is involved?

**ANNOTATE** by marking vocabulary and key passages you want to revisit.

**CONNECT** ideas within the selection to what you already know and what you have already read.

**RESPOND** by completing the Comprehension Check and by writing a brief summary of the selection.

First Read

≡ STANDARDS
**RI.9–10.10** By the end of grade 9, read and comprehend literary nonfiction in the grades 9–10 text complexity band proficiently, with scaffolding as needed at the high end of the range.

# "I Have a Dream"

## Dr. Martin Luther King, Jr.

### BACKGROUND

Because speeches are written to be spoken aloud, they are a more fluid form of literature than most other nonfiction. A strong speaker will react to unspoken signals from his or her listeners and adjust a speech accordingly. He or she might change words or add whole phrases. This is the case with Dr. Martin Luther King, Jr., one of the great speakers of the modern age. The text that appears here represents the speech exactly as it was delivered by Dr. King on the steps of the Lincoln Memorial.

SCAN FOR MULTIMEDIA

1    I am happy to join with you today in what will go down in history as the greatest demonstration for freedom in the history of our nation.

2    Five score[1] years ago, a great American, in whose symbolic shadow we stand today, signed the Emancipation Proclamation. This momentous decree came as a great beacon light of hope to millions of Negro slaves who had been seared in the flames of withering injustice. It came as a joyous daybreak to end the long night of their captivity.

3    But one hundred years later, the Negro still is not free. One hundred years later, the life of the Negro is still sadly crippled by the manacles of segregation and the chains of discrimination. One hundred years later, the Negro lives on a lonely island of poverty in the midst of a vast ocean of material prosperity. One hundred years later, the Negro is still languished in the corners of American society and finds himself an exile in his own land. And so we've come here today to dramatize a shameful condition.

4    In a sense we've come to our nation's capital to cash a check. When the architects of our republic wrote the magnificent words of the Constitution and the Declaration of Independence, they were signing a promissory note[2] to which every American was to fall heir.

**NOTES**

**prosperity** (pros PEHR uh tee) *n.* good fortune; success

---

1. **score** *n.* twenty. "Five score" is one hundred years.
2. **promissory note** (PROM ih sawr ee) *n.* written promise to pay a specific amount.

hallowed *adj.* (HAL ohd)
holy; sacred

**CLOSE READ**

**ANNOTATE:** In paragraphs 6 and 7, mark sentences that present two highly contrasting or opposing images or ideas.

**QUESTION:** What do these images suggest about the speaker's view of both the present and the future?

**CONCLUDE:** How do these images add urgency to the speaker's message?

This note was a promise that all men, yes, black men as well as white men, would be guaranteed the "unalienable Rights" of "Life, Liberty, and the pursuit of Happiness." It is obvious today that America has defaulted on this promissory note, insofar as her citizens of color are concerned. Instead of honoring this sacred obligation, America has given the Negro people a bad check, a check which has come back marked "insufficient funds."

5      But we refuse to believe that the bank of justice is bankrupt. We refuse to believe that there are insufficient funds in the great vaults of opportunity of this nation. And so, we've come to cash this check, a check that will give us upon demand the riches of freedom and the security of justice.

6      We have also come to this **hallowed** spot to remind America of the fierce urgency of Now. This is no time to engage in the luxury of cooling off or to take the tranquilizing drug of gradualism. Now is the time to make real the promises of democracy. Now is the time to rise from the dark and desolate valley of segregation to the sunlit path of racial justice. Now is the time to lift our nation from the quicksands of racial injustice to the solid rock of brotherhood. Now is the time to make justice a reality for all of God's children.

7      It would be fatal for the nation to overlook the urgency of the moment. This sweltering summer of the Negro's legitimate discontent will not pass until there is an invigorating autumn of freedom and equality. Nineteen sixty-three is not an end, but a beginning. And those who hope that the Negro needed to blow off steam and will now be content will have a rude awakening if the nation returns to business as usual. And there will be neither rest nor tranquility in America until the Negro is granted his citizenship rights. The whirlwinds of revolt will continue to shake the foundations of our nation until the bright day of justice emerges.

8      But there is something that I must say to my people, who stand on the warm threshold which leads into the palace of justice. In the process of gaining our rightful place, we must not be guilty of wrongful deeds. Let us not seek to satisfy our thirst for freedom by drinking from the cup of bitterness and hatred. We must forever conduct our struggle on the high plane of dignity and discipline. We must not allow our creative protest to degenerate into physical violence. Again and again, we must rise to the majestic heights of meeting physical force with soul force.

9      The marvelous new militancy which has engulfed the Negro community must not lead us to a distrust of all white people, for many of our white brothers, as evidenced by their presence here today, have come to realize that their destiny is tied up with our destiny. And they have come to realize that their freedom is inextricably bound to our freedom.

10      We cannot walk alone.

11      And as we walk, we must make the pledge that we shall always march ahead.

12      We cannot turn back.

13      There are those who are asking the devotees of civil rights, "When will you be satisfied?" We can never be satisfied as long as the Negro is the victim of the unspeakable horrors of police brutality. We can never be satisfied as long as our bodies, heavy with the fatigue of travel, cannot gain lodging in the motels of the highways and the hotels of the cities. We cannot be satisfied as long as the Negro's basic mobility is from a smaller ghetto to a larger one. We can never be satisfied as long as our children are stripped of their self-hood and robbed of their dignity by signs stating: "For Whites Only." We cannot be satisfied as long as a Negro in Mississippi cannot vote and a Negro in New York believes he has nothing for which to vote. No, no, we are not satisfied, and we will not be satisfied until "justice rolls down like waters, and righteousness like a mighty stream."

14      I am not unmindful that some of you have come here out of great trials and **tribulations**. Some of you have come fresh from narrow jail cells. And some of you have come from areas where your quest— quest for freedom left you battered by the storms of persecution and staggered by the winds of police brutality. You have been the veterans of creative suffering. Continue to work with the faith that unearned suffering is **redemptive**. Go back to Mississippi, go back to Alabama, go back to South Carolina, go back to Georgia, go back to Louisiana, go back to the slums and ghettos of our northern cities, knowing that somehow this situation can and will be changed.

15      Let us not wallow in the valley of despair, I say to you today, my friends.

16      And so even though we face the difficulties of today and tomorrow, I still have a dream. It is a dream deeply rooted in the American dream.

17      I have a dream that one day this nation will rise up and live out the true meaning of its creed: "We hold these truths to be self-evident, that all men are created equal."

18      I have a dream that one day on the red hills of Georgia, the sons of former slaves and the sons of former slave owners will be able to sit down together at the table of brotherhood.

19      I have a dream that one day even the state of Mississippi, a state sweltering with the heat of injustice, sweltering with the heat of **oppression**, will be transformed into an oasis of freedom and justice.

20      I have a dream that my four little children will one day live in a nation where they will not be judged by the color of their skin but by the content of their character.

21      I have a *dream* today!

22      I have a dream that one day, down in Alabama, with its vicious racists, with its governor having his lips dripping with the words of "interposition" and "nullification"[3]—one day right there in Alabama

**tribulations** (trihb yuh LAY shuhnz) *n.* great trouble or misery

**redemptive** (rih DEHMP tihv) *adj.* serving to deliver from sorrow; make amends or pay back

**oppression** (uh PREHSH uhn) *n.* cruel or unjust treatment

---

3. **"interposition"** (ihn tuhr puh ZIHSH uhn) **and "nullification"** (nuhl uh fih KAY shuhn) disputed doctrine that a state can reject federal laws considered to be violations of its rights. Governor George C. Wallace of Alabama used this doctrine to reject federal civil rights legislation.

exalted (ehg ZAWL tihd) *adj.* elevated

CLOSE READ

ANNOTATE: Mark words and phrases in paragraphs 26–27 that refer to sounds or music.

QUESTION: How do these references help define the transformation in society King is seeking?

CONCLUDE: What effect do these references have on both the meaning and the emotional impact of the speech?

little black boys and black girls will be able to join hands with little white boys and white girls as sisters and brothers.

23  I have a *dream* today!

24  I have a dream that one day every valley shall be **exalted**, and every hill and mountain shall be made low, the rough places will be made plain, and the crooked places will be made straight; "and the glory of the Lord shall be revealed and all flesh shall see it together."[4]

25  This is our hope, and this is the faith that I go back to the South with.

26  With this faith, we will be able to hew out of the mountain of despair a stone of hope. With this faith, we will be able to transform the jangling discords of our nation into a beautiful symphony of brotherhood. With this faith, we will be able to work together, to pray together, to struggle together, to go to jail together, to stand up for freedom together, knowing that we will be free one day.

27  And this will be the day—this will be the day when all of God's children will be able to sing with new meaning:

> My country 'tis of thee, sweet land of liberty, of thee I sing.
> Land where my fathers died, land of the Pilgrim's pride,
> From every mountainside, let freedom ring!

28  And if America is to be a great nation, this must become true.

29  And so let freedom ring from the prodigious hilltops of New Hampshire.

30  Let freedom ring from the mighty mountains of New York.

31  Let freedom ring from the heightening Alleghenies[5] of Pennsylvania.

32  Let freedom ring from the snow-capped Rockies of Colorado.

33  Let freedom ring from the curvaceous slopes of California.

34  But not only that:

35  Let freedom ring from Stone Mountain of Georgia.

36  Let freedom ring from Lookout Mountain of Tennessee.

37  Let freedom ring from every hill and molehill of Mississippi.

38  From every mountainside, let freedom ring.

39  And when this happens, when we allow freedom to ring, when we let it ring from every village and every hamlet, from every state and every city, we will be able to speed up that day when all of God's children, black men and white men, Jews and Gentiles,[6] Protestants and Catholics, will be able to join hands and sing in the words of the old Negro spiritual:

40  Free at last! Free at last!

41  Thank God Almighty, we are free at last! ◆

---

4. **every valley . . . all flesh shall see it together** reference to a biblical passage (Isaiah 40:4–5). King is likening the struggle of African Americans to the struggle of the Israelites.
5. **Alleghenies** (al uh GAY neez) mountain range that runs through Pennsylvania, Maryland, West Virginia, and Virginia.
6. **Gentiles** (JEHN tylz) people who are not Jewish; often refers to Christians.

"I Have a Dream"

**Discuss It** How does Dr. King's delivery contribute to the power and impact of the speech?

**Write your response before sharing your ideas.**

SCAN FOR
MULTIMEDIA

# Comprehension Check

Complete the following items after you finish your first read.

1. About how much time has passed between the signing of the Emancipation Proclamation and Dr. King's speech?

2. When his audience returns home after his speech, what does Dr. King want them to know about the situation African Americans face?

3. What dream does Dr. King have for his four children?

4. **Notebook** Write a summary of Dr. King's "I Have a Dream" speech.

---

## RESEARCH

**Research to Clarify** Choose at least one unfamiliar detail from the text. Briefly research that detail. In what way does the information you learned shed light on an aspect of the speech?

"I HAVE A DREAM"

## Close Read the Text

1. This model, from paragraph 8 of the text, shows two sample annotations, along with questions and conclusions. Close read the passage, and find another detail to annotate. Then, write a question and your conclusion.

ANNOTATE: The use of the word "thirst" relates to a physical need, something people must have in order to live.

QUESTION: How does this choice of words add intensity to King's argument?

CONCLUDE: The powerful choice of words shows that freedom isn't simply something King and his followers want; it is a basic human need.

ANNOTATE: This phrase develops the idea of thirst.

QUESTION: What does this phrase suggest about King's view of the struggle for freedom?

CONCLUDE: The phrase implies that thirst can be quenched in various ways. King warns his listeners against taking a dark path.

Let us not seek to satisfy our thirst for freedom by drinking from the cup of bitterness and hatred.

Close Read

ANNOTATE  QUESTION  CONCLUDE

🔧 **Tool Kit**
Close-Read Guide and
Model Annotation

2. For more practice, go back into the text, and complete the close-read notes.

3. Revisit a section of the text you found important during your first read. Read this section closely, and **annotate** what you notice. Ask yourself **questions** such as "Why did the author make this choice?" What can you **conclude**?

---

## Analyze the Text

CITE TEXTUAL EVIDENCE
to support your answers.

📓 **Notebook** Respond to these questions.

1. **Interpret** What does King mean when he refers to the African American as an "exile in his own land"?

2. **Summarize** Explain the comparison King makes between the African American struggle for equality and the cashing of a check.

3. **Paraphrase** (a) When you **paraphrase**, you restate a text in your own words. Paraphrase King's comments on the urgency of "Now." (b) **Speculate** To which group of people might King have been directing that part of his argument? Explain.

4. **Evaluate** What idea is King trying to convey when he says that "unearned suffering is redemptive"?

5. **Essential Question:** *How can words inspire change?* What have you learned about the power of words by reading this speech?

**STANDARDS**

**RI.9–10.1** Cite strong and thorough textual evidence to support analysis of what the text says explicitly as well as inferences drawn from the text.

**RI.9–10.6** Determine an author's point of view or purpose in a text and analyze how an author uses rhetoric to advance that point of view or purpose.

**RI.9–10.9** Analyze seminal U.S. documents of historical and literary significance, including how they address related themes and concepts.

# Analyze Craft and Structure

**Argument** In a **persuasive speech**, the speaker tries to convince listeners to think or act in a certain way. Strong persuasive speakers present information and supporting evidence clearly and logically so listeners can follow the reasoning. Persuasive speakers may charged language—language that appeals to emotions. In addition, they often use **rhetorical devices**—patterns of words and ideas that create emphasis and emotion. These devices include the following forms:

- **Parallelism:** repeating a grammatical structure or an arrangement of words to create rhythm and momentum

- **Repetition:** using the same words frequently to reinforce concepts and unify the speech

- **Analogy:** drawing a comparison that shows a similarity between two unlike things

## Practice

**CITE TEXTUAL EVIDENCE**
to support your answers.

**Notebook** Reread the speech. Then, respond to the questions.

1. In this speech, what is King attempting to persuade his listeners to think or do? Explain.

2. Use the chart to record at least one example of each type of rhetorical device used in this speech. Explain why each choice is a good example of that device.

| RHETORICAL DEVICE | EXAMPLE FROM THE SPEECH | EXPLANATION |
| --- | --- | --- |
| charged language | | |
| parallelism | | |
| repetition | | |
| analogy | | |

3. For each example from your chart, state whether the rhetorical device serves to clarify an idea, stir listeners' emotions, or both. For each determination, explain your reasoning.

4. This speech has become an iconic part of American history. Do you think it deserves this standing? Support your answer with text evidence and your analysis of King's use of rhetoric.

"I HAVE A DREAM"

## Concept Vocabulary

| | | |
|---|---|---|
| prosperity | tribulations | oppression |
| hallowed | redemptive | exalted |

**Why These Words?** The six concept vocabulary words are all related to overcoming a challenge. For example, Dr. Martin Luther King, Jr., speaks of overcoming the *tribulations* that African Americans face.

1. How does the concept vocabulary help express both the difficulties and the possible rewards of the struggle for equality?

2. What other words in the selection connect to this concept?

### Practice

Notebook Complete the activities.

1. Use each concept vocabulary word in a sentence that demonstrates its meaning.
2. Rewrite each of your sentences, replacing the concept vocabulary word with a synonym. How do your replacements change the meaning of each sentence?

## Word Study

**Patterns of Word Changes** When added to a base word, the suffix *-tion* changes a verb to a noun. In some words, that change requires other adjustments to spelling. For example, in the word *describe*, the letters *be* are deleted and replaced with a *p* plus *-tion* to get *description*.

1. Form nouns by adding the suffix *-tion* to each of the following verbs. Make any adjustments to spelling that might be required.

   a. **assume** ______________________

   b. **receive** ______________________

   c. **prescribe** ______________________

2. Now that you have changed the verbs into nouns, use them in your own sentences.

WORD NETWORK

Add interesting words related to civil rights from the text to your Word Network.

STANDARDS

**L.9–10.1** Demonstrate command of the conventions of standard English grammar and usage when writing or speaking.

**L.9–10.1.a** Use parallel structure.

**L.9–10.2.c** Spell correctly.

**L.9–10.4.b** Identify and correctly use patterns of word changes that indicate different meanings or parts of speech and continue to apply knowledge of Greek and Latin roots and affixes.

# Conventions

**Parallel Structure** Parallelism, or **parallel structure**, is the use of similar grammatical forms or patterns to express similar ideas. Effective use of parallelism adds rhythm and balance to your writing and strengthens connections among your ideas.

When writing lacks parallelism, it presents equal ideas in an unnecessary mix of grammatical forms. This inconsistency can be awkward, confusing, or distracting for readers. By contrast, parallel constructions place equal ideas in words, phrases, or clauses of similar types.

This chart shows examples of nonparallel and parallel structure.

| ELEMENTS | NONPARALLEL STRUCTURE | PARALLEL STRUCTURE |
|---|---|---|
| words | <u>Planning</u>, <u>drafting</u>, and **revision** are three steps in the writing process. | <u>Planning</u>, <u>drafting</u>, and **revising** are three steps in the writing process. |
| phrases | I could not wait <u>to try my new surfboard</u>, <u>to catch some waves</u>, and **for a visit to the beach**. | I could not wait <u>to try my new surfboard</u>, <u>to catch some waves</u>, and <u>to visit the beach</u>. |
| clauses | Olivia likes her school: <u>The teachers are good</u>, <u>the students are nice</u>, and **she likes the new building.** | Olivia likes her school: <u>The teachers are good</u>, <u>the students are nice</u>, and **the building is new.** |

### TIP

**CLARIFICATION**
Always check for parallelism when your writing contains items in a series, draws a comparison between two or more things, or includes a correlative conjunction, such as *both . . . and* or *not only . . . but also.*

## Read It

1. Read each sentence from Dr. King's "I Have a Dream" speech. Mark the elements that are parallel. Then, note what type of parallel structure is being used—words, phrases, or clauses.

   a. One hundred years later, the life of the Negro is still sadly crippled by the manacles of segregation and the chains of discrimination.

   b. This is no time to engage in the luxury of cooling off or to take the tranquilizing drug of gradualism.

   c. With this faith, we will be able to work together, to pray together, to struggle together, to go to jail together, to stand up for freedom together, knowing that we will be free one day.

## Write It

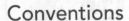 **Notebook** Add a parallel phrase or clause to each of the following sentences.

1. But we refuse to believe that the bank of justice is bankrupt.

2. And so, we've come to cash this check.

3. And so, even though we face the difficulties of today and tomorrow, I still have a dream.

"I HAVE A DREAM"

## Comparing Texts

In this part of the lesson, you will read Dr. King's "Letter From Birmingham Jail." First, complete the first read and close read activities. Then, compare the ways in which Dr. King uses language to appeal to different audiences.

LETTER FROM
BIRMINGHAM JAIL

## About the Author

**Dr. Martin Luther King, Jr.**
(1929–1968) was one of the most charismatic leaders of the civil rights movement. King first came to national attention in Montgomery, Alabama in 1956 when he organized a boycott by African-Americans of the city's segregated buses. He went on to lead other protests and to speak out against poverty and social injustice. He was assassinated on April 4, 1968.

🔧 **Tool Kit**
First-Read Guide and
Model Annotation

📋 STANDARDS
**RI.9–10.10** By the end of grade 9, read and comprehend literary nonfiction in the grades 9–10 text complexity band proficiently, with scaffolding as needed at the high end of the range.

# Letter From Birmingham Jail

## Concept Vocabulary

You will encounter the following words as you read "Letter From Birmingham Jail." Before reading, note how familiar you are with each word. Then, rank the words in order from most familiar (1) to least familiar (6).

| WORD | YOUR RANKING |
|------|--------------|
| idly | |
| postpone | |
| stagnation | |
| complacency | |
| yearning | |
| languished | |

After completing the first read, come back to the concept vocabulary and review your rankings. Mark changes to your original rankings as needed.

## First Read NONFICTION

Apply these strategies as you conduct your first read. You will have an opportunity to complete a close read after your first read.

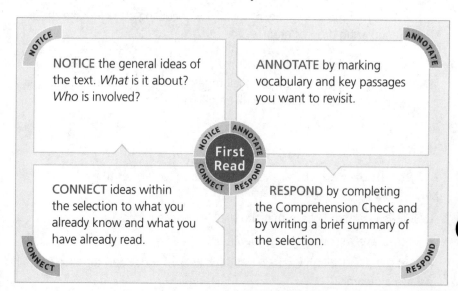

NOTICE the general ideas of the text. *What* is it about? *Who* is involved?

ANNOTATE by marking vocabulary and key passages you want to revisit.

First Read

CONNECT ideas within the selection to what you already know and what you have already read.

RESPOND by completing the Comprehension Check and by writing a brief summary of the selection.

# Letter From Birmingham Jail

## Dr. Martin Luther King, Jr.

SCAN FOR
MULTIMEDIA

## BACKGROUND

By the late 1950s, Dr. Martin Luther King, Jr. had emerged as a key figure of the Civil Rights movement. During the Kennedy administration, Dr. King was arrested in April, 1963, for protesting racial segregation in Birmingham, Alabama. As he sat in jail, he read a newspaper article in which eight white clergymen criticized him for "unwise and untimely" demonstrations. Without proper writing paper, Dr. King drafted a response—this letter—in the cramped margins of that newspaper.

16 April 1963

My Dear Fellow Clergymen:

1    While confined here in the Birmingham city jail, I came across your recent statement calling my present activities "unwise and untimely." Seldom do I pause to answer criticism of my work and ideas. If I sought to answer all the criticisms that cross my desk, my secretaries would have little time for anything other than such correspondence in the course of the day, and I would have no time for constructive work. But since I feel that you are men of genuine good will and that

NOTES

your criticisms are sincerely set forth, I want to try to answer your statement in what I hope will be patient and reasonable terms.

2   I think I should indicate why I am here in Birmingham, since you have been influenced by the view which argues against "outsiders coming in." I have the honor of serving as president of the Southern Christian Leadership Conference, an organization operating in every southern state, with headquarters in Atlanta, Georgia. We have some eighty five affiliated organizations across the South, and one of them is the Alabama Christian Movement for Human Rights. Frequently we share staff, educational, and financial resources with our affiliates. Several months ago the affiliate here in Birmingham asked us to be on call to engage in a nonviolent direct action program if such were deemed necessary. We readily consented, and when the hour came we lived up to our promise. So I, along with several members of my staff, am here because I was invited here. I am here because I have organizational ties here.

3   But more basically, I am in Birmingham because injustice is here. Just as the prophets of the eighth century B.C. left their villages and carried their "thus saith the Lord" far beyond the boundaries of their home towns, and just as the Apostle Paul left his village of Tarsus and carried the gospel of Jesus Christ to the far corners of the Greco-Roman world, so am I compelled to carry the gospel of freedom beyond my own home town. Like Paul, I must constantly respond to the Macedonian call for aid.

**idly** (YD lee) *adv.* lazily; without taking action

4   Moreover, I am cognizant of the interrelatedness of all communities and states. I cannot sit **idly** by in Atlanta and not be concerned about what happens in Birmingham. Injustice anywhere is a threat to justice everywhere. We are caught in an inescapable network of mutuality, tied in a single garment of destiny. Whatever affects one directly, affects all indirectly. Never again can we afford to live with the narrow, provincial "outside agitator" idea. Anyone who lives inside the United States can never be considered an outsider anywhere within its bounds.

**CLOSE READ**

**ANNOTATE:** In paragraph 5, mark details that reveal what King is apologizing for.

**QUESTION:** Why would King express his apology in this way?

**CONCLUDE:** How does this approach emphasize what King believes is the real problem to address?

5   You deplore the demonstrations taking place in Birmingham. But your statement, I am sorry to say, fails to express a similar concern for the conditions that brought about the demonstrations. I am sure that none of you would want to rest content with the superficial kind of social analysis that deals merely with effects and does not grapple with underlying causes. It is unfortunate that demonstrations are taking place in Birmingham, but it is even more unfortunate that the city's white power structure left the Negro community with no alternative.

6   In any nonviolent campaign there are four basic steps: collection of the facts to determine whether injustices exist; negotiation; self purification; and direct action. We have gone through all these steps in Birmingham. There can be no gainsaying[1] the fact that racial

---

1. **gainsaying** *v.* denying or disproving.

injustice engulfs this community. Birmingham is probably the most thoroughly segregated city in the United States. Its ugly record of brutality is widely known. Negroes have experienced grossly unjust treatment in the courts. There have been more unsolved bombings of Negro homes and churches in Birmingham than in any other city in the nation. These are the hard, brutal facts of the case. On the basis of these conditions, Negro leaders sought to negotiate with the city fathers. But the latter consistently refused to engage in good faith negotiation.

7    Then, last September, came the opportunity to talk with leaders of Birmingham's economic community. In the course of the negotiations, certain promises were made by the merchants—for example, to remove the stores' humiliating racial signs. On the basis of these promises, the Reverend Fred Shuttlesworth and the leaders of the Alabama Christian Movement for Human Rights agreed to a moratorium[2] on all demonstrations. As the weeks and months went by, we realized that we were the victims of a broken promise. A few signs, briefly removed, returned; the others remained.

8    As in so many past experiences, our hopes had been blasted, and the shadow of deep disappointment settled upon us. We had no alternative except to prepare for direct action, whereby we would present our very bodies as a means of laying our case before the conscience of the local and the national community. Mindful of the difficulties involved, we decided to undertake a process of self purification. We began a series of workshops on nonviolence, and we repeatedly asked ourselves: "Are you able to accept blows without retaliating?" "Are you able to endure the ordeal of jail?" We decided to schedule our direct action program for the Easter season, realizing that except for Christmas, this is the main shopping period of the year. Knowing that a strong economic-withdrawal program would be the by-product of direct action, we felt that this would be the best time to bring pressure to bear on the merchants for the needed change.

**postpone** (pohst POHN) *v.* delay

9    Then it occurred to us that Birmingham's mayoral election was coming up in March, and we speedily decided to **postpone** action until after election day. When we discovered that the Commissioner of Public Safety, Eugene "Bull" Connor, had piled up enough votes to be in the run off, we decided again to postpone action until the day after the run off so that the demonstrations could not be used to cloud the issues. Like many others, we waited to see Mr. Connor defeated, and to this end we endured postponement after postponement. Having aided in this community need, we felt that our direct action program could be delayed no longer.

10    You may well ask: "Why direct action? Why sit-ins, marches, and so forth? Isn't negotiation a better path?" You are quite right in calling for negotiation. Indeed, this is the very purpose of direct action.

---

2. **moratorium** (mawr uh TAWR ee uhm) *n.* time when a particular activity is not allowed.

Nonviolent direct action seeks to create such a crisis and foster such a tension that a community which has constantly refused to negotiate is forced to confront the issue. It seeks so to dramatize the issue that it can no longer be ignored. My citing the creation of tension as part of the work of the nonviolent resister may sound rather shocking. But I must confess that I am not afraid of the word "tension." I have earnestly opposed violent tension, but there is a type of constructive, nonviolent tension which is necessary for growth. Just as Socrates felt that it was necessary to create a tension in the mind so that individuals could rise from the bondage of myths and half truths to the unfettered realm of creative analysis and objective appraisal, so must we see the need for nonviolent gadflies[3] to create the kind of tension in society that will help men rise from the dark depths of prejudice and racism to the majestic heights of understanding and brotherhood.

11      The purpose of our direct action program is to create a situation so crisis-packed that it will inevitably open the door to negotiation. I therefore concur with you in your call for negotiation. Too long has our beloved Southland been bogged down in a tragic effort to live in monologue rather than dialogue.

12      One of the basic points in your statement is that the action that I and my associates have taken in Birmingham is untimely. Some have asked: "Why didn't you give the new city administration time to act?" The only answer that I can give to this query is that the new Birmingham administration must be prodded about as much as the outgoing one, before it will act. We are sadly mistaken if we feel that the election of Albert Boutwell as mayor will bring the millennium[4] to Birmingham. While Mr. Boutwell is a much more gentle person than Mr. Connor, they are both segregationists, dedicated to maintenance of the status quo. I have hope that Mr. Boutwell will be reasonable enough to see the futility of massive resistance to desegregation. But he will not see this without pressure from devotees of civil rights. My friends, I must say to you that we have not made a single gain in civil rights without determined legal and nonviolent pressure. Lamentably, it is an historical fact that privileged groups seldom give up their privileges voluntarily. Individuals may see the moral light and voluntarily give up their unjust posture; but, as Reinhold Niebuhr[5] has reminded us, groups tend to be more immoral than individuals.

13      We know through painful experience that freedom is never voluntarily given by the oppressor; it must be demanded by the oppressed. Frankly, I have yet to engage in a direct action campaign that was "well timed" in the view of those who have not suffered unduly from the disease of segregation. For years now I have heard

---

3. **gadflies** *n.* people who annoy others by being very critical.
4. **bring the millennium** In some forms of Christianity, the world is believed to enter a thousand-year period of peace and happiness before the end of time.
5. **Reinhold Niebuhr** (NEE bur) (1892–1971) American professor of theology who advocated nonviolence and social reform.

^ Police officers arrest Dr. King on September 3, 1958, in Montgomery, Alabama. Dr. King was charged with loitering outside the courtroom in which his colleague was testifying.

the word "Wait!" It rings in the ear of every Negro with piercing familiarity. This "Wait" has almost always meant "Never." We must come to see, with one of our distinguished jurists, that "justice too long delayed is justice denied."

14      We have waited for more than 340 years for our constitutional and God given rights. The nations of Asia and Africa are moving with jetlike speed toward gaining political independence, but we still creep at horse and buggy pace toward gaining a cup of coffee at a lunch counter. Perhaps it is easy for those who have never felt the stinging darts of segregation to say, "Wait." But when you have seen vicious mobs lynch your mothers and fathers at will and drown your sisters and brothers at whim; when you have seen hate filled policemen curse, kick and even kill your black brothers and sisters; when you see the vast majority of your twenty million Negro brothers smothering in an airtight cage of poverty in the midst of an affluent society; when you suddenly find your tongue twisted and your speech stammering as you seek to explain to your six year old daughter why she can't go to the public amusement park that has just been advertised on television, and see tears welling up in her eyes when she is told that Funtown is closed to colored children, and see ominous clouds of inferiority beginning to form in her little mental sky, and see her beginning to distort her personality by developing an unconscious bitterness toward white people; when you have to concoct an answer for a five year old son who is asking: "Daddy,

why do white people treat colored people so mean?"; when you take a cross-county drive and find it necessary to sleep night after night in the uncomfortable corners of your automobile because no motel will accept you; when you are humiliated day in and day out by nagging signs reading "white" and "colored"; when your first name becomes "nigger," your middle name becomes "boy" (however old you are) and your last name becomes "John," and your wife and mother are never given the respected title "Mrs."; when you are harried by day and haunted by night by the fact that you are a Negro, living constantly at tiptoe stance, never quite knowing what to expect next, and are plagued with inner fears and outer resentments; when you are forever fighting a degenerating sense of "nobodiness"— then you will understand why we find it difficult to wait. There comes a time when the cup of endurance runs over, and men are no longer willing to be plunged into the abyss of despair. I hope, sirs, you can understand our legitimate and unavoidable impatience.

> I would agree with St. Augustine that "an unjust law is no law at all."

15      You express a great deal of anxiety over our willingness to break laws. This is certainly a legitimate concern. Since we so diligently urge people to obey the Supreme Court's decision of 1954 outlawing segregation in the public schools, at first glance it may seem rather paradoxical for us consciously to break laws. One may well ask: "How can you advocate[6] breaking some laws and obeying others?" The answer lies in the fact that there are two types of laws: just and unjust. I would be the first to advocate obeying just laws. One has not only a legal but a moral responsibility to obey just laws. Conversely, one has a moral responsibility to disobey unjust laws. I would agree with St. Augustine that "an unjust law is no law at all."

16      Now, what is the difference between the two? How does one determine whether a law is just or unjust? A just law is a man made code that squares with the moral law or the law of God. An unjust law is a code that is out of harmony with the moral law. To put it in the terms of St. Thomas Aquinas:[7] An unjust law is a human law that is not rooted in eternal law and natural law. Any law that uplifts human personality is just. Any law that degrades human personality is unjust. All segregation statutes are unjust because segregation distorts the soul and damages the personality. It gives the segregator a false sense of superiority and the segregated a false sense of inferiority. Segregation, to use the terminology of the Jewish philosopher Martin Buber, substitutes an "I it" relationship for an "I thou" relationship and ends up relegating persons to the status of things. Hence segregation is not only politically, economically

---

6. **advocate** v. argue for or support a cause or policy.
7. **St. Thomas Aquinas** (uh KWY nuhs) (1225–1274) influential Christian philosopher who made lasting contributions to Western philosophy.

and sociologically unsound, it is morally wrong and sinful. Paul Tillich[8] has said that sin is separation. Is not segregation an existential expression of man's tragic separation, his awful estrangement, his terrible sinfulness? Thus it is that I can urge men to obey the 1954 decision of the Supreme Court, for it is morally right; and I can urge them to disobey segregation ordinances,[9] for they are morally wrong.

17    Let us consider a more concrete example of just and unjust laws. An unjust law is a code that a numerical or power majority group compels a minority group to obey but does not make binding on itself. This is difference made legal. By the same token, a just law is a code that a majority compels a minority to follow and that it is willing to follow itself. This is sameness made legal.

18    Let me give another explanation. A law is unjust if it is inflicted on a minority that, as a result of being denied the right to vote, had no part in enacting or devising the law. Who can say that the legislature of Alabama which set up that state's segregation laws was democratically elected? Throughout Alabama all sorts of devious methods are used to prevent Negroes from becoming registered voters, and there are some counties in which, even though Negroes constitute a majority of the population, not a single Negro is registered. Can any law enacted under such circumstances be considered democratically structured?

19    Sometimes a law is just on its face and unjust in its application. For instance, I have been arrested on a charge of parading without a permit. Now, there is nothing wrong in having an ordinance which requires a permit for a parade. But such an ordinance becomes unjust when it is used to maintain segregation and to deny citizens the First-Amendment privilege of peaceful assembly and protest.

20    I hope you are able to see the distinction I am trying to point out. In no sense do I advocate evading or defying the law, as would the rabid segregationist. That would lead to anarchy. One who breaks an unjust law must do so openly, lovingly, and with a willingness to accept the penalty. I submit that an individual who breaks a law that conscience tells him is unjust, and who willingly accepts the penalty of imprisonment in order to arouse the conscience of the community over its injustice, is in reality expressing the highest respect for law.

21    Of course, there is nothing new about this kind of civil disobedience. It was evidenced sublimely in the refusal of Shadrach, Meshach and Abednego to obey the laws of Nebuchadnezzar,[10] on the ground that a higher moral law was at stake. It was practiced superbly by the early Christians, who were willing to face hungry lions and the excruciating pain of chopping blocks rather than submit to certain unjust laws of the Roman Empire. To a degree, academic freedom is a reality today because Socrates practiced civil

© Pearson Education, Inc., or its affiliates. All rights reserved.

---

8. **Paul Tillich** (1886–1965) German American, Christian philosopher.
9. **ordinances** *n.* laws or regulations made by a city or town government.
10. **refusal . . . Nebuchadnezzar** story from the Bible about three Jews who refused to worship a golden statue; Nebuchadnezzar sentenced them to death by burning, but God protected them from harm.

NOTES

**CLOSE READ**
**ANNOTATE:** In paragraphs 17 and 18, mark words and phrases that sound as though King is actually speaking to his readers.

**QUESTION:** Why does King seem to be walking his readers through his reasoning?

**CONCLUDE:** How might this approach affect how King's readers understand and respond to his argument?

disebedience. In our own nation, the Boston Tea Party represented a massive act of civil disobedience.

22     We should never forget that everything Adolf Hitler did in Germany was "legal" and everything the Hungarian freedom fighters did in Hungary was "illegal." It was "illegal" to aid and comfort a Jew in Hitler's Germany. Even so, I am sure that, had I lived in Germany at the time, I would have aided and comforted my Jewish brothers. If today I lived in a Communist country where certain principles dear to the Christian faith are suppressed, I would openly advocate disobeying that country's antireligious laws.

23     I must make two honest confessions to you, my Christian and Jewish brothers. First, I must confess that over the past few years I have been gravely disappointed with the white moderate. I have almost reached the regrettable conclusion that the Negro's great stumbling block in his stride toward freedom is not the White Citizen's Counciler or the Ku Klux Klanner, but the white moderate, who is more devoted to "order" than to justice; who prefers a negative peace which is the absence of tension to a positive peace which is the presence of justice; who constantly says: "I agree with you in the goal you seek, but I cannot agree with your methods of direct action"; who paternalistically believes he can set the timetable for another man's freedom; who lives by a mythical concept of time and who constantly advises the Negro to wait for a "more convenient season." Shallow understanding from people of good will is more frustrating than absolute misunderstanding from people of ill will. Lukewarm acceptance is much more bewildering than outright rejection.

24     I had hoped that the white moderate would understand that law and order exist for the purpose of establishing justice and that when they fail in this purpose they become the dangerously structured dams that block the flow of social progress. I had hoped that the white moderate would understand that the present tension in the South is a necessary phase of the transition from an obnoxious negative peace, in which the Negro passively accepted his unjust plight, to a substantive and positive peace, in which all men will respect the dignity and worth of human personality. Actually, we who engage in nonviolent direct action are not the creators of tension. We merely bring to the surface the hidden tension that is already alive. We bring it out in the open, where it can be seen and dealt with. Like a boil that can never be cured so long as it is covered up but must be opened with all its ugliness to the natural medicines of air and light, injustice must be exposed, with all the tension its exposure creates, to the light of human conscience and the air of national opinion before it can be cured.

25     In your statement you assert that our actions, even though peaceful, must be condemned because they precipitate violence. But is this a logical assertion? Isn't this like condemning a robbed man because his possession of money precipitated the evil act of

robbery? Isn't this like condemning Socrates because his unswerving commitment to truth and his philosophical inquiries precipitated the act by the misguided populace in which they made him drink hemlock?[11] Isn't this like condemning Jesus because his unique God consciousness and never-ceasing devotion to God's will precipitated the evil act of crucifixion? We must come to see that, as the federal courts have consistently affirmed, it is wrong to urge an individual to cease his efforts to gain his basic constitutional rights because the quest may precipitate violence. Society must protect the robbed and punish the robber.

26    I had also hoped that the white moderate would reject the myth concerning time in relation to the struggle for freedom. I have just received a letter from a white brother in Texas. He writes: "All Christians know that the colored people will receive equal rights eventually, but it is possible that you are in too great a religious hurry. It has taken Christianity almost two thousand years to accomplish what it has. The teachings of Christ take time to come to earth." Such an attitude stems from a tragic misconception of time, from the strangely irrational notion that there is something in the very flow of time that will inevitably cure all ills. Actually, time itself is neutral; it can be used either destructively or constructively. More and more I feel that the people of ill will have used time much more effectively than have the people of good will. We will have to repent in this generation not merely for the hateful words and actions of the bad people but for the appalling silence of the good people. Human progress never rolls in on wheels of inevitability; it comes through the tireless efforts of men willing to be coworkers with God, and without this hard work, time itself becomes an ally of the forces of social stagnation. We must use time creatively, in the knowledge that the time is always ripe to do right. Now is the time to make real the promise of democracy and transform our pending national elegy[12] into a creative psalm[13] of brotherhood. Now is the time to lift our national policy from the quicksand of racial injustice to the solid rock of human dignity.

27    You speak of our activity in Birmingham as extreme. At first I was rather disappointed that fellow clergymen would see my nonviolent efforts as those of an extremist. I began thinking about the fact that I stand in the middle of two opposing forces in the Negro community. One is a force of complacency, made up in part of Negroes who, as a result of long years of oppression, are so drained of self respect and a sense of "somebodiness" that they have adjusted to segregation; and in part of a few middle-class Negroes who, because of a degree of academic and economic security and because in some ways they profit by segregation, have become insensitive to the problems of the masses. The other force is one of bitterness and hatred, and it

**stagnation** (stag NAY shuhn) *n.* state of being inactive and not moving or changing

**complacency** (kuhm PLAY suhn see) *n.* state of unthinking or satisfied acceptance

---

11. **hemlock** *n.* highly poisonous plant.
12. **elegy** (EHL uh jee) *n.* song expressing sorrow or grief.
13. **psalm** (sahm) *n.* biblical song that praises God.

∧ A crowd gathers on the steps of the Sixteenth Street Baptist Church in Birmingham, Alabama, during protests led by Dr. King in an effort to end racial segregation in the city.

© Pearson Education, Inc., or its affiliates. All rights reserved.

NOTES

comes perilously close to advocating violence. It is expressed in the various black nationalist groups that are springing up across the nation, the largest and best known being Elijah Muhammad's[14] Muslim movement. Nourished by the Negro's frustration over the continued existence of racial discrimination, this movement is made up of people who have lost faith in America, who have absolutely repudiated Christianity, and who have concluded that the white man is an incorrigible "devil."

28      I have tried to stand between these two forces, saying that we need emulate neither the "do-nothingism" of the complacent nor the hatred and despair of the black nationalist. For there is the more excellent way of love and nonviolent protest. I am grateful to God that, through the influence of the Negro church, the way of nonviolence became an integral part of our struggle.

29      If this philosophy had not emerged, by now many streets of the South would, I am convinced, be flowing with blood. And I am further convinced that if our white brothers dismiss as "rabble rousers" and "outside agitators" those of us who employ nonviolent direct action, and if they refuse to support our nonviolent efforts, millions of Negroes will, out of frustration and despair, seek solace

_____
14. **Elijah Muhammad** (1897–1975) African American leader of the Nation of Islam and a mentor to Malcolm X.

and security in black nationalist ideologies—a development that would inevitably lead to a frightening racial nightmare.

30    Oppressed people cannot remain oppressed forever. The **yearning** for freedom eventually manifests itself, and that is what has happened to the American Negro. Something within has reminded him of his birthright of freedom, and something without has reminded him that it can be gained. Consciously or unconsciously, he has been caught up by the Zeitgeist,[15] and with his black brothers of Africa and his brown and yellow brothers of Asia, South America and the Caribbean, the United States Negro is moving with a sense of great urgency toward the promised land of racial justice. If one recognizes this vital urge that has engulfed the Negro community, one should readily understand why public demonstrations are taking place. The Negro has many pent up resentments and latent frustrations, and he must release them. So let him march; let him make prayer pilgrimages to the city hall; let him go on freedom rides—and try to understand why he must do so. If his repressed emotions are not released in nonviolent ways, they will seek expression through violence; this is not a threat but a fact of history. So I have not said to my people: "Get rid of your discontent." Rather, I have tried to say that this normal and healthy discontent can be channeled into the creative outlet of nonviolent direct action. And now this approach is being termed extremist.

31    But though I was initially disappointed at being categorized as an extremist, as I continued to think about the matter I gradually gained a measure of satisfaction from the label. Was not Jesus an extremist for love: "Love your enemies, bless them that curse you, do good to them that hate you, and pray for them which despitefully use you, and persecute you." Was not Amos an extremist for justice: "Let justice roll down like waters and righteousness like an ever flowing stream." Was not Paul an extremist for the Christian gospel: "I bear on my body the marks of the Lord Jesus." Was not Martin Luther[16] an extremist: "Here I stand; I cannot do otherwise, so help me God." And John Bunyan:[17] "I will stay in jail to the end of my days before I make a butchery of my conscience." And Abraham Lincoln: "This nation cannot survive half slave and half free." And Thomas Jefferson: "We hold these truths to be self evident, that all men are created equal." So the question is not whether we will be extremists, but what kind of extremists we will be. Will we be extremists for hate or for love? Will we be extremists for the preservation of injustice or for the extension of justice? In that dramatic scene on Calvary's hill three men were crucified. We must never forget that all three were crucified for the same crime—the crime of extremism. Two were

NOTES

**yearning** (YUR nihng) *n.* strong desire; longing

**CLOSE READ**

**ANNOTATE:** In paragraph 31, mark references to historic figures.

**QUESTION:** What qualities do these historic figures have in common?

**CONCLUDE:** How is King attempting to redefine what the word "extremist" means?

---

15. **Zeitgeist** (ZYT gyst) *n.* general intellectual, moral, and cultural spirit of an era.
16. **Martin Luther** (1483–1546) German priest and professor of theology who was an important figure in the Protestant Reformation.
17. **John Bunyan** (1628–1688) English writer and preacher who wrote *The Pilgrim's Progress*.

extremists for immorality, and thus fell below their environment. The other, Jesus Christ, was an extremist for love, truth and goodness, and thereby rose above his environment. Perhaps the South, the nation, and the world are in dire need of creative extremists.

32  I had hoped that the white moderate would see this need. Perhaps I was too optimistic; perhaps I expected too much. I suppose I should have realized that few members of the oppressor race can understand the deep groans and passionate yearnings of the oppressed race, and still fewer have the vision to see that injustice must be rooted out by strong, persistent and determined action. I am thankful, however, that some of our white brothers in the South have grasped the meaning of this social revolution and committed themselves to it. They are still all too few in quantity, but they are big in quality. Some—such as Ralph McGill, Lillian Smith, Harry Golden, James McBride Dabbs, Ann Braden and Sarah Patton Boyle—have written about our struggle in eloquent and prophetic terms. Others have marched with us down nameless streets of the South. They have languished in filthy, roach infested jails, suffering the abuse and brutality of policemen who view them as "dirty nigger-lovers." Unlike so many of their moderate brothers and sisters, they have recognized the urgency of the moment and sensed the need for powerful "action" antidotes to combat the disease of segregation.

33  Let me take note of my other major disappointment. I have been so greatly disappointed with the white church and its leadership. Of course, there are some notable exceptions. I am not unmindful of the fact that each of you has taken some significant stands on this issue. I commend you, Reverend Stallings, for your Christian stand on this past Sunday, in welcoming Negroes to your worship service on a nonsegregated basis. I commend the Catholic leaders of this state for integrating Spring Hill College several years ago.

34  But despite these notable exceptions, I must honestly reiterate that I have been disappointed with the church. I do not say this as one of those negative critics who can always find something wrong with the church. I say this as a minister of the gospel, who loves the church; who was nurtured in its bosom; who has been sustained by its spiritual blessings and who will remain true to it as long as the cord of life shall lengthen.

35  When I was suddenly catapulted into the leadership of the bus protest in Montgomery, Alabama, a few years ago, I felt we would be supported by the white church. I felt that the white ministers, priests and rabbis of the South would be among our strongest allies. Instead, some have been outright opponents, refusing to understand the freedom movement and misrepresenting its leaders; all too many others have been more cautious than courageous and have remained silent behind the anesthetizing security of stained glass windows.

36  In spite of my shattered dreams, I came to Birmingham with the hope that the white religious leadership of this community would see the justice of our cause and, with deep moral concern, would serve as

**languished** (LANG gwihsht) *v.* grown weak; lived under distressing conditions

**CLOSE READ**

**ANNOTATE:** In paragraph 34, mark sentences in which King mentions his affection for and loyalty to the church.

**QUESTION:** Why does King present his religious credentials and emotions so emphatically?

**CONCLUDE:** What does King want his readers to understand about the target or point of his criticism?

the channel through which our just grievances could reach the power structure. I had hoped that each of you would understand. But again I have been disappointed.

37      I have heard numerous southern religious leaders admonish their worshipers to comply with a desegregation decision because it is the law, but I have longed to hear white ministers declare: "Follow this decree because integration is morally right and because the Negro is your brother." In the midst of blatant injustices inflicted upon the Negro, I have watched white churchmen stand on the sideline and mouth pious irrelevancies and sanctimonious trivialities. In the midst of a mighty struggle to rid our nation of racial and economic injustice, I have heard many ministers say: "Those are social issues, with which the gospel has no real concern." And I have watched many churches commit themselves to a completely other-worldly religion which makes a strange, un-Biblical distinction between body and soul, between the sacred and the secular.

38      I have traveled the length and breadth of Alabama, Mississippi, and all the other southern states. On sweltering summer days and crisp autumn mornings I have looked at the South's beautiful churches with their lofty spires pointing heavenward. I have beheld the impressive outlines of her massive religious education buildings. Over and over I have found myself asking: "What kind of people worship here? Who is their God? Where were their voices when the lips of Governor Barnett dripped with words of interposition and nullification? Where were they when Governor Wallace gave a clarion call for defiance and hatred? Where were their voices of support when bruised and weary Negro men and women decided to rise from the dark dungeons of complacency to the bright hills of creative protest?"

39      Yes, these questions are still in my mind. In deep disappointment I have wept over the laxity of the church. But be assured that my tears have been tears of love. There can be no deep disappointment where there is not deep love. Yes, I love the church. How could I do otherwise? I am in the rather unique position of being the son, the grandson and the great grandson of preachers. Yes, I see the church as the body of Christ. But, oh! How we have blemished and scarred that body through social neglect and through fear of being nonconformists.

40      There was a time when the church was very powerful—in the time when the early Christians rejoiced at being deemed worthy to suffer for what they believed. In those days the church was not merely a thermometer that recorded the ideas and principles of popular opinion; it was a thermostat that transformed the mores of society. Whenever the early Christians entered a town, the people in power became disturbed and immediately sought to convict the Christians for being "disturbers of the peace" and "outside agitators." But the Christians pressed on, in the conviction that they were "a colony of heaven," called to obey God rather than man. Small in number,

they were big in commitment. They were too God-intoxicated to be "astronomically intimidated." By their effort and example they brought an end to such ancient evils as infanticide and gladiatorial contests. Things are different now. So often the contemporary church is a weak, ineffectual voice with an uncertain sound. So often it is an arch defender of the status quo. Far from being disturbed by the presence of the church, the power structure of the average community is consoled by the church's silent—and often even vocal—sanction of things as they are.

41    But the judgment of God is upon the church as never before. If today's church does not recapture the sacrificial spirit of the early church, it will lose its authenticity, forfeit the loyalty of millions, and be dismissed as an irrelevant social club with no meaning for the twentieth century. Every day I meet young people whose disappointment with the church has turned into outright disgust.

**CLOSE READ**

**ANNOTATE:** In paragraph 42, mark King's use of a question.

**QUESTION:** Why do you think King begins the paragraph with a question?

**CONCLUDE:** Does the rest of the paragraph help us find an answer to the question? If so, what would that answer be?

42    Perhaps I have once again been too optimistic. Is organized religion too inextricably bound to the status quo to save our nation and the world? Perhaps I must turn my faith to the inner spiritual church, the church within the church, as the true ekklesia[18] and the hope of the world. But again I am thankful to God that some noble souls from the ranks of organized religion have broken loose from the paralyzing chains of conformity and joined us as active partners in the struggle for freedom. They have left their secure congregations and walked the streets of Albany, Georgia, with us. They have gone down the highways of the South on tortuous rides for freedom. Yes, they have gone to jail with us. Some have been dismissed from their churches, have lost the support of their bishops and fellow ministers. But they have acted in the faith that right defeated is stronger than evil triumphant. Their witness has been the spiritual salt that has preserved[19] the true meaning of the gospel in these troubled times. They have carved a tunnel of hope through the dark mountain of disappointment.

43    I hope the church as a whole will meet the challenge of this decisive hour. But even if the church does not come to the aid of justice, I have no despair about the future. I have no fear about the outcome of our struggle in Birmingham, even if our motives are at present misunderstood. We will reach the goal of freedom in Birmingham and all over the nation, because the goal of America is freedom. Abused and scorned though we may be, our destiny is tied up with America's destiny. Before the pilgrims landed at Plymouth, we were here. Before the pen of Jefferson etched the majestic words of the Declaration of Independence across the pages of history, we were here. For more than two centuries our forebears labored in this country without wages; they made cotton king; they built the homes of their masters while suffering gross injustice and shameful

---

18. **ekklesia** (ih KLEE zhee uh) *n.* Greek word for a group of believers.
19. **spiritual salt that has preserved** Salt has traditionally been used to preserve food so that it remains edible.

humiliation—and yet out of a bottomless vitality they continued to thrive and develop. If the inexpressible cruelties of slavery could not stop us, the opposition we now face will surely fail. We will win our freedom because the sacred heritage of our nation and the eternal will of God are embodied in our echoing demands.

44    Before closing I feel impelled to mention one other point in your statement that has troubled me profoundly. You warmly commended the Birmingham police force for keeping "order" and "preventing violence." I doubt that you would have so warmly commended the police force if you had seen its dogs sinking their teeth into unarmed, nonviolent Negroes. I doubt that you would so quickly commend the policemen if you were to observe their ugly and inhumane treatment of Negroes here in the city jail; if you were to watch them push and curse old Negro women and young Negro girls; if you were to see them slap and kick old Negro men and young boys; if you were to observe them, as they did on two occasions, refuse to give us food because we wanted to sing our grace together. I cannot join you in your praise of the Birmingham police department.

> If the inexpressible cruelties of slavery could not stop us, the opposition we now face will surely fail.

45    It is true that the police have exercised a degree of discipline in handling the demonstrators. In this sense they have conducted themselves rather "nonviolently" in public. But for what purpose? To preserve the evil system of segregation. Over the past few years I have consistently preached that nonviolence demands that the means we use must be as pure as the ends we seek. I have tried to make clear that it is wrong to use immoral means to attain moral ends. But now I must affirm that it is just as wrong, or perhaps even more so, to use moral means to preserve immoral ends. Perhaps Mr. Connor and his policemen have been rather nonviolent in public, as was Chief Pritchett in Albany, Georgia, but they have used the moral means of nonviolence to maintain the immoral end of racial injustice. As T. S. Eliot has said: "The last temptation is the greatest treason: To do the right deed for the wrong reason."

46    I wish you had commended the Negro sit inners and demonstrators of Birmingham for their sublime courage, their willingness to suffer and their amazing discipline in the midst of great provocation. One day the South will recognize its real heroes. They will be the James Merediths,[20] with the noble sense of purpose that enables them to face jeering and hostile mobs, and with the agonizing loneliness that characterizes the life of the pioneer. They will be old, oppressed, battered Negro women, symbolized in a seventy two year old woman in Montgomery, Alabama, who rose up with a sense of dignity and with her people decided not to

20. **James Meredith** (b. 1933) civil rights activist who, in 1962, became the first African American student admitted to the segregated University of Mississippi.

ride segregated buses, and who responded with ungrammatical profundity[21] to one who inquired about her weariness: "My feets is tired, but my soul is at rest." They will be the young high school and college students, the young ministers of the gospel and a host of their elders, courageously and nonviolently sitting in at lunch counters and willingly going to jail for conscience' sake. One day the South will know that when these disinherited children of God sat down at lunch counters, they were in reality standing up for what is best in the American dream and for the most sacred values in our Judeo-Christian heritage, thereby bringing our nation back to those great wells of democracy which were dug deep by the founding fathers in their formulation of the Constitution and the Declaration of Independence.

**CLOSE READ**

**ANNOTATE:** In paragraph 47, mark King's descriptions of himself.

**QUESTION:** What part of his character is King emphasizing in this paragraph?

**CONCLUDE:** What is the effect of King's describing himself like this at the very end of his letter?

47      Never before have I written so long a letter. I'm afraid it is much too long to take your precious time. I can assure you that it would have been much shorter if I had been writing from a comfortable desk, but what else can one do when he is alone in a narrow jail cell, other than write long letters, think long thoughts and pray long prayers?

48      If I have said anything in this letter that overstates the truth and indicates an unreasonable impatience, I beg you to forgive me. If I have said anything that understates the truth and indicates my having a patience that allows me to settle for anything less than brotherhood, I beg God to forgive me.

49      I hope this letter finds you strong in the faith. I also hope that circumstances will soon make it possible for me to meet each of you, not as an integrationist or a civil-rights leader but as a fellow clergyman and a Christian brother. Let us all hope that the dark clouds of racial prejudice will soon pass away and the deep fog of misunderstanding will be lifted from our fear-drenched communities, and in some not too distant tomorrow the radiant stars of love and brotherhood will shine over our great nation with all their scintillating beauty.

Yours for the cause of Peace and Brotherhood,

Martin Luther King, Jr. ❧

---

21. **profundity** (pruh FUHN duh tee) *n.* quality of having intellectual depth.

# Comprehension Check

Complete the following items after you finish your first read.

**1.** What circumstance or event is Dr. Martin Luther King, Jr., responding to in this letter?

**2.** According to Dr. King, what are the four basic steps that a nonviolent campaign must follow?

**3.** According to Dr. King, what are the two types of laws?

**4.** According to Dr. King, who are the South's real heroes?

📓 **Notebook**  Write a summary of "Letter From Birmingham Jail."

- - - - - - - - - - - - - - - - - - - - - - - - - - - - - - - - - - - - - - - - - - - - - - - - - -

## RESEARCH

**Research to Clarify**  Choose at least one unfamiliar detail from the text. Briefly research that detail. In what way does the information you learned shed light on an aspect of the letter?

**Research to Explore**  Choose something that interested you from the text, and formulate a research question.

LETTER FROM BIRMINGHAM JAIL

## Close Read the Text

1. This model, from paragraph 10 of the text, shows two sample annotations, along with questions and conclusions. Close read the passage, and find another detail to annotate. Then, write a question and your conclusion.

ANNOTATE: The author directly addresses the reader using the pronoun *you*.

QUESTION: What relationship with the reader is King trying to establish?

CONCLUDE: His use of "you" establishes a sense of connection; it suggests Dr. King is open to his critic's ideas.

ANNOTATE: The author asks a series of questions readers might ask.

QUESTION: What purpose do these questions serve?

CONCLUDE: The questions show that King is taking his readers' concerns into account. This makes his argument stronger.

> You may well ask: "Why direct action? Why sit-ins, marches, and so forth? Isn't negotiation a better path?" You are quite right in calling for negotiation. Indeed, this is the very purpose of direct action.

2. For more practice, go back into the selection and complete the close-read notes.

3. Revisit a section of the text you found important during your first read. Read this section closely, and **annotate** what you notice. Ask yourself **questions** such as "Why did the author make this choice?" What can you **conclude**?

**Tool Kit**
Close-Read Guide and Model Annotation

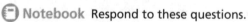

## Analyze the Text

CITE TEXTUAL EVIDENCE to support your answers.

**Notebook** Respond to these questions.

1. (a) In the first paragraph, what reasons does King give for his confidence in the outcome of the struggle? (b) **Infer** Why do you think he emphasizes his attitude about that outcome? Explain.

2. Reread paragraphs 13–18. How does Dr. King explain his decision to break the law?

3. Why is Dr. King more concerned with the attitudes of "white moderates" than he is with those of outright enemies of integration? Explain.

4. **Essential Question:** *How can words inspire change?* What have you learned about the power of words from reading this text?

**STANDARDS**

**RI.9–10.1** Cite strong and thorough textual evidence to support analysis of what the text says explicitly as well as inferences drawn from the text.

**RI.9–10.3** Analyze how the author unfolds an analysis or series of ideas or events, including the order in which the points are made, how they are introduced and developed, and the connections that are drawn between them.

**RI.9–10.9** Analyze seminal U.S. documents of historical and literary significance, including how they address related themes and concepts.

# Analyze Craft and Structure

**Argument** "Letter from Birmingham Jail" can be considered a persuasive essay in the form of a letter. A **persuasive essay** is a short nonfiction work in which a writer seeks to convince the reader to think or act in a certain way. Persuasive writers often use **rhetorical devices,** or special patterns of language that help to clarify ideas and evoke emotions. A persuasive essay may include the following types of rhetorical devices:

- **Antithesis:** a form of parallelism that emphasizes strong contrasts
  **Example:** It was the best of times; it was the worst of times.

- **Allusion:** a brief, unexplained reference to a well-known person, historical event, organization, literary work, or place
  **Example:** We all got the feeling that we were not in Kansas anymore. (reference to *The Wizard of Oz*)

- **Rhetorical Question:** a question asked to make a point rather than to invite an answer
  **Example:** If you poison us, do we not die?

## Practice

**CITE TEXTUAL EVIDENCE** to support your answers.

Go back and reread paragraph 27 in "Letter From Birmingham Jail."

📓 **Notebook** Respond to these questions.

1. In this letter, what is King attempting to persuade his listeners to think or do? Explain.

2. Use the chart to record at least one example of each type of rhetorical device used in King's letter.

3. For each example, explain whether the rhetorical device serves to clarify an idea, stir listeners' emotions, or both. For each determination, explain your reasoning.

| RHETORICAL DEVICE | EXAMPLE FROM THE LETTER | EXPLANATION |
| --- | --- | --- |
| antithesis | | |
| allusion | | |
| rhetorical question | | |

4. This letter is widely regarded as a powerful defense of nonviolent protest. Do you think it deserves this recognition? Support your answer with text evidence and your analysis of King's use of rhetoric.

LETTER FROM BIRMINGHAM JAIL

# Concept Vocabulary

| idly | stagnation | yearning |
|------|------------|----------|
| postpone | complacency | languished |

**Why These Words?** These concept words are related to inaction. For example, in paragraph 27 of the selection, Dr. King claims that he stands in the middle of two forces at work in the African American community. One of those forces is *complacency*. Those who are complacent are satisfied and passive. That is, they will not work for change.

1. Select two concept vocabulary words other than *complacency*. How does each word contribute to the idea of inaction? Explain.

2. What other words in the selection connect to the concept of inaction?

## Practice

🔲 **Notebook** The concept vocabulary words appear in "Letter From Birmingham Jail."

1. Use each concept word in a sentence that demonstrates your understanding of the word's meaning.

2. Challenge yourself to replace the concept word with one or two synonyms. How does each word affect the meaning of your sentence? For example, which sentence is stronger? Which has a more positive meaning?

# Word Study

**Latin Root: -*plac*-** The Latin root -*plac*- means "calm," "peaceful," or "pleasing." The word *complacency* suggests a sense of relaxed or satisfied pleasure in a situation. Using your understanding of the root -*plac*-, define each of the words listed here. Consult a dictionary if necessary.

**placate** _____

_____

**placid** _____

_____

**placebo** _____

_____

**implacable** _____

_____

---

**WORD NETWORK**

Add interesting words related to civil rights from the selection to your Word Network.

---

**STANDARDS**

**L.9–10.1.b** Use various types of phrases and clauses to convey specific meanings and add variety and interest to writing or presentations.

**L.9–10.4.b** Identify and correctly use patterns of word changes that indicate different meanings or parts of speech and continue to apply knowledge of Greek and Latin roots and affixes.

**L.9–10.5** Demonstrate understanding of figurative language, word relationships, and nuances in word meanings.

# Conventions

**Relative Clauses** A **clause** is a group of words that contains a subject and a verb. A **relative clause** is a type of clause that modifies a noun or pronoun in another clause by telling what kind or which one. It usually begins with a **relative pronoun**, such as that, which, who, whom, or whose.

This chart shows examples of sentences containing relative clauses. The relative pronouns are italicized, and the relative clauses are highlighted.

| SENTENCE | FUNCTION OF RELATIVE CLAUSE |
|---|---|
| The month *that* has 28 days is February. | modifies *month, telling which one* |
| The dinner, *which* includes dessert, is not expensive. | modifies *dinner,* telling *what kind* |
| This is the player *who* broke the record. | modifies *player,* telling *which one* |
| The next-door neighbor *whom* my sister has known since college is named Mario. | modifies *neighbor,* telling *which one* |
| The senator *whose* opinion was in question spoke to the press. | modifies *senator,* telling *which one* |

## Read It

1. Mark the relative pronoun and the relative clause in each of these sentences from "Letter From Birmingham Jail." Then, indicate the noun or pronoun each clause modifies.

   a. One who breaks an unjust law must do so openly, lovingly, and with a willingness to accept the penalty.

   b. Every day I meet young people whose disappointment with the church has turned into outright disgust.

   c. Now, there is nothing wrong in having an ordinance which requires a permit for a parade.

2. Reread paragraph 23 of "Letter From Birmingham Jail." Mark the relative clauses and relative pronouns, and tell what each clause modifies.

## Write It

📓 **Notebook** Add a relative clause to each sentence. Mark the relative clause and relative pronoun, and tell what word the clause modifies.

1. Segregation is an injustice.

2. Some church leaders stood up against discrimination.

"I HAVE A DREAM"

LETTER FROM BIRMINGHAM JAIL

# Writing to Compare

You have studied two famous works by Dr. Martin Luther King, Jr.—his "I Have a Dream" speech and his "Letter From Birmingham Jail." Now, deepen your analysis and formalize your observations in writing.

## Assignment

Both works by Dr. King are arguments, or persuasive texts, and use two main types of persuasive appeals.

- **Logical appeal,** or *logos*: using a clear line of reasoning supported by evidence, such as facts, data, or expert testimony
- **Emotional appeal,** or *pathos*: using loaded or charged language and other devices to arouse emotions

Write a **comparison-and-contrast essay** in which you analyze Dr. King's use of persuasive appeals in these two texts. Explain how the appeals he chooses fit the occasions and audiences for each text.

## Prewriting

**Clarify Audience and Occasion** Dr. King's use of the two main types of appeals reflects both the **occasion,** or circumstances of the writing, and the **audience,** or listeners and readers, he seeks to reach. Make sure you are clear about the audiences and occasions that prompted the writing of each text. If necessary, reread the Background notes to clarify that information.

"I Have a Dream" speech audience and occasion: _____

_____

"Letter From Birmingham Jail" audience and occasion: _____

_____

**Gather Evidence** Reread the two texts, and identify passages from each one that you feel are especially persuasive. Categorize each passage as an example of either logos or pathos. Explain why it fits that category.

| PASSAGE | LOGOS OR PATHOS | EXPLANATION |
|---------|-----------------|-------------|
|         |                 |             |
|         |                 |             |
|         |                 |             |
|         |                 |             |

📓 **Notebook** Respond to these questions.

1. What types of appeals would you expect Dr. King to use to persuade the audience for each of these texts? Were your expectations met? Explain.

2. Does one text use more pathos or more logos than the other? Explain.

## Drafting

**Determine Your Central Idea** In one sentence state the central idea or thesis you will develop:

Central Idea/Thesis: _____

_____

As you write, your ideas may come into clearer focus. If necessary, refine your thesis so that it expresses your position more precisely.

**Choose a Structure** Decide how best to organize your essay. Point-by-point organization and block organization are two commonly used structures for essays of comparison.

### Point-by-Point Organization

> I. Main Topic: Dr. King's Use of Logos in Two Texts
>   A. Appeals to Logic in "I Have a Dream" Speech
>   B. Appeals to Logic in "Letter from Birmingham Jail"
>
> II. Main Topic: Dr. King's Use of Pathos in Two Texts
>   A. Appeals to Emotion in "I Have a Dream" Speech
>   B. Appeals to Emotion in "Letter from Birmingham Jail"

### Block Organization

> I. Main Topic: Types of Appeals in Dr. King's "I Have a Dream" Speech
>   A. Appeals to Logic
>   B. Appeals to Emotion
>
> II. Main Topic: Types of Appeals in Dr. King's "Letter from Birmingham Jail"
>   A. Appeals to Logic
>   B. Appeals to Emotion

No matter the organizational structure you choose, weave in quotations from the two texts to support your analysis.

## Review, Revise and Edit

Once you are done drafting, review and revise your essay. Make sure you have given specific examples of Dr. King's use of logos and pathos. In addition, make sure you have explained how those appeals fit the occasion and audience of each text. If necessary, add support for your ideas by incorporating additional examples from the texts.

### ☑ EVIDENCE LOG

Before moving on to a new selection, go to your Evidence Log and record what you have learned from Dr. King's "I Have a Dream" speech and "Letter From Birmingham Jail."

## About the Author

**Robert F. Kennedy**
(1925–1968) was named
United States Attorney
General beginning when
his brother President John
F. Kennedy took office in
1961. Robert Kennedy was
known for fighting organized
crime and championing civil
rights. As Attorney General,
Kennedy fought for racial
equality and provided critical
help in passing the landmark
Civil Rights Act of 1964.
Kennedy was a leading
presidential candidate when
he was killed in Los Angeles,
a few months after the
assassination of Dr. Martin
Luther King, Jr.

# Remarks on the Assassination of Martin Luther King, Jr.

## Media Vocabulary

The following words or concepts will be useful to you as you analyze, discuss, and write about recordings of speeches.

| | |
|---|---|
| **oratory:** formal public speaking | • Speeches given on formal, serious, or ceremonial occasions are often examples of oratory.<br>• Oratory is typically more dramatic and passionate than everyday speech. |
| **delivery:** manner in which a speaker gives a speech | • Delivery involves all aspects of a speaker's presentation: his or her voice, tone, emotional expressiveness, use of gestures, and overall personality. |
| **gesture:** movement of the hands or body that conveys meaning | • Gestures play an important role in oratory, helping to emphasize the speaker's ideas or emotions.<br>• Gestures may help create a visual sense of a speaker's ideas. |
| **cadence:** rhythm and flow of language | • Cadence may have many different rhythms, from slow and steady to smooth and flowing.<br>• Effective speakers often vary cadence to emphasize ideas and add drama. |

## First Review MEDIA: VIDEO

Apply these strategies as you conduct your first review.

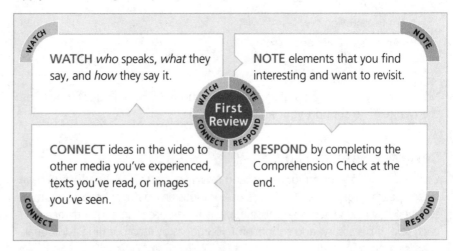

**WATCH** who speaks, what they say, and how they say it.

**NOTE** elements that you find interesting and want to revisit.

**CONNECT** ideas in the video to other media you've experienced, texts you've read, or images you've seen.

**RESPOND** by completing the Comprehension Check at the end.

First Review

WATCH • NOTE • CONNECT • RESPOND

## ▤ STANDARDS

**RI.9–10.10** By the end of grade 9, read and comprehend literary nonfiction in the grades 9–10 text complexity band proficiently, with scaffolding as needed at the high end of the range.

## Media Strategy: Tone and Context

🖹 **Notebook** Start your review of the speech by focusing on Kennedy's tone, or emotional attitude, and how it relates to the occasion. What makes the situation so difficult? What kind of assumptions must Kennedy have made about his audience? Why is his tone important in this situation?

# Remarks on the Assassination of Martin Luther King, Jr.

Robert F. Kennedy

SCAN FOR MULTIMEDIA

## BACKGROUND

Martin Luther King, Jr., was assassinated on April 4, 1968, in Memphis, Tennessee. On that day, Senator Robert F. Kennedy, who was then running for president, was in Indianapolis to give a campaign speech. After hearing news of King's murder, Kennedy chose not to give his planned speech. Instead, he announced that King had been killed and made the following impromptu remarks.

NOTES

# Comprehension Check

Complete the following items after you finish your first review.

1. What news does Kennedy communicate to his audience?

2. What fear does Kennedy have with respect to the African American members of his audience?

3. What response to the news does Kennedy urge his listeners to choose?

4. What poet does Kennedy quote at the end?

5. Where was Kennedy when he gave these remarks?

---

**MEDIA VOCABULARY**

Use these words as you discuss and write about the speech.

oratory
delivery
gesture
cadence

## 🔧 WORD NETWORK

Add interesting words related to civil rights from the video to your Word Network.

## ☰ STANDARDS

**SL.9–10.3** Evaluate a speaker's point of view, reasoning, and use of evidence and rhetoric, identifying any fallacious reasoning or exaggerated or distorted evidence.

## Close Review

Watch the video again. Write down any new observations that seem important. What **questions** do you have? What can you **conclude?**

---

## Analyze the Media

**CITE TEXTUAL EVIDENCE** to support your answers.

🗐 **Notebook Respond to these questions.**

1. **Infer** What does the response of the audience at the beginning of the speech tell you about the occasion and listeners' expectations? Explain.

2. **(a)** In what specific ways does Kennedy address his fear that the nation might erupt in violence? **(b) Evaluate** Do you think his approach is effective? Explain.

3. **Essential Question:** *How can words inspire change?* What have you learned about the power of words from reading this selection?

# Writing to Sources

Robert Kennedy was seeking election as president when Martin Luther King, Jr., was assassinated. He delivered this speech at an event that was supposed to be an ordinary campaign stop.

REMARKS ON THE ASSASSINATION OF MARTIN LUTHER KING, JR.

### Assignment

Imagine that you are a newspaper reporter assigned to Senator Kennedy's presidential campaign. You have been traveling with the Senator and are on the spot when he delivers this speech. Write the **newspaper report** that you post later that day.

- Answer the five journalistic questions about the event. These are as follows: *Who is involved? What happened? Where did it happen? When did it happen?* and *Why did it happen?*

- Use precise, descriptive language that accurately captures the circumstances of the events and provides readers with a sense of how people reacted and seemed to feel.

- A news report is not a personal, first-person account. Use third-person pronouns, such as "he," and "they," as well as an appropriately serious tone. Focus attention on the events you observed, not on personal feelings or experiences.

## ☑ EVIDENCE LOG

Before moving on to a new selection, go to your Evidence Log and record what you learned from "Remarks on the Assassination of Martin Luther King, Jr."

# Speaking and Listening

TV journalism follows many of the same rules as print journalism but requires strong speaking skills.

### Assignment

Adapt your newspaper report as a **newscast** that might have aired on national television. You may deliver your newscast live to the class. Alternatively, you may work with a partner to record it and present or post it.

- TV journalists do not usually read their reports. Work to memorize your article so that you can deliver it smoothly. You may need to shorten it or make other changes so that it works as a spoken text.

- As you deliver your report, pay attention to your cadence and do not rush. Use an appropriately serious, somber tone.

- Add realism by using an actual microphone or a prop.

- If you are recording your report, look into the camera. In addition, keep gestures to a minimum.

## ☰ STANDARDS

**W.9–10.2.b** Develop a topic with well-chosen, relevant, and sufficient facts, extended definitions, concrete details, quotations, or other information and examples appropriate to the audience's knowledge of the topic.

**W.9–10.2.e** Establish and maintain a formal style and objective tone while attending to the norms and conventions of the discipline in which they are writing.

**SL.9–10.4** Present information, findings, and supporting evidence clearly, concisely, and logically such that listeners can follow the line of reasoning and the organization, development, substance, and style are appropriate to purpose, audience, and task.

**SL.9–10.4.a** Plan and deliver an informative/explanatory presentation that: presents evidence in support of a thesis, conveys information from primary and secondary sources coherently, uses domain specific vocabulary, and provides a conclusion that summarizes the main points.

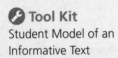 **Tool Kit**

Student Model of an Informative Text

## ACADEMIC VOCABULARY

As you craft your informative essay, consider using some of the academic vocabulary you learned in the beginning of the unit.

**coherent**
**aggregate**
**disrupt**
**notation**
**express**

## STANDARDS

**W.9–10.2.a–f** Write informative/ explanatory texts to examine and convey complex ideas, concepts, and information clearly and accurately through the effective selection, organization, and analysis of content.

**W.9–10.7** Conduct short as well as more sustained research projects to answer a question or solve a problem; narrow or broaden the inquiry when appropriate; synthesize multiple sources on the subject, demonstrating understanding of the subject under investigation.

**W.9–10.10** Write routinely over extended time frames and shorter time frames for a range of tasks, purposes, and audiences.

# Write an Informative Essay

You've read an essay, a speech, and a letter and viewed two videos of speeches, all of which have to do with the struggle for civil rights in the United States. In his "I Have a Dream" speech, Dr. Martin Luther King, Jr., speaks of the long struggle of the movement and of the need to persevere. In "Letter From Birmingham Jail," Dr. King writes to the white moderate religious leaders who would have him move more slowly to end segregation. Finally, in "Remarks on the Assassination of Martin Luther King, Jr.," Robert Kennedy announces to a crowd that Dr. King has been shot, and strives to give solace while appealing for peace and prayer. Now you will use your knowledge of the topic to write an informative text about the literature of civil rights.

> ### Assignment
> Think about how Dr. Martin Luther King, Jr., and Robert Kennedy choose to address the question of civil rights in the United States, and how their listeners would have responded at the time. Conduct research to write an **informative essay** on this question:
>
> > How did the selections in this section affect those who first heard them or read them?

## Elements of an Informative Text

A **informative text** presents and interprets information gathered through the extensive study of a subject.

An effective informative text includes these elements:

- a clear thesis statement
- facts and evidence from a variety of reliable, credited sources
- a clear organization that seamlessly integrates quotations, paraphrases, and analysis from various sources
- smooth transitions that show the relationships between ideas
- correct grammar, formal style, and an objective tone

**Model Informative Text** For a model of a well-crafted informative text, see the Launch Text, "1963: The Year That Changed Everything."

Challenge yourself to find all of the elements of effective informative writing in the text. You will have the opportunity to review these elements as you start to write your own informative text.

LAUNCH TEXT

**1963:** The Year That Changed Everything

# Prewriting / Planning

**Focus Your Research** Now that you have read the selections and thought about how words can inspire change, use the research question to focus your research. Plan to use a variety of sources. Consider:

- **primary sources**, which are firsthand or original accounts, such as newspaper articles

- **secondary sources**, such as encyclopedia entries

- **digital sources**, or material accessed on the Internet

- **print sources**, such as books or journal articles, which may be edited more carefully than digital material

- **original research**, such as eyewitness interviews or survey results

Create a list of sources to consult, and add new sources to your list as you find them.

Source List: _____

_____.

**Search Terms** Write down terms you plan to research online. Deciding on terms before going online may help you to stay focused on your topic. Use your search engine's advanced search function to narrow your results and find more relevant hits.

Search Terms: _____

_____.

**Evaluate Sources** To ensure that the sources you use are reliable, evaluate them carefully by asking yourself the following types of questions:

- Is the writer an authority on the subject?
- Is the information current, and does the publisher have a good reputation?
- Do other sources confirm the information in this source?

You can find out the answers to the first two questions by examining the author's and publisher's credentials. Do a quick Internet search to find out about the author's background, previous publications, and reputation. Consider the author's bias, or leanings, before accepting a conclusion. Check publication dates to make sure information is current. If you find conflicts in information between two sources, check the facts in a third source.

Take notes as you find relevant information, and keep a reference list of every source you use. Note each source's author, title, publisher, city, and date of publication. For Internet sources, record the name and Web address of the site, and the date you accessed the information. For print sources, note the page numbers on which you found useful information.

### EVIDENCE LOG

Review your Evidence Log and identify key details you may want to cite in your informative essay.

### STANDARDS

**W.9–10.8** Gather relevant information from multiple authoritative print and digital sources, using advanced searches effectively; assess the usefulness of each source in answering the research question; integrate information into the text selectively to maintain the flow of ideas, avoiding plagiarism and following a standard format for citation including footnotes and endnotes.

## Drafting

**Organize Your Informative Text** Start by writing a **thesis statement**—a sentence that states your position. Your thesis for this essay will be a concise statement that summarizes the impact of the words of Dr. Martin Luther King, Jr., and Robert F. Kennedy on their audiences. This thesis can help shape the way you choose to organize your essay beyond the introduction.

- If your thesis emphasizes the connections between the impact of the words of the two men, you might consider a *point-by-point organization*. Each section of the essay would examine a new aspect of the men's influence and show their similarities.

- If your thesis emphasizes distinctions, you might consider a *block organization*. First you would describe multiple aspects of one man's words on his audience. Then, you would examine those same aspects with the words of the second man as the focus.

**Adequate Support** One of the main ingredients of a strong informative essay is the evidence you assemble to support your ideas. For example, you might be making a point about how Kennedy's speech affected the mood of the crowd. You could support that point with an exact quotation from an eyewitness or with details about the emotions that people in the crowd experienced, based on your sources. If you use an exact quotation, be sure to cite the source.

- **Exact Quotation:** Vechel Rhodes, who was there that night, later described the Kennedy event for CBS News: "A white man coming in this neighborhood, especially seeking for [the office of] president, it was a big deal for the blacks [for Kennedy] to be in this area."

- **Details:** The Indianapolis police chief was afraid Kennedy would be attacked by the crowd if he told them that King had been shot… The crowd's mood seemed to shift during the course of the speech.

**Remember Your Audience** While selecting facts, details, and quotations, keep your audience and their knowledge level firmly in mind. For instance, if your audience has with very limited knowledge, you might have to supply an extended definition of *segregation*—explaining how the system of inequality came about and how it affected communities. Use this space to record some notes about who your audience is and what they might already know.

© Pearson Education, Inc., or its affiliates. All rights reserved.

**❚❚ STANDARDS**

**W.9–10.2.a** Introduce a topic or thesis statement, organize complex ideas, concepts, and information to make important connections and distinctions, include formatting, graphics, and multimedia when useful to aiding comprehension.

**W.9–10.2.b** Develop the topic with well-chosen, relevant, and sufficient facts, extended definitions, concrete details, quotations, or other information and examples appropriate to the audience's knowledge of the topic.

**W.9–10.2.d** Use precise language and domain-specific vocabulary to manage the complexity of the topic.

# Create Cohesion: Integrate Different Types of Information

As you write your draft, use the following methods to incorporate the facts, examples, and quotations you have found:

- **Direct Quotations:** Place a writer's exact words in quotation marks. Any omitted words or sentences should not alter the intent of the passage. Indicate omitted material with **ellipses,** or dots.
- **Paraphrase:** Restate a writer's specific ideas in your own words, accurately reflecting the writer's meaning.
- **Summary:** Condense an extended idea into a brief statement in your own words to introduce background information or review key ideas.

When paraphrasing or quoting text, provide proper credit for all sources. There are several citation formats that are widely accepted. Those offered by the Modern Language Association (MLA) and the American Psychological Association (APA) are two of the most common. Each has different rules about the source information to include, as well as how to order and punctuate it. The style guides treat quotations and in-text citations differently, as well. Follow the citation format your teacher specifies.

## Read It

These sentences from the Launch Text show the different methods of incorporating information.

- *"Injustice anywhere is a threat to justice everywhere," King wrote. He added, "Whatever affects one directly, affects all indirectly."* (uses direct quotation from "Letter From Birmingham Jail")
- *His message, the famous "Letter From Birmingham Jail," defends nonviolent resistance to injustice.* (paraphrases Dr. King's ideas)
- *In 1865, the Thirteenth Amendment to the United States Constitution ended slavery.* (summarizes the text of the Amendment)

## Write It

Use this chart to begin collecting source material and to plan your use of it.

| SOURCE MATERIAL | QUOTATION | PARAPHRASE | SUMMARY |
|---|---|---|---|
| | | | |
| | | | |

### STANDARDS

**W.9–10.8** Gather relevant information from multiple authoritative print and digital sources, using advanced searches effectively; assess the usefulness of each source in answering the research question; integrate information into the text selectively to maintain the flow of ideas, avoiding plagiarism and following a standard format for citation including footnotes and endnotes.

**L.9–10.3.a** Write and edit work so that it conforms to the guidelines in a style manual appropriate for the discipline and writing type.

# Revising

## Evaluating Your Draft

Use the following checklist to evaluate the effectiveness of your first draft. Then, use your evaluation and the instruction on this page to guide your revision.

| FOCUS AND ORGANIZATION | EVIDENCE AND ELABORATION | CONVENTIONS |
|---|---|---|
| ☐ Provides a clear thesis statement. | ☐ Includes specific reasons, details, facts, and quotations to support the thesis. | ☐ Attends to the norms and conventions of the discipline especially regarding crediting sources properly. |
| ☐ Includes a clear introduction, body, and conclusion. | ☐ Provides adequate support for each major idea. | |
| ☐ Uses facts and evidence from a variety of reliable, credited sources. | ☐ Uses precise language that is appropriate for the audience and purpose. | |
| ☐ Provides a logical text structure. | ☐ Establishes a formal, objective tone. | |
| ☐ Concludes with a summary of the thesis and supporting evidence. | | |

## Revising for Focus and Organization

**Review Your Conclusion** Reread your conclusion. Make sure that it fully addresses the prompt and summarizes information you presented in your essay.

**Use Transitions** Make sure the flow of your ideas is clear to your readers. Reread your draft, highlighting places where the addition of a transition word or phrase would clarify your thinking. Words or phrases such as *in contrast, finally, additionally,* and *similarly* serve as signposts for the next idea.

## Revising for Evidence and Elaboration

**Use Precise Language** Choose words that say exactly what you mean. The author of the Launch Text uses precise language to describe the effects of the Children's Crusade. Words such as *transform, under attack,* and *global outcry* help capture the dramatic impact of the events described.

As you choose precise words, make sure you avoid overgeneralizations. Look through your draft for clue words, such as *all, none,* or *never* that suggest an overgeneralization. Circle these words in your draft and—if you can't back them up with support—consider qualifying, or limiting, your statements.

> **Overgeneralization:** <u>Everyone</u> who heard King's words was inspired to change American society.
> **Qualified statement:** <u>Many</u> who heard King's words were inspired to change American society.

### ⬡ WORD NETWORK

Include interesting words from your Word Network in your informative text.

### ☰ STANDARDS

**W.9–10.2.c** Use appropriate and varied transitions to link the major sections of the text, create cohesion, and clarify the relationships among complex ideas and concepts.

**W.9–10.2.d** Use precise language and domain-specific vocabulary to manage the complexity of the topic.

**W.9–10.2.f** Provide a concluding statement or section that follows from and supports the information or explanation presented.

**PEER REVIEW**

Exchange papers with a classmate. Use the checklist to evaluate your classmate's informative essay and provide supportive feedback.

**1.** Is the thesis clear?

☐ yes ☐ no If no, explain what confused you.

**2.** Is the essay organized logically?

☐ yes ☐ no If no, what about the organization does not work?

**3.** Does the essay fully address the writing prompt?

☐ yes ☐ no If no, write a brief note explaining what you thought was missing.

**4.** What is the strongest part of your classmate's essay? Why?

_____

_____

_____

_____

## Editing and Proofreading

**Edit for Formal Language** Reread your draft to make sure that you did not use any slang or informal language. Also, keep in mind that informative writing requires an objective tone, so avoid adding personal opinions when presenting facts and information about the time period.

**Proofread for Accuracy** Read your draft carefully, looking for errors in spelling and punctuation. Double-check that you have used quotation marks correctly, and that there is an ending quotation mark for every beginning quotation mark.

## Publishing and Presenting

Create a final version of your draft. Share it with a small group so that your classmates can read it and make comments. In turn, review and comment on your classmate's work. Together, determine what your different reports convey about the initial impact of Dr. King's and Senator Kennedy's words. Listen and respond respectfully to comments about your work.

## Reflecting

Think about what you learned while writing your essay. What techniques did you learn that you could use when writing another informative text? How could you improve the process? For example, you might take more notes as you read over reliable sources of information.

**STANDARDS**
**W.9–10.2.e** Establish and maintain a formal style and objective tone while attending to the norms and conventions of the discipline in which they are writing.

ESSENTIAL QUESTION:

# How can words inspire change?

The 1960s marked a time of great change in American history. However, we should never forget the hardships of those who lived under segregation. The selections you will read present insights into different accounts of what took place during this important period. You will work in a group to continue your exploration of the civil rights movement.

## Small-Group Learning Strategies

Throughout your life, in school, in your community, in college, and in your career, you will continue to learn and work with others.

Look at these strategies and the actions you can take to practice them as you work in teams. Add ideas of your own for each step. Use these strategies during Small-Group Learning.

| STRATEGY | ACTION PLAN |
|---|---|
| Prepare | • Complete your assignments so that you are prepared for group work.<br>• Organize your thinking so you can contribute to your group's discussion.<br><br>• |
| Participate fully | • Make eye contact to signal that you are listening and taking in what is being said.<br>• Use text evidence when making a point.<br><br>• |
| Support others | • Build off ideas from others in your group.<br>• Invite others who have not yet spoken to join the discussion.<br><br>• |
| Clarify | • Paraphrase the ideas of others to ensure that your understanding is correct.<br>• Ask follow-up questions.<br><br>• |

SCAN FOR MULTIMEDIA

# CONTENTS

## Working as a Team

**1. Take a Position** In your group, discuss the following question:

> If you saw an injustice in your community, how might you start to change it?

As you take turns sharing your ideas, be sure to provide reasons. After all group members have shared, discuss the strengths and weaknesses of different types of approaches to social change.

**2. List Your Rules** As a group, decide on the rules that you will follow as you work together. Two samples are provided. Add two more of your own. As you work together, you may add or revise rules based on your experience together.

- Everyone should read all of the texts.
- People should stay focused during discussions.

- _____

  _____

- _____

  _____

**3. Apply the Rules** Share what you have learned about the Civil Rights movement. Make sure each person in the group contributes. Take notes and be prepared to share with the class one thing that you have heard from another member of your group.

**4. Name Your Group** Choose a name that reflects the unit topic.

Our group's decision: _____

**5. Create a Communication Plan** Decide how you want to communicate with one another. For example, you might use online collaboration tools, email, or instant messaging.

Our group's decision: _____

_____

## Making a Schedule

First, find out the due dates for the Small-Group activities. Then, preview the texts and activities with your group, and make a schedule for completing the tasks.

| SELECTION | ACTIVITIES | DUE DATE |
|-----------|-----------|----------|
| Remembering Civil Rights History, When "Words Meant Everything" | | |
| For My People<br><br>Incident | | |
| Lessons of Dr. Martin Luther King, Jr. | | |
| Traveling | | |

## Working on Group Projects

As your group works together, you'll find it more effective if each person has a specific role. Different projects require different roles. Before beginning a project, discuss the necessary roles, and choose one for each group member. Some possible roles are listed here. Add your own ideas to the list.

**Project Manager:** monitors the schedule and keeps everyone on task

**Researcher:** organizes information-gathering activities

**Recorder:** takes notes during group meetings

**Role:** _____

**Role:** _____

_____

_____

SCAN FOR MULTIMEDIA

## About the Newscast

The poet featured in this newscast, **Natasha Trethewey** (b. 1966), was born in Gulfport, Mississippi, the daughter of a biracial couple. Trethewey has won numerous awards and honors for her poetry. In 2007, her book *Native Guard* was awarded the Pulitzer Prize. In 2012, Trethewey was named the Poet Laureate of the United States, 2012–2014.

**Jeffrey Brown** (b. 1956) is the Chief Correspondent for Arts, Culture, and Society at *PBS NewsHour.* His work as both a correspondent and a news producer has been recognized with numerous honors, including an Emmy.

# Remembering Civil Rights History, When "Words Meant Everything"

## Media Vocabulary

The following words or concepts will be useful to you as you analyze, discuss, and write about media.

| | |
|---|---|
| **Point of View:** perspective from which the creators of a media piece approach a topic | • A media creator's perspective includes his or her attitudes and assumptions as well as his or her knowledge of a topic. |
| **Primary Source:** document, recording, image, or other source that was created at the same time as the events it describes or shows | • In journalism, someone with information to share or experience of an event may be referred to as a "source."<br>• Newspaper articles are one type of written primary source. |
| **Eyewitness:** someone who has firsthand experience of an event | • Information from eyewitnesses is often used in newscasts.<br>• Information from eyewitnesses is often seen as more credible than content from other sources. |
| **Secondary Source:** document, recording, image, or other source that is written or created after an event by someone who did not witness it firsthand | • Secondary sources include history books, documentary films, and other works.<br>• Secondary sources often include references to or interpretations of primary sources. |

## First Review MEDIA: VIDEO

Apply these strategies as you conduct your first review.

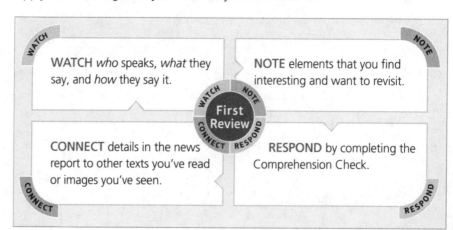

WATCH *who* speaks, *what* they say, and *how* they say it.

NOTE elements that you find interesting and want to revisit.

CONNECT details in the news report to other texts you've read or images you've seen.

RESPOND by completing the Comprehension Check.

# Remembering Civil Rights History, When "Words Meant Everything"

Jeffrey Brown

## BACKGROUND

This video describes key people, places, and events of the civil rights era, including the murder of activist Medgar Evers. Evers was an African American civil rights leader in Mississippi who helped desegregate the University of Mississippi in 1962. One year later, he was shot by a member of the Ku Klux Klan, a racist hate group, in his own driveway. His home, where this video begins, is now a museum.

SCAN FOR
MULTIMEDIA

NOTES

# Comprehension Check

Complete the following items after you finish your first review. Review and clarify details with your group..

1. What event did Jeffrey Brown and Natasha Trethewey attend?

2. How long did the pilgrimage last, where did it go, and how many people participated?

3. What is the topic of the poem that Natasha Trethewey reads during the newscast?

4. What special status does Representative John Lewis have among the marchers?

5. Who is Terri Sewell and how does her current status demonstrate the ways life in Selma has changed?

## MEDIA VOCABULARY

Use these words as you discuss and write about the newscast.

**point of view**
**primary source**
**eyewitness**
**secondary source**

### ⚓ WORD NETWORK

Add interesting words arelated to civil rights from the newscast to your Word Network.

### ▦ STANDARDS

**SL.9–10.2** Integrate multiple sources of information presented in diverse media or formats evaluating the credibility and accuracy of each source.

## Close Review

With your group, revisit the newscast and your first-review notes. Share your observations and brainstorm new ones that might seem important. What **questions** do you have? What can you **conclude?**

## Analyze the Media

1. **Present and Discuss** Choose the part of the newscast that you find most interesting or powerful. Share your choice with the group and discuss why you chose it. Explain what you notice in that portion, the questions it raises for you, and the conclusions you reached about it.

2. **Review and Synthesize** With your group, review all of the scenes included in the newscast. How do they work together? How does the newscast add to your understanding of the topic of civil rights? Explain.

3. 📓 **Notebook** Essential Question: *How can words inspire change?* Do you think the poem included in the newscast might help change someone's opinion about the Civil Rights era? Explain why or why not.

# Research

REMEMBERING CIVIL RIGHTS
HISTORY, WHEN "WORDS MEANT
EVERYTHING"

### Assignment

The newscast refers to a number of important events from the Civil Rights era. Choose one of those events to research. Then, write a **research report** of your findings. Consider these topics or choose another one that was mentioned in the newscast:

☐ the killing of Medgar Evers

☐ the murders of civil rights workers James Chaney, Andrew Goodman, and Michael Schwerner

☐ "Bloody Sunday" in Selma, Alabama

As you research, identify at least three reliable sources to cite. Then, note unique information from each source that you will synthesize, or weave together, to create a complete picture of events. As you write, include the following elements:

- background information that will help readers understand the context, or bigger social and historical issues, of the event.

- clear presentation of basic information, such as who was involved, what happened, and where it happened.

- explanation of the impact the event had on people both at the time and in years to follow.

# Writing to Sources

### Assignment

Starting at about the 3:50 point in the newscast, listen to Natasha Trethewey's description of "sacred language." Then, write a short **essay** in which you consider how various types of "sacred language"—such as songs, poetry, or stories—can affect what people understand, know, and feel about social problems. Use these questions to guide your thinking:

- What does Natasha Trethewey mean by the term "sacred language"?

- What role does Trethewey believe "sacred language" played in the Civil Rights movement?

- Does "sacred language" like Trethewey describes exist today? If you think it does, provide examples. If you think it does not, explain your thinking.

⬛ STANDARDS

**W.9–10.7** Conduct short as well as more sustained research projects to answer a question or solve a problem; narrow or broaden the inquiry when appropriate; synthesize multiple sources on the subject, demonstrating understanding of the subject under investigation.

# For My People

# Incident

## Concept Vocabulary

As you perform your first read of "For My People" and "Incident," you will encounter these words.

| | | |
|---|---|---|
| bewildered | blundering | trembling |

**Context Clues** If these words are unfamiliar to you, try using context clues. **Context clues** are other words and phrases that appear in a text and may provide hints about the meanings of unfamiliar words. There are various types of context clues that you may encounter as you read.

> **Definition:** Tonight there will be a **lunar** eclipse—an eclipse of the moon!
>
> **Synonym:** Oscar was known for his **acerbic,** or sharp, wit.
>
> **Elaborating Details:** Curtis angered his father and was **disinherited,** which left his siblings with a much larger portion of the family fortune.

Apply your knowledge of context clues and other vocabulary strategies to determine the meanings of unfamiliar words you encounter during your first read.

## First Read POETRY

Apply these strategies as you conduct your first read. You will have an opportunity to complete a close read after your first read.

**NOTICE** who or what is "speaking" the poem and whether the poem tells a story or describes a single moment.

**ANNOTATE** by marking vocabulary and key passages you want to revisit.

**First Read**

**CONNECT** ideas within the selection to what you already know and what you have already read.

**RESPOND** by completing the Comprehension Check.

### ☷ STANDARDS

**RL.9–10.10** By the end of grade 9, read and comprehend literature, including stories, dramas, and poems, in the grades 9–10 text complexity band proficiently, with scaffolding as needed at the high end of the range.

**L.9–10.4.a** Use context as a clue to the meaning of a word or phrase.

## About the Poets

A writer, a teacher, and an activist, **Margaret Walker** (1915–1998) was 22 years old when she published her first volume of poetry, *For My People*. In 1942, she became the first African American to win the Yale Younger Poets Prize. She is also known for her epic novel *Jubilee*, which was based on the life of her great-grandmother and took 30 years to write, and for establishing one of the first African American–studies centers in the nation.

**Natasha Trethewey** (b. 1966) was Poet Laureate, or official poet, of the United States from 2012 to 2014. Born in Mississippi to an African American mother and a white father, Trethewey grew up in the South at a time when laws enforcing segregation had just been overturned, but stark divisions between African Americans and whites were still common. Much of her poetry addresses her biracial heritage, as well as the forgotten histories of African American men and women in the deep South.

## Backgrounds

### For My People

Margaret Walker wrote this poem as part of a book of poetry, also titled *For My People*. True to its name, Walker's collection of sonnets, ballads, and free verse was intended to honor and celebrate the joys, struggles, and ordinary lives of African Americans— in her words, to "write the songs of my people—to frame their dreams into words, their souls into notes."

### Incident

During the 1960s, the Ku Klux Klan, a white supremacist hate group that had been active in the late nineteenth and early twentieth centuries, reemerged in response to the growing Civil Rights movement. One of their typical acts of terrorism was a cross-burning, during which a wooden cross would be set on fire in front of an African American home or church.

# For My People
## Margaret Walker

SCAN FOR
MULTIMEDIA

NOTES

For my people everywhere singing their slave songs
　　repeatedly: their dirges[1] and their ditties and their blues
　　and jubilees, praying their prayers nightly to an
　　unknown god, bending their knees humbly to an
5　　unseen power;

For my people lending their strength to the years, to the
　　gone years and the now years and the maybe years,
　　washing ironing cooking scrubbing sewing mending
　　hoeing plowing digging planting pruning patching
10　　dragging along never gaining never reaping never
　　knowing and never understanding;

For my playmates in the clay and dust and sand of Alabama
　　backyards playing baptizing and preaching and doctor
　　and jail and soldier and school and mama and cooking
15　　and playhouse and concert and store and hair and
　　Miss Choomby and company;[2]

For the cramped **bewildered** years we went to school to learn
　　to know the reasons why and the answers to and the
　　people who and the places where and the days when, in
20　　memory of the bitter hours when we discovered we
　　were black and poor and small and different and nobody
　　cared and nobody wondered and nobody understood;

Mark context clues or indicate
another strategy you used that
helped you determine meaning.

**bewildered** (bih WIHL duhrd)
*adj.*

MEANING:

---

1. **dirges** (DURJ uhz) *n.* slow songs expressing sorrow.
2. **Miss Choomby and company** Margaret Walker and her sister would play house, which
　　they referred to as playing "Miss Choomby," because her father had said that Miss
　　Choomby was a name for a black lady.

For the boys and girls who grew in spite of these things to
    be man and woman, to laugh and dance and sing and
25    play and drink their wine and religion and success, to
    marry their playmates and bear children and then die
    of consumption[3] and anemia[4] and lynching;

For my people thronging 47th Street in Chicago and Lenox
    Avenue in New York and Rampart Street in New
30    Orleans,[5] lost disinherited dispossessed[6] and happy
    people filling the cabarets and taverns and other
    people's pockets and needing bread and shoes and milk and
    land and money and something—something all our own;

For my people walking blindly spreading joy, losing time
35    being lazy, sleeping when hungry, shouting when
    burdened, drinking when hopeless, tied, and shackled
    and tangled among ourselves by the unseen creatures
    who tower over us omnisciently[7] and laugh;

For my people **blundering** and groping and floundering in
40    the dark of churches and schools and clubs
    and societies, associations and councils and committees and
    conventions, distressed and disturbed and deceived and
    devoured by money-hungry glory-craving leeches,
    preyed on by facile force of state and fad and novelty, by
45    false prophet and holy believer;

For my people standing staring trying to fashion a better way
    from confusion, from hypocrisy and misunderstanding,
    trying to fashion a world that will hold all the people,
    all the faces, all the adams and eves and their countless
50      generations;

Let a new earth rise. Let another world be born. Let a
    bloody peace be written in the sky. Let a second
    generation full of courage issue forth; let a people
    loving freedom come to growth. Let a beauty full of
55    healing and a strength of final clenching be the pulsing
    in our spirits and our blood. Let the martial songs
    be written, let the dirges disappear. Let a race of men now
    rise and take control.

Mark context clues or indicate another strategy you used that helped you determine meaning.

**blundering** (BLUHN duhr ihng) *adj.*

MEANING:

---

3. **consumption** (kuhn SUHMP shuhn) *n.* tuberculosis, a lung disease that was widespread in poor communities.
4. **anemia** (uh NEE mee uh) *n.* blood disease caused by a lack of iron, often due to a lack of good nutrition suffered by the poor.
5. **47th Street . . . New Orleans** African American communities which were thriving but poor.
6. **dispossessed** *adj.* deprived of the possession of something, especially land or a house.
7. **omnisciently** (om NIHSH uhnt lee) *adv.* acting with complete knowledge of the world.

# Incident

## Natasha Trethewey

SCAN FOR
MULTIMEDIA

NOTES

Mark context clues or indicate
another strategy you used that
helped you determine meaning.

**trembling** (TREHM blihng) v.

MEANING:

We tell the story every year—
how we peered from the windows, shades drawn—
though nothing really happened,
the charred grass now green again.

5  We peered from the windows, shades drawn,
at the cross trussed[1] like a Christmas tree,
the charred grass still green. Then
we darkened our rooms, lit the hurricane lamps.

At the cross trussed like a Christmas tree,
10  a few men gathered, white as angels in their gowns.
We darkened our rooms and lit hurricane lamps,
the wicks[2] trembling in their fonts of oil.

It seemed the angels had gathered, white men in their gowns.
When they were done, they left quietly. No one came.
15  The wicks trembled all night in their fonts of oil;
by morning the flames had all dimmed.

When they were done, the men left quietly. No one came.
Nothing really happened.
By morning all the flames had dimmed.
20  We tell the story every year.

1. **trussed** v. tied up tightly.
2. **wicks** n. strings in lamps or candles that are lit to burn off oil or wax.

# Comprehension Check

Complete the following items after you finish your first read. Review and clarify details with your group.

### FOR MY PEOPLE

**1.** Who are the "people" that the speaker refers to in the title and text of the poem "For My People"?

**2.** In stanza four, what discovery does the speaker say "we" made?

**3.** What wish does the speaker express in the final stanza of the poem?

### INCIDENT

**1.** What story does the speaker's family tell every year?

**2.** To the speaker, what do the gathered men look like?

**3.** At the end of the poem, what has happened by morning?

## RESEARCH

**Research to Clarify**  Choose at least one unfamiliar detail from one of the poems. Briefly research that detail. In what way does the information you learned shed light on an aspect of the poem?

## Close Read the Text

With your group, revisit sections of the text you marked during your first read. **Annotate** details that you notice. What **questions** do you have? What can you **conclude**?

---

## Analyze the Text

 **Notebook** Complete the activities.

1. **Review and Clarify** With your group, reread stanza 4 (lines 17–22) of "For My People." Discuss what the speaker claims African American children learned in school. Why does the speaker refer to "the reasons why and the answers to and the / people who and the places where and the days when," rather than provide specific examples of people, places, and events?

2. **Analyze** How does the speaker begin and end "Incident"? Does this line support or contradict the speaker's statement in the final stanza, "Nothing really happened"? Discuss why you think the poet made these choices.

3. **Essential Question:** *How can words inspire change?* What have you learned about the literature of civil rights from reading these poems?

## Concept Vocabulary

| bewildered | blundering | trembling |

**Why These Words?** The three concept vocabulary words are related. With your group, determine what the words have in common. Write your ideas, and add at least one other word that fits the category.

### Practice

 **Notebook** Use a print or online dictionary to confirm your understanding of each concept vocabulary word. Then, use each word in an original sentence. What emotions might a person be feeling if he or she were *trembling, bewildered,* or *blundering*?

## Word Study

**Latin Root: *-trem-*** The word *trembling* contains the Latin root *-trem-*, meaning "to shake" or "to shiver." Use an online thesaurus to look up these words that also contain the root *-trem-*: *tremor, tremendous, tremulous.* Write a synonym for each word.

---

### Sidebar

**GROUP DISCUSSION**
Remember that personal experiences can affect how a reader perceives a poem. Some readers will be familiar with the imagery and context of a poem, whereas other readers may not relate to these poetic elements. Keep these differences in mind as your group discusses the poems.

 **WORD NETWORK**

Add interesting words related to civil rights from the text to your Word Network.

 **STANDARDS**

**RL.9–10.5** Analyze how an author's choices concerning how to structure a text, order events within and manipulate time create such effects as mystery, tension, or surprise.

**L.9–10.4.b** Identify and correctly use patterns of word changes that indicate different meanings or parts of speech and continue to apply knowledge of Greek and Latin roots and affixes.

**L.9–10.4.c** Consult general and specialized reference materials, both print and digital, to find the pronunciation of a word or determine or clarify its precise meaning, its part of speech, or its etymology.

# Analyze Craft and Structure

**Poetic Structure** A **lyric poem** expresses the thoughts and feelings of a single speaker, often in vivid, musical language. Although it may describe characters and events, a lyric poem does not tell a complete story. Instead, it captures an emotion or a moment in time. Lyric poems may follow a particular **poetic form**, or structure. This may involve a pattern of lines, stanzas, rhyme, meter, or a combination of all of those elements. Stanzas are named for the number of lines they contain:

**CLARIFICATION**
Repeating lines in a poem may not be identical. Look for similar lines that share many—but perhaps not all—of the same words.

**Couplet:** two-line stanza    **Sextet:** six-line stanza

**Tercet:** three-line stanza    **Septet:** seven-line stanza

**Quatrain:** four-line stanza    **Octet:** eight-line stanza

The form of a poem may contribute to its effect in different ways. The form may emphasize words or sounds, create rhythm or flow, or build a sense of order or sequence.

Natasha Trethewey's poem "Incident" is an example of an ancient form called a **pantoum**. Margaret Walker's "For My People" is **free verse**, or a poem that does not follow a set pattern. Nevertheless, Walker includes elements that add structure and help organize the poem.

## Practice

**CITE TEXTUAL EVIDENCE** to support your answers.

📔 **Notebook** Work independently to answer the questions and complete the activities. Then, share your responses with your group.

1. (a) What basic type of stanza appears in "Incident"? Explain. (b) Use the chart to identify by number which lines from stanza 1 repeat in stanza 2, which lines from stanza 2 repeat in stanza 3, and so on.

| STANZA | LINES REPEATED FROM PREVIOUS STANZAS |
|--------|--------------------------------------|
| 2 | |
| 3 | |
| 4 | |
| 5 | |

2. (a) At what point does the first line of "Incident" repeat? (b) Does the meaning of the first line change when it is repeated? Explain.

3. Using "Incident" as a model, outline the structure of a pantoum.

4. (a) Which elements of "For My People" repeat, either exactly or very closely? (b) What qualities connect the separate images in each stanza? (c) In what ways does the final stanza differ from the preceding stanzas?

POETRY COLLECTION

# Author's Style

**Punctuation** Poets respect the rules of grammar and punctuation, but they may break them to add emphasis or to create a particular effect. Before examining how poets use interior punctuation (punctuation *within* a sentence), review the functions of commas, semicolons, and dashes.

**Commas** separate independent clauses linked by a coordinating conjunction (*and, but, or, nor, so, yet,* or *for*). Commas also separate words, phrases, or clauses in a series.

**Semicolons** separate independent clauses without a conjunction or items in a series, especially when one or more of the items already includes a comma.

**Dashes** set off a word, phrase, or clause from the rest of a sentence.

| COMMAS | SEMICOLONS | DASHES |
|---|---|---|
| I caught my bus, yet was still late to practice. | I just missed my bus; Coach Carlos was pretty upset. | The bus—ten feet away—belched fumes in my face. |
| Our grocery list started with beef, onions, and peas. | We needed beef, peas, and onions; sugar for cookies; and fruit. | Start with beef, peas, and onions—for stew. |

In "For My People," Margaret Walker breaks some of the traditional rules of punctuation. In "Incident," Natasha Trethewey uses conventional punctuation—commas, semicolons, and dashes—throughout. Complete this organizer with your group. The first and last items are done.

| POEM | PUNCTUATION | HOW IT IS USED | EFFECT |
|---|---|---|---|
| "For My People" | comma | separates phrases in a series (lines 23–27) | creates a simple style that reinforces the humble images |
| | semicolon | | |
| | dash | | |
| "Incident" | comma | | |
| | semicolon | | |
| | dash | sets off explanatory material | creates suspense |

## Read It

**Notebook** Work individually to identify and record examples of conventional and unconventional punctuation from the second stanza of "For My People." Think about the effect of the punctuation on the poem's meaning, and jot down your ideas. Then, discuss your findings with your group.

## Write It

**Notebook** Write a poem that describes an "incident" from your life. You may want to write it in complete sentences. You could then delete parts of sentences to leave meaningful phrases, and then make line breaks to create stanzas of free verse. Use commas, semicolons, and dashes for effect.

**STANDARDS**

**L.9–10.2** Demonstrate command of the conventions of standard English capitalization, punctuation, and spelling when writing.

**L.9–10.2.a** Use a semicolon to link two or more closely related independent clauses.

# Speaking and Listening

### Assignment

Create a **multimedia presentation** using the poem of your choice. In your presentation, combine text with audio, graphics, or both. When delivering your presentation, pay special attention to your pronunciation, tone, speaking rate, and voice modulation. Be sure to make eye contact with your audience and to use body language to add emphasis or reflect your meaning. Choose from among the following options.

☐ **Soundtrack or Playlist** Record a soundtrack or playlist to accompany an oral reading of one of the poems. Decide what type of music you will include to enhance or support your oral reading. Practice your oral presentation of the poem using your finished soundtrack or playlist in the background. Prepare brief explanations of why you selected the music or songs you used.

☐ **Historical Context Report** Prepare an oral report that explains the circumstances of the era one of the poems reflects. In your report, be sure to include factual details and events of the period and explain how these elements relate to images and language used in the poem.

☐ **Annotated Illustration** Select images from period photographs and art that show a vision of the "new earth" the speaker imagines at the end of "For My People." Prepare comments and excerpts from the poem to accompany and explain how each image is related to the speaker's vision.

Use this chart or one like it to help gather and record the text excerpts, images, musical selections, and notes/comments you will use in your multimedia presentation.

Poem: _____

| TEXT EXCERPT | IMAGE | MUSIC/SONG | NOTES/COMMENTS |
|---|---|---|---|
| | | | |
| | | | |
| | | | |
| | | | |

### ✐ EVIDENCE LOG

Before moving on to a new selection, go to your Evidence Log and record what you learned from "For My People" and "Incident."

### ☷ STANDARDS

**SL.9–10.4.b** Plan, memorize, and present a recitation that: conveys the meaning of the selection and includes appropriate performance techniques to achieve the desired aesthetic effect.

**SL.9–10.5** Make strategic use of digital media in presentations to enhance understanding of findings, reasoning, and evidence and to add interest.

**SL.9–10.6** Adapt speech to a variety of contexts and tasks, demonstrating command of formal English when indicated or appropriate.

About the Speaker

**Cesar Chavez** (1927–1993) was the founder of the United Farm Workers Union (UFW). In the 1960s, Chavez recognized that the predominantly Latino field workers who picked grapes, lettuce, and other crops were being poorly treated. Chavez tried to put an end to this mistreatment by organizing the workers into the UFW, a union that fought for higher wages and better treatment.

# Lessons of Dr. Martin Luther King, Jr.

## Concept Vocabulary

As you perform your first read, you will encounter these words.

| activist | radical | advocating |

**Context Clues** To infer the meaning of an unfamiliar word, look to the context, the text that surrounds the word. Consider these lines from "Lessons of Dr. Martin Luther King, Jr."

### Context Clues: Word Position

*Our nation continues to **wage** war upon its neighbors, and upon itself.*

You can gather clues about a word's meaning based on its role in a sentence. Here, *wage* is a verb; it is something that a nation is doing to another nation in the context of warfare. That helps you understand that the correct meaning of *wage* here is to "carry on a war."

### Context Clue: Series

*When our workers complain, or try to organize, they are fired, **assaulted**, and even murdered.*

The sequence of *fired, assaulted,* and *murdered* is arranged so that each term names a more serious offense than the previous term. Since *assaulted* is the middle term, it must refer to something more serious than *fired* but less serious than *murdered*. So, assaulted may mean "attacked."

Apply your knowledge of context clues and other vocabulary strategies to help you determine the meanings of unfamiliar words you encounter during your first read.

## First Read NONFICTION

Apply these strategies as you conduct your first read. You will have an opportunity to complete a close read after your first read.

**NOTICE** the general ideas of the text. *What* is it about? *Who* is involved?

**ANNOTATE** by marking vocabulary and key passages you want to revisit.

**First Read**

**CONNECT** ideas within the selection to what you already know and what you have already read.

**RESPOND** by completing the Comprehension Check and by writing a brief summary of the selection.

**STANDARDS**

**RI.9–10.10** By the end of grade 9, read and comprehend literary nonfiction in the grades 9–10 text complexity band proficiently, with scaffolding as needed at the high end of the range.

**L.9–10.4.a** Use context as a clue to the meaning of a word or phrase.

# Lessons of
# Dr. Martin Luther King, Jr.

### Cesar Chavez

## BACKGROUND

Starting with the 1962 publication of *Silent Spring,* by Rachel Carson, an American anti-pesticide movement worked to reduce the amount and variety of toxic chemicals used to kill insects that feed on crops or spread disease. Cesar Chavez, shown here at an anti-pesticide rally in 1985, was one such activist. Chavez gave many speeches, including the following, against the use of pesticides on California grapes. One major success of the anti-pesticide movement was the banning of DDT, a powerful pesticide, in cases other than disease control.

SCAN FOR
MULTIMEDIA

1   January 12, 1990

2       My friends, today we honor a giant among men: today we honor the reverend Martin Luther King, Jr.

3       Dr. King was a powerful figure of destiny, of courage, of sacrifice, and of vision. Few people in the long history of this nation can rival his accomplishment, his reason, or his selfless dedication to the cause of peace and social justice.

4       Today we honor a wise teacher, an inspiring leader, and a true visionary, but to truly honor Dr. King we must do more than say words of praise.

5       We must learn his lessons and put his views into practice, so that we may truly be free at last.

6       Who was Dr. King?

7       Many people will tell you of his wonderful qualities and his many accomplishments, but what makes him special to me, the truth many

NOTES

NOTES

Mark context clues or indicate another strategy you used that helped you determine meaning.

**activist** (AK tuh vihst) *n.*

MEANING:

**radical** (RAD uh kuhl) *adj.*

MEANING:

**advocating** (AD vuh kayt ihng) *v.*

MEANING:

people don't want you to remember, is that Dr. King was a great **activist**, fighting for **radical** social change with radical methods.

8    While other people talked about change, Dr. King used direct action to challenge the system. He welcomed it, and used it wisely.

9    In his famous letter from the Birmingham jail, Dr. King wrote that "The purpose of direct action is to create a situation so crisis-packed that it will inevitably open the door to negotiation."

10   Dr. King was also radical in his beliefs about violence. He learned how to successfully fight hatred and violence with the unstoppable power of nonviolence.

11   He once stopped an armed mob, saying: "We are not **advocating** violence. We want to love our enemies. I want you to love our enemies. Be good to them. This is what we live by. We must meet hate with love."

12   Dr. King knew that he very probably wouldn't survive the struggle that he led so well. But he said "If I am stopped, the movement will not stop. If I am stopped, our work will not stop. For what we are doing is right. What we are doing is just, and God is with us."

13   My friends, as we enter a new decade, it should be clear to all of us that there is an unfinished agenda,[1] that we have miles to go before we reach the promised land.

14   The men who rule this country today never learned the lessons of Dr. King, they never learned that non-violence is the only way to peace and justice.

15   Our nation continues to wage war upon its neighbors, and upon itself.

16   The powers that be rule over a racist society, filled with hatred and ignorance.

17   Our nation continues to be segregated along racial and economic lines.

18   The powers that be make themselves richer by exploiting the poor. Our nation continues to allow children to go hungry, and will not even house its own people. The time is now for people, of all races and backgrounds, to sound the trumpets of change. As Dr. King proclaimed "There comes a time when people get tired of being trampled over by the iron feet of oppression."

19   My friends, the time for action is upon us. The enemies of justice want you to think of Dr. King as only a civil rights leader, but he had a much broader agent. He was a tireless crusader for the rights of the poor, for an end to the war in Vietnam long before it was popular to take that stand, and for the rights of workers everywhere.

20   Many people find it convenient to forget that Martin was murdered while supporting a desperate strike on that tragic day in Memphis, Tennessee. He died while fighting for the rights of sanitation workers.

---

1. **agenda** (uh JEHN duh) *n.* plan or goal that guides someone's behavior.

21     Dr. King's dedication to the rights of the workers who are so often exploited by the forces of greed has profoundly touched my life and guided my struggle.

22     During my first fast in 1968, Dr. King reminded me that our struggle was his struggle too. He sent me a telegram which said "Our separate struggles are really one. A struggle for freedom, for dignity, and for humanity."

23     I was profoundly moved that someone facing such a tremendous struggle himself would take the time to worry about a struggle taking place on the other side of the continent.

24     Just as Dr. King was a disciple of Ghandi[2] and Christ, we must now be Dr. King's disciples.

25     Dr. King challenged us to work for a greater humanity. I only hope that we are worthy of his challenge.

26     The United Farm Workers are dedicated to carrying on the dream of reverend Martin Luther King, Jr. My friends, I would like to tell you about the struggle of the farm workers who are waging a desperate struggle for our rights, for our children's rights and for our very lives.

27     Many decades ago the chemical industry promised the growers that pesticides would bring great wealth and bountiful harvests to the fields.

28     Just recently, the experts are learning what farm workers, and the truly organized farmers have known for years.

29     The prestigious National Academy of Sciences recently concluded an exhaustive five-year study which determined that pesticides do not improve profits and do not produce more crops.

30     What, then, is the effect of pesticides? Pesticides have created a legacy of pain, and misery, and death for farm workers and consumers alike.

31     The crop which poses the greatest danger, and the focus of our struggle, is the table grape crop. These pesticides soak the fields, drift with the wind, pollute the water, and are eaten by unwitting consumers.

32     These poisons are designed to kill, and pose a very real threat to consumers and farm workers alike. The fields are sprayed with pesticides: like Captan, Parathion, Phosdrin, and Methyl Bromide. These poisons cause cancer, DNA mutation, and horrible birth defects.

33     The Central Valley of California is one of the wealthiest agricultural regions in the world. In its midst are clusters of children dying from cancer.

34     The children live in communities surrounded by the grape fields that employ their parents. The children come into contact with the poisons when they play outside, when they drink the water, and when they hug their parents returning from the fields.

---

2. **Gandhi** Mohandas Karamchand Gandhi (1869–1948), an Indian leader who used nonviolent resistance to fight for Indian independence from Britain. He is considered to have been a major influence on Dr. Martin Luther King, Jr.

35    And the children are dying.

36    They are dying slow, painful, cruel deaths in towns called cancer clusters, in cancer clusters like McFarland, where the children cancer rate is 800 percent above normal. A few months ago, the parents of a brave little girl in the agricultural community of Earlimart came to the United Farm Workers to ask for help.

37    The Ramirez family knew about our protests in nearby McFarland and thought there might be a similar problem in Earlimart. Our union members went door to door in Earlimart, and found that the Ramirez family's worst fears were true:

38    There are at least four other children suffering from cancer in the little town of Earlimart, a rate 1200 percent above normal.

39    In Earlimart, little Jimmy Caudillo died recently from leukemia at the age of three.

40    Three other young children in Earlimart, in addition to Jimmy and Natalie, are suffering from similar fatal diseases that the experts believe are caused by pesticides.

41    These same pesticides can be found on the grapes you buy in the stores.

42    My friends, the suffering must end. So many children are dying, so many babies are born without limbs and vital organs, so many workers are dying in the fields.

43    We have no choice, we must stop the plague of pesticides.

44    The growers responsible for this outrage are blinded by greed, by racism, and by power.

45    The same inhumanity displayed at Selma, in Birmingham, in so many of Dr. King's battlegrounds, is displayed every day in the vineyards of California.

46    The farm labor system in place today is a system of economic slavery.

47    My friends, even those farm workers who do not have to bury their young children are suffering from abuse, neglect, and poverty.

48    Our workers labor for many hours every day under the hot sun, often without safe drinking water or toilet facilities.

49    Our workers are constantly subjected to incredible pressures and intimidation to meet excessive quotas.[3]

50    When our workers complain, or try to organize, they are fired, assaulted, and even murdered.

51    Just as Bull Connor turned the dogs loose on non-violent marchers in Alabama, the growers turn armed foremen on innocent farm workers in California.

52    The stench of injustice in California should offend every American. Some people, especially those who just don't care, or don't understand, like to think that the government can take care of these problems. The government should, but won't.

---

3. **quotas** (KWOHT uhz) *n.* specific amounts that are expected to be achieved.

Posters like the one pictured here were used to gain support for Chavez's cause.

understand, like to think that the government can take care of these problems. The government should, but won't.

53     The growers used their wealth to buy good friends like Governor George Deukmajian, Ronald Reagan, and George Bush.

54     My friends, if we are going to end the suffering, we must use the same people power that vanquished injustice in Montgomery, Selma and Birmingham.

55     I have seen many boycotts succeed. Dr. King showed us the way with the bus boycott, and with our first boycott we were able to get DDT, Aldrin, and Dieldrin banned in our first contracts with grape growers. Now, even more urgently, we are trying to get deadly pesticides banned.

56     The growers and their allies have tried to stop us for years with intimidation, with character assassination,[4] with public relations campaigns, with outright lies, and with murder.

57     But those same tactics did not stop Dr. King, and they will not stop us.

58     Once social change begins, it cannot be reversed.

59     You cannot uneducate the person who has learned to read. You cannot humiliate the person who feels pride. And you cannot oppress the people who are not afraid anymore.

---

4. **character assassination** *n.* saying false things about a person in order to make the public stop liking or trusting that person.

60    In our life and death struggle for justice we have turned to the court of last resort: the American people. And the people are ruling in our favor.

61    As a result, grape sales keep falling. We have witnessed truckloads of grapes being dumped because no one would stop to buy them. As demand drops, so do prices and profits. The growers are under tremendous economic pressure.

62    We are winning, but there is still much hard work ahead of us. I hope that you will join our struggle.

63    The simple act of refusing to buy table grapes laced with pesticides is a powerful statement that the growers understand.

64    Economic pressure is the only language the growers speak, and they are beginning to listen.

65    Please, boycott table grapes. For your safety, for the workers, and for the children, we must act together.

66    My friends, Dr. King realized that the only real wealth comes from helping others.

67    I challenge each and every one of you to be a true disciple of Dr. King, to be truly wealthy.

68    I challenge you to carry on his work by volunteering to work for a just cause you believe in.

69    Consider joining our movement because the farm workers, and so many other oppressed peoples, depend upon the unselfish dedication of its volunteers, people just like you.

70    Thousands of people have worked for our cause and have gone on to achieve success in many different fields.

71    Our non-violent cause will give you skills that will last a lifetime. When Dr. King sounded the call for justice, the freedom riders answered the call in droves. I am giving you the same opportunity to join the same cause, to free your fellow human beings from the yoke[5] of oppression.

72    I have faith that in this audience there are men and women with the same courage and the same idealism, that put young Martin Luther King, Jr. on the path to social change.

73    I challenge you to join the struggle of the United Farm Workers. And if you don't join our cause, then seek out the many organizations seeking peaceful social change.

74    Seek out the many outstanding leaders who will speak to you this week, and make a difference.

75    If we fail to learn that each and every person can make a difference, then we will have betrayed Dr. King's life's work. The reverend Martin Luther King, Jr. had more than just a dream, he had the love and the faith to act.

76    God Bless You. ❧

---

5. **yoke** (yohk) *n.* type of collar used on working animals to pull wagons or plows; here, used figuratively to indicate something that causes people to be treated cruelly and unfairly.

# Comprehension Check

Complete the following items after you finish your first read. Review and clarify details with your group.

1. According to Chavez, what must people do to truly honor Dr. Martin Luther King, Jr.?

2. What was the primary message that Dr. Martin Luther King, Jr., wanted to communicate in the telegram he sent to Chavez?

3. What evidence does Chavez offer to make the case for banning pesticides?

4. What was Chavez doing to fight back against what he saw as oppression of the farm workers in California's central valley?

5. 📝 **Notebook** Write a summary of "Lessons of Dr. Martin Luther King, Jr." to confirm your understanding of the text.

- - - - - - - - - - - - - - - - - - - - - - - - - - - - - - - - - - - - - - - - - - - - - -

## RESEARCH

**Research to Clarify** Choose at least one unfamiliar detail from the text. Briefly research that detail. In what way does the information you learned shed light on an aspect of the speech?

**Research to Explore** Choose something that interested you from the text, and formulate a research question.

LESSONS OF
DR. MARTIN LUTHER KING, JR.

## Close Read the Text

With your group, revisit sections of the text you marked during your first read. **Annotate** details that you notice. What **questions** do you have? What can you **conclude**?

Close
Read

ANNOTATE
QUESTION
CONCLUDE

---

## Analyze the Text

**CITE TEXTUAL EVIDENCE**
to support your answers.

📓 **Notebook** Complete the activities.

1. **Review and Clarify** With your group, reread paragraphs 45–50 of "Lessons of Dr. Martin Luther King, Jr." What does Chavez mean when he refers to "economic slavery"? Do you think Chavez's use of this term is justified based on the evidence he presents? Explain.

2. **Present and Discuss** Now, work with your group to share other key passages from "Lessons of Dr. Martin Luther King, Jr." What made you choose these particular sections? Take turns presenting your choices. Discuss parts of the text that you found to be most meaningful, the questions you asked, and the conclusions you reached as a result of reading those passages.

3. **Essential Question:** *How can words inspire change?* What have your learned about the power of words from reading this speech?

---

**TIP**

**GROUP DISCUSSION**
Keep in mind that the struggle for fair pay and good working conditions is ongoing in today's world. Different people have different ideas for how to solve these problems in the best possible way.

---

🔗 **WORD NETWORK**

Add interesting words related to civil rights from the selection to your Word Network.

---

### ▤ STANDARDS

**RI.9–10.3** Analyze how the author unfolds an analysis or series of ideas or events, including the order in which the points are made, how they are introduced and developed, and the connections that are drawn between them.

**L.9–10.4.b** Identify and correctly use patterns of word changes that indicate different meanings or parts of speech and continue to apply knowledge of Greek and Latin roots and affixes.

---

LANGUAGE DEVELOPMENT

## Concept Vocabulary

| activist | radical | advocating |

**Why These Words?** Use a print or online dictionary to confirm your definitions of the three vocabulary words. Write a sentence using each vocabulary word. In what news stories would you hear these words commonly used? Discuss.

### Practice

📓 **Notebook** Confirm your understanding of these words from the text by using them in sentences. Be sure to use context clues that hint at each word's meaning.

## Word Study

**Latin root: *-voc-*** In this speech, Cesar Chavez discusses Dr. King's assertion that he was not advocating violence. The word *advocating* contains the Latin root *-voc-* or *-vok-*, meaning "to call," "to name," or "voice." Find several other words that were formed from this same root. Record the words and their meanings.

# Analyze Craft and Structure

**Development of Ideas** One way in which an author can build a persuasive argument is by identifying **cause-and-effect relationships,** showing how one event or situation leads to another. Many complex issues, such as those Cesar Chavez discusses in this speech, have multiple causes or multiple, different effects.

To show the true seriousness of a problem, an author may present related aspects of an issue in a **cause-and-effect chain**. This means that the author demonstrates how a single cause results in an effect, which leads to a second effect, which causes a third effect, and so on. Cause-and-effect organization allows an author to show how one issue is part of a series or network of connected issues.

**TIP**

CLARIFICATION
Keep in mind the difference between a cause-and-effect chain and a single cause with multiple effects. Imagine the chain as having a linear shape, and a cause with multiple effects having a fanlike shape.

## Practice

**CITE TEXTUAL EVIDENCE** to support your answers.

1. Work with your group to complete the chart. (a) Identify three effects resulting from each of the causes noted. (b) Identify another cause from the speech and at least two of its effects.

| TRACING CAUSE AND EFFECT |
| --- |
| **CAUSE:** *The men who rule this country today never learned the lessons of Dr. King, they never learned that non-violence is the only way to peace and justice. (par. 14)* <br> **EFFECT:** <br> **EFFECT:** <br> **EFFECT:** |
| **CAUSE:** *Many decades ago the chemical industry promised the growers that pesticides would bring great wealth and bountiful harvests to the fields. (par. 27)* <br> **EFFECT:** <br> **EFFECT:** <br> **EFFECT:** |
| **CAUSE:** <br><br> **EFFECT:** <br> **EFFECT:** |

📝 **Notebook** Answer the following questions.

2. What connections does Chavez make between Dr. King's approach to social change and the work of the UFW?

3. What effects does Chavez say those who volunteer to work for a just cause will experience?

# Author's Style

**Cohesion and Clarity Transitions** are the words and phrases that link sections of a text. Writers and speakers use transitions to create cohesion and to clarify the relationships among the ideas they are presenting.

When a transitional word or phrase begins a sentence, or when it joins two closely related independent clauses connected with a semicolon, follow it with a comma. When it appears in the middle of a word or phrase, set it off with two commas.

Here are examples of transitions and the types of relationships they indicate.

> **Similarity:** *also, likewise, similarly, in the same way*
> **Example:** Dr. King advocated for nonviolent resistance. *Similarly*, Chavez encourages the community to seek peaceful social change.
>
> **Contrast:** *although, however, nevertheless, on the other hand*
> **Example:** The workers protested; *however,* the growers refused to change.
>
> **Addition of Ideas:** *also, in addition, moreover, even more so*
> **Example:** Workers were underpaid. *Moreover*, they were treated poorly.
>
> **Cause-and-effect:** *so, thus, therefore, consequently, as a result*
> **Example:** Buyers boycotted. *As a result*, growers changed their practices.
>
> **Example:** *for example, for instance, specifically, in particular*
> **Example:** Growers were paying to receive favorable treatment. One grower, *for example*, gave over a million dollars to the governor.

**≔ STANDARDS**

**W.9–10.2.c** Use appropriate and varied transitions to link the major sections of the text, create cohesion, and clarify the relationships among complex ideas and concepts.

**W.9–10.7** Conduct short as well as more sustained research projects to answer a question, or solve a problem; narrow or broaden the inquiry when appropriate; synthesize multiple sources on the subject, demonstrating understanding of the subject under investigation.

**L.9–10.2.a** Use a semicolon to link two or more closely related independent clauses.

## Read It

Work individually. Read these pairs of sentences based on the "Lessons of Dr. Martin Luther King, Jr." For each pair, indicate a transitional word or phrase that could be used to effectively link the sentences. Then, write the type of relationship the transition is conveying.

| PASSAGE | TRANSITION | RELATIONSHIP |
|---|---|---|
| Dr. King knew that he probably would not survive the struggle. He believed that if he were stopped, the movement would not stop. | | |
| The children live in communities surrounded by grape fields. They come into contact with poisons whenever they play outside. | | |
| Our workers labor for man hours every day under the hot sun. They are subjected to incredible pressures to meet excessive quotas. | | |

## Write It

🗒 **Notebook** Write a short description of the issues the farm workers faced. In your description, use at least three different transitional words or phrases. Identify the relationship each transition conveys.

# Research

### Assignment

Write a **team report** on one of the following topics:

☐ A **strategy analysis** that addresses the following questions: *Was Chavez's strategy of asking consumers to boycott grapes morally responsible? Were Chavez and the UFW able to make the plight of farm workers clear and compelling? How likely was it that some consumers feel manipulated or resentful at being told what they could and could not buy? Given what happened in other boycotts, was Chavez's strategy likely to be successful?*

☐ A **public opinion report** that addresses the following questions: *How did the general public view Chavez's work during the era of the grape boycott? Did workers in general support Chavez and the UFW? How does the public view Chavez's legacy today?*

☐ A **status report** that addresses the following questions: *How are farm workers in California and other places treated today? Do they have full rights? Are their wages comparable to workers in other industries? Have working conditions improved since Chavez's time? Have the problems presented by pesticides been solved?*

**Research Plan** Before you write, work together to identify a variety of sources, including the following types:

- **Primary Sources:** firsthand or original accounts
- **Secondary Sources:** texts that analyze, retell, or report on events
- **Specialized Sources:** almanacs, government publications, and other texts that provide specific information or data

List the sources you consult and consider their usefulness. Make sure the authors have the knowledge to speak with authority on the topic. In addition, determine whether any show bias or make unfair judgments. You can then decide whether to use the information or to discard it.

| EVALUATING USEFULNESS OF SOURCES | |
|---|---|
| Primary Source(s) | authoritative? <br><br> fair and unbiased? |
| Secondary Source(s) | authoritative? <br><br> fair and unbiased? |
| Specialized Source(s) | authoritative? <br><br> fair and unbiased? |

> **EVIDENCE LOG**
>
> Before moving on to a new selection, go to your Evidence Log and record what you learned from "Lessons of Dr. Martin Luther King, Jr."

### About the Author

**Grace Paley** (1922–2007) grew up in New York, the daughter of Russian Jewish immigrants. Before writing as a career, she spent many hours in parks with her children, getting to know the women who would eventually become the focus of her literary output. In addition to writing, Paley also participated in many activist causes, such as the feminist and peace movements.

# Traveling

## Concept Vocabulary

As you perform your first read of "Traveling," you will encounter these words.

| absolute | sheer | adamant |
|---|---|---|

**Context Clues** If these words are unfamiliar to you, try using **context clues**—other words and phrases that appear in a text—to help you determine their meanings. There are various types of context clues that you may encounter as you read.

**Definition:** Her mood yesterday seemed **pensive,** or deeply thoughtful.

**Elaborating Details:** Many of their comments were **unintelligible**— because they mumbled or spoke too quietly to be heard.

**Contrast of Ideas and Topics:** Failing to display his usual **tenacity,** Patrick decided to abandon his science project.

Apply your knowledge of context clues and other vocabulary strategies to determine the meanings of unfamiliar words you encounter during your first read. Use a resource such as a dictionary or a thesaurus to verify the meanings you identify.

## First Read NONFICTION

Apply these strategies as you conduct your first read. You will have an opportunity to complete a close read after your first read.

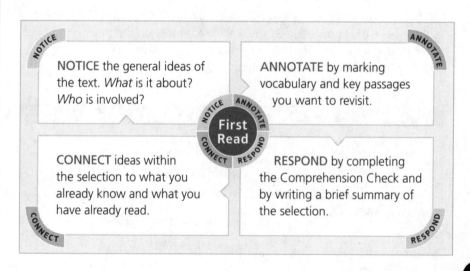

NOTICE the general ideas of the text. *What* is it about? *Who* is involved?

ANNOTATE by marking vocabulary and key passages you want to revisit.

CONNECT ideas within the selection to what you already know and what you have already read.

RESPOND by completing the Comprehension Check and by writing a brief summary of the selection.

### STANDARDS

**RI.9–10.10** By the end of grade 9, read and comprehend literary nonfiction in the grades 9–10 text complexity band proficiently, with scaffolding as needed at the high end of the range.

**L.9–10.4.a** Use context as a clue to the meaning of a word or phrase.

**L.9–10.4.d** Verify the preliminary determination of the meaning of a word or phrase.

# Traveling

*from* Just as I Thought

Grace Paley

## BACKGROUND

Some of the most visible Jim Crow laws (state laws establishing segregation between African American and white citizens) were those affecting public transportation. During the Civil Rights era, laws requiring African American travelers to sit in the back of buses became the focus of organized protest.

SCAN FOR MULTIMEDIA

1   My mother and sister were traveling south. The year was 1927. They had begun their journey in New York. They were going to visit my brother, who was studying in the South Medical College of Virginia. Their bus was an express and had stopped only in Philadelphia, Wilmington, and now Washington. Here, the darker people who had gotten on in Philadelphia or New York rose from their seats, put their bags and boxes together, and moved to the back of the bus. People who boarded in Washington knew where to seat themselves. My mother had heard that something like this would happen. My sister had heard of it, too. They had not lived in it. This reorganization of passengers by color happened in silence. My mother and sister remained in their seats, which were about three-quarters of the way back.

2   When everyone was settled, the bus driver began to collect tickets. My sister saw him coming. She pinched my mother: Ma! Look! Of

NOTES

course, my mother saw him, too. What frightened my sister was the quietness. The white people in front, the black people in back—silent.

3    The driver sighed, said, You can't sit here, ma'am. It's for them, waving over his shoulder at the Negroes, among whom they were now sitting. Move, please.

4    My mother said, No.

5    He said, You don't understand, ma'am. It's against the law. You have to move to the front.

6    My mother said, No.

7    When I first tried to write this scene, I imagined my mother saying, That's all right, mister, we're comfortable. I can't change my seat every minute. I read this invention to my sister. She said it was nothing like that. My mother did not try to be friendly or pretend innocence. While my sister trembled in the silence, my mother said, for the third time, quietly, No.

8    Somehow finally, they were in Richmond. There was my brother in school among so many American boys. After hugs and my mother's anxious looks at her young son, my sister said, Vic, you know what Mama did?

9    My brother remembers thinking, What? Oh! She wouldn't move? He had a classmate, a Jewish boy like himself, but from Virginia, who had had a public confrontation with a Negro man. He had punched that man hard, knocked him down. My brother couldn't believe it. He was stunned. He couldn't imagine a Jewish boy wanting to knock anyone down. He had never wanted to. But he thought, looking back, that he had been set down to work and study in a nearly foreign place and had to get used to it. Then he told me about the Second World War, when the disgrace of black soldiers being forced to sit behind white German POWs[1] shook him. Shamed him.

10    About fifteen years later, in 1943, in early summer, I rode the bus for about three days from New York to Miami Beach, where my husband in sweaty fatigues,[2] along with hundreds of other boys, was trudging up and down the streets and beaches to prepare themselves for war.

11    By late afternoon of the second long day, we were well into the South, beyond Richmond, maybe South Carolina or Georgia. My excitement about travel in the wide world was damaged a little by a sudden fear that I might not recognize Jess or he, me. We hadn't seen each other for two months. I took a photograph out of my pocket; yes, I would know him.

12    I had been sleeping waking reading writing dozing waking. So many hours, the movement of the passengers was something like a tide that sometimes ebbed[3] and now seemed to be noisily rising. I opened my eyes to the sound of new people brushing past my aisle seat. And looked up to see a colored woman holding a large sleeping

---

1. **POWs** abbreviation for "prisoners of war."
2. **fatigues** (fuh TEEGZ) *n.* uniforms soldiers wear while doing physical work.
3. **ebbed** *v.* flowed outward from the land, lowering the level of the water.

This photograph depicts how segregation looked on public buses in the Jim Crow South.

baby, who, with the heaviness of sleep, his arms so tight around her neck, seemed to be pulling her head down. I looked around and noticed that I was in the last white row. The press of travelers had made it impossible for her to move farther back. She seemed so tired and I had been sitting and sitting for a day and a half at least. Not thinking, or maybe refusing to think, I offered her my seat.

13    She looked to the right and left as well as she could. Softly she said, Oh no. I became fully awake. A white man was standing right beside her, but on the other side of the invisible **absolute** racial border. Of course, she couldn't accept my seat. Her sleeping child hung mercilessly from her neck. She shifted a little to balance the burden. She whispered to herself, Oh, I just don't know. So I said, Well, at least give me the baby. First, she turned, barely looking at the man beside her. He made no move. So, to my surprise, but obviously out of **sheer** exhaustion, she disengaged the child from her body and placed him on my lap. He was deep in child-sleep. He stirred, but not enough to bother himself or me. I liked holding him, aligning him along my twenty-year-old young woman's shape. I thought ahead to that holding, that breathing together that would happen in my life if this war would ever end.

14    I was so comfortable under his nice weight. I closed my eyes for a couple of minutes, but suddenly opened them to look up into the face of a white man talking. In a loud voice he addressed me: Lady, I wouldn't of touched that thing with a meat hook.

15    I thought, Oh, this world will end in ice. I could do nothing but look straight into his eyes. I did not look away from him. Then I held that boy a little tighter, kissed his curly head, pressed him even closer so that he began to squirm. So sleepy, he reshaped himself

NOTES

Mark context clues or indicate another strategy you used that helped you determine meaning.

**absolute** (AB suh loot) *adj.*

MEANING:

**sheer** (sheer) *adj.*

MEANING:

inside my arms. His mother tried to narrow herself away from that dangerous border, too frightened at first to move at all. After a couple of minutes, she leaned forward a little, placed her hand on the baby's head, and held it there until the next stop. I couldn't look up into her mother face.

16  I write this remembrance more than fifty years later. I look back at that mother and child. How young she is. Her hand on his head is quite small, though she tries by spreading her fingers wide to hide him from the white man. But the child I'm holding, his little face as he turns toward me, is the brown face of my own grandson, my daughter's boy, the open mouth of the sleeper, the full lips, the thick little body of a child who runs wildly from one end of the yard to the other, leaps from dangerous heights with certain experienced caution, muscling his body, his mind, for coming realities.

17  Of course, when my mother and sister returned from Richmond, the family at home wanted to know: How was Vic doing in school among all those gentiles?[4] Was the long bus ride hard, was the anti-Semitism really bad or just normal? What happened on the bus? I was probably present at that supper, the attentive listener and total forgetter of information that immediately started to form me.

18  Then last year, my sister, casting the net of old age (through which recent experience easily slips), brought up that old story. First I was angry. How come you never told me about your bus ride with Mama? I mean, really, so many years ago.

19  I don't know, she said, anyway you were only about four years old, and besides, maybe I did.

20  I asked my brother why we'd never talked about that day. He said he thought now that it had had a great effect on him; he had tried unraveling its meaning for years—then life family work happened. So I imagined him, a youngster really, a kid from the Bronx in Virginia in 1927; why, he was a stranger there himself.

21  In the next couple of weeks, we continued to talk about our mother, the way she was principled, **adamant**, and at the same time so shy. What else could we remember . . . Well, I said, I have a story about those buses, too. Then I told it to them: How it happened on just such a journey, when I was still quite young, that I first knew my grandson, first held him close, but could protect him for only about twenty minutes fifty years ago.  — 1997 ❧

---

4. **gentiles** (JEHN tylz)  *n.* people who are not Jewish.

Mark context clues or indicate another strategy you used that helped you determine meaning.

**adamant** (AD uh muhnt) *adj.*

MEANING:

# Comprehension Check

Complete the following items after you finish your first read. Review and clarify details with your group.

1. Why does the bus driver ask the author's mother and sister to change their seats?

2. On her way by bus to Miami, how does the author attempt to help one of her fellow passengers?

3. How does the author react when a white man addresses her in a loud voice?

4. About how much time separates the third part of the memoir from the second part?

5. In the last part of the memoir, what does the author come to realize about her mother?

6. 🗐 **Notebook** Confirm your understanding of "Traveling" by writing a timeline of events.

- - - - - - - - - - - - - - - - - - - - - - - - - - - - - - - - - - - - - - - - - - - - -

## RESEARCH

**Research to Clarify** Choose at least one unfamiliar detail from the text. Briefly research that detail. In what way does the information you learned shed light on an aspect of the memoir?

**Research to Explore** Choose something that interested you from the text, and formulate a research question.

TRAVELING

## Close Read the Text

With your group, revisit sections of the text you marked during your first read. **Annotate** details that you notice. What **questions** do you have? What can you **conclude**?

## Analyze the Text

**CITE TEXTUAL EVIDENCE**
to support your answers.

📔 **Notebook** Complete the activities.

1. **Review and Clarify** Reread paragraphs 1–4 of the selection. Discuss why you think that the author's mother refused to change her seat.

2. **Present and Discuss** Now work with your group to share the passages from the selection that you found especially important. Take turns presenting your passages. Discuss what you notice in the selection, the questions you asked, and the conclusions you reached.

3. **Essential Question:** *How can words inspire change?* What has this text taught you about the power of words to effect change?

---

LANGUAGE DEVELOPMENT

## Concept Vocabulary

| absolute | sheer | adamant |

**Why These Words?** The three concept vocabulary words are related. With your group, discuss the words, and determine what they have in common. How do these word choices enhance the impact of the text?

### Practice

📔 **Notebook** Confirm your understanding of these words by using them in sentences. Include context clues that hint at each word's meaning.

## Word Study

📔 **Notebook Etymology** A word's origins are called its **etymology**. You will find every word's etymology in its dictionary entry. For example, if you look up the word *adamant* in a dictionary, you will see that it comes from the Greek word *adamas*, which was formed in Greek from the prefix *a-*, meaning "not," and the root *-daman-*, meaning "to subdue" or "to tame." Thus, the original meaning of *adamant* was "untameable" or "unbreakable."

Use a good dictionary to research the etymology of the following words: *invention, disengaged, attentive,* and *remembrance*. Write each word's etymology, and then write its meaning.

---

**TIP**

**GROUP DISCUSSION**

Keep in mind that group members will have different interpretations of the text. These different perspectives will help you to learn from one another and clarify your own thoughts. Very often there is no single interpretation or conclusion.

---

### ⊞ WORD NETWORK

Add interesting words related to civil rights from the text to your Word Network.

---

### ▤ STANDARDS

**RI.9–10.3** Analyze how the author unfolds an analysis or series of ideas or events, including the order in which the points are made, how they are introduced and developed, and the connections that are drawn between them.

**RI.9–10.5** Analyze in detail how an author's ideas or claims are developed and refined by particular sentences, paragraphs, or larger portions of a text.

**L.9–10.4.b** Identify and correctly use patterns of word changes that indicate different meanings or parts of speech and continue to apply knowledge of Greek and Latin roots and affixes.

# Analyze Craft and Structure

**Author's Choices: Point of View and Structure** The **author's point of view** is the perspective from which events are related. In a memoir like "Traveling," the author's point of view can be compared to a physical position. For example, an author may look at events from a distance, reflecting on them from the perspective of an older, wiser self. Alternatively, a writer may choose a much closer perspective, perhaps attempting to recreate the feeling of a long ago moment.

The **structure** of a work is its overall shape, including the relationship of its different parts or sections to one another. In this memoir, Grace Paley employs a different point of view in each of the work's three sections. The point of view and the structure she uses are fully intertwined.

**TIP**

**GROUP DISCUSSION**
Members of your group may have responded in various ways to these questions. As you discuss your responses, be sure to allow group members to explain their thinking.

## Practice

**CITE TEXTUAL EVIDENCE** to support your answers.

📓 **Notebook** Work independently to answer these questions. Then, share your responses with the group.

1. Reread paragraphs 1–6. Did Paley herself live through the experience she describes in those paragraphs? Explain.

2. (a) What shift in author's perspective happens in paragraph 7? (b) How does this shift allow the author to clarify the memoir's opening scene? Explain.

3. (a) What is the author's perspective in the memoir's second section, paragraphs 1 through 15? (b) Explain the shift in perspective that happens at paragraph 16. (c) How does the perspective shift again in the final section, paragraphs 17–21?

4. Explain how the changes in perspective in each section of the memoir follow the chronology of the author's life.

5. Why do you think the author chose to structure the memoir as she did? What does the shifting chronology and point of view allow that a more basic story structure might not?

6. (a) "Traveling" is a work of nonfiction. Identify at least two sections in which Paley uses techniques commonly found in works of fiction. (b) How does her use of fictional elements add to or detract from the power of the story? Explain.

7. Does the fact that this is a true story make it more powerful or less powerful than a fictionalized version might be? Explain.

TRAVELING

# Author's Style

**Punctuation** In her memoir, Paley uses a nonstandard format for punctuating **dialogue.** In standard English, a speaker's exact words are enclosed by punctuation marks in a direct quotation. When Paley quotes the words spoken by her mother, her sister, her brother, and the bus driver in paragraphs 1–9 of "Traveling," however, she does not use quotation marks.

In addition, Paley occasionally omits punctuation marks, such as commas, that are standard for lists or series. For example, in paragraph 12, she writes this way about her bus ride to Miami: "I had been sleeping waking reading writing dozing waking."

## Read It

Work individually. For each quotation from dialogue in the left column of the chart, examine the context. Then, write a note in the right column that comments on Paley's use of direct speech without standard quotation marks. Include your thoughts about the effect of Paley's punctuation choices.

| QUOTATION | NOTES ON DIALOGUE |
|---|---|
| *The driver sighed, said, You can't sit here, ma'am. . . .*<br><br>(paragraph 3) | |
| *My mother said, No.*<br><br>(paragraph 6) | |
| *Softly she said, Oh no.*<br><br>(paragraph 13) | |
| *In a loud voice, he addressed me: Lady, I wouldn't of touched that thing with a meat hook.*<br><br>(paragraph 14) | |
| *I don't know, she said, anyway you were only about four years old, and besides, maybe I did.*<br><br>(paragraph 19) | |
| *Well, I said, I have a story about those buses, too.*<br><br>(paragraph 21) | |

## Write It

🗒 **Notebook** Write a brief anecdote about something that happened recently to you and someone you know, such as a friend or classmate. Include some direct speech without the use of quotation marks.

**:≡ STANDARDS**

**L.9–10.2** Demonstrate command of the conventions of standard English capitalization, punctuation, and spelling when writing.

## Speaking and Listening

### Assignment

In the memoir "Traveling," two generations of women make difficult choices in the segregated South. Each decision has the potential to produce both positive and negative results for all of those involved. With a group, plan a **debate** about a question raised by Paley's memoir. Choose from among these options for your debate.

☐ Was Paley's mother right to refuse to move to the front of the bus? Was her attitude helpful?

☐ Was Paley right to hold the baby on the bus to Miami? Was she standing up for her principles, or was she endangering the child?

☐ Which story—Paley's experience on a segregated bus or her mother's—best reflects the tensions caused by the belief in "separate but equal" treatment?

**Support Your Position** Working individually, identify at least three specific supporting reasons for your position as well as passages from Paley's memoir that you could use to support your position. Collect your ideas in the chart.

**STANDARDS**

**SL.9–10.1.c** Propel conversations by posing and responding to questions that relate the current discussion to broader themes or larger ideas; actively incorporate others into the discussion; and clarify, verify, or challenge ideas and conclusions.

| SUPPORTING REASONS | SUPPORTING PASSAGES OR OTHER EVIDENCE |
|---|---|
| 1 | |
| 2 | |
| 3 | |

**Come to a Consensus** Invite each member of your group to share their positions on the debate questions. Discuss one another's positions, asking questions and clarifying your responses. Work together to reach a conclusion that identifies the strongest argument. This conclusion may draw on points from several group members.

# Multimedia Presentation

**Assignment**

You have read stories, poems, and a speech that deal with the struggle for civil rights in the United States. Work with your group to develop a **multimedia presentation** that addresses this question:

> Why do words and actions in some time periods produce meaningful change—and in others do not?

## Plan With Your Group

**Analyze the Text** With your group, analyze each selection and consider what it suggests about the ways in which words and actions either did or could lead to change. Use the chart to record your notes.

| TITLE | WHAT ACTIONS OR WORDS LEAD TO CHANGE? |
|---|---|
| Remembering Civil Rights History, When "Words Meant Everything" | |
| For My People | |
| Incident | |
| Lessons of Dr. Martin Luther King, Jr. | |
| Traveling | |

**Gather Evidence and Media Examples** After your group has finished filling in the chart, list ways in which the words of civil rights leaders and political activists produced change in the 1960s. This will help you draw comparisons and contrasts with other eras, such as today. Consider using audio clips from speeches or news programs to emphasize points in your presentation. You may also include music and other sound effects. Allow each group member to make suggestions for how to integrate media that is appropriate for your audience and task.

**STANDARDS**

**SL.9–10.4** Present information, findings, and supporting evidence clearly, concisely, and logically such that listeners can follow the line of reasoning and the organization, development, substance, and style are appropriate to purpose, audience, and task.

**Organize Your Ideas** As a group, organize the script for your presentation. Decide who will do what job in each part of the presentation. Then, take note of when each section begins, and record what the speaker will say. Also, note when you will use excerpts from texts in this section, other sources, sound effects, and music.

| MULTIMEDIA PRESENTATION SCRIPT | | |
|---|---|---|
| | Media Cues | Script |
| Speaker 1 | | |
| Speaker 2 | | |
| Speaker 3 | | |

## Rehearse With Your Group

**Practice With Your Group** As you work through the script for your presentation, use this checklist to evaluate the effectiveness of your group's first run-through. Then, use your evaluation and the instruction here to guide your revision.

| CONTENT | USE OF MEDIA | PRESENTATION TECHNIQUES |
|---|---|---|
| ☐ The presentation has a clear purpose and focus. | ☐ The media support and enhance understanding of the topic. | ☐ Media are audible. |
| ☐ Main ideas are supported with evidence from the texts and from research. | ☐ Media are used evenly throughout the report. | ☐ Transitions are smooth. |
| | ☐ Equipment functions properly. | ☐ Each speaker speaks clearly and with conviction. |

**Fine-Tune the Content** Work with your group to identify key points that are not clear to listeners. Add material to support your points or find another way to word these ideas. Make sure that you address the main prompt by offering an analysis of why some eras produce meaningful change, while others do not.

**Improve Your Use of Media** Review all audio clips, music, and sound effects to make sure they add interest and help create a cohesive presentation. If a sound cue is not clearly related to the presentation, replace it with a more relevant item.

## Present and Evaluate

When you present, be sure that each member has taken into account each of the checklist items. As you listen to other groups' presentations, evaluate how well they meet the items on checklist.

### ▦ STANDARDS

**SL.9–10.5** Make strategic use of digital media in presentations to enhance understanding of findings, reasoning, and evidence and to add interest.

**SL.9–10.6** Adapt speech to a variety of contexts and tasks, demonstrating command of formal English when indicated or appropriate.

ESSENTIAL QUESTION:

# How can words inspire change?

Words, as well as actions, were crucial to the fight for civil rights. In this section, you will complete your study of the literature of civil rights by exploring an additional selection related to the topic. You'll then share what you learn with classmates. To choose a text, follow these steps.

**Look Back** Think about the selections you have already studied. What more do you want to know about the topic of civil rights?

**Look Ahead** Preview the texts by reading the descriptions. Which one seems most interesting and appealing to you?

**Look Inside** Take a few minutes to scan the text you chose. Choose a different one if this text doesn't meet your needs.

## Independent Learning Strategies

Throughout your life, in school, in your community, and in your career, you will need to rely on yourself to learn and work on your own. Review these strategies and the actions you can take to practice them during Independent Learning. Add ideas of your own for each category.

| STRATEGY | ACTION PLAN |
|---|---|
| Create a schedule | • Understand your goals and deadlines.<br>• Make a plan for what to do each day.<br><br>• |
| Practice what you've learned | • Use first-read and close-read strategies to deepen your understanding.<br>• After you read, evaluate the usefulness of the evidence to help you understand the topic.<br>• Consider the quality and reliability of the source.<br><br>• |
| Take notes | • Record important ideas and information.<br>• Review your notes before preparing to share with a group.<br><br>• |

SCAN FOR MULTIMEDIA

# CONTENTS

Choose one selection. Selections are available online only.

 SCAN FOR MULTIMEDIA

## First-Read Guide

Use this page to record your first-read ideas.

🔧 **Tool Kit**
First-Read Guide and
Model Annotation

Selection Title: _____

**NOTICE** new information or ideas you learn about the unit topic as you first read this text.

**ANNOTATE** by marking vocabulary and key passages you want to revisit.

**First Read**

NOTICE ANNOTATE CONNECT RESPOND

**CONNECT** ideas within the selection to other knowledge and the selections you have read.

**RESPOND** by writing a brief summary of the selection.

**STANDARD**

**Anchor Reading Standard 10** Read and comprehend complex literary and informational texts independently and proficiently.

# Close-Read Guide

Use this page to record your close-read ideas.

Selection Title: _____

🔧 **Tool Kit**
Close-Read Guide and
Model Annotation

## Close Read the Text

Revisit sections of the text you marked during your first read. Read these sections closely and **annotate** what you notice. Ask yourself **questions** about the text. What can you **conclude?** Write down your ideas.

ANNOTATE QUESTION
**Close Read**
CONCLUDE

## Analyze the Text

Think about the author's choices of patterns, structure, techniques, and ideas included in the text. Select one, and record your thoughts about what this choice conveys.

## QuickWrite

Pick a paragraph from the text that grabbed your interest. Explain the power of this passage.

**:≡ STANDARD**
**Anchor Reading Standard 10** Read and comprehend complex literary and informational texts independently and proficiently.

# Share Your Independent Learning

## Prepare to Share

How can words inspire change?

Even when you read or learn you learn something independently, you can continue to grow by sharing what you've learned with others. Reflect on the text you explored independently and write notes about its connection to the unit. In your notes, consider why this text belongs in this unit.

## Learn From Your Classmates

**Discuss It** Share your ideas about the text you explored on your own. As you talk with your classmates, jot down ideas that you learn from them.

## Reflect

Review your notes and underline the most important insight you gained from these writing and discussion activities. Explain how this idea adds to your understanding of the literature of civil rights.

# Review Evidence for an Informative Essay

At the beginning of the unit, you expressed your ideas in response to the following direction:

Explain how words have the power to provoke, calm, or inspire.

## ✏ EVIDENCE LOG

Review your Evidence Log and your QuickWrite from the beginning of the unit. Did you learn anything new?

### NOTES

Identify at least three pieces of information that interested you about the Civil Rights movement and its literature.

1.

2.

3.

Identify a real-life experience that illustrates one of your revised ideas about literature and the Civil Rights movement:

_____

Develop your thoughts into a topic sentence for an informative essay. Complete this sentence starter:
*I learned a great deal about the literature of civil rights when*

_____

**Evaluate Your Evidence** Consider the information you learned. Did the texts you read expand your knowledge? If not, make a plan.

☐ Do more research

☐ Reread a selection

☐ Talk with my classmates

☐ Ask an expert

☐ Other:_____

**≡ STANDARDS**
**W.9–10.2** Write informative/
explanatory texts to examine
and convey ideas, concepts, and
information clearly and accurately
through the effective selection,
organization, and analysis of content.

SOURCES

• WHOLE-CLASS SELECTIONS

• SMALL-GROUP SELECTIONS

• INDEPENDENT LEARNING

## WORD NETWORK

As you write and revise your informative essay, use your Word Network to help vary your word choices.

## STANDARDS

**W.9–10.2.a** Introduce a topic or thesis statement; organize complex ideas, concepts, and information to make important connections and distinctions; include formatting, graphics, and multimedia when useful to aiding comprehension.

**W.9–10.2.b** Develop a topic with well-chosen, relevant, and sufficient facts, extended definitions, concrete details, quotations, or other information and examples appropriate to the audience's knowledge of the topic.

**W.9–10.8** Gather relevant information from multiple authoritative print and digital sources, using advanced searches effectively; assess the usefulness of each source in answering the research question; integrate information into the text selectively to maintain the flow of ideas, avoiding plagiarism and following a standard format for citation including footnotes and endnotes.

**W.9–10.9** Draw evidence from literary or informational texts to support analysis, reflection, and research.

**W.9–10.10** Write routinely over extended time frames and shorter time frames for a range of tasks, purposes, and audiences.

## PART 1

# Writing to Sources: Informative Essay

In this unit, you read about various characters, both real and fictional, who are a part of the struggle for civil rights. Some used words to inspire others and share their own experiences, while others used words as a call to action.

**Assignment**

Write an **informative essay** on the following:

> Explain how words have the power to provoke, calm, or inspire.

Use evidence from at least three of the selections you read and researched in this unit to express and support your thesis. If time permits, do outside research, using credible sources, to support your ideas with examples, facts, and quotations. Ensure that your ideas are fully supported, that you use a formal, objective tone, and that your organization is logical and coherent.

**Reread the Assignment** Review the assignment to be sure you fully understand it. The task may reference some of the academic words presented at the beginning of the unit. Be sure you understand each of the words given below in order to complete the assignment correctly.

**Academic Vocabulary**

| | | |
|---|---|---|
| disrupt | coherent | notation |
| aggregate | express | |

**Review the Elements of an Informational Text** Before you begin writing, read the Informational Text Rubric. Once you have completed your first draft, check it against the rubric. If one or more of the elements are missing or not as strong as they could be, revise your essay to add or strengthen those components.

# Informative Text Rubric

| | Focus and Organization | Evidence and Elaboration | Conventions |
|---|---|---|---|
| **4** | The introduction engages the reader and states a thesis in a compelling way.<br><br>The informative essay includes a clear introduction, body, and conclusion.<br><br>The essay uses facts and evidence from a variety of reliable sources.<br><br>The conclusion summarizes ideas and offers fresh insight into the thesis. | The essay includes specific reasons, details, facts, and quotations from selections and outside resources to support thesis.<br><br>The tone of the essay is always formal and objective.<br><br>The language is always precise and appropriate for the audience and purpose. | The essay consistently uses standard English conventions of usage and mechanics. |
| **3** | The introduction engages the reader and sets forth the thesis.<br><br>The essay includes an introduction, body, and conclusion.<br><br>The essay uses facts and evidence from a variety of sources.<br><br>The conclusion summarizes ideas. | The essay includes some specific reasons, details, facts, and quotations from selections and outside resources to support the thesis.<br><br>The tone of the essay is mostly formal and objective.<br><br>The language is generally precise and appropriate for the audience and purpose. | The essay demonstrates general accuracy in standard English conventions of usage and mechanics. |
| **2** | The introduction sets forth the thesis.<br><br>The essay includes an introduction, body, and conclusion, but one or more parts is weak.<br><br>The essay uses facts and evidence from a few sources.<br><br>The conclusion partially summarizes ideas. | The essay includes a few reasons, details, facts, and quotations from selections and outside resources to support the thesis.<br><br>The tone of the essay is occasionally formal and objective.<br><br>The language is somewhat precise and appropriate for the audience and purpose. | The essay demonstrates some accuracy in standard English conventions of usage and mechanics. |
| **1** | The introduction does not state the thesis clearly.<br><br>The essay does not include an introduction, body, and conclusion.<br><br>The essay does not use a variety of facts and evidence.<br><br>The conclusion does not summarize ideas. | Reliable and relevant evidence is not included.<br><br>The tone of the essay is not objective or formal.<br><br>The language used is imprecise and not appropriate for the audience and purpose. | The essay contains mistakes in standard English conventions of usage and mechanics. |

## PART 2

# Speaking and Listening: Multimedia Presentation

**STANDARDS**

**SL.9–10.4** Present information, findings, and supporting evidence clearly, concisely, and logically such that listeners can follow the line of reasoning and the organization, development, substance, and style are appropriate to purpose, audience, and task.

**SL.9–10.5** Make strategic use of digital media in presentations to enhance understanding of findings, reasoning, and evidence and to add interest.

**SL.9–10.6** Adapt speech to a variety of contexts and tasks, demonstrating command of formal English when indicated or appropriate.

**Assignment**

After completing the final draft of your informative essay, use it as the foundation for a three-to five-minute **multimedia presentation**.

Do not simply read your essay aloud. Instead, take the following steps to make your presentation lively and engaging.

- Go back to your essay and annotate the most important ideas and details.
- Choose audio clips and visuals to support your presentation.
- Deliver your presentation with conviction, maintaining eye contact with your audience.

**Review the Multimedia Presentation Rubric** The criteria by which your multimedia presentation will be evaluated appear in the rubric below. Review these criteria before presenting to ensure that you are prepared.

| | Content | Use of Media | Presentation Techniques |
|---|---|---|---|
| 3 | The introduction engages the audience and establishes the thesis in a compelling way. | The speaker focuses the right amount of time on each part. | The speaker maintains eye contact and speaks effectively. |
| | The presentation provides strong, valid reasons and evidence that support the thesis. | The media add interest to the presentation. | Media are audible and visible. |
| | The media support the thesis. | Media are used evenly throughout the presentation. | The speaker presents with strong conviction and energy. |
| | The conclusion restates thesis and offers fresh insight. | Listeners can follow presentation. | |
| 2 | The introduction sets out a thesis. | The speaker focuses the right amount of time on most parts. | The speaker mostly maintains eye contact and speaks effectively sometimes. |
| | The presentation includes some valid reasons and evidence that support the thesis. | Media add some interest to the presentation. | Media are mostly audible and visible. |
| | The media offer some support for the thesis. | Media are used in some parts of the presentation but not others. | The speaker presents with some level of conviction and energy. |
| | The conclusion offers some insight into the thesis. | Listeners can mostly follow presentation. | |
| 1 | The introduction does not set out a thesis. | The speaker spends too much time on some parts of the presentation, and too little on others. | The speaker does not maintain eye contact or speak effectively. |
| | The presentation does not include reasons or evidence to support the thesis. | Media do not add interest to the presentation. | Media are not visible or audible. |
| | The media do not support the thesis. | Media are used poorly throughout the presentation. | The speaker presents with little conviction or energy. |
| | The conclusion does not restate the thesis. | Listeners cannot follow presentation. | |

## Reflect on the Unit

Now that you've completed the unit, take a few moments to reflect on your learning. Use the questions below to think about where you succeeded, what skills and strategies helped you, and where you can continue to grow in the future.

### Reflect on the Unit Goals

Look back at the goals at the beginning of the unit. Use a different colored pen to rate yourself again. Think about readings and activities that contributed the most to the growth of your understanding. Record your thoughts.

### Reflect on the Learning Strategies

**Discuss It** Write a reflection on whether you were able to improve your learning based on your Action Plans. Think about what worked, what didn't, and what you might do to keep working on these strategies. Record your ideas before a class discussion.

### Reflect on the Text

Choose a selection that you found challenging and explain what made it difficult.

Explain something that surprised you about a text in the unit.

Which activity taught you the most about the literature of civil rights? What did you learn?

SCAN FOR
MULTIMEDIA

# RESOURCES

## CONTENTS

## Marking the Text: Strategies and Tips for Annotation

When you close read a text, you read for comprehension and then reread to unlock layers of meaning and to analyze a writer's style and techniques. Marking a text as you read it enables you to participate more fully in the close-reading process.

Following are some strategies for text mark-ups, along with samples of how the strategies can be applied. These mark-ups are suggestions; you and your teacher may want to use other mark-up strategies.

| | |
|---|---|
| * | Key Idea |
| ! | I love it! |
| ? | I have questions |
| ◯ | Unfamiliar or important word |
| ---- | Context Clues |

### Suggested Mark-Up Notations

| WHAT I NOTICE | HOW TO MARK UP | QUESTIONS TO ASK |
|---|---|---|
| Key Ideas and Details | • Highlight key ideas or claims.<br>• Underline supporting details or evidence. | • What does the text say? What does it leave unsaid?<br>• What inferences do you need to make?<br>• What details lead you to make your inferences? |
| Word Choice | • Circle unfamiliar words.<br>• Put a dotted line under context clues, if any exist.<br>• Put an exclamation point beside especially rich or poetic passages. | • What inferences about word meaning can you make?<br>• What tone and mood are created by word choice?<br>• What alternate word choices might the author have made? |
| Text Structure | • Highlight passages that show key details supporting the main idea.<br>• Use arrows to indicate how sentences and paragraphs work together to build ideas.<br>• Use a right-facing arrow to indicate foreshadowing.<br>• Use a left-facing arrow to indicate flashback. | • Is the text logically structured?<br>• What emotional impact do the structural choices create? |
| Author's Craft | • Circle or highlight instances of repetition, either of words, phrases, consonants, or vowel sounds.<br>• Mark rhythmic beats in poetry using checkmarks and slashes.<br>• Underline instances of symbolism or figurative language. | • Does the author's style enrich or detract from the reading experience?<br>• What levels of meaning are created by the author's techniques? |

TOOL KIT: CLOSE READING

TOOL KIT: CLOSE READING

**First Read**
NOTICE · ANNOTATE · RESPOND · CONNECT

\* Key Idea

! I love it!

? I have questions

◯ Unfamiliar or important word

---- Context Clues

NOTES

In a first read, work to get a sense of the main idea of a text. Look for key details and ideas that help you understand what the author conveys to you. Mark passages which prompt a strong response from you.

Here is how one reader marked up this text.

MODEL

INFORMATIONAL TEXT

# *from* Classifying the Stars

## Cecilia H. Payne

\*

1   Sunlight and starlight are composed of waves of various lengths, which the eye, even aided by a telescope, is unable to separate. We must use more than a telescope. In order to sort out the component colors, the light must be dispersed by a prism, or split up by some other means. For instance, sunbeams passing through rain drops, are transformed into the myriad-tinted rainbow. The familiar rainbow spanning the sky is Nature's most glorious demonstration that light is composed of many colors.

\*

2   The very beginning of our knowledge of the nature of a star dates back to 1672, when Isaac Newton gave to the world the results of his experiments on passing sunlight through a prism. To describe the beautiful band of rainbow tints, produced when sunlight was dispersed by his three-cornered piece of glass, he took from the Latin the word *spectrum*, meaning an appearance. The rainbow is the spectrum of the Sun. . . .

\*

3   In 1814, more than a century after Newton, the spectrum of the Sun was obtained in such purity that an amazing detail was seen and studied by the German optician, Fraunhofer. He saw that the multiple spectral tints, ranging from delicate violet to deep red, were crossed by hundreds of fine dark lines. In other words, there were narrow gaps in the spectrum where certain shades were wholly blotted out. We must remember that the word spectrum is applied not only to sunlight, but also to the light of any glowing substance when its rays are sorted out by a prism or a grating.

# First-Read Guide

**Use this page to record your first-read ideas.**

Selection Title: _____Classifying the Stars_____

**NOTICE**

**NOTICE** new information or ideas you learned about the unit topic as you first read this text.

Light = different waves of colors. (Spectrum)

Newton - the first person to observe these waves using a prism.

Faunhofer saw gaps in the spectrum.

**ANNOTATE**

**ANNOTATE** by marking vocabulary and key passages you want to revisit.

Vocabulary
myriad
grating
component colors

Different light types = different lengths

Isaac Newton also worked theories of gravity.

Multiple spectral tints? "colors of various appearance"

Key Passage:
Paragraph 3 shows that Fraunhofer discovered more about the nature of light spectrums: he saw the spaces in between the tints.

**First Read**
NOTICE ANNOTATE CONNECT RESPOND

**CONNECT**

**CONNECT** ideas within the selection to other knowledge and the selections you have read.

I remember learning about prisms in science class.

Double rainbows! My favorite. How are they made?

**RESPOND**

**RESPOND** by writing a brief summary of the selection.

Science allows us to see things not visible to the naked eye. What we see as sunlight is really a spectrum of colors. By using tools, such as prisms, we can see the components of sunlight and other light. They appear as single colors or as multiple colors separated by gaps of no color. White light contains a rainbow of colors.

# CLOSE READING

**Close Read**

ANNOTATE QUESTION CONCLUDE

\* Key Idea

! I love it!

? I have questions

◯ Unfamiliar or important word

---- Context Clues

In a close read, go back into the text to study it in greater detail. Take the time to analyze not only the author's ideas but the way that those ideas are conveyed. Consider the genre of the text, the author's word choice, the writer's unique style, and the message of the text.

Here is how one reader close read this text.

**MODEL**

**INFORMATIONAL TEXT**

## *from* Classifying the Stars

### Cecilia H. Payne

**NOTES**

explanation of sunlight and starlight

What is light and where do the colors come from?

1 \* Sunlight and starlight are composed of waves of various lengths, which the eye, even aided by a telescope, is unable to separate. We must use more than a telescope. In order to sort out the component colors, the light must be dispersed by a prism, or split up by some other means. For instance, sunbeams passing through rain drops, are transformed into the myriad-tinted rainbow. The familiar rainbow spanning the sky is Nature's most glorious demonstration that light is composed of many colors.

This paragraph is about Newton and the prism.

What discoveries helped us understand light?

2 \* The very beginning of our knowledge of the nature of a star dates back to 1672, when Isaac Newton gave to the world the results of his experiments on passing sunlight through a prism. To describe the beautiful band of rainbow tints, produced when sunlight was dispersed by his three-cornered piece of glass, he took from the Latin the word *spectrum*, meaning an appearance. The rainbow is the spectrum of the Sun. . . .

Fraunhofer and gaps in spectrum

3 \* In 1814, more than a century after Newton, the spectrum of the Sun was obtained in such purity that an amazing detail was seen and studied by the German optician, Fraunhofer. He saw that the multiple spectral tints, ranging from delicate violet to deep red, were crossed by hundreds of fine dark lines. In other words, there were narrow gaps in the spectrum where certain shades were wholly blotted out. We must remember that the word spectrum is applied not only to sunlight, but also to the light of any glowing substance when its rays are sorted out by a prism or a grating.

# Close-Read Guide

Use this page to record your close-read ideas.

Selection Title: ___Classifying the Stars___

You can use the Close-Read Guide to help you dig deeper into the text. Here is how a reader completed a Close-Read Guide.

## Close Read the Text

Revisit sections of the text you marked during your first read. Read these sections closely and **annotate** what you notice. Ask yourself **questions** about the text. What can you **conclude?** Write down your ideas.

Paragraph 3: Light is composed of waves of various lengths. Prisms let us see different colors in light. This is called the spectrum. Fraunhofer proved that there are gaps in the spectrum, where certain shades are blotted out.

More than one researcher studied this and each built off the ideas that were already discovered.

## Analyze the Text

Think about the author's choices of patterns, structure, techniques, and ideas included in the text. Select one, and record your thoughts about what this choice conveys.

The author showed the development of human knowledge of the spectrum chronologically. Helped me see how ideas were built upon earlier understandings. Used dates and "more than a century after Newton" to show time.

## QuickWrite

Pick a paragraph from the text that grabbed your interest. Explain the power of this passage.

The first paragraph grabbed my attention, specifically the sentence "The familiar rainbow spanning the sky is Nature's most glorious demonstration that light is composed of many colors." The paragraph began as a straightforward scientific explanation. When I read the word "glorious," I had to stop and deeply consider what was being said. It is a word loaded with personal feelings. With that one word, the author let the reader know what was important to her.

## Argument

When you think of the word *argument*, you might think of a disagreement between two people, but an argument is more than that. An argument is a logical way of presenting a belief, conclusion, or stance. A good argument is supported with reasoning and evidence.

Argument writing can be used for many purposes, such as to change a reader's point of view or opinion or to bring about an action or a response from a reader.

### Elements of an Argumentative Text

An **argument** is a logical way of presenting a viewpoint, belief, or stand on an issue. A well-written argument may convince the reader, change the reader's mind, or motivate the reader to take a certain action.

An effective argument contains these elements:

- a precise claim
- consideration of counterclaims, or opposing positions, and a discussion of their strengths and weaknesses
- logical organization that makes clear connections among claim, counterclaim, reasons, and evidence
- valid reasoning and evidence
- a concluding statement or section that logically completes the argument
- formal and objective language and tone
- error-free grammar, including accurate use of transitions

ARGUMENT: SCORE 1

## Selfies, Photoshop, and You: Superficial Image Culture is Hurtful for Teens

Selfies are kind of cool, also kind of annoying, and some say they might be bad for you if you take too many. Selfies of celebrities and ordinary people are everywhere. People always try to smile and look good, and they take a lot of selfies when they are somewhere special, like at the zoo or at a fair. Some people spend so much time taking selfies they forget to just go ahead and have fun.

TV and other media are full of beautiful people. Looking at all those model's and celebrities can make kids feel bad about their one bodies, even when they are actually totally normal and fine and beautiful they way they are. Kids start to think they should look like the folks on TV which is mostly impossible. It's also a cheat because lots of the photos we see of celebrities and model's have been edited so they look even better.

Selfies make people feel even worse about the way they look. They're always comparing themselves and feeling that maybe they aren't as good as they should be. Selfies can make teens feel bad about their faces and bodies, and the stuff they are doing every day.

Regular people edit and change things before they post their pictures. That means, the pictures are kind of fake and it's impossible to compete with something that is fake. It's sad to think that teens can start to hate themselves and feel depressed just because they don't and can't look like a faked photo of a movie star.

Kids and teens post selfies to hear what others think about them, to show off, and to see how they compare with others. It can be kind of full of pressure always having to look great and smile. Even if you get positive comments about a selfie that you post, and everyone says you look beautiful, that feeling only lasts for a few minutes. After all, what you look like is just something on the outside. What's more important is what you are on the inside and what you do.

It's great for those few minutes, but then what? If you keep posting, people will not want to keep writing nice comments. Kids and teens should take a break from posting selfies all the time. It's better to go out and have fun rather than always keeping on posting selfies.

The writer does not clearly state the claim in the introduction.

The argument contains mistakes in standard English conventions of usage and mechanics.

The tone of the argument is informal, and the vocabulary is limited or ineffective.

The writer does not address counterclaims.

The conclusion does not restate any information that is important.

TOOL KIT: WRITING

# WRITING

MODEL

ARGUMENT: SCORE 2

## Selfies and You: Superficial Image Culture is Hurtful for Teens

Selfies are bad for teens and everyone else. Selfies of celebrities and ordinary people are everywhere. It seems like taking and posting selfies is not such a big deal and not harmful, but that's not really true. Actually, taking too many selfies can be really bad.

TV and other media are full of beautiful people. Looking at all those models and celebrities can make kids feel bad about their own bodies. Kids start to think they should look like the folks on TV which is mostly impossible. It's also a cheat because lots of the photos we see of celebrities and model's have been edited so they look even better.

Regular people use image editing software as well. They edit and change things before they post their pictures. That means, the pictures are kind of fake and it's impossible to compete with something that is fake.

Selfies make people feel even worse about the way they look. They're always comparing themselves and feeling that maybe they aren't as good as they should be. Selfies can make teens feel bad about their faces and bodies.

But maybe selfies are just a fun way to stay in touch, but that's not really how people use selfies, I don't think. Kids and teens post selfies show off. It can be full of pressure always having to look great and smile.

Sometimes posting a selfie can make you feel good if it gets lots of 'likes' and positive comments. But you can never tell. Someone also might say something mean. Also, even if you get positive comments and everyone says you look beautiful, that feeling only lasts for a few minutes. It's great for those few minutes, but then what? If you keep posting and posting, people will not want to keep writing nice comments.

The selfie culture today is just too much. Kids and teens can't be happy when they are always comparing themselves and worrying about what they look like. It's better to go out and have fun rather than always keeping on posting selfies.

The introduction establishes the writer's claim.

The tone of the argument is occasionally formal and objective.

The writer briefly acknowledges one counterclaim.

The conclusion offers some insight into the claim and restates information.

## ARGUMENT: SCORE 3

### Selfies and You: Superficial Image Culture is Hurtful for Teens

Selfies are everywhere. Check out any social media site and you'll see an endless parade of perfect smiles on both celebrities and ordinary people. It may seem as if this flood of seflies is harmless, but sadly that is not true. Selfies promote a superficial image culture that is harmful and dangerous for teens.

The problem starts with the unrealistic: idealized images teens are exposed to in the media. Most models and celebrities are impossibly beautiful and thin. Even young children can feel that there is something wrong with they way they look. According to one research group, more than half of girls and one third of boys ages 6-8 feel their ideal body is thinner than their current body weight. Negative body image can result in serious physical and mental health problems.

When teens look at selfies they automatically make comparisons with the idealized images they have in their minds. This can make them feel inadequate and sad about themselves, their bodies, and their lives. And with social media sites accessible 24/7, it's difficult to get a break from the constant comparisons, competition, and judgment.

Image editing software plays a role too. A recent study carried out by the Renfrew Center Foundation said that about 50% of people edit pictures of themselves before posting. They take away blemishes, change skin tone, maybe even make themselves look thinner. And why not? Even the photos of models and celebrities are heavily edited. Teens can start to hate themselves and feel depressed just because they don't and can't look like a faked photo of a movie star.

Some say that posting a selfie is like sending a postcard to your friends and family, but that's not how selfies are used: teens post selfies to get feedback, to compare themselves with others, and to present a false image to the world. There is a lot of pressure to look great and appear happy.

It's true that sometimes a selfie posted on social media gets 'likes' and positive comments that can make a person feel pretty. However, the boost you get from feeling pretty for five minutes doesn't last.

A million selfies are posted every day—and that's way too many. Selfies promote a superficial image culture that is harmful to teens. In the end, the selfie life is not a healthy way to have fun. Let's hope the fad will fade.

---

The argument's claim is clearly stated.

The tone of the argument is mostly formal and objective.

The writer includes reasons and evidence that address and support claims.

The ideas progress logically, and the writer includes sentence transitions that connect the reader to the argument.

The conclusion restates important information.

TOOL KIT: WRITING

# WRITING

MODEL

ARGUMENT: SCORE 4

## Selfies and You: Superficial Image Culture Is Hurtful for Teens

*Smile, Snap, Edit, Post—Repeat!* That's the selfie life, and it's everywhere. A million selfies are posted every day. But this **tsunami** of self-portraits is not as harmless as it appears. Selfies promote a superficial image culture that is hurtful and dangerous for teens.

It all starts with the unrealistic: When teens look at selfies they automatically make comparisons with the idealized images they have in their minds. This can cause them to feel inadequate and sad about themselves, their bodies, and their lives. According to Common Sense Media, more than half of girls and one third of boys ages 6-8 feel their ideal body is thinner than their current body weight. Negative body image can result in serious physical and mental health problems such as anorexia and other eating disorders.

To make matter worse, many or even most selfies have been edited. A recent study carried out by the Renfrew Center Foundation concluded that about 50% of people edit their own images before posting. They use image-editing software to take away blemishes, change skin tone, maybe even make themselves look thinner. And why not? Even the photos of models and celebrities are heavily edited.

Some say that selfies are a harmless and enjoyable way to communicate: posting a selfie is like sending a postcard to your friends and family, inviting them to share in your fun. But that is not how selfies are used: teens post selfies to get feedback, to compare themselves with others, and to present an (often false) image to the world.

It's true that posting a selfie on social media can generate 'likes' and positive comments that can make a person feel good.

However, the boost one gets from feeling pretty for five minutes is like junk food: it tastes good but it is not nourishing.

The selfie culture that is the norm today is out of control. The superficial image culture promoted by selfies is probably behind the recent 20 percent increase in plastic surgery—something with its own dangers and drawbacks. Let's hope the fad will fade, and look forward to a future where people are too busy enjoying life to spend so much time taking, editing, and posting pictures of themselves.

---

The introduction is engaging, and the writer's claim is clearly stated at the end of the paragraph.

The writer has included a variety of sentence transitions such as "To make matters worse..." "Some say..." "Another claim..." "It is true that..."

The sources of evidence are specific and contain relevant information.

The writer clearly acknowledges counterclaims.

The conclusion offers fresh insights into the claim.

# Argument Rubric

| | Focus and Organization | Evidence and Elaboration | Conventions |
|---|---|---|---|
| 4 | The introduction engages the reader and establishes a claim in a compelling way. The argument includes valid reasons and evidence that address and support the claim while clearly acknowledging counterclaims. The ideas progress logically, and transitions make connections among ideas clear. The conclusion offers fresh insight into the claim. | The sources of evidence are comprehensive and specific and contain relevant information. The tone of the argument is always formal and objective. The vocabulary is always appropriate for the audience and purpose. | The argument intentionally uses standard English conventions of usage and mechanics. |
| 3 | The introduction engages the reader and establishes the claim. The argument includes reasons and evidence that address and support my claim while acknowledging counterclaims. The ideas progress logically, and some transitions are used to help make connections among ideas clear. The conclusion restates the claim and important information. | The sources of evidence contain relevant information. The tone of the argument is mostly formal and objective. The vocabulary is generally appropriate for the audience and purpose. | The argument demonstrates general accuracy in standard English conventions of usage and mechanics. |
| 2 | The introduction establishes a claim. The argument includes some reasons and evidence that address and support the claim while briefly acknowledging counterclaims. The ideas progress somewhat logically. A few sentence transitions are used that connect readers to the argument. The conclusion offers some insight into the claim and restates information. | The sources of evidence contain some relevant information. The tone of the argument is occasionally formal and objective. The vocabulary is somewhat appropriate for the audience and purpose. | The argument demonstrates some accuracy in standard English conventions of usage and mechanics. |
| 1 | The introduction does not clearly state the claim. The argument does not include reasons or evidence for the claim. No counterclaims are acknowledged. The ideas do not progress logically. Transitions are not included to connect ideas. The conclusion does not restate any information that is important. | Reliable and relevant evidence is not included. The vocabulary used is limited or ineffective. The tone of the argument is not objective or formal. | The argument contains mistakes in standard English conventions of usage and mechanics. |

# WRITING

## Informative/Explanatory Texts

Informative and explanatory writing should rely on facts to inform or explain. Informative writing serves several purposes: to increase readers' knowledge of a subject, to help readers better understand a procedure or process, or to provide readers with an enhanced comprehension of a concept. It should also feature a clear introduction, body, and conclusion.

### Elements of Informative/Explanatory Texts

**Informative/explanatory texts** present facts, details, data, and other kinds of evidence to give information about a topic. Readers turn to informational and explanatory texts when they wish to learn about a specific idea, concept, or subject area, or if they want to learn how to do something.

An effective informative/explanatory text contains these elements:

- a topic sentence or thesis statement that introduces the concept or subject
- relevant facts, examples, and details that expand upon a topic
- definitions, quotations, and/or graphics that support the information given
- headings (if desired) to separate sections of the essay
- a structure that presents information in a direct, clear manner
- clear transitions that link sections of the essay
- precise words and technical vocabulary where appropriate
- formal and object language and tone
- a conclusion that supports the information given and provides fresh insights

## *Moai:* The Giant Statues of Easter Island

Easter Island is a tiny Island. It's far out in the middle of the pacific ocean, 2200 miles off the coast. The closest country is Chile, in south america. The nearest island where people live is called Pitcairn, and that's about 1,300 miles away, and only about 60 people live so their most of the time. Easter island is much bigger than Pitcairn, and lots more people live there now—about 5,000-6,000. Although in the past there were times when only about 111 people lived there.

Even if you don't really know what it is, you've probably seen pictures of the easter island Statues. You'd recognize one if you saw it, with big heads and no smiles. Their lots of them on the island. Almost 900 of them. But some were never finished They're called *moai.* They are all different sizes. All the sizes together average out to about 13 feet tall and 14 tons of heavy.

Scientists know that Polynesians settled Easter Island (it's also called Rapa Nui, and the people are called the Rapanui people). Polynesians were very good at boats. And they went big distances across the Pacific. When these Polynesians arrived was probably 300, but it was probably 900 or 1200.

The island was covered with forests. They can tell by looking at pollin in lakes. The Rapanui people cut trees, to build houses. They didn't know that they wood run out of wood). They also carved *moai.*

The *moai* were made for important chiefs. They were made with only stone tools. They have large heads and narrow bodies. No 2 are the same. Although they look the same as far as their faces are concerned. They are very big and impressive and special.

Over the years, many of the statues were tipped over and broken. But some years ago scientists began to fix some of them and stand them up again. They look more better like that. The ones that have been fixed up are probably the ones you remember seeing in photographs.

The essay does not include a thesis statement.

The writer includes many details that are not relevant to the topic of the essay.

The essay has many errors in grammar, spelling, capitalization, punctuation. The errors detract from the fluency and effectiveness of the essay.

The sentences are often not purposeful, varied, or well-controlled.

The essay ends abruptly and lacks a conclusion.

TOOL KIT: WRITING

# WRITING

INFORMATIVE/EXPLANATORY: SCORE 2

## *Moai:* The Giant Statues of Easter Island

Easter Island is a tiny Island. It's far out in the middle of the pacific ocean, 2200 miles off the coast. The closest South American country is Chile. The nearest island where people live is called Pitcairn, and that's almost 1,300 miles away. Even if don't know much about it, you've probably seen pictures of the Easter Island statues. You'd recognize one if you saw it. They're almost 900 of them. They're called *moai.* The average one is about 13 feet high (that's tall) and weighs a lot—almost 14 tons.

Scientists know that Polynesians settled Easter Island (it's also called Rapa Nui, and the people are called the Rapanui). Polynesians were very good sailers. And they traveled big distances across the Pacific. Even so, nobody really can say exactly *when* these Polynesians arrived and settled on the Island. Some say 300 A.D., while others say maybe as late as 900 or even 1200 A.D.

Scientists can tell that when the settlers first arrived, the island was covered with forests of palm and hardwood. They can tell by looking at pollin deposits in lakes on the island. The Rapanui people cut trees, built houses, planted crops, and a thriving culture. They didn't know that cutting so many trees would cause problems later on (like running out of wood). They also began to carve *moai.*

The *moai* were built to honor important Rapanui ancestors or chiefs. The statutes all have large heads and narrow bodies, but no too are exactly the same. There faces are all similar. Some have places where eyes could be inserted.

Why did the Rapanui stopped making *moai*? Part of it might have been because there were no more trees and no more of the wood needed to transport them. Part of it was maybe because the people were busy fighting each other because food and other necessary things were running out. In any case, they stopped making moai and started tipping over and breaking the ones that were there already. Later on, archeologists began to try to restore some of the statues and set them up again. But even now that some have been set up again, we still don't know a lot about them. I guess some things just have to remain a mystery!

The writer does not include a thesis statement.

Some of the ideas are reasonably well developed.

The essay has many errors in grammar, spelling, capitalization, punctuation. The errors decrease the effectiveness of the essay.

The writer's word choice shows that he is not fully aware of the essay's purpose and tone.

The writer does not include a clear conclusion.

INFORMATIVE/EXPLANATORY: SCORE 3

## *Moai:* The Giant Statues of Easter Island

Easter Island is a tiny place, far out in the middle of the Pacific Ocean, 2200 miles off the coast of South America. Another name for the island is Rapa Nui. Even if you don't know much about it, you would probably recognize the colossal head-and-torso carvings known as *moai.* Even after years of research by scientists, many questions about these extraordinary statues remain unanswered.

> The thesis statement is clearly stated.

Scientists now agree that it was Polynesians who settled Easter Island. Earlier some argued South American voyagers were the first. But the Polynesians were expert sailors and navigators known to have traveled huge distances across the Pacific Ocean. However, scientists do not agree about *when* the settlers arrived. Some say A.D. 300, while others suggest as late as between A.D. 900 and 1200.

Scientists say that when the settlers first arrived on Rapa Nui, the island was covered with forests of palm and hardwood. They can tell by looking at the layers of pollen deposited over the years in the lakes on the island. The Rapa Nui began to carve *moai.* They developed a unique artistic and architectural tradition all of their own.

> The essay has many interesting details, but some do not relate directly to the topic.

Archeologists agree that the *moai* were created to honor ancestor's or chief's. Most *moai* are made from a soft rock called *tuff* that's formed from hardened volcanic ash. The statues all have large heads on top of narrow bodies, but no two are exactly the same. Some have indented eye sockets where eyes could be inserted.

> There are very few errors in grammar, usage, and punctuation. These errors do not interrupt the fluency and effectiveness of the essay.

At some point, the Rapanui stopped making *moai.* Why? Was it because there were no more trees and no longer enough wood needed to transport them? Was it because the people were too busy fighting each other over resources which had begun to run out? No one can say for sure. Rival groups began toppling their enemys' *moai* and breaking them. By the 19th century, most of the statues were tipped over, and many were destroyed. It wasn't until many years later that archeologists began to restore some of the statues.

The *moai* of Easter Island are one of the most awe-inspiring human achievements ever. Thanks to scientific studies, we know much more about the *moai, ahu,* and Rapanui people than we ever did in the past. But some questions remain unanswered. At least for now, the *moai* are keeping their mouths shut, doing a good job of guarding their secrets.

> The writer's conclusion sums up the main points of the essay and supports the thesis statement.

INFORMATIVE/EXPLANATORY: SCORE 4

## *Moai:* The Giant Statues of Easter Island

Easter Island, 2200 miles off the coast of South America, is "the most remote inhabited island on the planet." Few have visited this speck in the middle of the vast Pacific Ocean, but we all recognize the colossal statues that bring this tiny island its fame: the head-and-torso carvings known as *moai.* Yet even after years of research by scientists, many questions about the *moai* remain unanswered.

Scientists now agree that it was Polynesians, not South Americans, who settled Easter Island (also known as Rapa Nui). Polynesians were expert sailors and navigators known to have traveled huge distances across the Pacific Ocean. Even so, there is little agreement about *when* the settlers arrived. Some say A.D. 300, while others suggest as late as between A.D. 900 and 1200.

Most archeologists agree that the *moai* were created to honor ancestors, chiefs, or other important people. Most *moai* are made from a soft rock called *tuff* that's formed from hardened volcanic ash. The statues have large heads atop narrow torsos, with eyes wide open and lips tightly closed. While the moai share these basic characteristics, no two are exactly the same: while all are huge, some are bigger than others. Some are decorated with carvings. Some have indented eye sockets where white coral eyes could be inserted. It's possible that the eyes were only put in for special occasions.

In the late 1600s, the Rapanui stopped carving *moai.* Was it because the forests had been depleted and there was no longer enough wood needed to transport them? Was it because they were too busy fighting each other over dwindling resources? No one can say for sure. What is known is that rival groups began toppling their enemies' *moai* and breaking them. By the 19th century, most of the statues were tipped over, and many were destroyed. It wasn't until many years later that archeologists began restoration efforts.

The *moai* of Easter Island are one of humanity's most awe-inspiring cultural and artistic achievements. Part of Rapa Nui was designated as a World Heritage Site in 1995 to recognize and protect these extraordinary creations. Thanks to scientific studies, we know much more about the *moai* than we ever did in the past. But some questions remain unanswered, some mysteries unsolved. Don't bother asking the *moai*: their lips are sealed.

The thesis statement of is clearly stated in an engaging manner.

The ideas in the essay relate to the thesis statement and focus on the topic.

The writer includes many specific and well-chosen details that add substance to the essay.

The fluency of the writing and effectiveness of the essay are unaffected by errors.

The conclusion relates to the thesis statement and is creative and memorable.

# Informative/Explanatory Rubric

| | Focus and Organization | Evidence and Elaboration | Conventions |
|---|---|---|---|
| **4** | The introduction engages the reader and states a thesis in a compelling way.<br><br>The essay includes a clear introduction, body, and conclusion.<br><br>The conclusion summarizes ideas and offers fresh insight into the thesis. | The essay includes specific reasons, details, facts, and quotations from selections and outside resources to support the thesis.<br><br>The tone of the essay is always formal and objective.<br><br>The language is always precise and appropriate for the audience and purpose. | The essay uses standard English conventions of usage and mechanics.<br><br>The essay contains no spelling errors. |
| **3** | The introduction engages the reader and sets forth the thesis.<br><br>The essay includes an introduction, body, and conclusion.<br><br>The conclusion summarizes ideas and supports the thesis. | The essay includes some specific reasons, details, facts, and quotations from selections and outside resources to support the thesis.<br><br>The tone of the essay is mostly formal and objective.<br><br>The language is generally precise and appropriate for the audience and purpose. | The essay demonstrates general accuracy in standard English conventions of usage and mechanics.<br><br>The essay contains few spelling errors. |
| **2** | The introduction sets forth the thesis.<br><br>The essay includes an introduction, body, and conclusion, but one or more parts are weak.<br><br>The conclusion partially summarizes ideas but may not provide strong support of the thesis. | The essay includes a few reasons, details, facts, and quotations from selections and outside resources to support the thesis.<br><br>The tone of the essay is occasionally formal and objective.<br><br>The language is somewhat precise and appropriate for the audience and purpose. | The essay demonstrates some accuracy in standard English conventions of usage and mechanics.<br><br>The essay contains some spelling errors. |
| **1** | The introduction does not state the thesis clearly.<br><br>The essay does not include an introduction, body, and conclusion.<br><br>The conclusion does not summarize ideas and may not relate to the thesis. | Reliable and relevant evidence is not included.<br><br>The tone of the essay is not objective or formal.<br><br>The language used is imprecise and not appropriate for the audience and purpose. | The essay contains mistakes in standard English conventions of usage and mechanics.<br><br>The essay contains many spelling errors. |

TOOL KIT: WRITING

# WRITING

## Narration

Narrative writing conveys experience, either real or imaginary, and uses time to provide structure. It can be used to inform, instruct, persuade, or entertain. Whenever writers tell a story, they are using narrative writing. Most types of narrative writing share certain elements, such as characters, setting, a sequence of events, and, often, a theme.

### Elements of a Narrative Text

A **narrative** is any type of writing that tells a story, whether it is fiction, nonfiction, poetry, or drama.

An effective nonfiction narrative usually contains these elements:

- an engaging beginning in which characters and setting are established
- characters who participate in the story events
- a well-structured, logical sequence of events
- details that show time and place
- effective story elements such as dialogue, description, and reflection
- the narrator's thoughts, feelings, or views about the significance of events
- use of language that brings the characters and setting to life

An effective fictional narrative usually contains these elements:

- an engaging beginning in which characters, setting, or a main conflict is introduced
- a main character and supporting characters who participate in the story events
- a narrator who relates the events of the plot from a particular point of view
- details that show time and place
- conflict that is resolved in the course of the narrative
- narrative techniques such as dialogue, description, and suspense
- use of language that vividly brings to life characters and events

NARRATIVE: SCORE 1

## The Remark-a-Ball

Eddie decided to invent a Remark-a-Ball. Eddie thought Barnaby should be able to speak to him.

> The story's beginning is choppy and vague.

That's when he invited the Remark-a-Ball.

Barnaby had a rubber ball. It could make a bunchs of sounds that made Barnaby bark. It had always seemed that Barnaby was using his squeaky toy to talk, almost.

> The sequence of events is unclear and hard to follow.

This was before Barnaby got hit by a car and died. This was a big deal. He took his chemistry set and worked real hard to created a thing that would make the toy ball talk for Barnaby, his dog.

> The narrative lacks descriptive details and sensory language.

Eddie made a Remark-a-Ball that worked a little too well, tho. Barnaby could say anything he wanted too. And now he said complaints—his bed didn't feel good, he wanted to be walks, he wanted to eat food.

> The narrative contains many errors in standard English conventions of usage and mechanics.

Barnaby became bossy to Eddy to take him on walks or wake up. It was like he became his boss. Like my dad's boss. Eddy didn't like having a mean boss for a dog.

Eddy wished he hadn't invented the Remark-a-Ball.

> The conclusion is abrupt and unsatisfying.

TOOL KIT: WRITING

# WRITING

NARRATIVE: SCORE 2

## The Remark-a-Ball

Eddie couldn't understand what his dog was barking about, so he decided to invent a Remark-a-Ball. Eddie thought Barnaby should be able to speak to him.

> The story's beginning provides few details to establish the situation.

That's when he invented the Remark-a-Ball.

Barnaby had a rubber ball the size of an orange. It could make a bunch of sounds that made Barnaby bark. It had always seemed to Eddie that Barnaby was almost talking with his squeaky toy.

This was a big deal. Eddy would be the first human ever to talk to a dog, which was a big deal! He took his chemistry set and worked real hard to created a thing that would make the toy ball talk for Barnaby, his dog.

Eddie made a Remark-a-Ball that worked a little too well, tho. Barnaby could say anything he wanted now. And now he mostly said complaints—his bed didn't feel good, he wanted to be walked all the time, he wanted to eat people food.

> Narrative techniques such as dialogue, pacing, and description are used sparingly.

Barnaby became bossy to Eddy to take him on walks or wake him up. It was like he became his boss. His really mean boss, like my dad's boss. Eddy didn't like having a mean boss for a dog.

> The narrative contains some errors in standard English conventions of usage and mechanics.

Eddy started to ignore his best friend, which used to be his dog named Barnaby. He started tot think maybe dogs shouldn't be able to talk.

Things were much better when Barnaby went back to barking

> The conclusion comes abruptly and provides little insight about the story's meaning.

NARRATIVE: SCORE 3

## The Remark-a-Ball

Any bark could mean anything: *I'm hungry*, *Take me outside*, or *There's that dog again*. Eddie thought Barnaby should be able to speak to him.

And that's how the Remark-a-Ball was born.

Barnaby had a rubber ball the size of an orange. It could make a wide range of sounds that made Barnaby howl. It had always seemed to Eddie that Barnaby was almost communicating with his squeaky toy.

This was big. This was epic. He would be the first human ever to bridge the communication gap between species! He dusted off his old chemistry set and, through trial and error, created a liquid bath that would greatly increase the toy's flexibility, resilience, and mouth-feel.

Eddie had a prototype that worked—perhaps too well. Barnaby was ready to speak his mind. This unleashed a torrent of complaints— his bed was lumpy, he couldn't *possibly* exist on just three walks a day, he wanted table food like the poodle next door.

Barnaby made increasingly specific demands to Eddie to take him on walks or wake him up. This kind of conversation did not bring them closer, as Eddie had thought, but instead it drove them apart.

Eddie started to avoid his former best friend, and he came to the realization that there is a good reason different species don't have a common language.

So Eddie quit letting Barnaby use the toy.

"Hey, Barn, want to go outside?" Eddie would say, and the dog, as if a switch was turned on, would shake, wag, pant, run in circles, and bark—just like he used to.

The story's beginning establishes the situation and the narrator's point of view but leaves some details unclear.

The narrative consistently uses standard English conventions of usage and mechanics.

Narrative techniques such as dialogue and description are used occasionally.

The conclusion resolves the situation or problem, but does not clearly convey the significance of the events in the story.

TOOL KIT: WRITING

# WRITING

NARRATIVE: SCORE 4

## The Remark-a-Ball

Barnaby, for no apparent reason, leapt up and began to bark like a maniac. "Why are you barking?" asked Eddie, holding the leash tight. But Barnaby, being a dog, couldn't say. It could have been anything—a dead bird, a half-eaten sandwich, the Taj Mahal.

> The story's beginning is engaging, sets up a point of view, and establishes characters and tone.

This was one of those times Eddie wished that Barnaby could talk. Any bark could mean anything: *I'm hungry, Take me outside,* or *There's that dog again.* Eddie thought, as buddies, they should be able to understand each other.

And that's how the Remark-a-Ball was born.

> The narrative uses standard English conventions of usage and mechanics, except where language is manipulated for effect.

Barnaby had a squeaky toy—a rubber ball the size of an orange. It could emit a wide range of sounds. It made Barnaby howl even as he was squeaking it. And it had always seemed to Eddie that through this process Barnaby was almost communicating.

This was big. This was epic. He, Edward C. Reyes III, would be the first human ever to bridge the communication gap between species! He dusted off his old chemistry set and, through trial and error, created a liquid bath that would greatly increase the toy's flexibility, resilience, and mouth-feel.

> Events are presented in a logical sequence, and the progression from one even to another is smooth.

By the end of the week Eddie had a prototype that worked— perhaps too well. Barnaby was ready to speak his mind. This unleashed a torrent of complaints—his bed was lumpy, he couldn't *possibly* exist on just three walks a day, he wanted table food like the poodle next door.

Barnaby made increasingly specific demands, such as "Wake me in ten minutes," and "I want filtered water." This kind of conversation did not bring them closer, as Eddie had thought, but instead it drove them apart.

> Narrative techniques are used effectively to develop characters and events.

Eddie started to avoid his former best friend, and he came to the realization that there is a good reason different species don't have a common language. It didn't take long for the invention to be relegated to the very bottom of Barnaby's toy chest, too far down for him to get.

There followed a period of transition, after which Eddie and Barnaby returned to their former mode of communication, which worked out just fine.

> The conclusion resolves the situation or problem and clearly conveys the significance of the events in the story.

"Hey, Barn, want to go outside?" Eddie would say, and the dog, as if a switch was turned on, would shake, wag, pant, run in circles, and bark—just like he used to.

"You're a good boy, Barnaby," Eddie would say, scratching him behind the ears.

TOOL KIT: WRITING

**R22** RESOURCES: TOOL KIT

# Narrative Rubric

| | Focus and Organization | Development of Ideas/Elaboration | Conventions |
|---|---|---|---|
| 4 | The introduction establishes a clear context and point of view.<br><br>Events are presented in a clear sequence, building to a climax, then moving toward the conclusion.<br><br>The conclusion follows from and reflects on the events and experiences in the narrative. | Narrative techniques such as dialogue, pacing, and description are used effectively to develop characters, events, and setting.<br><br>Descriptive details, sensory language, and precise words and phrases are used to convey the experiences in the narrative and to help the reader imagine the characters and setting.<br><br>Voice is established through word choice, sentence structure, and tone. | The narrative uses standard English conventions of usage and mechanics. Deviations from standard English are intentional and serve the purpose of the narrative.<br><br>Rules of spelling and punctuation are followed. |
| 3 | The introduction gives the reader some context and sets the point of view.<br><br>Events are presented logically, though there are some jumps in time.<br><br>The conclusion logically ends the story, but provides only some reflection on the experiences related in the story. | Narrative techniques such as dialogue, pacing, and description are used occasionally.<br><br>Descriptive details, sensory language, and precise words and phrases are used occasionally.<br><br>Voice is established through word choice, sentence structure, and tone occasionally, though not evenly. | The narrative mostly uses standard English conventions of usage and mechanics, though there are some errors.<br><br>There are few errors in spelling and punctuation. |
| 2 | The introduction provides some description of a place. The point of view can be unclear at times.<br><br>Transitions between events are occasionally unclear.<br><br>The conclusion comes abruptly and provides only a small amount of reflection on the experiences related in the narrative. | Narrative techniques such as dialogue, pacing, and description are used sparingly.<br><br>The story contains few examples of descriptive details and sensory language.<br><br>Voice is not established for characters, so that it becomes difficult to determine who is speaking. | The narrative contains some errors in standard English conventions of usage and mechanics.<br><br>There are many errors in spelling and punctuation. |
| 1 | The introduction fails to set a scene or is omitted altogether. The point of view is not always clear.<br><br>The events are not in a clear sequence, and events that would clarify the narrative may not appear.<br><br>The conclusion does not follow from the narrative or is omitted altogether. | Narrative techniques such as dialogue, pacing, and description are not used.<br><br>Descriptive details are vague or missing. No sensory language is included.<br><br>Voice has not been developed. | The text contains mistakes in standard English conventions of usage and mechanics.<br><br>Rules of spelling and punctuation have not been followed. |

## Conducting Research

We are lucky to live in an age when information is accessible and plentiful. However, not all information is equally useful, or even accurate. Strong research skills will help you locate and evaluate information.

### Narrowing or Broadening a Topic

The first step of any research project is determining your topic. Consider the scope of your project and choose a topic that is narrow enough to address completely and effectively. If you can name your topic in just one or two words, it is probably too broad. Topics such as Shakespeare, jazz, or science fiction are too broad to cover in a single report. Narrow a broad topic into smaller subcategories.

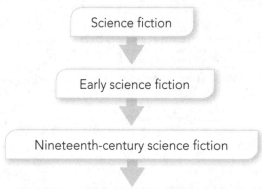

Science fiction

↓

Early science fiction

↓

Nineteenth-century science fiction

↓

Nineteenth-century science fiction that predicted the future accurately

When you begin to research a topic, pay attention to the amount of information available. If you feel overwhelmed by the number of relevant sources, you may need to narrow your topic further.

If there isn't enough information available as your research, you might need to broaden your topic. A topic is too narrow when it can be thoroughly presented in less space than the required size of your assignment. It might also be too narrow if you can find little or no information in library and media sources, so consider broadening your topic to include other related ideas.

### Generating Research Questions

Use research questions to focus your research. Specific questions can help you avoid time-wasting digressions. For example, instead of simply hunting for information about Mark Twain, you might ask, "What jobs did Mark Twain have, other than being a writer?" or "Which of Twain's books was most popular during his lifetime?"

In a research report, your research question often becomes your thesis statement, or may lead up to it. The question will also help you focus your research into a comprehensive but flexible search plan, as well as prevent you from gathering unnecessary details. As your research teaches you more about your topic, you may find it necessary to refocus your original question.

## Consulting Print and Digital Sources

Effective research combines information from several sources, and does not rely too heavily on a single source. The creativity and originality of your research depends on how you combine ideas from multiple sources. Plan to consult a variety of resources, such as the following:

- **Primary and Secondary Sources:** To get a thorough view of your topic, use primary sources (firsthand or original accounts, such as interview transcripts, eyewitness reports, and newspaper articles) and secondary sources (accounts, created after an event occurred, such as encyclopedia entries).

- **Print and Digital Resources:** The Internet allows fast access to data, but print resources are often edited more carefully. Use both print and digital resources in order to guarantee the accuracy of your findings.

- **Media Resources:** You can find valuable information in media resources such as documentaries, television programs, podcasts, and museum exhibitions. Consider attending public lectures given by experts to gain an even more in-depth view of your topic.

- **Original Research:** Depending on your topic, you may wish to conduct original research to include among your sources. For example, you might interview experts or eyewitnesses, or conduct a survey of people in your community.

**Using Online Encyclopedias**

Online encyclopedias are often written by anonymous contributors who are not required to fact-check information. These sites can be very useful as a launching point for research, but should not be considered accurate. Look for footnotes, endnotes, or hyperlinks that support facts with reliable sources that have been carefully checked by editors.

**Evaluating Sources** It is important to evaluate the credibility, validity, and accuracy of any information you find, as well as its appropriateness for your purpose and audience. You may find the information you need to answer your research question in specialized and authoritative sources, such as almanacs (for social, cultural, and natural statistics), government publications (for law, government programs, and subjects such as agriculture), and information services. Also, consider consumer, workplace, and public documents.

Ask yourself questions such as these to evaluate these additional sources:

- **Authority:** Is the author well known? What are the author's credentials? Does the source include references to other reliable sources? Does the author's tone win your confidence? Why or why not?

- **Bias:** Does the author have any obvious biases? What is the author's purpose for writing? Who is the target audience?

- **Currency:** When was the work created? Has it been revised? Is there more current information available?

TOOL KIT: RESEARCH

# RESEARCH

## Using Search Terms

Finding information on the Internet can be both easy and challenging. Type a word or phrase into a general search engine and you will probably get hundreds—or thousands—of results. However, those results are not guaranteed to be relevant or accurate.

These strategies can help you find information from the Internet:

- Create a list of keywords that apply to your topic before you begin using a search engine. Consult a thesaurus to expand your list.

- Enter six to eight keywords.

- Choose precise nouns. Most search engines ignore articles and prepositions. Verbs may be used in multiple contexts, leading to sources that are not relevant. Use modifiers, such as adjectives, when necessary to specify a category.

- Use quotation marks to focus a search. Place a phrase in quotation marks to find pages that include exactly that phrase. Add several phrases in quotation marks to narrow your results.

- Spell carefully. Many search engines autocorrect spelling, but they cannot produce accurate results for all spelling errors.

- Scan search results before you click them. The first result isn't always the most relevant. Read the text and consider the domain before make a choice.

- Utilize more than one search engine.

### Evaluating Internet Domains

Not everything you read on the Internet is true, so you have to evaluate sources carefully. The last three letters of an Internet URL identify the Website's domain, which can help you evaluate the information of the site.

- **.gov**—Government sites are sponsored by a branch of the United States federal government, such as the Census Bureau, Supreme Court, or Congress. These sites are considered reliable.

- **.edu**—Education domains include schools from kindergartens to universities. Information from an educational research center or department is likely to be carefully checked. However, education domains can also include student pages that are not edited or monitored.

- **.org**—Organizations are nonprofit groups and usually maintain a high level of credibility. Keep in mind that some organizations may express strong biases.

- **.com** and **.net**—Commercial sites exist to make a profit. Information may be biased to show a product or service in a good light. The company may be providing information to encourage sales or promote a positive image.

## Taking Notes

Take notes as you locate and connect useful information from multiple sources, and keep a reference list of every source you use. This will help you make distinctions between the relative value and significance of specific data, facts, and ideas.

For long-term research projects, create source cards and notecards to keep track of information gathered from multiple resources.

### Source Cards
Create a card that identifies each source.

- For print materials, list the author, title, publisher, date of publication, and relevant page numbers.
- For Internet sources, record the name and Web address of the site, and the date you accessed the information.
- For media sources, list the title, person, or group credited with creating the media, and the year of production.

### Notecards
Create a separate notecard for each item of information.

- Include the fact or idea, the letter of the related source card, and the specific page(s) on which the fact or idea appears.
- Use quotation marks around words and phrases taken directly from print or media resources.
- Mark particularly useful or relevant details using your own annotation method, such as stars, underlining, or colored highlighting.

| Source Card | [A] |
| --- | --- |

Marsh, Peter. *Eye to Eye: How People Interact.* Salem House Publishers, 1988.

**Notecard**

Gestures vary from culture to culture. The American "OK" symbol (thumb and forefinger) is considered insulting in Greece and Turkey.

Source Card: A, p. 54.

**Quote Accurately** Responsible research begins with the first note you take. Be sure to quote and paraphrase your sources accurately so you can identify these sources later. In your notes, circle all quotations and paraphrases to distinguish them from your own comments. When photocopying from a source, include the copyright information. When printing out information from an online source, include the Web address.

# Reviewing Research Findings

While conducting research, you will need to review your findings, checking that you have collected enough accurate and appropriate information.

## Considering Audience and Purpose

Always keep your audience in mind as you gather information, since different audiences may have very different needs. For example, if you are writing an in-depth analysis of a text that your entire class has read together and you are writing for your audience, you will not need to gather background information that has been thoroughly discussed in class. However, if you are writing the same analysis for a national student magazine, you cannot assume that all of your readers have the same background information. You will need to provide facts from reliable sources to help orient these readers to your subject. When considering whether or not your research will satisfy your audience, ask yourself:

- Who am I writing for?
- Have I collected enough information to explain my topic to this audience?
- Are there details in my research that I can omit because they are already familiar to my audience?

Your purpose for writing will also influence your review of research. If you are researching a question to satisfy your own curiosity, you can stop researching when you feel you understand the answer completely. If you are writing a research report that will be graded, you need to consider the criteria of the assignment. When considering whether or not you have enough information, ask yourself:

- What is my purpose for writing?
- Will the information I have gathered be enough to achieve my purpose?
- If I need more information, where might I find it?

## Synthesizing Sources

Effective research writing does not merely present facts and details; it synthesizes—gathers, orders, and interprets—them. These strategies will help you synthesize information effectively:

- Review your notes and look for connections and patterns among the details you have collected.
- Arrange notes or notecards in different ways to help you decide how to best combine related details and present them in a logical way.
- Pay close attention to details that support one other, emphasizing the same main idea.
- Also look for details that challenge each other, highlighting ideas about which there is no single, or consensus, opinion. You might decide to conduct additional research to help you decide which side of the issue has more support.

## Types of Evidence

When reviewing your research, also consider the kinds of evidence you have collected. The strongest writing contains a variety of evidence effectively. This chart describes three of the most common types of evidence: statistical, testimonial, and anecdotal.

| TYPE OF EVIDENCE | DESCRIPTION | EXAMPLE |
|---|---|---|
| **Statistical evidence** includes facts and other numerical data used to support a claim or explain a topic. | Examples of statistical evidence include historical dates and information, quantitative analyses, poll results, and quantitative descriptions. | "Although it went on to become a hugely popular novel, the first edition of William Goldman's book sold fewer than 3,000 copies." |
| **Testimonial evidence** includes any ideas or opinions presented by others, especially experts in a field. | Firsthand testimonies present ideas from eyewitnesses to events or subjects being discussed. | "The ground rose and fell like an ocean at ebb tide." —Fred J. Hewitt, eyewitness to the 1906 San Francisco earthquake |
| | Secondary testimonies include commentaries on events by people who were not involved. You might quote a well-known literary critic when discussing a writer's most famous novel, or a prominent historian when discussing the effects of an important event | Gladys Hansen insists that "there was plenty of water in hydrants throughout [San Francisco] . . . The problem was this fire got away." |
| **Anecdotal evidence** presents one person's view of the world, often by describing specific events or incidents. | Compelling research should not rely solely on this form of evidence, but it can be very useful for adding personal insights and refuting inaccurate generalizations. An individual's experience can be used with other forms of evidence to present complete and persuasive support. | Although many critics claim the novel is universally beloved, at least one reader "threw the book against a wall because it made me so angry." |

TOOL KIT: RESEARCH

# RESEARCH

## Incorporating Research Into Writing

### Avoiding Plagiarism

Plagiarism is the unethical presentation of someone else's ideas as your own. You must cite sources for direct quotations, paraphrased information, or facts that are specific to a single source. When you are drafting and revising, circle any words or ideas that are not your own. Follow the instructions on pages R32 and R33 to correctly cite those passages.

**Review for Plagiarism** Always take time to review your writing for unintentional plagiarism. Read what you have written and take note of any phrases or sentences that do not have your personal writing voice. Compare those passages with your resource materials. You might have copied them without remembering the exact source. Add a correct citation to give credit to the original author. If you cannot find the questionable phrase in your notes, revise it to ensure that your final report reflects your own thinking and not someone else's work.

### Quoting and Paraphrasing

When including ideas from research into your writing, you will decide to quote directly or paraphrase.

**Direct Quotation** Use the author's exact words when they are interesting or persuasive. You might decide to include direct quotations for these reasons:

- to share an especially clear and relevant statement
- to reference a historically significant passage
- to show that an expert agrees with your position
- to present an argument that you will counter in your writing.

Include complete quotations, without deleting or changing words. If you need to omit words for space or clarity, use ellipsis points to indicate the omission. Enclose direct quotations in quotation marks and indicate the author's name.

**Paraphrase** A paraphrase restates an author's ideas in your own words. Be careful to paraphrase accurately. Beware of making sweeping generalizations in a paraphrase that were not made by the original author. You may use some words from the original source, but a legitimate paraphrase does more than simply rearrange an author's phrases, or replace a few words with synonyms.

| Original Text | "*The Tempest* was written as a farewell to art and the artist's life, just before the completion of his forty-ninth year, and everything in the play bespeaks the touch of autumn." Brandes, Georg. "Analogies Between *The Tempest* and *A Midsummer Night's Dream*." *The Tempest*, by William Shakespeare, William Heinemann, 1904, p. 668. |
|---|---|
| **Patchwork Plagiarism**<br><br>phrases from the original are rearranged, but too closely follows the original text. | A farewell to art, Shakespeare's play, *The Tempest*, was finished just before the completion of his forty-ninth year. The artist's life was to end within three years. The touch of autumn is apparent in nearly everything in the play. |
| **Good Paraphrase** | Images of autumn occur throughout *The Tempest*, which Shakespeare wrote as a way of saying goodbye to both his craft and his own life. |

## Maintaining the Flow of Ideas

Effective research writing is much more that just a list of facts. Be sure to maintain the flow of ideas by connecting research information to your own ideas. Instead of simply stating a piece of evidence, use transition words and phrases to explain the connection between information you found from outside resources and your own ideas and purpose for writing. The following transitions can be used to introduce, compare, contrast, and clarify.

## Useful Transitions

**When providing examples:**

for example        for instance        to illustrate        in [name of resource], [author]

**When comparing and contrasting ideas or information:**

in the same way        similarly        however        on the other hand

**When clarifying ideas or opinions:**

in other words        that is        to explain        to put it another way

Choosing an effective organizational structure for your writing will help you create a logical flow of ideas. Once you have established a clear organizational structure, insert facts and details from your research in appropriate places to provide evidence and support for your writing.

| ORGANIZATIONAL STRUCTURE | USES |
| --- | --- |
| **Chronological order** presents information in the sequence in which it happens. | historical topics; science experiments; analysis of narratives |
| **Part-to-whole order** examines how several categories affect a larger subject. | analysis of social issues; historical topics |
| **Order of importance** presents information in order of increasing or decreasing importance. | persuasive arguments; supporting a bold or challenging thesis |
| **Comparison-and-contrast organization** outlines the similarities and differences of a given topic. | addressing two or more subjects |

# RESEARCH

## Formats for Citing Sources

In research writing, cite your sources. In the body of your paper, provide a footnote, an endnote, or a parenthetical citation, identifying the sources of facts, opinions, or quotations. At the end of your paper, provide a bibliography or a Works Cited list, a list of all the sources referred to in your research. Follow an established format, such as Modern Language Association (MLA) style.

### Parenthetical Citations (MLA Style)

A parenthetical citation briefly identifies the source from which you have taken a specific quotation, factual claim, or opinion. It refers readers to one of the entries on your Works Cited list. A parenthetical citation has the following features:

- It appears in parentheses.
- It identifies the source by the last name of the author, editor, or translator, or by the title (for a lengthy title, list the first word only).
- It provides a page reference, the page(s) of the source on which the information cited can be found.

A parenthetical citation generally falls outside a closing quotation mark but within the final punctuation of a clause or sentence. For a long quotation set off from the rest of your text, place the citation at the end of the excerpt without any punctuation following.

### Sample Parenthetical Citations

It makes sense that baleen whales such as the blue whale, the bowhead whale, the humpback whale, and the sei whale (to name just a few) grow to immense sizes (Carwardine et al. 19–21). The blue whale has grooves running from under its chin to partway along the length of its underbelly. As in some other whales, these grooves expand and allow even more food and water to be taken in (Ellis 18–21).

Authors' last names

Page numbers where information can be found

### Works Cited List (MLA Style)

A Works Cited list must contain accurate information to enable a reader to locate each source you cite. The basic components of an entry are as follows:

- name of the author, editor, translator, and/or group responsible for the work
- title of the work
- publisher
- date of publication

For print materials, the information for a citation generally appears on the copyright and title pages. For the format of a Works Cited list, consult the examples on this page and in the MLA Style for Listing Sources chart.

### Sample Works Cited List (MLA 8th Edition)

Carwardine, Mark, et al. *The Nature Company Guides: Whales, Dolphins, and Porpoises.* Time-Life, 1998.

"Discovering Whales." *Whales on the Net.* Whales in Danger, 1998, www.whales.org.au/discover/index.html. Accessed 11 Apr. 2017.

Neruda, Pablo. "Ode to Spring." *Odes to Opposites,* translated by Ken Krabbenhoft, edited and illustrated by Ferris Cook, Little, 1995, p. 16.

*The Saga of the Volsungs.* Translated by Jesse L. Byock, Penguin, 1990.

List an anonymous work by title.

List both the title of the work and the collection in which it is found.

### Works Cited List or Bibliography?

A Works Cited list includes only those sources you paraphrased or quoted directly in your research paper. By contrast, a bibliography lists all the sources you consulted during research—even those you did not cite.

# MLA (8th Edition) Style for Listing Sources

| | |
|---|---|
| **Book with one author** | Pyles, Thomas. *The Origins and Development of the English Language.* 2nd ed., Harcourt Brace Jovanovich, 1971.<br>[Indicate the edition or version number when relevant.] |
| **Book with two authors** | Pyles, Thomas, and John Algeo. *The Origins and Development of the English Language.* 5th ed., Cengage Learning, 2004. |
| **Book with three or more authors** | Donald, Robert B., et al. *Writing Clear Essays.* Prentice Hall, 1983. |
| **Book with an editor** | Truth, Sojourner. *Narrative of Sojourner Truth.* Edited by Margaret Washington, Vintage Books, 1993. |
| **Introduction to a work in a published edition** | Washington, Margaret. Introduction. *Narrative of Sojourner Truth,* by Sojourner Truth, edited by Washington, Vintage Books, 1993, pp. v–xi. |
| **Single work in an anthology** | Hawthorne, Nathaniel. "Young Goodman Brown." *Literature: An Introduction to Reading and Writing,* edited by Edgar V. Roberts and Henry E. Jacobs, 5th ed., Prentice Hall, 1998, pp. 376–385.<br>[Indicate pages for the entire selection.] |
| **Signed article from an encyclopedia** | Askeland, Donald R. "Welding." *World Book Encyclopedia,* vol. 21, World Book, 1991, p. 58. |
| **Signed article in a weekly magazine** | Wallace, Charles. "A Vodacious Deal." *Time,* 14 Feb. 2000, p. 63. |
| **Signed article in a monthly magazine** | Gustaitis, Joseph. "The Sticky History of Chewing Gum." *American History,* Oct. 1998, pp. 30–38. |
| **Newspaper article** | Thurow, Roger. "South Africans Who Fought for Sanctions Now Scrap for Investors." *Wall Street Journal,* 11 Feb. 2000, pp. A1+.<br>[For a multipage article that does not appear on consecutive pages, write only the first page number on which it appears, followed by the plus sign.] |
| **Unsigned editorial or story** | "Selective Silence." Editorial. *Wall Street Journal,* 11 Feb. 2000, p. A14.<br>[If the editorial or story is signed, begin with the author's name.] |
| **Signed pamphlet or brochure** | [Treat the pamphlet as though it were a book.] |
| **Work from a library subscription service** | Ertman, Earl L. "Nefertiti's Eyes." *Archaeology,* Mar.–Apr. 2008, pp. 28–32. *Kids Search,* EBSCO, New York Public Library. Accessed 7 Jan. 2017.<br>[Indicating the date you accessed the information is optional but recommended.] |
| **Filmstrips, slide programs, videocassettes, DVDs, and other audiovisual media** | *The Diary of Anne Frank.* 1959. Directed by George Stevens, performances by Millie Perkins, Shelley Winters, Joseph Schildkraut, Lou Jacobi, and Richard Beymer, Twentieth Century Fox, 2004.<br>[Indicating the original release date after the title is optional but recommended.] |
| **CD-ROM (with multiple publishers)** | Simms, James, editor. *Romeo and Juliet.* By William Shakespeare, Attica Cybernetics / BBC Education / Harper, 1995. |
| **Radio or television program transcript** | "Washington's Crossing of the Delaware." *Weekend Edition Sunday,* National Public Radio, 23 Dec. 2013. Transcript. |
| **Web page** | "Fun Facts About Gum." ICGA, 2005–2017, www.gumassociation.org/index.cfm/facts-figures/fun-facts-about-gum. Accessed 19 Feb. 2017.<br>[Indicating the date you accessed the information is optional but recommended.] |
| **Personal interview** | Smith, Jane. Personal interview, 10 Feb. 2017. |

All examples follow the style given in the MLA Handbook, 8th edition, published in 2016.

MODEL

# Evidence Log

Unit Title: _Discovery_

Perfomance-Based Assessment Prompt:
Do all discoveries benefit humanity?

My initial thoughts:
Yes - all knowledge moves us forward.

As you read multiple texts about a topic, your thinking may change. Use an Evidence Log like this one to record your thoughts, to track details you might use in later writing or discussion, and to make further connections.

Here is a sample to show how one reader's ideas deepened as she read two texts.

---

Title of Text: _Classifying the Stars_     Date: _Sept. 17_

| CONNECTION TO THE PROMPT | TEXT EVIDENCE/DETAILS | ADDITIONAL NOTES/IDEAS |
|---|---|---|
| Newton shared his discoveries and then other scientists built on his discoveries. | Paragraph 2: "Isaac Newton gave to the world the results of his experiments on passing sunlight through a prism." Paragraph 3: "In 1814 . . . the German optician, Fraunhofer . . . saw that the multiple spectral tints . . . were crossed by hundreds of fine dark lines." | It's not always clear how a discovery might benefit humanity in the future. |

How does this text change or add to my thinking? This confirms what I think.     Date: _Sept. 20_

---

Title of Text: _Cell Phone Mania_     Date: _Sept. 21_

| CONNECTION TO THE PROMPT | TEXT EVIDENCE/DETAILS | ADDITIONAL NOTES/IDEAS |
|---|---|---|
| Cell phones have made some forms of communication easier, but people don't talk to each other as much as they did in the past. | Paragraph 7: "Over 80% of young adults state that texting is their primary method of communicating with friends. This contrasts with older adults who state that they prefer a phone call." | Is it good that we don't talk to each other as much?<br><br>Look for article about social media to learn more about this question. |

How does this text change or add to my thinking?     Date: _Sept. 25_
Maybe there are some downsides to discoveries. I still think that knowledge moves us forward, but there are sometimes unintended negative effects.

# Word Network

A word network is a collection of words related to a topic. As you read the selections in a unit, identify interesting theme-related words and build your vocabulary by adding them to your Word Network.

Use your Word Network as a resource for your discussions and writings. Here is an example:

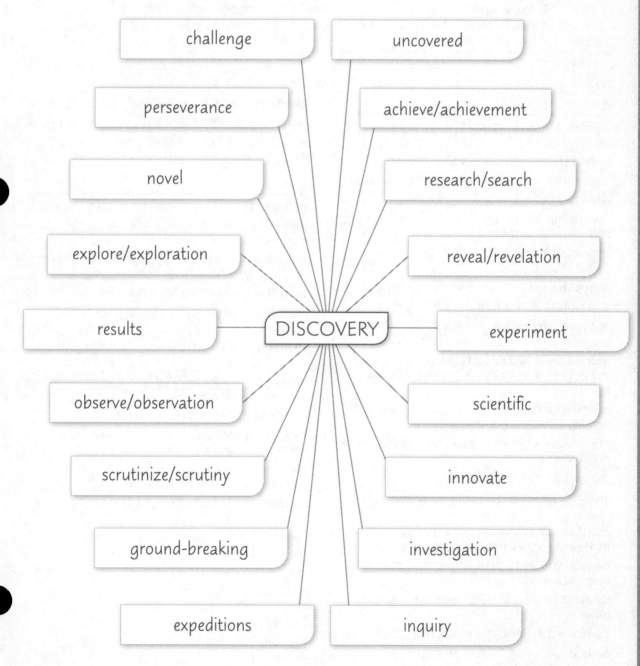

# ACADEMIC / CONCEPT VOCABULARY

Academic vocabulary appears in **blue type**.

## Pronunciation Key

| Symbol | Sample Words | Symbol | Sample Words |
|---|---|---|---|
| a | *at, catapult, Alabama* | oo | *boot, soup, crucial* |
| ah | *father, charms, argue* | ow | *now, stout, flounder* |
| ai | *care, various, hair* | oy | *boy, toil, oyster* |
| aw | *law, maraud, caution* | s | *say, nice, press* |
| awr | *pour, organism, forewarn* | sh | *she, abolition, motion* |
| ay | *ape, sails, implication* | u | *full, put, book* |
| ee | *even, teeth, really* | uh | *ago, focus, contemplation* |
| eh | *ten, repel, elephant* | ur | *bird, urgent. perforation* |
| ehr | *merry, verify, terribly* | y | *by, delight, identify* |
| ih | *it, pin, hymn* | yoo | *music, confuse, few* |
| o | *shot, hopscotch, condo* | zh | *pleasure, treasure, vision* |
| oh | *own, parole, rowboat* | | |

## A

**absolute** (AB suh loot) *adj.* certain; positive; perfectly whole

**activist** (AK tuh vihst) *n.* active supporter of a cause

**adamant** (AD uh muhnt) *adj.* not giving in; stubborn

**adversary** (AD vuhr sehr ee) *n.* opponent; enemy

**advocating** (AD vuh kayt ihng) *v.* speaking or writing in favor of a cause or person

**aggregate** (AG ruh giht) *n.* collection; sum of many parts

**anticipated** (an TIHS uh payt ihd) *v.* eagerly expected

**apocryphal** (uh POK ruh fuhl) *adj.* fake; not genuine

**applicant information** (AP luh kuhnt) (ihn fuhr MAY shuhn) *n.* data about a person applying for a job

**archival audio** (ahr KY vuhl) (AW dee oh) *n.* sound recorded from radio broadcasts, television shows, or films of past decades

**assimilation** (uh sihm uh LAY shuhn) *n.* process of adapting to the culture of an adopted country

**attending** (uh TEHND ihng) *adj.* being present; taking care of things

**avenge** (uh VEHNJ) *v.* get revenge for

**awesome** (AW suhm) *adj.* impressive; causing awe

## B

**bade** (bayd) *v.* past tense of *bid;* requested

**banishment** (BAN ihsh muhnt) *n.* state of having been banished, or exiled

**banter** (BAN tuhr) *n.* friendly exchange between speakers

**bemusing** (bih MYOOZ ihng) *adj.* confusing; bewildering

**besieged** (bih SEEJD) *adj.* under military attack

**bewildered** (bih WIHL duhrd) *adj.* confused completely

**blundering** (BLUHN duhr ihng) *adj.* clumsy

**burden** (BUR duhn) *n.* something that is carried with difficulty or obligation

## C

**cadence** (KAY duhns) *n.* rhythm and flow of language

**caption** (KAP shuhn) *n.* words in a separate box in a graphic novel or comic strip

**check box** (chehk) (boks) *n.* place on a form to indicate "yes," signifying that a certain statement is true

**chimed** (chymd) *v.* rang; made the sound of a bell

**chirruped** (CHIHR uhpt) *v.* made bird-like chirping sounds

**coalescing** (koh uh LEHS ihng) *n.* coming together in one body or place

**coherent** (koh HIHR ihnt) *adj.* sticking together; holding together; logically consistent

**compact** (kuhm PAKT) *adj.* firmly packed

**compelling** (kuhm PEHL ihng) *adj.* interesting and attractive; persuasive

**complacency** (kuhm PLAY suhn see) *n.* state of unthinking or satisfied acceptance

**composed** (kuhm POHZD) *n.* created music or literary work

**composition** (kom puh ZIHSH uhn) *n.* arrangement of the parts of a picture

**concessions** (kuhn SEHSH uhnz) *n.* special allowances

**confidence** (KON fuh duhns) *n.* meeting, especially one held in secret

**conflict** (KON flihkt) *n.* struggle; problem; fight

**conjecture** (kuhn JEHK chuhr) *n.* guess; *v.* guess

**conscience** (KON shuhns) *n.* inner sense of what is morally right or wrong in one's actions

**correspondents** (kawr uh SPON duhnts) *n.* reporters who send news from far away or on a special subject

**counterfeit** (KOWN tuhr fiht) *n.* something made to deceive

**craft** (kraft) *n.* activity that requires skill

**credible** (KREHD uh buhl) *adj.* believable; convincing

**credulity** (kruh DYOO luh tee) *n.* readiness to believe

**culpability** (kuhl puh BIHL uh tee) *n.* guilt or blame that is deserved; blameworthiness

**cunning** (KUHN ihng) *n.* skill in deception

**customs** (KUHS tuhmz) *n.* traditions; actions that are commonly done by a group of people

## D

**deceived** (dih SEEVD) *v.* lied to; tricked

**deftly** (DEHFT lee) *adv.* in a way that is skillfull and quick

**delicately** (DEHL uh kiht lee) *adv.* carefully; with grace and gentleness

**delivery** (dih LIHV uhr ee) *n.* manner in which a speaker gives a speech

**dependency** (dih PEHN duhn see) *n.* act of leaning on another for support or help

**depiction** (dih PIHK shuhn) *n.* picture, description, or explanation

**descendants** (dih SEHN duhnts) *n.* people who are the offspring of an ancestor

**description** (dih SKRIHP shuhn) *n.* writing or speech that tells about something

**desperate** (DEHS puhr iht) *adj.* involving extreme danger or disaster; driven to action by a loss of hope

**destined** (DEHS tihnd) *adj.* caused by fate; meant to do; meant for

**devoted** (dih VOHT ihd) *adj.* loving, loyal, and concerned with another's well-being

**dialogue** (DY uh log) *n.* conversation between characters in writing, film, or drama

**discordant** (dihs KAWR duhnt) *adj.* unrelated; out of place

**disparate** (DIHS puhr iht) *adj.* essentially different in kind

**dispatched** (dihs PACHT) *v.* finished something quickly

**disrupt** (dihs RUHPT) *v.* break up; upset; interrupt

**dissemble** (dih SEHM buhl) *v.* put on an appearance or disguise

**distressed** (dihs TREHST) *adj.* full of anxiety and suffering

**diversity** (duh VUR suh tee) *n.* variety of different ethnic or cultural groups

## E

**eerily** (EER uh lee) *adv.* strangely; weirdly

**elation** (ih LAY shuhn) *n.* great happiness and excitement

**elucidate** (ih LOO suh dayt) *v.* explain; make clear

**empathic** (ehm PATH ihk) *adj.* characterized by empathy, the ability to identify with the feelings or thoughts of others

**endure** (ehn DUR) *v.* last; continue; put up with

**enthralled** (ehn THRAWLD) *v.* captivated

**entranced** (ehn TRANST) *adj.* in a state of wonder or amazement

**entrusted** (ehn TRUHST ihd) *v.* given the responsibility of doing something or caring for someone or something

**establishing shot** (ehs TAB lihsh ihng) (shot) *n.* shot that shows the context of a scene in a film or video

**eternal** (ih TUR nuhl) *adj.* timeless; everlasting

**evidence** (EHV uh duhns) *n.* facts or details that support a position or claim

**exalted** (ehg ZAWL tihd) *adj.* elevated

**exile** (EHG zyl) *v.* punish someone by forcing that person to leave a place permanently

**expedite** (EHKS puh dyt) *v.* make easy and quick; do quickly

**expert commentary** (EHKS purht) (KOM ehn tair ee) *n.* information delivered by a person who has special knowledge of the subject

**exposition** (ehks spuh ZIH shuhn) *n.* writing or speech that explains or shows

**express** (ehks PREHS) *v.* say; convey; reveal

**eyewitness** (Y wiht nihs) *n.* someone who has firsthand experience of an event

## F

**factions** (FAK shuhnz) *n.* groups of people inside a political party, club, government, etc., working against another group

**faithless** (FAYTH lihs) *adj.* without faith; unbelieving

**fasting** (FAS tihng) *v.* intentionally not eating, often for religious or spiritual reasons

**fluttered** (FLUH tuhrd) *v.* waved gently

**forbidden** (fuhr BIHD uhn) *adj.* prevented or prohibited

**formulate** (FAWR myuh layt) *v.* build; state definitely; develop

**fugitives** (FYOO juh tihvz) *n.* group of persons who have run away from danger

## G

**gesture** (JEHS chuhr) *n.* movement of the hands or body that conveys meaning

**guise** (gyz) *n.* outward appearance

**gutter** (GUHT uhr) *n.* space between panels in a graphic novel

# H

**hallowed** (HAL ohd) *adj.* holy; sacred

**hallucination** (huh loo suh NAY shuhn) *n.* something perceived that has no reality

**heretics** (HEHR uh tihks) *n.* people who hold a different belief from the official belief of their church

**human interest story** (HYOO muhn) (IHN trihst) (STAWR ee) *n.* story that focuses on the personal issues of people

# I

**idly** (YD lee) *adv.* lazily; without taking action

**impulse** (IHM puhls) *n.* sudden urge to act or do something

**incredulity** (ihn kruh DYOO luh tee) *n.* doubt

**indignation** (ihn dihg NAY shuhn) *n.* righteous anger; hostility

**inevitable** (ihn EHV uh tuh buhl) *adj.* certain to occur; unavoidable

**infantile** (IHN fuhn tyl) *adj.* babyish; childish

**infatuated** (ihn FACH oo ayt ihd) *adj.* briefly but intensely in love

**innovate** (IHN uh vayt) *v.* make changes; introduce something new

**inscribed** (ihn SKRYBD) *adj.* written or engraved upon

**interpreter** (ihn TUR pruh tuhr) *n.* person who changes the words of one language into another for the benefit of listeners

**intervened** (ihn tuhr VEEND) *v.* came between groups

**interwoven** (ihn tuhr WOH vuhn) *adj.* intermingled; combined

**intrigued** (ihn TREEGD) *v.* interested and curious

**introduction** (ihn truh DUHK shuhn) *n.* context and background information about the topic of a radio broadcast, provided at its beginning

**introspective** (ihn truh SPEHK tihv) *adj.* having the habit of examining one's own thoughts and feelings

**iridescent** (ihr uh DEHS uhnt) *adj.* changing in color when seen from different angles

**irresolvable** (ihr ih ZOL vuh buhl) *adj.* impossible to resolve or settle

# L

**lamentable** (luh MEHN tuh buhl) *adj.* grievous; mournful; sorrowful

**languished** (LANG gwihsht) *v.* grown weak; lived under distressing conditions

**lighting and color** (LY tihng) (KUHL uhr) *n.* use of light, shadow, and color in a picture

**logical** (LOJ uh kuhl) *adj.* based on reason or sound judgment

**luminous** (LOO muh nuhs) *adj.* shining; radiating light

# M

**macabre** (muh KAH bruh) *adj.* grim and horrible

**manipulated** (muh NIHP yuh layt ihd) *v.* managed or controlled through clever moves

**meager** (MEE guhr) *adj.* extremely thin

**meditative** (MEHD uh tay tihv) *adj.* given to extended thought

**melancholy** (MEHL uhn kol ee) *adj.* sad and depressed

**memento** (muh MEHN toh) *n.* souvenir; keepsake

**minority** (muh NAWR uh tee) *n.* group of people that differs in some way from the larger population

**misery** (MIHZ uhr ee) *n.* condition of great wretchedness

**montage** (mon TOZH) *n.* group of images shown quickly, one after another, to create a single impression

**mortality** (mawr TAL uh tee) *n.* condition of being sure to die sometime

**mutiny** (MYOO tuh nee) *n.* open rebellion against lawful authority, especially by sailors or soldiers against their officers

# N

**naturalization** (nach uhr uh luh ZAY shuhn) *n.* process of becoming a citizen

**notation** (noh TAY shuhn) *n.* brief note added to a text to explain, elaborate, remind, etc.

# O

**oppression** (uh PREHSH uhn) *n.* cruel or unjust treatment

**oratory** (AWR uh tawr ee) *n.* formal public speaking

# P

**panel** (PAN uhl) *n.* one of the drawings on a page, usually framed by a border

**pardon** (PAHR duhn) *n.* forgiveness for a crime

**pathos** (PAY thos) *n.* quality that creates a feeling of sadness or pity

**penury** (PEHN yuhr ee) *n.* destitution or poverty

**perspective or angle** (puhr SPEHK tihv) (ANG guhl) *n.* vantage point from which a photo is taken

**physiology** (fihz ee OL uh jee) *n.* all functions and activites of living things and their parts

**pipes** (pyps) *v.* says in a loud, clear, or shrill voice

**pitched** (pihcht) *v.* moved up and down

**plotted** (PLOT ihd) *v.* planned a strategy or activity

**plundered** (PLUHN duhrd) *v.* took something by force

**pluralistic** (pluhr uh LIHS tihk) *adj.* having multiple parts or aspects

**point of view** (poynt) (uhv) (vyoo) *n.* perspective from which the creators of a media piece approach a topic

**postpone** (pohst POHN) *v.* delay

**prayerful** (PRAIR fuhl) *adj.* appearing as if praying

**predatory** (PREHD uh tawr ee) *adj.* living by capturing and feeding on other animals

**premonition** (prehm uh NIHSH uhn) *n.* feeling that something bad will happen

**primary source** (PRY mehr ee) (sawrs) *n.* document, recording, image, or other source that was created at the same time as the events it describes or shows

**privacy** statement (PRY vuh see) (STAYT muhnt) *n.* statement from an institution that guarantees personal information will not be given out

**procedure** (pruh SEE juhr) *n.* steps to complete an action

**profound** (pruh FOWND) *adj.* intense; deep

**prophet** (PROF iht) *n.* person who predicts the future

**propose** (pruh POHZ) *v.* suggest

**prosperity** (pros PEHR uh tee) *n.* good fortune; success

**proximity** (prok SIHM uh tee) *n.* quality of being near or close to

**psyche** (SY kee) *n.* human mind or spirit

**purified** (PYUR uh fyd) *v.* cleaned by removing harmful or unwanted materials or qualities

## R

**radical** (RAD uh kuhl) *adj.* extreme; fundamental

**recurrent** (rih KUR uhnt) *adj.* repeating

**redemptive** (rih DEHMP tihv) *adj.* serving to deliver from sorrow, make amends, or pay back

**reeling** (REE lihng) *adj.* going around and around in a whirling motion

**reincarnation** (ree ihn kahr NAY shuhn) *n.* belief that the soul reappears after death in another bodily form

**relented** (rih LEHNT ihd) *v.* agreed to do something after resisting it before

**remorse** (rih MAWRS) *n.* deep sense of regret for having done wrong

**reporter stand-ups** (rih POHR tuhr) (STAND uhps) *n.* shots that show a reporter looking into the camera and delivering information about a story

**retaliating** (rih TAL ee ayt ihng) *v.* paying back for injury; returning evil for evil

## S

**salient** (SAY lee uhnt) *adj.* noticeable; prominent

**secondary source** (SEHK uhn dehr ee) (sawrs) *n.* document, recording, image, or other source that is written or created after an event by someone who did not witness it firsthand

**sensationalized** (sehn SAY shuh nuh lyzd) *v.* exaggerated for effect

**sequence** (SEE kwuhns) *n.* order, as a linear order of steps or events

**serpentine** (SUR puhn teen) *adj.* twisting; winding; like a serpent

**sheer** (sheer) *adj.* absolute; complete; utter

**specter** (SPEHK tuhr) *n.* ghost

**speech bubble** (speech) (BUHB uhl) *n.* rounded shape containing a character's words

**splash** (splash) *n.* large, full-page illustration

**sprawling** (SPRAWL ihng) *adj.* spread out

**stagnation** (stag NAY shuhn) *n.* state of being inactive and not moving or changing

**steal** (steel) *v.* move in a way that is secret or quiet

**stern** (sturn) *adj.* strict; severe

**stock** (stok) *n.* descendants of a particular individual or ethnic group; family or lineage

**subsequent** (SUHB suh kwuhnt) *adj.* coming after; following

**summoned** (SUHM uhnd) *v.* ordered someone or something to come to a place

**surrounding** (suh ROWN dihng) *adj.* enclosing on all sides

## T

**tactics** (TAK tihks) *n.* military procedures

**teased** (teezd) *v.* made an affectionate, good-humored personal joke

**technique** (tehk NEEK) *n.* special method or skill

**tier** (tihr) *n.* row of panels in a graphic novel

**tone** (tohn) *n.* attitude a speaker takes toward a subject

**transgression** (tranz GREHSH uhn) *n.* act of breaking a law or command, or of committing a sin

**treasure** (TREHZH uhr) *v.* value greatly; cherish

**trembling** (TREHM blihng) *v.* shaking because of fear, excitement, or weakness, etc.

**tremulous** (TREHM yuh luhs) *adj.* trembling; quivering; timid; fearful

**tribulations** (trihb yuh LAY shuhnz) *n.* great trouble or misery

**tryst** (trihst) *n.* secret romantic meeting

## U

**understatement** (UHN duhr stayt muhnt) *n.* downplaying a topic to make it seem less important

**upheaval** (uhp HEE vuhl) *n.* a lifting up

## V

**valid** (VAL ihd) *adj.* well-founded; sound; effective

**ventured** (VEHN chuhrd) *v.* tried something dangerous

**voluntary** (VOL uhn tehr ee) *adj.* done freely

## Y

**yearning** (YUR nihng) *n.* strong desire; longing

# VOCABULARIO ACADÉMICO/ VOCABULARIO DE CONCEPTOS

## A

**absolute / absoluto** *adj.* innegable; definitivo; completo

**activist / activista** *s.* partidario o defensor activo de una causa

**adamant / inflexible** *adj.* firme; terco

**adversary / adversario** *s.* oponente; enemigo

**advocating / abogar** *v.* hablar o escribir en favor de una causa o persona

**aggregate / total** *s.* conjunto; suma de varias partes

**anticipated / esperado** *adj.* deseado con ansias

**apocryphal / apócrifo** *adj.* falso; no legítimo

**applicant information / información sobre el solicitante** *s.* datos de una persona que está solicitando un trabajo

**archival audio / grabación de archivo** *s.* sonido de programas de radio, de televisión o de películas grabado en décadas pasadas

**assimilation / asimilación** *s.* proceso de adaptación a la cultura del país de adopción

**attending / asistir** *v.* estar presente; cuidar; ocuparse de o atender a alguien

**avenge / vengar** *v.* tomar revancha; vengarse

**awesome / impresionante** *adj.* imponente; que causa asombro

## B

**bade / demandó** *v.* pasado de *demandar*; pidió; requirió

**banishment / destierro** *s.* el estado de encontrarse desterrado o exiliado

**banter / cotorreo** *s.* intercambio amistoso entre dos interlocutores

**bemusing / desconcertante** *adj.* que confunde mucho; que deja perplejo

**besieged / sitiado** *adj.* bajo ataque militar

**bewildered / perplejo** *adj.* profundamente confundido

**blundering / torpe** *adj.* desmañado, inhábil

**burden / carga** *s.* algo que se hace o se lleva con dificultad o por obligación

## C

**cadence / cadencia** *s.* el ritmo y la fluidez del lenguaje

**caption / cartela** *s.* texto que está en un recuadro aparte en las novelas gráficas o en los cómics

**check box / casillero de verificación** *s.* espacio en un formulario para indicar "sí", y que señala que un enunciado es verdadero

**chimed / repicó** *v.* sonó del modo en que suena una campana

**chirruped / gorjeó** *v.* hizo un sonido similar al gorjeo de un pájaro

**coalescing / fusión** *s.* acto de fundirse o juntarse en un solo cuerpo o lugar

**coherent / cohesivo** *adj.* que produce adherencia; que junta o pega

**compact / compacto** *adj.* denso, abarrotado; *v.* to compress / comprimir

**compelling / cautivador** *adj.* interesante y atractivo; convincente

**complacency / complacencia** *s.* estado de aceptación despreocupada o irreflexiva

**composed / compuesta** *adj* escrita, creada, especialmente cuando se refiere a una obra musical o literaria

**composition/ composición** *s.* distribución o arreglo de las partes de un cuadro

**concessions / concesiones** *s.* permisos o prestaciones especiales

**confidence / confianza** *s.* reunión, especialmente la que se lleva a cabo en secreto

**conflict / conflicto** *s.* lucha; problema; pelea

**conjecture / conjetura** *s.* suposición; *v.* to guess / adivinar

**conscience / conciencia** *s.* sentido interior de lo que es moralmente correcto o incorrecto en nuestras acciones

**correspondents / corresponsales** *s.* reporteros que envían noticias sobre un determinado tema desde lugares lejanos

**counterfeit / falsificación** *s.* algo hecho para engañar

**craft / oficio** *s.* actividad que requiere ciertas destrezas

**credible / creíble** *adj.* verosímil; convincente

**credulity / credulidad** *s.* diposición a creer

**culpability / culpabilidad** *s.* culpa o responsabilidad en algún hecho censurable; reprobabilidad

**cunning / astucia** *s.* habilidad para mentir o engañar

**customs / costumbres** *s.* tradiciones; las acciones que por lo general realizan un grupo de personas

## D

**deceived / engañado** *v.* alguien a quien se le ha mentido; que ha sido burlado

**deftly / hábilmente** *adv.* de manera diestra y rápida

**delicately / delicadamente** *adv.* cuidadosamente; con gracia y suavidad

**delivery / presentación oral** *s.* la manera en que un orador pronuncia su discurso

**dependency / dependencia** *s.* supeditarse al apoyo o ayuda de otra persona

**depiction / representación** *s.* retrato, descripción o explicación de algo

**descendents / descendientes** *s.* las personas que son sucesoras de un ancestro

**description / descripción** *s.* texto o discurso que informa acerca de algo

**desperate / desesperado** *adj.* que implica algún desastre o peligro extremo

**desperate / desesperanzado** *adj.* que actúa a partir de la pérdida de esperanza

**destined / destinado** *adj.* causado por el destino; llamado a hacer; nacido para realizar algo

**devoted / dedicado** *adj.* cariñoso, leal y preocupado por el bienestar de otra persona

**dialogue / diálogo** *s.* conversación entre los personajes de un texto, película u obra de teatro

**discordant / discordante** *adj.* no relacionado; fuera de lugar

**disparate / dispar** *adj.* de un tipo esencialmente distinto

**dispatched / despachado** *adj.* que se terminó rápidamente

**disrupt / irrumpir** *v.* interrumpir; perturbar

**dissemble / disimular** *v.* simular, pretender

**distressed / angustiado** *adj.* lleno de ansiedad y preocupación

**diversity / diversidad** *s.* una variedad de distintos grupos étnicos o culturales

## E

**eerily / misteriosamente** *adv.* extrañamente; inquietantemente o siniestramente

**elation / euforia** *s.* gran felicidad y entusiasmo

**elucidate / elucidar** *v.* explicar, aclarar

**empathic / empático** *adj.* que se caracteriza por la empatía, es decir, por la habilidad de identificarse con los sentimientos o pensamientos de otras personas

**endure / perdurar** *v.* durar, continuar; aguantar o tolerar algo

**enthralled / embelesado** *adj.* cautivado o fascinado

**entranced / extasiado** *adj.* maravillado o asombrado

**entrusted / encargado** *adj.* que se le ha asignado la responsabilidad de hacer algo o de cuidar de alguien o de algo

**establishing shot / plano de situación** *s.* plano que muestra el contexto de una escena en una película o video

**eternal / eterno** *adj.* atemporal; perpetuo

**evidence / evidencia** *s.* datos o detalles que respaldan una posición o reclamo

**exalted / exaltado** *adj.* elevado

**exile / exiliar** *v.* castigar a una persona forzándola a abandonar un lugar de manera permanente

**expedite / acelerar** *v.* facilitar algo; hacer algo rápidamente

**exposition / presentación** *s.* texto o discurso que explica o muestra algo

**express / expresar** *v.* decir; transmitir; revelar

**eyewitness / testigo presencial** *s.* persona que ha presenciado un evento histórico o importante

## F

**factions / facciones** *s.* grupos de personas que pertenecen a un partido político, club, gobierno, etc. y que se oponen a las posturas de otros grupos

**faithless / ateo** *adj.* persona que no profesa una fe religiosa; no creyente

**fasting / ayunar** *v.* privarse voluntariamente de la comida, generalmente por razones religiosas o espirituales

**fluttered / aleteó** *v.* ondeó suavemente

**forbidden / prohibido** *adj.* que se impide o se veta

**formulate / formular** *v.* construir; enunciar de forma precisa; desarrollar

**framework script / borrador de guión** *s.* se usa para bosquejar escenas de una película o video

**fugitives / fugitivos** *s.* personas que escaparon de un peligro

## G

**gesture / gesto** *s.* movimiento de las manos o de otras partes del cuerpo

**guise / aspecto** *s.* apariencia exterior

**gutter / canaleta** *s.* en una novela gráfica, el espacio entre dos viñetas

## H

**hallowed / santificado** *adj.* sagrado

**hallucination / alucinación** *s.* algo que se percibe pero que no tiene una existencia real

**heretics / herejes** *s.* personas que tienen creencias distintas de las aceptadas por su religión

**human interest story / relato de interés humano** *s.* una historia que se centra en los problemas personales de la gente

## I

**idly / descuidadamente** *adv.* perezosamente; que no actúa

**impulse / impulso** *s.* súbita urgencia de actuar o de hacer algo

**incredulity / incredulidad** *s.* duda

**indignation / indignación** *s.* ira justificada; hostilidad

**inevitable / inevitable** *adj.* que ocurrirá; que no puede evitarse

**infantile / infantil** *adj.* ingenuo; propio de un niño pequeño

**infatuated / prendado** *adj.* estar breve pero intensamente enamorado

**innovate / innovar** *v.* hacer cambios; introducir algo nuevo

**inscribed / inscripto** *adj.* escrito o grabado

**interpreter / intérprete** *s.* persona que traduce de una lengua a otra de forma oral

**intervened / intervino** *v.* que terció entre dos grupos para ayudar a resolver diferencias

**interwoven / entretejido** *adj.* entrelazado; combinado

**intrigued / intrigado** *adj.* interesado, curioso

**introduction / presentación** *s.* contexto e información sobre el tema al inicio de un programa de radio

**introspective / introspectivo** *adj.* que tiene por costumbre analizar sus propios pensamientos y sentimientos

**iridescent / iridiscente** *adj.* que cambia de color cuando se lo mira desde distintos ángulos

**irresolvable / irresoluble** *adj.* que no se puede resolver o solucionar

## L

**lamentable / lamentable** *adj.* penoso; doloroso; lastimoso

**languished / languideció** *v.* se debilitó poco a poco bajo condiciones angustiosas

**lighting and color / luz y color** *s.* uso de la luz, la sombra y el color en un cuadro

**logical / lógico** *adj.* que se basa en la razón o en un juicio sensato

**luminous / luminoso** *adj.* brillante, que irradia luz

## M

**macabre / macabro** *adj.* lúgubre y horroroso

**manipulated / manipulado** *adj.* manejado o controlado por medio de movimientos atinados

**meager / raquítico** *adj.* sumamente delgado

**meditative / meditativo** *adj.* que tiende a pensar prolongadamente

**melancholy / melancólico** *adj.* triste y deprimido

**memento / recuerdo** *s.* souvenir; objeto que se da como recuerdo

**minority / minoría** *s.* grupo de personas que se distingue de alguna manera de la mayor parte de la población

**misery / miseria** *s.* estado de gran infortunio o desgracia

**montage / montaje** *s.* grupo de imágenes que se muestran rápidamente, una tras otra, para dar la impresión de que es una sola imagen

**mortality / mortalidad** *s.* seguridad de que en algún momento se va a morir

**mutiny / motín** *s.* rebelión o revuelta contra la autoridad legítima, especialmente la llevada a cabo por los marineros o los soldados contra los oficiales

## N

**naturalization / naturalización** *s.* proceso de hacerse ciudadano de un país que no es el de su nacimiento

**notation / anotación** *s.* apunte; información que se pone por escrito

## O

**oppression / opresión** *s.* tratamiento cruel o injusto

**oratory / oratoria** *s.* arte formal de hablar en público

## P

**panel / viñeta** *s.* cada dibujo de una página, por lo genera enmarcado por un borde

**pardon / perdón** *s.* indulto de un delito

**pathos / patetismo** *s.* cualidad que produce un sentimiento de tristeza o de compasión

**penury / penuria** *s.* indigencia o pobreza

**perspective or angle / ángulo o perspectiva** *s.* punto desde el cual se toma una foto

**physiology / fisiología** *s.* conjunto de funciones y actividades de los seres vivos y sus partes

**pipes / chillar** *v.* hablar en voz alta, clara o muy aguda

**pitched / cabeceó** *v.* se movió hacia arriba y hacia abajo

**plotted / tramó** *v.* planificó una estrategia o actividad

**plundered / saqueó** *v.* tomó algo por la fuerza

**pluralistic / pluralista** *adj.* que tiene múltiples partes o aspectos

**point of view / punto de vista** *s.* perspectiva desde la cual se observa lo que se narra

**postpone / posponer** *v.* retrasar

**prayerful / piadoso** *adj.* que parece que estuviera rezando

**predatory / predatorio** *adj.* que se alimenta de los animales que captura

**premonition / premonición** *s.* sensación de que algo malo va a pasar

**primary source / fuente primaria** *s.* documento, grabación, imagen u otra fuente original creada al mismo tiempo que los eventos que describe o muestra

**privacy statement / aviso de privacidad** *s.* garantía de una institución de que no se compartirá información personal

**procedure / procedimiento** *s.* conjunto de pasos para realizar una acción

**profound / profundo** *adj.* intenso; hondo

**prophet / profeta** *s.* persona que predice el futuro

**propose / proponer** *v.* sugerir

**prosperity / prosperidad** *s.* buena suerte; éxito

**proximity / proximidad** *s.* cualidad de estar cerca o próximo a algo

**psyche / psiquis** *s.* espíritu o mente humana

**purified / purificado** *adj.* limpio de todo atributo o materia dañina o no deseada

## R

**radical / radical** *s.* persona que apoya los cambios extremos; *adj.* muy cambiado

**recurrent / recurrente** *adj.* que se repite

**redemptive / redentor** *adj.* que sirve para librar del dolor; para reparar o compensar

**reeling / girar** *v.* dar vueltas y más vueltas en un movimiento circular

**reincarnation / reencarnación** *s.* creencia de que, después de la muerte, el alma reaparece en otro cuerpo o forma material

**relented / cedió** *v.* accedió a hacer algo a lo que se había negado en el pasado

**remorse / remordimiento** *s.* un profundo sentido de arrepentimiento por haber hecho algo malo

**reporter stand-ups / reportero** *in situ s.* toma que muestra al reportero mirando a la cámara e informando sobre el evento que está cubriendo

**retaliating / tomar represalias** *v.* vengarse por un daño recibido; devolver un perjuicio con otro

## S

**salient / sobresaliente** *adj.* notable, prominente

**secondary source / fuente secundaria** *s.* recuento y análisis de un suceso ocurrido en el pasado que se hace a partir de fuentes primarias y de otro tipo

**sensationalized / hacer sensacionalismo** *v.* exagerar una situación para provocar un efecto sensacionalista o tremendista

**sequence / secuencia** *s.* serie u orden lineal de pasos o sucesos

**serpentine / serpentino** *adj.* sinuoso; serpenteante, como el movimiento de una serpiente

**sheer / transparente** *adj.* muy fino; cuerpo a través del cual se puede ver

**specter / espectro** *s.* fantasma

**speech bubble / globo (historieta)** *s.* en una novela gráfica o cómic, forma circular que contiene las palabras de los personajes

**splash (splash) /** *splash page s.* en una novela gráfica o cómic un dibujo de toda una página

**sprawling / expandido** *adj.* extendido

**stagnation / estancamiento** *s.* estado de inactividad, de no moverse ni cambiar

**steal / escabullirse** *v.* moverse en secreto o silenciosamente

**stern / estricto** *adj.* rígido; severo

**stock / linaje** *s.* línea de descendencia de un determinado individuo o grupo étnico; familia o antepasados

**subsequent / subsecuente** *adj.* que viene después; siguiente

**summoned / convocó** *v.* le ordenó a alguien o algo que fuera a un lugar determinado

**surrounding / rodear** *v.* cercar por todos lados

## T

**tactics / tácticas** *s.* métodos militares

**teased / bromeó** *v.* hizo un chiste afectuoso, con buen humor

**technique / técnica** *s.* destreza o método especial

**tier / hilera** *s.* cada fila de viñetas de una novela gráfica

**tone / tono** *s.* la actitud que tiene el hablante hacia su tema

**transgression / transgresión** *s.* la acción de violar una ley o un mandato, o de cometer un pecado

**treasure / atesorar** *v.* valorar enormemente; estimar mucho

**trembling / tembloroso** *adj.* que se agita o tirita por temor, entusiasmo, debilidad, etc.

**tremulous / trémulo** *adj.* tembloroso; estremecido; tímido; temeroso

**tribulations / tribulaciones** *s.* conjunto de adversidades o penurias

**tryst / cita** *s.* encuentro amoroso secreto

## U

**understatement / subestimación** *s.* la acción de minimizar un tema para que parezca menos importante

**upheaval / revuelta** *s.* levantamiento

**valid / válido** *adj.* bien fundamentado; sensato; efectivo

**ventured / arriesgado** *adj.* se dice de alguien que intenta algo peligroso

**voluntary / voluntario** *adj.* algo que se eligió hacer libremente

## Y

**yearning / anhelo** *s.* deseo profundo; añoranza

# LITERARY TERMS HANDBOOK

**ADAPTATION** An *adaptation* is a work of art that uses the characters and tells the story originally presented in another work of art. Often, the adaptation is in a different form. A novel or play becomes a film, for example, or a poem becomes a story.

**ALLITERATION** *Alliteration* is the repetition of initial consonant sounds. Writers use alliteration to give emphasis to words, to imitate sounds, and to create musical effects.

**ALLUSION** An *allusion* is a reference to a well-known person, place, event, literary work, or work of art.

**ANALOGY** An *analogy* makes a comparison between two or more things that are similar in some ways but otherwise unalike.

**ANECDOTE** An *anecdote* is a brief story about an interesting, amusing, or strange event told to entertain or to make a point.

**ANTAGONIST** An *antagonist* is a character or force in conflict with a main character, or protagonist.

**ANTITHESIS** *Antithesis* is a form of parallelism that emphasizes strong contrasts.

**ARCHETYPE** An *archetype* is is a type of character, detail, image, or situation that appears in literature throughout history. Some critics believe that archetypes reveal deep truths about human experience.

**ARGUMENT** An *argument* is writing or speech that attempts to convince the reader to adopt a particular opinion or course of action. An argument is a logical way of presenting a belief, conclusion, or stance. A good argument is supported with reasoning and evidence.

**ASIDE** An *aside* is a short speech delivered by a character in a play in order to express his or her true thoughts and feelings. Traditionally, the aside is directed to the audience and is presumed to be inaudible to the other actors.

**ASSONANCE** *Assonance* is the repetition of vowel sounds followed by different consonants in two or more stressed syllables.

**AUTHOR'S PURPOSE** An *author's purpose* is his or her reason for writing. The four general purposes for writing are to inform, to persuade, to entertain, and to reflect.

**AUTOBIOGRAPHICAL WRITING** *Autobiographical writing* is any type of nonfiction in which an author tells his or her own story.

**AUTOBIOGRAPHY** An *autobiography* is a form of nonfiction in which a writer tells his or her own life story. An autobiography may tell about the person's whole life or only a part of it.

**BIBLIOGRAPHY** A *bibliography* or "works cited" lists all research sources used for an informative essay in an approved style.

**BIOGRAPHY** A *biography* is a form of nonfiction in which a writer tells the life story of another person. Biographies have been written about many famous people, historical and contemporary, but they can also be written about "ordinary" people.

**BLANK VERSE** *Blank verse* is poetry written in unrhymed iambic pentameter lines. This verse form was widely used by William Shakespeare.

**CAUSE-AND-EFFECT CHAIN** A single cause, which results in an effect, which leads to a second effect, which causes a third effect, and so on, is a *cause-and-effect chain.*

**CAUSE-AND-EFFECT RELATIONSHIP** A cause-and-effect relationship shows how one event or situation leads to another.

**CENTRAL IDEA** The *central idea* is the main idea the author wants the audience to understand and remember

**CHARACTER** A *character* is a person or an animal that takes part in the action of a literary work. The main character, or protagonist, is the most important character in a story. This character often changes in some important way as a result of the story's events.

Characters are sometimes classified as round or flat, dynamic or static. A complex, or *round character*, shows many different traits—faults as well as virtues. A *flat character* shows only one trait. A *dynamic character* develops and grows during the course of the story; a *static character* does not change.

**CHARACTERIZATION** *Characterization* is the act of creating and developing a character. In *direct characterization,* the author directly states a character's traits.

In *indirect characterization,* an author provides clues about a character by describing what a character looks like, does, and says, as well as how other characters react to him or her. It is up to the reader to draw conclusions about the character based on this indirect information.

The most effective indirect characterizations usually result from showing characters acting or speaking.

**CHARGED LANGUAGE** Words or phrases that evoke strong positive or negative reactions are referred to as *charged language.*

**CLAIM** The *claim* of a text is the key message that the writer wants to communicate about a topic.

**CLARIFICATION** A *clarification* focuses on a specific part of a response, sometimes simplifying the original idea and other times providing more detail.

**COMIC RELIEF** *Comic relief* is a technique that is used to interrupt a serious part of a literary work by introducing a humorous character or situation.

**CONFLICT** A *conflict* is a struggle between opposing forces. Characters in conflict form the basis of stories, novels, and plays.

There are two kinds of conflict: external and internal. In an *external conflict,* the main character struggles against an outside force.

An *internal conflict* involves a character in conflict with himself or herself.

**CONNOTATION** The *connotation* of a word is the set of ideas associated with it in addition to its explicit meaning.

**CONSONANCE** *Consonance* is the repetition of final consonant sounds in stressed syllables with different vowel sounds, as in *hat* and *sit*.

**COUPLET** A *couplet* is a pair of rhyming lines, usually of the same length and meter. Couplets are often found in poems and in plays written in verse.

**CRITICISM** *Criticism* is a form of argumentative writing in which an author expresses an opinion about a created work, such as a book, a film, or a performance.

**DENOTATION** The *denotation* of a word is its dictionary meaning, independent of other associations that the word may have.

**DESCRIPTION** A *description* is a portrait in words of a person, a place, or an object. Descriptive writing uses sensory details, those that appeal to the senses: sight, hearing, taste, smell, and touch. Description can be found in all types of writing. Rudolfo Anaya's essay "A Celebration of Grandfathers" contains descriptive passages.

**DIALOGUE** A *dialogue* is a conversation between characters that may reveal their traits and advance the action of a narrative. In fiction or nonfiction, quotation marks indicate a speaker's exact words, and a new paragraph usually indicates a change of speaker.

**DICTION** *Diction* refers to an author's choice of words, especially with regard to range of vocabulary, use of slang and colloquial language, and level of formality.

**DRAMA** A *drama* is a story written to be performed by actors. The script of a drama is made up of **dialogue**—the words the actors say—and **stage directions,** which are comments on how and where action happens.

The drama's **setting** is the time and place in which the action occurs. It is indicated by one or more sets, including furniture and backdrops, that suggest interior or exterior scenes. *Props* are objects, such as a sword or a cup of tea, that are used onstage.

At the beginning of most plays, a brief **exposition** gives the audience some background information about the characters and the situation. Just as in a story or novel, the plot of a drama is built around characters in conflict.

Dramas are divided into large units called **acts,** which are divided into smaller units called **scenes**. A long play may include many sets that change with the scenes, or it may indicate a change of scene with lighting.

**DRAMATIC IRONY** *Dramatic irony* is a contradiction between what a character thinks and what the audience knows to be true. For example: If a character tries desperately to crack a safe when the audience already knows the safe is empty, dramatic irony is created, causing humor or tension.

**ELLIPSES** *Ellipses* are used to show omitted words or sentences in quoted texts.

**END-STOPPED LINE** An *end-stopped line* is one in which both the grammatical structure and sense are complete at the end of the line.

**EPIC** An *epic* is a long narrative poem about the deeds of gods or heroes.

An epic is elevated in style and usually follows certain patterns. The poet begins by announcing the subject and asking a Muse—one of the nine goddesses of the arts, literature, and sciences—to help. An *epic hero* is the larger-than-life central character in an epic. Through behavior and deeds, the epic hero displays qualities that are valued by the society in which the epic originated.

See also **Epic Simile** and **Narrative Poem.**

**EPIC SIMILE** An *epic simile*, also called **Homeric simile,** is an elaborate comparison of unlike subjects.

**ESSAY** An *essay* is a short nonfiction work about a particular subject. While classification is difficult, four types of essays are sometimes identified.

A *descriptive essay* seeks to convey an impression about a person, place, or object.

A *narrative essay* tells a true story.

An *expository essay* gives information, discusses ideas, or explains a process.

An *explanatory* essay describes and summarizes information gathered from a number of sources on a concept.

A *persuasive essay* tries to convince readers to do something or to accept the writer's point of view.

**EXPOSITION** *Exposition* is writing or speech that explains a process or presents information. In the plot of a story or drama, the exposition is the part of the work that introduces the characters, the setting, and the basic situation.

**EXTENDED METAPHOR** In an *extended metaphor,* as in regular metaphor, a writer speaks or writes of a subject as though it were something else. An extended metaphor sustains the comparison for several lines or for an entire poem.

**FATE** *Fate* is a destiny over which a hero has little or no control.

**FEATURE ARTICLES** *Feature articles* are a type of journalism that focuses on a specific event or situation.

**FICTION** *Fiction* is prose writing that tells about imaginary characters and events. The term is usually used for novels and short stories, but it also applies to dramas and narrative poetry. Some writers rely on their imaginations alone to create their works of fiction. Others base their fiction on actual events and people, to which they add invented characters, dialogue, and plot situations.

**FIGURATIVE LANGUAGE** *Figurative language* is writing or speech not meant to be interpreted literally. It is often used to create vivid impressions by setting up comparisons between dissimilar things.

Some frequently used figures of speech are **metaphors, similes,** and **personifications.**

**FLASHBACK** A *flashback* is a means by which authors present material that occurred earlier than the present tense of the narrative. Authors may include this material in a character's memories, dreams, or accounts of past events.

**FOIL** A *foil* is a character who provides a contrast to another character. In *Romeo and Juliet*, the fiery temper of Tybalt serves as a foil to the good nature of Benvolio.

**FOLLOW-UP QUESTION** A *follow-up question* builds on the interview subject's response, clarifying and deepening answers.

**FORESHADOWING** *Foreshadowing* is the use in a literary work of clues that suggest events that have yet to occur. This technique helps create suspense, keeping readers wondering about what will happen next.

**FRAME STORY** A *frame story* is a story that brackets— or frames—another story or group of stories. This device creates a story-within-a-story narrative structure.

**FREE VERSE** *Free verse* is poetry not written in a regular pattern of meter or rhyme.

**GENRE** A *genre* is a category or type of literature. Literature is commonly divided into three major genres:

poetry, prose, and drama. Each major genre is in turn divided into smaller genres, as follows:

1. **Poetry:** Lyric Poetry, Concrete Poetry, Dramatic Poetry, Narrative Poetry, and Epic Poetry
2. **Prose:** Fiction (Novels and Short Stories) and Nonfiction (Biography, Autobiography, Letters, Essays, and Reports)
3. **Drama:** Serious Drama and Tragedy, Comic Drama, Melodrama, and Farce

**HYPERBOLE** A *hyperbole* is a deliberate exaggeration or overstatement.

**IAMB** An *iamb* is an unstressed syllable followed by a stressed syllable.

**IAMBIC PENTAMETER** Blank verse written in *iambic pentameter* has five iambs, called "feet," in each line.

**IN MEDIA RES** *In media res* means "in the middle of things."

**IDIOM** An *idiom* is an expression that is characteristic of a language, region, community, or class of people. *Idiomatic expressions* often arise from figures of speech and therefore cannot be understood literally.

**INTERVIEW** An *interview* is an exchange of ideas between an interviewer and an expert or someone who has had a unique experience. The basic structure of an interview is the Q&A (question and answer) format.

**IMAGE** An *image* is a word or phrase that appeals to one or more of the five senses—sight, hearing, touch, taste, or smell. Writers use images to re-create sensory experiences in words.

**IMAGERY** *Imagery* is the descriptive or figurative language used in literature to create word pictures for the reader. These pictures, or images, are created by details of sight, sound, taste, touch, smell, or movement.

**INTERNAL MONOLOGUE** To show a character's thoughts with more dimension, an author uses *internal monologue,* a kind of "conversation" a character has with himself or herself.

**INTERVIEW** An *interview* is an exchange of ideas between an interviewer and an expert or someone who has had a unique experience.

**IRONY** *Irony* is the general term for literary techniques that portray differences between appearance and reality, or expectation and result. In **verbal irony,** words are used to suggest the opposite of what is meant. In **dramatic irony,** there is a contradiction between what a character thinks and what the reader or audience knows to be true. In **situational irony,** an event occurs that directly contradicts the expectations of the characters, the reader, or the audience.

**JOURNALISM** *Journalism* is a type of nonfiction writing that focuses on current events and nonfiction subjects of general interest to the public.

**LYRIC POEM** A *lyric poem* is a highly musical verse that expresses the thoughts, observations, and feelings of a single speaker.

**MEMOIR** A *memoir* is a limited kind of autobiographical writing that focuses on one period or aspect of the writer's life.

**METAPHOR** A *metaphor* is a figure of speech in which one thing is spoken of as though it were something else. Unlike a simile, which compares two things using *like* or *as,* a metaphor implies a comparison between them.

**MONOLOGUE** A *monologue* in a play is a speech by one character that, unlike a *soliloquy,* is addressed to another character or characters.

**MOOD** *Mood,* or *atmosphere,* is the feeling created in the reader by a literary work or passage. The mood is often suggested by descriptive details. Often the mood can be described in a single word, such as lighthearted, frightening, or despairing.

**MOTIVE** A *motive* is a reason for an action.

**NARRATION** *Narration* is writing that tells a story. The act of telling a story in speech is also called narration. Novels and short stories are fictional narratives. Nonfiction works—such as news stories, biographies, and autobiographies—are also narratives. A narrative poem tells a story in verse.

**NARRATIVE** A *narrative* is a story told in fiction, nonfiction, poetry, or drama.

**NARRATIVE NONFICTION** Writing that tells a real-life story is called *narrative nonfiction.*

**NARRATIVE POINT OF VIEW** A *narrative point of view* is the vantage point from which a fiction writer chooses to tell a story.

**NARRATOR** A *narrator* is a speaker or character who tells a story. The writer's choice of narrator determines the story's *point of view*, which directs the type and amount of information the writer reveals.

When a character in the story tells the story, that character is a *first-person narrator*. This narrator may be a major character, a minor character, or just a witness. Readers see only what this character sees, hear only what he or she hears, and so on. The first-person narrator may or may not be reliable.

When a voice outside the story narrates, the story has a third-person narrator. An omniscient, or all-knowing, third-person narrator can tell readers what any character thinks and feels. A limited third-person narrator sees the world through one character's eyes and reveals only that character's thoughts.

**NONFICTION** *Nonfiction* is prose writing that presents and explains ideas or that tells about real people, places, ideas, or events. To be classified as nonfiction, a work must be true. "Single Room, Earth View" is a nonfictional account of the view of Earth from space.

**NOVEL** A *novel* is a long work of fiction. It has a plot that explores characters in conflict. A novel may also have one or more subplots, or minor stories, and several themes.

**ONOMATOPOEIA** *Onomatopoeia* is the use of words that imitate sounds. *Whirr, thud,* and *hiss* are examples.

**ORAL TRADITION** The *oral tradition* is the passing of songs, stories, and poems from generation to generation by word of mouth. Many folk songs, ballads, fairy tales, legends, and myths originated in the oral tradition.

See also *Myth.*

**OXYMORON** An *oxymoron* is a combination of words, or parts of words, that contradict each other. Examples are "deafening silence," "honest thief," "wise fool," and "bittersweet."

**PANTOUM** A *pantoum* is an old, formal poetic structure consisting of a series of quatrains, or four-line stanzas.

**PARADOX** A *paradox* is a statement that seems contradictory but may actually be true. Because a paradox is surprising, it catches the reader's attention.

**PARALLELISM** *Parallelism* is the repetition of a grammatical structure in order to create a rhythm and make words more memorable.

**PARAPHRASE** A *paraphrase* is a restatement of a passage from an original text

**PERSONIFICATION** *Personification* is a type of figurative language in which a nonhuman subject is given human characteristics.

**PERSUASION** *Persuasion* is writing or speech that attempts to convince the reader to adopt a particular opinion or course of action. An *argument* is a logical way of presenting a belief, conclusion, or stance. A good argument is supported with reasoning and evidence.

**PERSUASIVE APPEALS** *Persuasive appeals* are methods of informing or convincing readers to see something in a new way.

**PERSUASIVE ESSAY** A *persuasive essay* is a short nonfiction work in which a writer seeks to convince the reader to think or act in a certain way.

**PERSUASIVE SPEECH** In a *persuasive speech,* the speaker uses rhetoric, logic, and oral-presentation techniques to convince listeners to think or act in a certain way.

**PLOT** *Plot* is the sequence of events in a literary work. In most novels, dramas, short stories, and narrative poems, the plot involves both characters and a central conflict. The plot usually begins with an *exposition* that introduces the setting, the characters, and the basic situation. This is followed by the *inciting incident*, which introduces the central conflict. The conflict then increases during the *development* until it reaches a high point of interest or suspense, the *climax*. All the events leading up to the climax make up the *rising action*. The climax is followed by the *falling action*, which leads to the *denouement*, or *resolution*, in which a general insight or change is conveyed.

**POETIC STRUCTURE** The basic structures of poetry are lines and stanzas. A *line* is a group of words arranged in a row. A line of poetry may break, or end, in different ways. An *end-stopped line* is one in which both the grammatical structure and sense are complete at the end of the line. A *run-on*, or *enjambed, line* is one in which both the grammatical structure and sense continue past the end of the line.

**POETRY** *Poetry* is one of the three major types of literature, the others being prose and drama. Most poems make use of highly concise, musical, and emotionally charged language. Many also make use of imagery, figurative language, and special devices of sound such as rhyme. Poems are often divided into lines and stanzas and often employ regular rhythmical patterns, or meters. However, some poems are written out just like prose, while others are written in free verse.

**POINT OF VIEW** An author's *point of view* is the perspective from which events are told or described.

**PRIMARY SOURCE** A *primary source* is raw material or first-hand information about what is being studied.

**PROSE** *Prose* is the ordinary form of written language. Most writing that is not poetry, drama, or song is considered prose. Prose is one of the major genres of literature and occurs in two forms: fiction and nonfiction.

**PUN** A *pun* is a play on words involving a word with two or more different meanings or two words that sound alike but have different meanings. In *Romeo and Juliet,* the dying Mercutio makes a pun involving two meanings of the word *grave*, "serious" and "burial site": "Ask for me tomorrow, and you shall find me a grave man" (Act III, Scene i, lines 92–93).

**QUATRAIN** A *quatrain* is a stanza or poem made up of four lines, usually with a definite rhythm and rhyme scheme.

**QUOTATION** A speaker's exact words are a *direct quotation* and are shown using quotation marks.

**REPETITION** *Repetition* is the use of any element of language—a sound, a word, a phrase, a clause, or a sentence—more than once.

Poets use many kinds of repetition. Alliteration, assonance, rhyme, and rhythm are repetitions of certain sounds and sound patterns. A refrain is a repeated line or group of lines. In both prose and poetry, repetition is used for musical effects and for emphasis.

**RESTATEMENT** *Restatements,* or paraphrases, help an interviewer make sure the audience understands the main point the interviewee is communicating.

**RHETORIC** *Rhetoric* refers to language devices, especially the art of speaking or writing effectively.

**RHETORICAL DEVICES** *Rhetorical devices* are special patterns of words and ideas that create emphasis and stir emotion, especially in speeches or other oral presentations. *Parallelism,* for example, is the repetition of a grammatical structure in order to create a rhythm and make words more memorable.

Other common rhetorical devices include: *analogy*, drawing comparisons between two unlike things; *charged language*, words that appeal to the emotions; *restatement*, expressing the same idea in different words; and *rhetorical questions*, questions with obvious answers.

**RUN-ON, OR ENJAMBED, LINE** A *run-on, or enjambed, line* is one in which both the grammatical structure and sense continue past the end of the line.

See also *Meter*.

**SCIENCE FICTION** *Science fiction* is writing that tells about imaginary events involving science or technology. Many science-fiction stories are set in the future.

**SENSORY LANGUAGE** *Sensory language* is writing or speech that uses details to appeal to one or more of the senses.

**SETTING** The *setting* of a literary work is the time and lace of the action. Time can include not only the historical period—past, present, or future—but also a specific year, season, or time of day. Place may involve not only the geographical place—a region, country, state, or town—but also the social, economic, or cultural environment.

In some stories, setting serves merely as a backdrop for action, a context in which the characters move and speak. In others, however, setting is a crucial element.

**SHORT STORY** A *short story* is a brief work of fiction. In most short stories, one main character faces a conflict that is resolved in the plot of the story. Great craftsmanship must go into the writing of a good story, for it has to accomplish its purpose in relatively few words.

**SIMILE** A *simile* is a figure of speech in which the words *like* or *as* are used to compare two apparently dissimilar items. The comparison, however, surprises the reader into a fresh perception by finding an unexpected likeness.

**SITUATIONAL IRONY** *Situational irony* occurs when events in a story go directly against the expectations of the main characters or the readers.

**SOCIAL AND HISTORICAL CONTEXT** The circumstances of the time and place in which a story occurs are referred to as *social and historical context.*

**SOLILOQUY** A *soliloquy* is a long speech expressing the thoughts of a character alone on stage.

**SOUND DEVICES** A *sound device* is a technique used by a poets and writers to emphasize the sound relationships among words in order to create musical and emotional effects and emphasize a poem's meaning. These devices include *alliteration, consonance, assonance, onomatopoeia,* and *rhyme.*

**SPEAKER** The *speaker* is the imaginary voice assumed by the writer of a poem. In many poems, the speaker is not identified by name, and may be may be a person, an animal, a thing, or an abstraction.

**SPECIFIC DETAILS** *Specific details* are used by both fiction and nonfiction writers to support and develop a central idea or theme.

**STAGE DIRECTIONS** *Stage directions* are notes included in a drama to describe how the work is to be performed or staged. These instructions are printed in italics and are not spoken aloud. They are used to describe sets, lighting, sound effects, and the appearance, personalities, and movements of characters.

**STANZA** A *stanza* is a repeated grouping of two or more lines in a poem that often share a pattern of rhythm and rhyme. Stanzas are sometimes named according to the number of lines they have—for example, a *couplet,* two lines; a *quatrain,* four lines; a *sestet,* six lines; and an *octave,* eight lines.

**STYLE** *Style* refers to an author's unique way of writing. Elements determining style include diction; tone; characteristic use of figurative language, dialect, or rhythmic devices; and syntax.

**SUMMARY** A *summary* is a concise, complete, and accurate overview of a text.

**SUPPORTING DETAILS** Pieces of information that illustrate, expand on, or prove an author's ideas are called *supporting details.* Supporting details can validate an argument, provide information, or add interest.

**SYMBOL** A *symbol* is anything that stands for something else. In addition to having its own meaning and reality, a symbol also represents abstract ideas. For example, a flag is a piece of cloth, but it also represents the idea of a country.

**THEME** A *theme* is a central message or insight into life revealed through a literary work. The theme of a literary work may be stated directly or implied. When the theme of a work is implied, readers think about what the work suggests about people or life.

*Archetypal themes* are those that occur in folklore and literature across the world and throughout history.

**TONE** The *tone* of a literary work is the writer's attitude toward his or her audience and subject.

**TRAGEDY** A *tragedy* is a work of literature, especially a play, that results in a catastrophe or great misfortune for the main character, or *tragic hero.* In ancient Greek drama, the main character was always a significant person—a king or a hero—and the cause of the tragedy was a *tragic flaw,* or weakness, in his or her character. In modern drama, the main character can be an ordinary person, and the cause of the tragedy can be some evil in society itself.

**TRAGIC FLAW** A *tragic flaw* is a personality defect that contributes to a hero's choice, and thus, to his or her tragic downfall.

**TRAVEL JOURNALISM** *Travel journalism* is a type of literary nonfiction in which a writer describes the experience of visiting a particular place.

**VISUAL ESSAY** A *visual essay* is an exploration of a topic that conveys its ideas through visual elements as well as language. Like a standard essay, a visual essay presents an author's views of a single topic. Unlike other essays, however, much of the meaning in a visual essay is conveyed through illustrations or photographs.

**VIVID LANGUAGE** *Vivid language* is strong, precise words that bring ideas to life.

**VOICE** *Voice* is a writer's distinctive "sound" or way of "speaking" on the page. It is related to such elements as word choice, sentence structure, and tone. It is similar to an individual's speech style and can be described in the same way—fast, slow, blunt, meandering, breathless, and so on.

Voice resembles *style,* an author's typical way of writing, but style usually refers to a quality that can be found throughout an author's body of work, while an author's voice may sometimes vary from work to work.

# MANUAL DE TÉRMINOS LITERARIOS

**ADAPTACIÓN** Una *adaptación* es una obra de arte que incluye los personajes y cuenta la misma historia que se presentó originalmente en otra obra de arte. A menudo, la adaptación adopta una forma diferente. Una novela u obra de teatro puede transformarse en una película, por ejemplo, o un poema puede transformarse en un cuento.

**ALITERACIÓN** La *aliteración* es la repetición de los sonidos consonantes iniciales. Los escritores usan la aliteración para dar énfasis a las palabras, para imitar sonidos y para crear efectos de musicalida.

**ALUSIÓN** Una *alusión* es una referencia a una persona, lugar, hecho, obra literaria u obra de arte muy conocida.

**ANALOGÍA** Una *analogía* establece una comparación entre dos o más cosas que son parecidas en algunos aspectos pero se diferencian en otros.

**ANÉCDOTA** Una *anécdota* es un relato breve sobre un hecho interesante, divertido o extraño, que se narra con el fin de entretener o decir algo importante.

**ANTAGONISTA** Un *antagonista* es un personaje o fuerza en conflicto con el personaje principal o protagonista.

**ANTÍTESIS** Una *antítesis* es una forma de paralelismo que enfatiza los contrastes más importantes.

**ARQUETIPO** Un *arquetipo* es un tipo de personaje, detalle, imagen o situación que reaparece en la literatura a través de la historia. Algunos críticos piensan que los arquetipos revelan verdades profundas sobre la experiencia humana.

**ARGUMENTO** Un *argumento* es un escrito o discurso que trata de convencer al lector para que siga una acción o adopte una opinión en particular. Un argumento es una manera lógica de presentar una creencia, una conclusión o una postura. Un buen argumento se respalda con razonamientos y pruebas.

**APARTE** Un *aparte* es un parlamento breve en boca de un personaje en una obra de teatro, en el que expresa sus verdaderos pensamientos y sentimientos. Tradicionalmente, los apartes se dirigen a la audiencia y se suponen inaudibles a los otros personajes.

**ASONANCIA** La *asonancia* es la repetición de los sonidos vocálicos seguidos de distintas consonantes en dos o más sílabas acentuadas.

**PROPÓSITO DEL AUTOR** El *propósito del autor* es su razón para escribir. Los cuatro propósitos generales del autor son: informar, persuadir, entretener y reflexionar.

**ESCRITURA AUTOBIOGRÁFICA** La *escritura autobiográfica* es cualquier forma de no-ficción en la que el autor narra la historia de su vida

**AUTOBIOGRAFÍA** Una *autobiografía* es una forma de no-ficción en la que el escritor cuenta su propia vida. Una autobiografía puede contar toda la vida de una persona o solo una parte de ella.

**BIBLIOGRAFÍA** Una *bibliografía* o lista de "obras citadas" enumera todas las fuentes de investigación usadas para escribir un ensayo informativo en un estilo aprobado.

**BIOGRAFÍA** Una *biografía* es una forma de no-ficción en la que un escritor cuenta la vida de otra persona. Se han escrito biografías de muchas personas famosas de la historia o del mundo contemporáneo, pero también pueden escribirse biografías de personas comunes.

**VERSO BLANCO** El *verso blanco* es poesía escrita en líneas de pentámetros yámbicos sin rima. Esta forma de verso fue muy utilizada por William Shakespeare.

**CADENA DE CAUSA Y CONSECUENCIA** Una causa única, que tiene como resultado una consecuencia, la cual lleva a una segunda consecuencia, que a su vez causa una tercera consecuencia, etcétera, constituye una *cadena de causa y consecuencia.*

**RELACIÓN DE CAUSA Y CONSECUENCIA** Una *relación de causa y consecuencia* muestra como un suceso o situación lleva a otro.

**IDEA CENTRAL** La *idea central* es la idea principal que el autor quiere que la audiencia comprenda y recuerde.

**PERSONAJE** Un *personaje* es una persona o animal que participa de la acción en una obra literaria. El personaje principal, o protagonista, es el personaje más importante del relato. Este personaje a menudo cambia de una manera importante como resultado de los eventos que se suceden en el cuento.

Los personajes a veces son clasificados como complejos o chatos, dinámicos o estáticos. Un *personaje complejo* muestra muchos rasgos diferentes—tanto faltas como virtudes. Un *personaje chato* muestra solo un rasgo. Un *personaje dinámico* se desarrolla y crece en el curso del relato; mientras que un *personaje estático* no cambia.

**CARACTERIZACIÓN** La *caracterización* es el acto de crear y desarrollar un personaje. En una *caracterización directa*, el autor expresa explícitamente los rasgos de un personaje. En una *caracterización indirecta*, el autor proporciona claves sobre el personaje, describiendo el aspecto del personaje, qué hace, qué dice, así como la manera en que otros personajes lo ven y reaccionan a él. Al lector le corresponde sacar conclusiones sobre los personajes basándose en información indirecta.

La caracterización indirecta más efectiva resulta por lo general de mostrar cómo hablan y actúan los personajes.

**LENGUAJE EMOCIONALMENTE CARGADO** Se conoce como *lenguaje emocionalmente cargado* a las palabras o frases que evocan reacciones intensas, ya sean positivas o negativas.

**AFIRMACIÓN** La *afirmación* de un texto es el mensaje clave que el escritor quiere comunicar acerca de un tema.

**ACLARACIÓN** La *aclaración* se centra en una parte determinada de la respuesta, simplificando la idea original o aportando más detalles.

**ALIVIO CÓMICO** El *alivio cómico* es una técnica que se usa para interrumpir una parte seria de una obra literaria introduciendo personajes o situaciones jocosas.

**CONFLICTO** Un *conflicto* es una lucha entre fuerzas opuestas. Los personajes en conflicto forman la base de cuentos, novelas y obras de teatro.

Hay dos tipos de conflicto: externos e internos. En un *conflicto externo*, el personaje principal lucha contra una fuerza externa.

Un *conflicto interno* atañe a un personaje que entra en conflicto consigo mismo.

**CONNOTACIÓN** La *connotación* de una palabra es el conjunto de ideas que se asocian a ella, además de su significado explícito.

**CONSONANCIA** La *consonancia* es la repetición de los sonidos consonantes finales de sílabas acentuadas con distintos sonidos vocálicos, como en *hat* and *sit*.

**PAREADO** Un *dístico* o *pareado* es un par de versos rimados, por lo general de la misma extensión y metro. Por lo general, los pareados se usan en poemas y en obras de teatro escritas en verso.

**CRÍTICA** La *crítica* es un texto argumentativo en el que un autor expresa su opinión acerca de una obra como, por ejemplo, un libro, una película o una actuación.

**DENOTACIÓN** La *denotación* de una palabra es su significado en un diccionario, independientemente de otras asociaciones que la palabra suscita.

**DESCRIPCIÓN** Una *descripción* es un retrato en palabras de una persona, un lugar o un objeto. La escritura descriptiva utiliza detalles sensoriales, es decir, aquellos que apelan a los sentidos: la vista, el oído, el gusto, el olfato y el tacto. La descripción puede encontrarse en todo tipo de escritores. El ensayo de Rudolfo Anaya, "Una celebración de los abuelos" incluye pasajes descriptivos.

**DIÁLOGO** Un *diálogo* es una conversación entre personajes que puede revelar sus rasgos y hacer progresar la acción de un relato. Ya sea en un género de ficción o de no ficción —en inglés— las comillas reproducen las palabras exactas de un personaje, y un nuevo párrafo indica un cambio de personaje.

**DICCIÓN** La *dicción* comprende la elección de palabras que hace el autor, especialmente en relación a un abanico de posibilidades, al uso de un lenguaje coloquial o jerga, y al nivel de formalidad que utilizan tanto el narrador como los personajes.

**DRAMA** Un *drama* es una historia escrita para ser representada por actores. El guión de un drama está constituido por *diálogo* —las palabras que dicen los actores— y por *direcciones escénicas*, que son los comentarios acerca de cómo y dónde se sitúa la acción.

La *ambientación* es la época y el lugar donde sucedes la acción. Se indica a través de una o varias escenografías, que incluyen el mobiliario y el fondo, o telón de fondo, que sugieren si las escenas son interiores o exteriores. La *tramoya o utilería* son los objetos, tales como una espada o una taza de té, que se usan en escena.

Al principio de la mayoría de los dramas, una breve *exposición* le da a la audiencia cierta información de contexto sobre los personajes y la situación. Al igual que en un cuento o una novela, el argumento o trama de una obra dramática se construye a partir de personajes en conflicto.

Los dramas se dividen a grandes unidades llamadas *actos*, que a su vez se dividen en unidades más breves llamadas *escenas*. Un drama de cierta extensión puede incluir muchas escenografías que cambian con las escenas, o pueden indicar un cambio de escena por medio de la iluminación.

**IRONÍA DRAMÁTICA** La *ironía dramática* es una contradicción entre lo que el personaje cree y lo que la audiencia sabe. Por ejemplo: se produce ironía dramática que provoca humor o tensión si el personaje intenta desesperadamente forzar una caja fuerte cuando la audiencia ya sabe que la caja está vacía.

**PUNTOS SUSPENSIVOS** Los *puntos suspensivos* se usan para indicar que se han omitido palabras u oraciones de un texto que se cita.

**VERSO NO ENCABALGADO** Un *verso no encabalgado* es aquel en el que tanto la estructura gramatical como el sentido se completan al final del renglón.

**ÉPICA** Un *poema épico* es un poema narrativo extenso sobre las hazañas de dioses o héroes.

Los poemas épicos son de estilo elevado y por lo general siguen ciertos patrones. El poeta comienza por anunciar el tema y le pide ayuda a la Musa —una de las nueve diosas de las artes, la literatura y las ciencias. Un *héroe épico* es el personaje principal de un poema épico y suele tener características sobrehumanas. A través de su conducta y sus hazañas, el héroe épico demuestra tener cualidades muy valoradas por la sociedad en la que se originó el poema.

Ver también *Comparativo épico y Poema narrativo*

**COMPARATIVO ÉPICO** El *comparativo épico*, también llamado *comparativo homérico*, es una comparación muy elaborada de dos objetos disímiles.

**ENSAYO** Un *ensayo* es una obra breve de no-ficción sobre un tema en particular. Si bien es difícil llegar a una clasificación, suelen diferenciarse cinco tipos de ensayos.

El *ensayo descriptivo* se propone transmitir una impresión acerca de una persona, un lugar o un objeto.

El *ensayo narrativo* narra una historia real.

El *ensayo expositivo* proporciona información, discute ideas o explica un proceso.

El *ensayo explicativo* describe y resume información sobre un determinado concepto recogida de cierto número de fuentes.

El *ensayo persuasivo* intenta convencer a los lectores de que hagan algo o que acepten el punto de vista del escritor.

**EXPOSICIÓN** Una *exposición* es un escrito o un discurso que explica un proceso o presenta información. En un cuento o un drama, la exposición es la parte donde se presenta a los personajes, la ambientación y la situación básica.

**METÁFORA EXTENDIDA** En una *metáfora extendida*, al igual que en una metáfora habitual, el escritor escribe o habla de algo como si fuera otra cosa. Una metáfora extendida prolonga la comparación a lo largo de varios versos o de un poema entero.

**DESTINO** El *destino* es la suerte del héroe, algo sobre lo que no tiene control.

**ARTÍCULOS DESTACADOS** Los *artículos destacados* son una forma de periodismo que se centra en una situación o suceso específico.

**FICCIÓN** Una obra de *ficción* es un escrito en prosa que cuenta algo sobre personajes y hechos imaginarios. El término se usa por lo general para referirse a novelas y cuentos, pero también se aplica a dramas y poemas narrativos. Algunos escritores se basan solamente en su imaginación para crear sus obras de ficción. Otros basan su ficción en hechos y personas reales, a las que agregan personajes, diálogos y situaciones de su propia invención.

**LENGUAJE FIGURADO** El *lenguaje figurado* es un escrito o discurso que no se debe interpretar literalmente. A menudo se usa para crear impresiones vívidas, estableciendo comparaciones entre cosas disímiles.

Algunas de las formas más usadas del lenguaje figurado son las *metáforas*, los *símiles* y las *personificaciones*.

**FLASHBACK** Un *flashback* o *escena retrospectiva* es una de las maneras a través de las que los autores presentan materiales de algo que ocurrió antes del tiempo presente del relato. Los autores pueden incluir estos materiales en los recuerdos o sueños de un personaje, o como relatos de hechos pasados

**PERSONAJE COMPLEMENTARIO** Un *personaje complementario* es un personaje que se presenta como la contraposición de otro. En *Romeo y Julieta*, el mal carácter de Teobaldo sirve de complementario a la buena disposición de Benvolio.

**PREGUNTA COMPLEMENTARIA** En las entrevistas, una *pregunta complementaria* clarifica y profundiza en las respuestas del entrevistado.

**PREFIGURACIÓN** La *prefiguración* es el uso, en una obra literaria, de claves que sugieren hechos que van a suceder. Esta técnica ayuda a crear suspenso, manteniendo a los lectores interesados preguntándose qué sucederá.

**CUENTO DE ENMARQUE** Un *cuento de enmarque* es un relato dentro del cual se incluyen otros relatos. Este recurso permite crear una estructura narrativa del tipo "cuento dentro del cuento".

**VERSO LIBRE** El *verso libre* es una forma poética en la que no se sigue un patrón regular de metro ni de rima.

**GÉNERO** Un *género* es una categoría o tipo de literatura. La literatura se divide por lo general en tres géneros principales: poesía, prosa y drama. Cada uno de estos géneros principales se dividen a su vez en géneros más pequeños. Por ejemplo:

1. **Poesía:** Poesía lírica, Poesía concreta, Poesía dramática, Poesía narrativa y Poesía épica.

2. **Prosa:** Ficción (Novelas y Cuentos) y No-ficción (Biografía, Autobiografía, Cartas, Ensayos, Artículos).

3. **Drama:** Drama serio y Tragedia, Comedia dramática, Melodrama y Farsa.

**HIPÉRBOLE** Una *hipérbole* es una exageración o magnificación deliberada.

**YAMBO** Una sílaba átona seguida por una tónica constituyen un *yambo.*

**PENTÁMETRO YÁMBICO** El verso libre escrito en *pentámetro yámbico* tiene cinco yambos, llamados "pies", en cada verso.

**EXPRESIÓN IDIOMÁTICA** Una *expresión idiomática* es una expresión propia de una lengua, región, comunidad, o clase de personas. Las *expresiones idiomáticas* surgen a menudo a partir de expresiones del lenguaje figurado y por lo tanto no pueden entenderse literalmente.

**IN MEDIA RES** La frase *in media res* significa "en el medio de las cosas".

**ENTREVISTA** Una *entrevista* es un intercambio de ideas entre un entrevistador y un experto o alguien que ha tenido una experiencia inusual. La estructura básica de una entrevista es una sucesión de preguntas y respuestas.

**IMAGEN** Una *imagen* es una palabra o frase que apela a uno o más de los cinco sentidos: la vista, el oído, el tacto, el gusto y el olfato. Los escritores usan imágenes para recrear en palabras las experiencias sensoriales.

**IMÁGENES** Las *imágenes* son el lenguaje figurado o descriptivo que se usa en la literatura para crear una descripción verbal para los lectores. Estas descripciones verbales, o imágenes, se crean incluyendo detalles visuales, auditivos, gustativos, táctiles, olfativos o de movimiento.

**MONÓLOGO INTERIOR** Para mostrar los pensamientos de un personaje con mayor profundidad, los autores usan *monólogo interior,* una especie de "conversación" que el personaje tiene consigo mismo.

**ENTREVISTA** Una *entrevista* es un intercambio de ideas entre el entrevistador y un experto o alguien que haya tenido una experiencia singular.

**IRONÍA** *Ironía* es un término general para distintas técnicas literarias que subrayan las diferencias entre apariencia y realidad, o entre expectativas y resultado. En una *ironía verbal*, las palabras se usan para sugerir lo opuesto a los que se dice. En la *ironía dramática* hay una contradicción entre los que el personaje piensa y lo que el lector o la audiencia sabe que es verdad. En una *ironía situacional,* ocurre un suceso que contradice directamente las expectativas de los personajes, y del lector o la audiencia.

**PERIODISMO** El *periodismo* es un fipo de escritura de no-ficción que se centra en hechos presentes y en temas de no-ficción de interés general.

**POEMA LÍRICO** Un *poema lírico* es una sucesión de versos de mucha musicalidad que expresan los pensamientos, observaciones y sentimientos de un único hablante.

**MEMORIAS** Un libro de *memorias* es un tipo limitado de escrito autobiográfico que se centra en un período o aspecto de la vida del autor.

**METÁFORA** Una *metáfora* es una figura retórica en la que el escritor se refiere a algo como si fuera otra cosa. Al contrario del símil, que compara dos cosas con las palabras *como* o *tal como*, la metáfora insinúa la comparación.

**MONÓLOGO** Un *monólogo* en una obra de teatro es un parlamento por parte de un personaje que, a diferencia del *soliloquio*, se dirige a otro u otros personajes.

**TONO** El *tono* o la *atmósfera* es la sensación que un pasaje u obra literaria crea en el lector. Por lo general, el tono se crea a partir de detalles descriptivos. A menudo puede ser descrito con una sola palabra, tal como desenfadado, aterrador o desesperante.

**MOTIVO** El *motivo* es la razón de una acción.

**NARRACIÓN** Una *narración* es un escrito que cuenta una historia. El acto de contar una historia de forma oral también se llama narración. Las novelas y los cuentos son obras narrativas de ficción. Las obras de no-ficción, como las noticias, las biografías y las autobiografías, también son narraciones. Un poema narrativo cuenta una historia en verso.

**RELATO** Se llama *relato* a la historia que se narra, en una obra de ficción, de no-ficción, en un poema o en un drama.

**RELATO DE NO-FICCIÓN** Se le llama *relato de no-ficción* al escrito que cuenta una historia de la vida real.

**PUNTO DE VISTA NARRATIVO** El *punto de vista narrativo* es la perspectiva desde la que el escritor de ficción cuenta la historia.

**NARRADOR** Un *narrador* es el hablante o el personaje que cuenta una historia. La elección del narrador por parte del autor determina el *punto de vista* desde el que se va a narrar la historia, lo que determina el tipo y la cantidad de información que se revelará.

Cuando el que cuenta la historia es uno de los personajes, a ese personaje se lo llama *narrador en primera persona*. Este narrador puede ser uno de los personajes principales, un personaje menor, o solo un testigo. Los lectores ven solo lo que este personaje ve, oyen solo lo que este personaje oye, etc. El narrador en primera persona puede ser confiable o no.

Cuando la que cuenta la historia es una voz exterior a la historia, hablamos de un *narrador en tercera persona*. Un narrador en tercera persona, omnisciente —es decir, que todo lo sabe— puede decirles a los lectores lo que cualquier personaje piensa o siente. Un narrador en tercera persona limitado ve el mundo a través de los ojos de un solo personaje y revela solo los pensamientos de ese personaje.

**NO-FICCIÓN** La *no-ficción* es un escrito en prosa que presenta y explica ideas o cuenta algo acerca de personas, lugares, ideas o hechos reales. Para ser clasificado como no-ficción un escrito debe ser verdadero. "Single Room, Earth View" es un relato no ficcional acerca de cómo se ve la Tierra desde el espacio.

**NOVELA** Una *novela* es una obra extensa de ficción. Tiene una trama que explora los personajes en conflicto. Una novela también puede tener una o más tramas secundarias —es decir, historias de menor importancia—, así como tocar varios temas.

**ONOMATOPEYA** La *onomatopeya* es el uso de palabras que imitan sonidos, tales como *pío-pío, tic-tac* o susurro.

**TRADICIÓN ORAL** La *tradición oral* es la transmisión de canciones, cuentos y poemas de una generación a otra, de boca a boca. Muchas canciones folklóricas, baladas, cuentos de hadas, leyendas y mitos se originaron en la tradición oral.

**OXÍMORON** Un *oxímoron* es una combinación de palabras, o partes de palabras, que se contradicen mutuamente. Por ejemplo, "un silencio ensordecedor", "un ladrón honesto", "la música callada".

**CUARTETAS ENCADENADAS** Las *cuartetas encadenadas* son una antigua estructura poética que consiste en un serie de cuartetas, o estrofas de cuatro versos.

**PARADOJA** Una *paradoja* es un enunciado que parece contradictorio, pero que sin embargo puede ser verdadero. Por ser siempre sorpresiva, la paradoja suele captar la atención de los lectores.

**PARALELISMO** El *paralelismo* es la repetición de una estructura gramatical con el fin de crear un ritmo y que las palabras resulten más memorables.

**PARÁFRASIS** La *paráfrasis* es reescribir o volver a contar una historia con nuestras propias palabras.

**PERSONIFICACIÓN** La *personificación* es un tipo de figura retórica en la que se dota a una instancia no humana de rasgos y actitudes humanas.

**PERSUASIÓN** La *persuasión* es un recurso escrito u oral por el que se intenta convencer al lector de que adopte una opinión o actúe de determinada manera. Un *argumento* es una manera lógica de presentar una creencia, una conclusión o una postura. Un buen argumento se respalda con razones y evidencias.

**APELACIONES PERSUASIVAS** Las *apelaciones persuasivas* son métodos que se utilizan para informar o convencer a los lectores de que vean algo desde una nueva perspectiva.

**ENSAYO PERSUASIVO** Un *ensayo persuasivo* es una obra corta de no-ficción en la que el escritor tiene como objetivo convencer al lector para que piense o actúe de una manera determinada.

**DISCURSO PERSUASIVO** En un *discurso persuasivo* el hablante utiliza técnicas de la retórica, la lógica y las presentaciones orales para convencer a los oyentes de que piensen o actúen de una manera determinada.

**TRAMA o ARGUMENTO** La *trama* o *argumento* es la secuencia de los eventos que suceden en una obra literaria. En la mayoría de las novelas, dramas, cuentos y poemas narrativos, la trama implica tanto a los personajes como al conflicto central. La trama por lo general empieza con una *exposición* que introduce la ambientación, los personajes y la situación básica. A ello le sigue el *suceso desencadenante*, que introduce el conflicto central. Este conflicto aumenta durante el *desarrollo* hasta que alcanza el punto más alto de interés o suspenso, llamado *clímax*. Todos los sucesos que conducen al clímax contribuyen a la *acción dramática creciente*. Al clímax le sigue la *acción dramática decreciente* que conduce al *desenlace*, o *resolución*, en el que se produce un cambio significativo.

**ESTRUCTURA POÉTICA** Las *estructuras poéticas* básicas son los versos y las estrofas. Un verso es un grupo de palabras ordenadas en una misma hilera. Un verso puede terminar, o cortarse, de distintas maneras. En un *verso no encabalgado* la estructura gramatical y el sentido se completan al final de esa línea. En un verso encabalgado tanto la estructura gramatical como el sentido de una línea continúa en el verso que sigue.

**POESÍA** La *poesía* es uno de los tres géneros literarios más importantes. Los otros dos son la prosa y el drama. La mayoría de los poemas están escritos en un lenguaje altamente conciso, musical y emocionalmente rico. Muchos también hacen uso de imágenes, de figuras retóricas y de recursos especiales de sonido, tales como la rima. Los poemas a menudo se dividen en versos y estrofas y emplean patrones rítmicos regulares, llamados metros. Sin embargo, algunos poemas están escritos en un lenguaje similar al de la prosa, mientras que otros están escritos en verso libre.

**PUNTO DE VISTA** El *punto de vista* es la perspectiva desde la cual se narran o describen los hechos.

**FUENTE PRIMARIA** Una *fuente primaria* es el material o la información de primera mano acerca de lo que se estudia.

**PROSA** La *prosa* es la forma común del lenguaje escrito. La mayoría de los escritos que no son poesía, ni drama, ni canciones, se consideran prosa. La prosa es uno de los géneros literarios más importantes y puede ser de dos formas: de ficción y de no-ficción.

**JUEGO DE PALABRAS** Un *juego de palabras* es una frase que comprende una palabra con dos o más significados distintos, o dos palabras que suenan igual pero tienen distinto significado. En *Romeo y Julieta*, Mercurio, moribundo, hace un juego de palabras a partir de los dos sentidos que tiene en inglés la palabra "grave" (serio y tumba): "Pregunta por mí mañana, y me encontrarás serio/ enterrado". (Acto 3, Escena i, versos 92–93).

**CUARTETA** Una *cuarteta* es una estrofa o poema de cuatro versos, por lo general con un esquema de ritmo y rima determinados.

**CITA** Las palabras exactas que pronuncia un hablante constituyen una *cita directa* y se indican encerrándolas entre comillas.

**REPETICIÓN** La *repetición* es el uso de cualquier elemento del lenguaje —un sonido, una palabra, una frase, una cláusula o una oración— más de una vez.

Los poetas usan muchos tipos de repeticiones. La aliteración, la asonancia, la rima y el ritmo son repeticiones de ciertos sonidos o patrones sonoros. Un estribillo es un verso o grupo de versos que se repiten. Tanto en prosa como en poesía, la repetición se usa tanto para lograr efectos de musicalidad como para dar énfasis.

**REAFIRMACIÓN** Las *reafirmaciones* o paráfrasis le ayudan al entrevistador a asegurarse de que la audiencia entienda el mensaje del entrevistado.

**RETÓRICA** La *retórica* se refiere a recursos lingüísticos, en especial el arte de hablar o escribir eficazmente.

**FIGURAS RETÓRICAS** Las *figuras retóricas* son patrones especiales de palabras e ideas que dan énfasis y producen emoción, especialmente en discursos y otras presentaciones orales. El *paralelismo*, por ejemplo, es la repetición de una estructura gramatical con el propósito de crear un ritmo y hacer que las palabras resulten más memorables.

Otras figuras retóricas muy frecuentes son: la *analogía*, que establece una comparación entre dos cosas diferentes; el *lenguaje emocionalmente cargado*, en el que las palabras apelan a las emociones; la *reafirmación*, en la que se expresa la misma idea con distintas palabras y las *preguntas retóricas*, que son preguntas cuyas respuestas son obvias.

**VERSO ENCABALGADO** Un *verso encabalgado* es aquel en el que tanto la estructura gramatical como el sentido no se completan al final del verso, sino que continúan en el verso siguiente.

**CIENCIA FICCIÓN** La *ciencia ficción* es un escrito que narra hechos imaginarios relacionados con la ciencia o la tecnología. Muchos relatos de ciencia ficción están ambientados en el futuro.

**LENGUAJE SENSORIAL** El *lenguaje sensorial* es un escrito o discurso que incluye detalles que apelan a uno o más de los sentidos.

**AMBIENTACIÓN** La *ambientación* de una obra literaria es la época y el lugar en el que se desarrolla la acción. La época incluye no solo el período histórico —pasado, presente o futuro—, sino también el año específico, la estación, la hora del día. El lugar puede incluir no solo el espacio geográfico —una región, un país, un estado, un pueblo— sino también el entorno social, económico o cultural.

En algunos cuentos, la ambientación sirve solo como un telón de fondo para la acción, un contexto en el que los personajes se mueven y hablan. En otros casos, en cambio, la ambientación es un elemento crucial.

**CUENTO** Un *cuento* es una obra breve de ficción. En la mayoría de los cuentos, un personaje principal se enfrenta a un conflicto que se resuelve a lo largo de la trama. Para escribir un buen cuento se necesita mucho dominio técnico, porque el cuento debe cumplir su cometido en relativamente pocas palabras.

**SÍMIL** Un *símil* es una figura retórica en la que se usa la palabra *como* para establecer una comparación entre dos cosas aparentemente disímiles. La comparación sorprende al lector permitiéndole una nueva percepción que se deriva de descubrir una semejanza inesperada.

**IRONÍA SITUACIONAL** La *ironía situacional* tiene lugar cuando los eventos de una historia suceden de manera opuesta a lo esperado por los personajes principales o los lectores.

**CONTEXTO SOCIAL E HISTÓRICO** Se conoce como *contexto social e histórico* a las circunstancias de tiempo y lugar en las que se desarrolla la historia.

**SOLILOQUIO** Un *soliloquio* es un largo parlamento en el que un personaje, solo en escena, expresa sus sentimientos.

**RECURSOS SONOROS** Un *recurso sonoro* es una técnica usada por poetas y prosistas para enfatizar la relación sonora entre las palabras con el fin de crear efectos musicales y emotivos, y de subrayar el significado del texto. Estos recursos incluyen la *aliteración*, la *consonancia*, la *asonancia*, la *onomatopeya* y la *rima*.

**HABLANTE** El *hablante* es la voz imaginaria que asume el escritor en un poema. En muchos poemas, el hablante no se identifica con un nombre. Al leer un poema, recuerda que el hablante que habla en el poema puede ser una persona, un animal, un objeto, o una abstracción.

**DETALLES ESPECÍFICOS** Tanto los escritores de ficción como los de no-ficción utilizan *detalles específicos* para respaldar una idea central o un tema.

**DIRECCIONES ESCÉNICAS** Las *direcciones escénicas* son notas que se incluyen en una obra de teatro para describir cómo debe ser actuada o puesta en escena. Estas instrucciones aparecen en itálicas y no se pronuncian durante la representación. Se usan para describir decorados, la iluminación, los efectos sonoros y el aspecto, la personalidad y los movimientos de los personajes.

**ESTROFA** Una *estrofa* es un grupo de dos o más versos cuya estructura se repite. Las distintas estrofas de un poema suelen seguir un mismo patrón de ritmo y de rima. Las estrofas a menudo reciben su nombre del número de versos que las componen. Por ejemplo, un *dístico* o *pareado* (dos versos), una *cuarteta* (cuatro versos), una *sextina* (seis versos), una *octava real* (ocho versos endecasílabos).

**ESTILO** El *estilo* es la manera particular en que escribe un autor. Los elementos que determinan el estilo son: la dicción, el tono; el uso característico de ciertas figuras retóricas, del dialecto, o de los recursos rítmicos; y la sintaxis, es decir, los patrones y estructuras gramaticales que usa con más fecuencia.

**RESUMEN** Un *resumen* es una síntesis concisa, completa y precisa de un texto.

**DETALLES DE APOYO** Se conoce como *detalles de apoyo* a la información que explica, amplía o demuestra las ideas del autor. Los detalles de apoyo validan un argumento, informan o añaden interés al texto.

**SÍMBOLO** Un *símbolo* es algo que representa otra cosa. Además de tener su propio significado y realidad, un símbolo también representa ideas abstractas. Por ejemplo, una bandera es un trozo de tela, pero también representa la idea de un país. Los escritores a veces usan símbolos convencionales como las banderas. Con frecuencia, sin embargo, crean sus propios símbolos, a veces a través del énfasis o la repetición.

**TEMA** Un *tema* es el mensaje central o la concepción de la vida que revela una obra literaria.

El tema de una obra literaria puede estar implícito o bien puede expresarse directamente. Cuando el tema de una obra está implícito, los lectores piensan qué sugiere la obra acerca de la vida o la gente.

Los *temas arquetípicos* son aquellos temas que aparecen en el folklore y en la literatura de todo el mundo, y a lo largo de toda la historia.

**TONO** El *tono* de una obra literaria es la actitud del escritor hacia su tema y su audiencia.

**TRAGEDIA** Una *tragedia* es una obra literaria, por lo general una obra de teatro, que termina en una catástrofe, un desastre o un gran infortunio para el personaje principal, también llamado *héroe trágico*. En el drama de la antigua Grecia, el personaje principal siempre era una persona importante —un rey o un héroe— y la causa de la tragedia era un *error trágico,* una debilidad de su carácter. En el drama moderno, el personaje principal puede ser una persona común, y la causa de la tragedia puede ser algún problema o falla de la sociedad misma. La tragedia no solo despierta miedo y piedad en la audiencia, sino también, en algunos casos, transmite un sentido de la majestuosidad y la nobleza del espíritu humano.

**ERROR TRÁGICO** Un *error trágico* es un defecto de la personalidad que contribuye a las decisiones del héroe y, por lo tanto, a su ruina.

**PERIODISMO DE VIAJES** El *periodismo de viajes* es un tipo de literatura de no-ficción en la que el escritor describe la experiencia de visitar un lugar determinado.

**ENSAYO VISUAL** Un *ensayo visual* es una exploración de un tema que transmite sus ideas tanto con el lenguaje como con los elementos visuales. Al igual que un ensayo estándar, un ensayo visual presenta las opiniones del autor acerca de un tema en particular. A diferencia de otros tipos de ensayos, sin embargo, gran parte del sentido del ensayo visual se expresa en las ilustraciones o fotografías.

**LENGUAJE VÍVIDO** Las palabras convincentes y precisas que dan vida a las ideas y las comunican de manera contundente constituyen *lenguaje vívido.*

**VOZ** La *voz* es el "sonido" distintivo de un escritor, o la manera en que "habla" en la página. Se relaciona a elementos tales como la elección del vocabulario, la estructura de las oraciones y el tono. Es similar al estilo en que habla un individuo y puede describirse de la misma manera: rápida, lenta, directa, dispersa, entrecortadamente, etc.

La voz se parece al *estilo*, es decir, a la manera típica en que escribe un autor, pero el estilo por lo general se refiere a una cualidad que puede encontrarse a lo largo de toda la obra de un autor, mientras que la voz de un autor puede variar de una obra a otra.

## PARTS OF SPEECH

Every English word, depending on its meaning and its use in a sentence, can be identified as one of the eight parts of speech. These are nouns, pronouns, verbs, adjectives, adverbs, prepositions, conjunctions, and interjections. Understanding the parts of speech will help you learn the rules of English grammar and usage.

**Nouns** A **noun** names a person, place, or thing. A **common noun** names any one of a class of persons, places, or things. A **proper noun** names a specific person, place, or thing.

| Common Noun | Proper Noun |
|---|---|
| writer, country, novel | Charles Dickens, Great Britain, *Hard Times* |

**Pronouns** A **pronoun** is a word that stands for one or more nouns. The word to which a pronoun refers (whose place it takes) is the **antecedent** of the pronoun.

A **personal pronoun** refers to the person speaking (first person); the person spoken to (second person); or the person, place, or thing spoken about (third person).

|  | Singular | Plural |
|---|---|---|
| First Person | I, me, my, mine | we, us, our, ours |
| Second Person | you, your, yours | you, your, yours |
| Third Person | he, him, his, she, her, hers, it, its | they, them, their, theirs |

A **reflexive pronoun** reflects the action of a verb back on its subject. It indicates that the person or thing performing the action also is receiving the action.

I keep *myself* fit by taking a walk every day.

An **intensive pronoun** adds emphasis to a noun or pronoun.

It took the work of the president *himself* to pass the law.

A **demonstrative** pronoun points out a specific person(s), place(s), or thing(s).

this, that, these, those

A **relative pronoun** begins a subordinate clause and connects it to another idea in the sentence.

that, which, who, whom, whose

An **interrogative pronoun** begins a question.

what, which, who, whom, whose

An **indefinite pronoun** refers to a person, place, or thing that may or may not be specifically named.

all, another, any, both, each, everyone, few, most, none, no one, somebody

**Verbs** A **verb** expresses action or the existence of a state or condition.
An **action verb** tells what action someone or something is performing.

gather, read, work, jump, imagine, analyze, conclude

A **linking verb** connects the subject with another word that identifies or describes the subject. The most common linking verb is *be.*

appear, be, become, feel, look, remain, seem, smell, sound, stay, taste

A **helping verb,** or **auxiliary verb,** is added to a main verb to make a verb phrase.

be, do, have, should, can, could, may, might, must, will, would

**Adjectives** An **adjective** modifies a noun or pronoun by describing it or giving it a more specific meaning. An adjective answers the questions:

| What kind? | *purple* hat, *happy* face, *loud* sound, |
| Which one? | *this* bowl |
| How many? | *three* cars |
| How much? | *enough* food |

The articles *the, a,* and *an* are adjectives.

A **proper adjective** is an adjective derived from a proper noun.

French, Shakespearean

**Adverbs** An **adverb** modifies a verb, an adjective, or another adverb by telling *where, when, how,* or *to what extent.*

will answer *soon,* *extremely* sad, calls *more* often

**Prepositions** A **preposition** relates a noun or pronoun that appears with it to another word in the sentence.

Dad made a meal *for* us. We talked *till* dusk. Bo missed school *because of* his illness.

**Conjunctions** A **conjunction** connects words or groups of words. A **coordinating conjunction** joins words or groups of words of equal rank.

bread *and* cheese, brief *but* powerful

**Correlative conjunctions** are used in pairs to connect words or groups of words of equal importance.

*both* Luis *and* Rosa, *neither* you *nor* I

**Subordinating conjunctions** indicate the connection between two ideas by placing one below the other in rank or importance. A subordinating conjunction introduces a subordinate, or dependent, clause.

> We will miss her *if* she leaves. Hank shrieked *when* he slipped on the ice.

**Interjections** An **interjection** expresses feeling or emotion. It is not related to other words in the sentence.

> ah, hey, ouch, well, yippee

## PHRASES AND CLAUSES

**Phrases** A **phrase** is a group of words that does not have both a subject and a verb and that functions as one part of speech. A phrase expresses an idea but cannot stand alone.

**Prepositional Phrases** A **prepositional phrase** is a group of words that begins with a preposition and ends with a noun or pronoun that is the **object of the preposition.**

> before dawn          as a result of the rain

An **adjective phrase** is a prepositional phrase that modifies a noun or pronoun.

> Eliza appreciates the beauty **of a well-crafted poem.**

An **adverb phrase** is a prepositional phrase that modifies a verb, an adjective, or an adverb.

> She reads Spenser's sonnets **with great pleasure.**

**Appositive Phrases** An **appositive** is a noun or pronoun placed next to another noun or pronoun to add information about it. An **appositive phrase** consists of an appositive and its modifiers.

> Mr. Roth, **my music teacher,** is sick.

**Verbal Phrases** A **verbal** is a verb form that functions as a different part of speech (not as a verb) in a sentence. **Participles, gerunds,** and **infinitives** are verbals.

A **verbal phrase** includes a verbal and any modifiers or complements it may have. Verbal phrases may function as nouns, as adjectives, or as adverbs.

A **participle** is a verb form that can act as an adjective. Present participles end in *-ing;* past participles of regular verbs end in *-ed.*

A **participial phrase** consists of a participle and its modifiers or complements. The entire phrase acts as an adjective.

> Jenna's backpack, **loaded with equipment,** was heavy.
> **Barking incessantly,** the dogs chased the squirrels out of sight.

A **gerund** is a verb form that ends in *-ing* and is used as a noun.

A **gerund phrase** consists of a gerund with any modifiers or complements, all acting together as a noun.

> **Taking photographs of wildlife** is her main hobby. [acts as subject]
> We always enjoy **listening to live music.** [acts as object]

An **infinitive** is a verb form, usually preceded by *to,* that can act as a noun, an adjective, or an adverb.

An **infinitive phrase** consists of an infinitive and its modifiers or complements, and sometimes its subject, all acting together as a single part of speech.

> She tries **to get out into the wilderness often.** [acts as a noun; direct object of *tries*]
> The Tigers are the team **to beat.** [acts as an adjective; describes *team*]
> I drove twenty miles **to witness the event.** [acts as an adverb; tells why I drove]

**Clauses** A **clause** is a group of words with its own subject and verb.

**Independent Clauses** An independent clause can stand by itself as a complete sentence.

> George Orwell wrote with extraordinary insight.

**Subordinate Clauses** A subordinate clause, also called a dependent clause, cannot stand by itself as a complete sentence. Subordinate clauses always appear connected in some way with one or more independent clauses.

> George Orwell, **who wrote with extraordinary insight,** produced many politically relevant works.

An **adjective clause** is a subordinate clause that acts as an adjective. It modifies a noun or a pronoun by telling *what kind* or *which one.* Also called relative clauses, adjective clauses usually begin with a **relative pronoun:** *who, which, that, whom,* or *whose.*

> "The Lamb" is the poem **that I memorized for class.**

An **adverb clause** is a subordinate clause that, like an adverb, modifies a verb, an adjective, or an adverb. An adverb clause tells *where, when, in what way, to what extent, under what condition,* or *why.*

The students will read another poetry collection **if their schedule allows.**
**When I recited the poem,** Mr. Lopez was impressed.

A **noun clause** is a subordinate clause that acts as a noun.

William Blake survived on **whatever he made as an engraver.**

## SENTENCE STRUCTURE

**Subject and Predicate** A **sentence** is a group of words that expresses a complete thought. A sentence has two main parts: a *subject* and a *predicate*.

A **fragment** is a group of words that does not express a complete thought. It lacks an independent clause.

The **subject** tells *whom* or *what* the sentence is about. The **predicate** tells what the subject of the sentence does or is.

A subject or a predicate can consist of a single word or of many words. All the words in the subject make up the **complete subject.** All the words in the predicate make up the **complete predicate.**

| Complete Subject | Complete Predicate |
|---|---|
| Both of those girls | have already read *Macbeth*. |

The **simple subject** is the essential noun, pronoun, or group of words acting as a noun that cannot be left out of the complete subject. The **simple predicate** is the essential verb or verb phrase that cannot be left out of the complete predicate.

**Both** of those girls | **have** already **read** *Macbeth*.
[Simple subject: *Both*; simple predicate: *have read*]

A **compound subject** is two or more subjects that have the same verb and are joined by a conjunction.
*Neither the horse nor the driver* looked tired.

A **compound predicate** is two or more verbs that have the same subject and are joined by a conjunction.
She *sneezed and coughed* throughout the trip.

**Complements** A **complement** is a word or word group that completes the meaning of the predicate. There are four kinds of complements: *direct objects, indirect objects, objective complements,* and *subject complements.*

A **direct object** is a noun, a pronoun, or a group of words acting as a noun that receives the action of a transitive verb.
We watched the **liftoff**.
She drove **Zach** to the launch site.

An **indirect object** is a noun or pronoun that appears with a direct object and names the person or thing to which or for which something is done.
He sold the **family** a mirror. [The direct object is *mirror*.]

An **objective complement** is an adjective or noun that appears with a direct object and describes or renames it.
The decision made her **unhappy**.
[The direct object is *her*.]
Many consider Shakespeare the greatest **playwright.** [The direct object is *Shakespeare*.]

A **subject complement** follows a linking verb and tells something about the subject. There are two kinds: *predicate nominatives* and *predicate adjectives.*

A **predicate nominative** is a noun or pronoun that follows a linking verb and identifies or renames the subject.
"A Modest Proposal" is a **pamphlet.**

A **predicate adjective** is an adjective that follows a linking verb and describes the subject of the sentence.
"A Modest Proposal" is **satirical.**

## Classifying Sentences by Structure

Sentences can be classified according to the kind and number of clauses they contain. The four basic sentence structures are *simple, compound, complex,* and *compound-complex.*

A **simple sentence** consists of one independent clause.
Terrence enjoys modern British literature.

A **compound sentence** consists of two or more independent clauses. The clauses are joined by a conjunction or a semicolon.
Terrence enjoys modern British literature, but his brother prefers the classics.

A **complex sentence** consists of one independent clause and one or more subordinate clauses.
Terrence, who reads voraciously, enjoys modern British literature.

A **compound-complex sentence** consists of two or more independent clauses and one or more subordinate clauses.
Terrence, who reads voraciously, enjoys modern British literature, but his brother prefers the classics.

## Classifying Sentences by Function

Sentences can be classified according to their function or purpose. The four types are *declarative, interrogative, imperative,* and *exclamatory.*

A **declarative sentence** states an idea and ends with a period.

An **interrogative sentence** asks a question and ends with a question mark.

An **imperative sentence** gives an order or a direction and ends with either a period or an exclamation mark.

An **exclamatory sentence** conveys a strong emotion and ends with an exclamation mark.

## PARAGRAPH STRUCTURE

An effective paragraph is organized around one **main idea,** which is often stated in a **topic sentence.** The other sentences support the main idea. To give the paragraph **unity,** make sure the connection between each sentence and the main idea is clear.

**Max** went to the bakery, but **he** can't buy mints there. [consistent]

### Unnecessary Shift in Voice

Do not change needlessly from active voice to passive voice in your use of verbs.

Elena and I **searched** the trail for evidence, but no clues **were found.** [shift from active voice to passive voice]

Elena and I **searched** the trail for evidence, but we **found** no clues. [consistent]

### Unnecessary Shift in Person

Do not change needlessly from one grammatical person to another. Keep the person consistent in your sentences.

**Max** went to the bakery, but **you** can't buy mints there. [shift from third person to second person]

## AGREEMENT

### Subject and Verb Agreement

A singular subject must have a singular verb. A plural subject must have a plural verb.

**Dr. Boone uses** a telescope to view the night sky.
The **students use** a telescope to view the night sky.

A phrase or clause that comes between a subject and verb does not affect subject-verb agreement.

His **theory**, as well as his claims, **lacks** support.

Two subjects joined by *and* usually take a plural verb.
The **dog** and the **cat are** healthy.

Two singular subjects joined by *or* or *nor* take a singular verb.
The **dog** or the **cat is** hiding.

Two plural subjects joined by *or* or *nor* take a plural verb.
The **dogs** or the **cats are** coming home with us.

When a singular and a plural subject are joined by *or* or *nor,* the verb agrees with the closer subject.
Either the **dogs** or the **cat is** behind the door.
Either the **cat** or the **dogs are** behind the door.

### Pronoun and Antecedent Agreement

Pronouns must agree with their antecedents in number and gender. Use singular pronouns with singular antecedents and plural pronouns with plural antecedents.

**Doris Lessing** uses **her** writing to challenge ideas about women's roles.
**Writers** often use **their** skills to promote social change.

Use a singular pronoun when the antecedent is a singular indefinite pronoun such as *anybody, each, either, everybody, neither, no one, one,* or *someone.*
Judge **each** of the articles on **its** merits.

Use a plural pronoun when the antecedent is a plural indefinite pronoun such as *both, few, many,* or *several.*
**Both** of the articles have **their** flaws.

The indefinite pronouns *all, any, more, most, none,* and *some* can be singular or plural depending on the number of the word to which they refer.
**Most** of the *books* are in **their** proper places.
**Most** of the *book* has been torn from **its** binding.

### Principal Parts of Regular and Irregular Verbs

A verb has four principal parts:

| Present | Present Participle | Past | Past Participle |
|---------|--------------------|------|-----------------|
| learn | learning | learned | learned |
| discuss | discussing | discussed | discussed |
| stand | standing | stood | stood |
| begin | beginning | began | begun |

**Regular verbs** such as *learn* and *discuss* form the past and past participle by adding *-ed* to the present form. **Irregular verbs** such as *stand* and *begin* form the past and past participle in other ways. If you are in doubt about the principal parts of an irregular verb, check a dictionary.

### The Tenses of Verbs

The different tenses of verbs indicate the time an action or condition occurred.

The **present tense** expresses an action that happens regularly or states a general truth.

> Tourists **flock** to the site yearly.

Daily exercise **is** good for your heallth.

The **past tense** expresses a completed action or a condition that is no longer true.

> The squirrel **dropped** the nut and **ran** up the tree.
> I **was** very tired last night by 9:00.

The **future tense** indicates an action that will happen in the future or a condition that will be true.

> The Glazers **will visit** us tomorrow.
> They **will be** glad to arrive from their long journey.

The **present perfect tense** expresses an action that happened at an indefinite time in the past or an action that began in the past and continues into the present.

> Someone **has cleaned** the trash from the park.
> The puppy **has been** under the bed all day.

The **past perfect tense** shows an action that was completed before another action in the past.

> Gerard **had revised** his essay before he turned it in.

The **future perfect tense** indicates an action that will have been completed before another action takes place.

> Mimi **will have painted** the kitchen by the time we finish the shutters.

### Degrees of Comparison

Adjectives and adverbs take different forms to show the three degrees of comparison: the *positive*, the *comparative*, and the *superlative*.

| Positive | Comparative | Superlative |
|----------|-------------|-------------|
| fast | faster | fastest |
| crafty | craftier | craftiest |
| abruptly | more abruptly | most abruptly |
| badly | worse | worst |
| much | more | most |

### Using Comparative and Superlative Adjectives and Adverbs

Use comparative adjectives and adverbs to compare two things. Use superlative adjectives and adverbs to compare three or more things.

> This season's weather was **drier** than last year's.
> This season has been one of the **driest** on record.
> Jake practices **more often** than Jamal.
> Of everyone in the band, Jake practices **most often.**

### Pronoun Case

The **case** of a pronoun is the form it takes to show its function in a sentence. There are three pronoun cases: *nominative*, *objective*, and *possessive*.

| Nominative | Objective | Possessive |
|------------|-----------|------------|
| I, you, he, she, it, we, you, they | me, you, him, her, it, us, you, them | my, your, yours, his, her, hers, its, our, ours, their, theirs |

Use the **nominative case** when a pronoun functions as a *subject* or as a *predicate nominative.*

> **They** are going to the movies. [subject]
> The biggest movie fan is **she.** [predicate nominative]

Use the **objective case** for a pronoun acting as a *direct object*, an *indirect object,* or the *object of a preposition.*

> The ending of the play surprised **me.** [direct object]
> Mary gave **us** two tickets to the play. [indirect object]
> The audience cheered for **him.** [object of preposition]

Use the **possessive case** to show ownership.

> The red suitcase is **hers.** [belongs to her]

**Diction** The words you choose contribute to the overall effectiveness of your writing. **Diction** refers to word choice and to the clearness and correctness of those words. You can improve one aspect of your diction by choosing carefully between commonly confused words, such as the pairs listed below.

### accept, except

*Accept* is a verb that means "to receive" or "to agree to." *Except* is a preposition that means "other than" or "leaving out."

> Please **accept** my offer to buy you lunch this weekend.

> He is busy every day **except** the weekends.

### affect, effect

*Affect* is normally a verb meaning "to influence" or "to bring about a change in." *Effect* is usually a noun meaning "result."

> The distractions outside **affect** Steven's ability to concentrate.

> The teacher's remedies had a positive **effect** on Steven's ability to concentrate.

### among, between

*Among* is usually used with three or more items, and it emphasizes collective relationships or indicates distribution. *Between* is generally used with only two items, but it can be used with more than two if the emphasis is on individual (one-to-one) relationships within the group.

> I had to choose a snack **among** the various vegetables.

> He handed out the booklets **among** the conference participants.

> Our school is **between** a park and an old barn.

> The tournament included matches **between** France, Spain, Mexico, and the United States.

### amount, number

*Amount* refers to overall quantity and is mainly used with mass nouns (those that can't be counted). *Number* refers to individual items that can be counted.

> The **amount** of attention that great writers have paid to Shakespeare is remarkable.

> A **number** of important English writers have been fascinated by the legend of King Arthur.

### assure, ensure, insure

*Assure* means "to convince [someone of something]; to guarantee." *Ensure* means "to make certain [that something happens]." *Insure* means "to arrange for payment in case of loss."

> The attorney **assured** us we'd win the case.

> The rules **ensure** that no one gets treated unfairly.

> Many professional musicians **insure** their valuable instruments.

### bad, badly

Use the adjective *bad* before a noun or after linking verbs such as *feel, look,* and *seem.* Use *badly* whenever an adverb is required.

> The situation may seem **bad**, but it will improve over time.

> Though I **badly** mismanaged my time, I might be able to recover over the weekend.

### beside, besides

*Beside* means "at the side of" or "close to." *Besides* means "in addition to."

> The stapler sits **beside** the pencil sharpener in our classroom.

> **Besides** being very clean, the classroom is also very organized.

### can, may

The helping verb *can* generally refers to the ability to do something. The helping verb *may* generally refers to permission to do something.

> I **can** run one mile in six minutes.

> **May** we have a race during recess?

### complement, compliment

The verb *complement* means "to enhance"; the verb *compliment* means "to praise."

> Online exercises **complement** the textbook lessons.

> Ms. Lewis **complimented** our team on our excellent debate.

### compose, comprise

*Compose* means "to make up; constitute." *Comprise* means "to include or contain." Remember that the whole comprises its parts or is composed of its parts, and the parts compose the whole.

> The assignment **comprises** three different tasks.

> The assignment is **composed** of three different tasks.

> Three different tasks **compose** the assignment.

### different from, different than

*Different* from is generally preferred over *different than,* but *different than* can be used before a clause. Always use *different from* before a noun or pronoun.

> Your point of view is so **different from** mine.

> His idea was so **different from** [or **different than**] what we had expected.

### farther, further

Use *farther* when you refer to distance. Use *further* when you mean "to a greater degree or extent" or "additional."

> Stephon has traveled **farther** than anybody else in the class.

> If I want **further** details about his travels, I can read his blog.

### fewer, less

Use *fewer* for things that can be counted. Use *less* for amounts or quantities that cannot be counted. *Fewer* must be followed by a plural noun.

**Fewer** students drive to school since the weather improved.

There is **less** noise outside in the mornings.

### good, well

Use the adjective *good* before a noun or after a linking verb. Use *well* whenever an adverb is required, such as when modifying a verb.

I feel **good** after sleeping for eight hours.

I did **well** on my test, and my soccer team played **well** in that afternoon's game. It was a **good** day!

### its, it's

The word *its* with no apostrophe is a possessive pronoun. The word *it's* is a contraction of "it is."

Angelica will try to fix the computer and **its** keyboard.

**It's** a difficult job, but she can do it.

### lay, lie

*Lay* is a transitive verb meaning "to set or put something down." Its principal parts are *lay, laying, laid, laid. Lie* is an intransitive verb meaning "to recline" or "to exist in a certain place." Its principal parts are *lie, lying, lay, lain.*

Please **lay** that box down and help me with the sofa.

When we are done moving, I am going to **lie** down.

My hometown **lies** sixty miles north of here.

### like, as

*Like* is a preposition that usually means "similar to" and precedes a noun or pronoun. The conjunction *as* means "in the way that" and usually precedes a clause.

**Like** the other students, I was prepared for a quiz.

**As** I said yesterday, we expect to finish before noon.

Use **such as,** not **like,** before a series of examples.

Foods **such as** apples, nuts, and pretzels make good snacks.

### of, have

Do not use *of* in place of *have* after auxiliary verbs such as *would, could, should, may, might,* or *must.* The contraction of *have* is formed by adding *-ve* after these verbs.

I **would have** stayed after school today, but I had to help cook at home.

Mom **must've** called while I was still in the gym.

### principal, principle

*Principal* can be an adjective meaning "main; most important." It can also be a noun meaning "chief officer of a school." *Principle* is a noun meaning "moral rule" or "fundamental truth."

His strange behavior was the **principal** reason for our concern.

Democratic **principles** form the basis of our country's laws.

### raise, rise

*Raise* is a transitive verb that usually takes a direct object. *Rise* is intransitive and never takes a direct object.

Iliana and Josef **raise** the flag every morning.

They **rise** from their seats and volunteer immediately whenever help is needed.

### than, then

The conjunction *than* is used to connect the two parts of a comparison. The adverb *then* usually refers to time.

My backpack is heavier **than** hers.

I will finish my homework and **then** meet my friends at the park.

### that, which, who

Use the relative pronoun *that* to refer to things or people. Use *which* only for things and *who* only for people.

*That* introduces a restrictive phrase or clause, that is, one that is essential to the meaning of the sentence. *Which* introduces a nonrestrictive phrase or clause—one that adds information but could be deleted from the sentence—and is preceded by a comma.

Ben ran to the park **that** just reopened.

The park, **which** just reopened, has many attractions.

The man **who** built the park loves to see people smiling.

### when, where, why

Do not use *when, where,* or *why* directly after a linking verb, such as *is.* Reword the sentence.

*Incorrect:* The morning is when he left for the beach.

*Correct:* He left for the beach in the morning.

### who, whom

In formal writing, use *who* only as a subject in clauses and sentences. Use *whom* only as the object of a verb or of a preposition.

**Who** paid for the tickets?

**Whom** should I pay for the tickets?

I can't recall to **whom** I gave the money for the tickets.

### your, you're

*Your* is a possessive pronoun expressing ownership. *You're* is the contraction of "you are."

Have you finished writing **your** informative essay?

**You're** supposed to turn it in tomorrow. If **you're** late, **your** grade will be affected.

## Capitalization

### First Words

Capitalize the first word of a sentence.

**S**tories about knights and their deeds interest me.

Capitalize the first word of direct speech.

**S**haron asked, "**D**o you like stories about knights?"

Capitalize the first word of a quotation that is a complete sentence.

**E**instein said, "**A**nyone who has never made a mistake has never tried anything new."

### Proper Nouns and Proper Adjectives

Capitalize all proper nouns, including geographical names, historical events and periods, and names of organizations.

| | | |
|---|---|---|
| **T**hames **R**iver | **J**ohn **K**eats | the **R**enaissance |
| **U**nited **N**ations | **W**orld **W**ar II | **S**ierra **N**evada |

Capitalize all proper adjectives.

| | |
|---|---|
| **S**hakespearean play | **B**ritish invaision |
| **A**merican citizen | **L**atin **A**merican literature |

### Academic Course Names

Capitalize course names only if they are language courses, are followed by a number, or are preceded by a proper noun or adjective.

| | | |
|---|---|---|
| **S**panish | **H**onors **C**hemistry | **H**istory 101 |
| **g**eology | **a**lgebra | **s**ocial **s**tudies |

### Titles

Capitalize personal titles when followed by the person's name.

**M**s. Hughes    **D**r. Perez    **K**ing George

Capitalize titles showing family relationships when they are followed by a specific person's name, unless they are preceded by a possessive noun or pronoun.

**U**ncle Oscar      Mangan's **s**ister      his **a**unt Tessa

Capitalize the first word and all other key words in the titles of books, stories, songs, and other works of art.

*Frankenstein*          "**S**hooting an **E**lephant"

## Punctuation

### End Marks

Use a **period** to end a declarative sentence or an imperative sentence.

We are studying the structure of sonnets.
Read the biography of Mary Shelley.

Use periods with initials and abbreviations.

| | |
|---|---|
| D. H. Lawrence | Mrs. Browning |
| Mt. Everest | Maple St. |

Use a **question mark** to end an interrogative sentence.

What is Macbeth's fatal flaw?

Use an **exclamation mark** after an exclamatory sentence or a forceful imperative sentence.

That's a beautiful painting!      Let me go now!

## Commas

Use a **comma** before a coordinating conjunction to separate two independent clauses in a compound sentence.

The game was very close, but we were victorious.

Use commas to separate three or more words, phrases, or clauses in a series.

William Blake was a writer, artist, and printer.

Use commas to separate coordinate adjectives.

It was a witty, amusing novel.

Use a comma after an introductory word, phrase, or clause.

When the novelist finished his book, he celebrated with his family.

Use commas to set off nonessential expressions.

Old English, of course, requires translation.

Use commas with places and dates.

Coventry, England          September 1, 1939

## Semicolons

Use a **semicolon** to join closely related independent clauses that are not already joined by a conjunction.

Tanya likes to write poetry; Heather prefers prose.

Use semicolons to avoid confusion when items in a series contain commas.

They traveled to London, England; Madrid, Spain; and Rome, Italy.

## Colons

Use a **colon** before a list of items following an independent clause.

Notable Victorian poets include the following: Tennyson, Arnold, Housman, and Hopkins.

Use a colon to introduce information that summarizes or explains the independent clause before it.

She just wanted to do one thing: rest.
Malcolm loves volunteering: He reads to sick children every Saturday afternoon.

## Quotation Marks

Use **quotation marks** to enclose a direct quotation.

"Short stories," Ms. Hildebrand said, "should have rich, well-developed characters."

An **indirect quotation** does not require quotation marks.

Ms. Hildebrand said that short stories should have well-developed characters.

Use quotation marks around the titles of short written works, episodes in a series, songs, and works mentioned as parts of collections.

"The Lagoon"          "Boswell Meets Johnson"

## Italics

Italicize the titles of long written works, movies, television and radio shows, lengthy works of music, paintings, and sculptures.

*Howards End*　　*60 Minutes*　　*Guernica*

For handwritten material, you can use underlining instead of italics.

<u>The Princess Bride</u>　　<u>Mona Lisa</u>

## Dashes

Use **dashes** to indicate an abrupt change of thought, a dramatic interrupting idea, or a summary statement.

> I read the entire first act of *Macbeth*—you won't believe what happens next.

> The director—what's her name again?—attended the movie premiere.

## Hyphens

Use a **hyphen** with certain numbers, after certain prefixes, with two or more words used as one word, and with a compound modifier that comes before a noun.

> seventy-two
> self-esteem
> well-being
> five-year contract

## Parentheses

Use **parentheses** to set off asides and explanations when the material is not essential or when it consists of one or more sentences. When the sentence in parentheses interrupts the larger sentence, it does not have a capital letter or a period.

> He listened intently (it was too dark to see who was speaking) to try to identify the voices.

When a sentence in parentheses falls between two other complete sentences, it should start with a capital letter and end with a period.

> The quarterback threw three touchdown passes. (We knew he could do it.) Our team won the game by two points.

## Apostrophes

Add an **apostrophe** and an *s* to show the possessive case of most singular nouns and of plural nouns that do not end in *-s* or *-es*.

> Blake's poems　　　the mice's whiskers

Names ending in *s* form their possessives in the same way, except for classical and biblical names, which add only an apostrophe to form the possessive.

> Dickens's　　　Hercules'

Add an apostrophe to show the possessive case of plural nouns ending in *-s* and *-es*.

> the girls' songs　　　the Ortizes' car

Use an apostrophe in a contraction to indicate the position of the missing letter or letters.

> She's never read a Coleridge poem she didn't like.

## Brackets

Use **brackets** to enclose clarifying information inserted within a quotation.

> Columbus's journal entry from October 21, 1492, begins as follows: "At 10 o'clock, we arrived at a cape of the island [San Salvador], and anchored, the other vessels in company."

## Ellipses

Use three ellipsis points, also known as an **ellipsis,** to indicate where you have omitted words from quoted material.

> Wollestonecraft wrote, "The education of women has of late been more attended to than formerly; yet they are still . . . ridiculed or pitied . . . ."

In the example above, the four dots at the end of the sentence are the three ellipsis points plus the period from the original sentence.

Use an ellipsis to indicate a pause or interruption in speech.

> "When he told me the news," said the coach, "I was . . . I was shocked . . . completely shocked."

## Spelling

### Spelling Rules

Learning the rules of English spelling will help you make **generalizations** about how to spell words.

### Word Parts

The three word parts that can combine to form a word are roots, prefixes, and suffixes. Many of these word parts come from the Greek, Latin, and Anglo-Saxon languages.

The **root word** carries a word's basic meaning.

| Root and Origin | Meaning | Examples |
|---|---|---|
| -leg- (-log-) [Gr.] | to say, speak | *legal, logic* |
| -pon- (-pos-) [L.] | to put, place | *postpone, deposit* |

A **prefix** is one or more syllables added to the beginning of a word that alter the meaning of the root.

| Prefix and Origin | Meaning | Examples |
|---|---|---|
| anti- [Gr.] | against | *antipathy* |
| inter- [L.] | between | *international* |
| mis- [A.S.] | wrong | *misplace* |

A **suffix** is a letter or group of letters added to the end of a root word that changes the word's meaning or part of speech.

| Suffix and Origin | Meaning | Part of Speech |
|---|---|---|
| -ful [A.S.] | full of: *scornful* | adjective |
| -ity [L.] | state of being: *adversity* | noun |
| -ize (-ise) [Gr.] | to make: *idolize* | verb |
| -ly [A.S.] | in a manner: *calmly* | adverb |

### Rules for Adding Suffixes to Root Words

When adding a suffix to a root word ending in *y* preceded by a consonant, change *y* to *i* unless the suffix begins with *i*.

  ply + -able = pliable    happy + -ness = happiness

  defy + -ing = defying    cry + -ing = crying

For a root word ending in *e*, drop the *e* when adding a suffix beginning with a vowel.

  drive + -ing = driving    move + -able = movable

  SOME EXCEPTIONS: traceable, seeing, dyeing

For root words ending with a consonant + vowel + consonant in a stressed syllable, double the final consonant when adding a suffix that begins with a vowel.

  mud + -y = muddy    submit + -ed = submitted

  SOME EXCEPTIONS: mixing, fixed

### Rules for Adding Prefixes to Root Words

When a prefix is added to a root word, the spelling of the root remains the same.

  un- + certain = uncertain    mis- + spell = misspell

With some prefixes, the spelling of the prefix changes when joined to the root to make the pronunciation easier.

  in- + mortal = immortal    ad- + vert = avert

### Orthographic Patterns

Certain letter combinations in English make certain sounds. For instance, *ph* sounds like *f*, *eigh* usually makes a long *a* sound, and the *k* before an *n* is often silent.

  **ph**armacy    n**eigh**bor    **k**nowledge

Understanding **orthographic patterns** such as these can help you improve your spelling.

### Forming Plurals

The plural form of most nouns is formed by adding *-s* to the singular.

  computer**s**    gadget**s**    Washington**s**

For words ending in *s, ss, x, z, sh,* or *ch,* add *-es.*

  circus**es**    tax**es**    wish**es**    bench**es**

For words ending in *y* or *o* preceded by a vowel, add *-s.*

  key**s**    patio**s**

For words ending in *y* preceded by a consonant, change the *y* to an *i* and add *-es.*

  cit**ies**    enem**ies**    troph**ies**

For most words ending in *o* preceded by a consonant, add *-es.*

  echo**es**    tomato**es**

Some words form the plural in irregular ways.

  women    oxen    children    teeth    deer

### Foreign Words Used in English

Some words used in English are actually foreign words that have been adopted. Learning to spell these words requires memorization. When in doubt, check a dictionary.

  sushi    enchilada    au pair    fiancé

  laissez faire    croissant

**Boldface numbers** indicate pages where terms are defined.

## Vocabulary

## Writing

# INDEX OF AUTHORS AND TITLES

The following authors and titles appear in the print and online versions of *my*Perspectives.

# ADDITIONAL SELECTIONS: AUTHOR AND TITLE INDEX

The following authors and titles appear in the Online Literature Library.

## Acknowledgments

The following selections appear in this grade level (Grade 9) of *my*Perspectives. Some selections appear online only.

**ABC News - Permissions Dept.** "Amazing Stories of Rescues and Survival in Nepal" ©ABC News; "Misty Copeland's Hard-Fought Journey to Ballet Stardom" ©ABC News; "Doomsday Plane Ready for Nuclear Attack" ©ABC News.

**Abner Stein.** "Rules of the Game" by Amy Tan, from *The Joy Luck Club*. Used with permission of Abner Stein.

**Alfred A. Knopf.** "The Seventh Man" by Haruki Murakami, translated by Jay Rubin; from *Blind Willow Sleeping Woman* by Haruki Murakami and translated by Philip Gabriel and Jay Rubin, copyright © 2006 by Haruki Murakami. Used by permission of Alfred A. Knopf, an imprint of the Knopf Doubleday Publishing Group, a division of Penguin Random House LLC. All rights reserved. Any third party use of this material, outside of this publication, is prohibited. Interested parties must apply directly to Penguin Random House LLC for permission; "The Voyage of the James Caird" from *The Endurance: Shackleton's Legendary Antarctic Expedition* by Caroline Alexander, copyright © 1998 by Caroline Alexander. Used by permission of Alfred A. Knopf, an imprint of the Knopf Doubleday Publishing Group, a division of Penguin Random House LLC. All rights reserved. Any third party use of this material, outside of this publication, is prohibited. Interested parties must apply directly to Penguin Random House LLC for permission.

**Apostrophe S Productions, Inc.** "The Hero's Adventure" from *The Power of Myth* by Joseph Campbell. Used with permission of Apostrophe S Productions.

**Arte Publico Press.** "Legal Alien" is reprinted with permission from the publisher of *Chants* by Pat Mora ©1994 Arte Publico Press - University of Houston).

**BBC Worldwide Americas, Inc.** "Grace Abbott and the Fight for Immigrant Rights in America" ©BBC Worldwide Learning; "Civil Rights Movement and the MLK Assassination" ©BBC Worldwide Learning; "Fannie Lou Hamer" ©BBC Worldwide Learning; "A Modern Take on Romeo and Juliet" ©BBC Worldwide Learning.

**BOA Editions, Ltd.** Lucille Clifton, excerpt from "mulberry fields" from *The Collected Poems of LucilleClifton*. Copyright © 2004 by Lucille Clifton. Reprinted with the permission of The Permissions Company, Inc. on behalf of BOA Editions Ltd.; Lucille Clifton, "the beginning of the end of the world" from *The Collected Poems of Lucille Clifton*. Copyright ©1991 by Lucille Clifton. Reprinted with the permission of The Permissions Company, Inc. on behalf of BOA Editions Ltd.

**Brandt & Hochman Literary Agents Inc.** "The Most Dangerous Game" by Richard Connell. Copyright ©1924 by Richard Connell. Copyright renewed © 1952 by Louise Fox Connell. Used by permission of Brandt & Hochman Literary Agents, Inc. Any copying or distribution of this text is expressly forbidden. All rights reserved.; "By the Waters of Babylon" by Stephen Vincent Benet. Copyright ©1937 by Stephen Vincent Benet Copyright renewed ©1965 by Thomas C. Benet, Stephanie Mahin and Rachel B. Lewis. Used by permission of Brandt & Hochman Literary Agents, Inc. Any copying or distribution of this text is expressly forbidden. All rights reserved.

**Candlewick Press.** *The Odyssey*. Copyright © 2010 by Gareth Hinds. Reproduced by permission of the publisher, Candlewick Press, Somerville, MA.

**Canongate Books Limited.** *From The Life of Pi*. Used with permission of Canongate Books Ltd.; Used with permission of Canongate Books Ltd.

**Carnegie Mellon University Press.** Gregory Djanikian, "Immigrant Picnic" from *So I Will Till the Ground*. Originally published in Poetry (July 1999). Copyright ©1999, 2007 by Gregory Djanikian. Reprinted with the permission of The Permissions Company, Inc., on behalf of Carnegie Mellon University Press.

**CBS News.** "A Visit to the Doomsday Vault," CBS, 60 Minutes. Used with permission of CBS News.

**CBS Rights & Permissions.** "A Visit to the Doomsday Vault," CBS, 60 Minutes, Copyright ©2008.

**Center for Disease Control.** "Preparedness 101: Zombie Apocalypse" by Ali S. Khan (CDC, 2011).

**Cesar Chavez Foundation.** "Lessons of Dr. Martin Luther King, Jr." TM/©2015 The Cesar Chavez Foundation.

**CNN ImageSource.** CNN newscast of "Tragic Romeo and Juliet Offers Bosnia Hope" ©CNN.

**Copyright Clearance Center.** "Ithaka" republished with permission of Princeton University Press, from *Collected Poems* by C.P. Cavafy, translated by Keeley & Sherrard, 1992; permission conveyed through Copyright Clearance Center, Inc.

**Define American.** "Define American." Hiep Le, Culver City, CA ©Define American.

**Don Congdon Associates.** "There Will Come Soft Rains." Reprinted by permission of Don Congdon Associates, Inc. Copyright ©1950 by the Crowell Collier Publishing Company, renewed 1977 by Ray Bradbury.

**Dunbar, Paul Laurence.** "We Wear the Mask" by Paul Laurence Dunbar.

**Dungy, Camille.** "The Writing on the Wall." First published on Harriet, the blog for the Poetry Foundation. Reprinted with permission of the author.

**Farrar, Straus and Giroux.** "Traveling" from *Just as I Thought* by Grace Paley. Copyright ©1998 by Grace Paley. Reprinted by permission Farrar, Straus and Giroux, LLC. CAUTION: Users are warned that this work is protected under copyright laws and downloading is strictly prohibited. The right to reproduce or transfer the work via any medium must be secured with Farrar, Straus and Giroux, LLC.; Excerpts from *The Odyssey* by Homer, translated by Robert Fitzgerald. Copyright ©1961, 1963 by Robert Fitzgerald. Copyright renewed 1989 by Benedict R.C. Fitzgerald, on behalf of the Fitzgerald children. Reprinted by permission of Farrar, Straus and Giroux, LLC. CAUTION: Users are warned that this work is protected under copyright laws and downloading is strictly prohibited. The right to reproduce or transfer the work via any medium must be secured with Farrar, Straus and Giroux, LLC.

**Farrell, Joanna.** "Popocatepetl and Ixtlaccihuatl" by permission of Mrs. J.S.E. Farrell.

**Fitzgerald, Benedict.** From *The Odyssey* translated by Robert Fitzgerald. Reprinted with permission of Benedict R.C. Fitzgerald.

**Frost, Robert.** "Fire and Ice" by Robert Frost (1920).

ACKNOWLEDGMENTS AND CREDITS

# ACKNOWLEDGMENTS AND CREDITS

**Watkins/Loomis Agency.** "The Return" from *Secret Lives* by Ngugi wa Thiong'o. Reprinted by Permission of Ngugi wa' Thiong'o and the Watkins Loomis Agency.

**Westwood Creative Artists.** From *Life of Pi* by Yann Martel (Harcourt, 2001). Copyright ©2001 Yann Martel. With permission of the author.

**Writers House LLC.** "I Have a Dream" / "Letter From a Birmingham City Jail"—Reprinted by arrangement with The Heirs to the Estate of Martin Luther King Jr., c/o Writers House as agent for the proprietor New York, NY; Reprinted by arrangement with the Heirs to the Estate of Martin Luther King Jr., c/o Writers House as agent for the proprietor New York, NY. Copyright ©1963 Dr. Martin Luther King, Jr. Copyright renewed 1991 Coretta Scott King; Reprinted by arrangement with The Heirs to the Estate of Martin Luther King Jr., c/o Writers House as agent for the proprietor New York, NY. Copyright ©1963 Dr. Martin Luther King, Jr. Copyright renewed 1991 Coretta Scott King.

**WUNC.** "Franklin McCain Dies—Helped Start Sit-In Movement At Greensboro Lunch Counter" ©National Public Radio, Inc.

**Wylie Agency.** "A Song on the End of the World" by Czeslaw Milosz, collected in *New and Collected Poems: 1931–2001.* Copyright ©1988, 1991, 1995, 2001 by Czeslaw Milosz Royalties, Inc., used by permission of The Wylie Agency LLC.

**Yale University Press.** "The Many Lives of Hazel Bryan" from *Elizabeth & Hazel: Two Women of Little Rock* by David Margolick. Copyright ©2011. Used with permission of the publisher, Yale University Press.

**YGS Group.** "Seven Steps to Surviving a Disaster" used with permission of Bloomberg L.P. Copyright ©2015. All rights reserved.

**Zachary Shuster Harmsworth Literary Agency.** From *Wild* by Cheryl Strayed; copyright ©2012 by Cheryl Strayed. Used by permission of Zachary Shuster Harmsworth Literary Agency.

# Credits

**Photo locators denoted as follows: Top (T), Center (C), Bottom (B), Left (L), Right (R), Background (Bkgd)**

**vi** P_Wei/Getty Images; **viii** All Canada Photos/Alamy: **x** William James Warren/Getty Images; **xii** Archivart/Alamy; **xiv** Soft_light/Shutterstock; **2** P_Wei/Getty Images; **3** (BC) Gary Carter/Corbis, (BL) Roni Ben Ishay/Shutterstock, (B) Don Mason/Blend Images/Corbis, (CL) Everett Historical/Shutterstock, (CT) Brant Ward/San Francisco Chronicle/Corbis, (T) Juanmonino/Getty Images, (C) Zerophoto/Fotolia, (TL) Blvdone/Shutterstock; **6** Juanmonino/Getty Images; **11**(B) Roni Ben Ishay/Shutterstock, (C) Everett Historical/Shutterstock, (T) Blvdone/Shutterstock; **12** (CL) Dpa picture alliance/Alamy, (TL) Blvdone/Shutterstock, (TR) Everett Historical/Shutterstock; **13, 18, 20** Blvdone/Shutterstock; **22** (CL) National Archives/Handout/Hulton Archive/Getty Images, (TL) Blvdone/Shutterstock, (TR) Everett Historical/Shutterstock; **23** Everett Historical/Shutterstock; **25** Everett Historical/Shutterstock; **30, 32, 34** Everett Historical/Shutterstock; **36** Photo by Tanya Cofer; **37** Roni Ben Ishay/Shutterstock; **41** Peopleimages/Getty Images; **46, 48, 50** Roni Ben Ishay/Shutterstock; **59** (B) Gary Carter/Corbis, (CB) Don Mason/Blend Images/Corbis, (CT) Brant Ward/San Francisco Chronicle/Corbis, (T) Zerophoto/Fotolia; **62** J.J. GUILLEN/EPA/Newscom; **63** Zerophoto/Fotolia; **69** Peter Dazeley/Getty Images; **74** Zerophoto/Fotolia; **76** Zerophoto/Fotolia; **78** Frazer Harrison/Getty Images; **79** Brant Ward/San Francisco Chronicle/Corbis; **81** Camille Dungy; **82** Kurt Rogers/San Francisco Chronicle/Corbis; **84, 86** Brant Ward/San Francisco Chronicle/Corbis; **88** Lynn Goldsmith/Corbis; **89, 96** Don Mason/Blend Images/Corbis; **98** Gary Carter/Corbis; **99** (C) Alysa Bennett, (T) Chris Felver/Getty Images; **100** Gary Carter/Corbis; **102** Lauri Patterson/Getty Images; **122** All Canada Photos/Alamy, (BCL) Wonderlust/Photonica/Getty Images, (C) AF archive/Alamy, (L) Guylain Doyle/AGE fotostock, (BL) FUKUSHIMA MINPO/AFP/Getty Images, (T) Scazza/Fotolia, (TC) Dmytro Pylypenko/Shutterstock, (TCL) Deposit Photos/Glow Images, (TL) Water Rights/SuperStock; **131** (B) FUKUSHIMA MINPO/AFP/Getty Images, **131** (C) Deposit Photos/Glow Images, (T) Water Rights/SuperStock; **132** Jeremy sutton hibbert/Alamy; **133** Water Rights/SuperStock; **137** Olga Ptashko/Shutterstock; **142** Vetryanaya/o/Shutterstock; **146, 148, 150** Water Rights/SuperStock; **152** Patrick McMullan Co/McMullan/Sipa USA/Newscom; **153, 158, 160, 162** Deposit Photos/Glow Images; **165** FUKUSHIMA MINPO/AFP/Getty Images; **168** Scazza/Fotolia; **175** (B) Wonderlust/Photonica/Getty Images, (BC) Guylain Doyle/AGE footstock, (C) AF archive/Alamy; (T) Dmytro Pylypenko/Shutterstock; **178** (CL) Janette Beckman/Getty Images, (TL) Dmytro Pylypenko/Shutterstock, (TR) Library of Congress Prints and Photographs Division [LC 3a11347u]; **183** Nejron/123RF; **187** Maksimilian/Shutterstock; **191, 194** Dmytro Pylypenko/Shutterstock; **194** (CL) Hulton Deutsch Collection/Corbis, (TR) Library of Congress Prints and Photographs Division [LC 3a11347u]; **195** Library of Congress Prints and Photographs Division [LC 3a11347u]; **196** (B) Library of Congress Prints and Photographs Division [LC 3a12748u], (T) Library of Congress Prints and Photographs Division [LC 3a19377u]; **197** (B) Library of Congress Prints and Photographs Division [LC 3a11986u], (T) Hulton Archive/Getty Images; **198** Library of Congress Prints and Photographs Division [LC 3a12746u]; **199** Library of Congress Prints and Photographs Division [LC 3a11347u]; **200** (B) Library of Congress Prints and Photographs Division [LC 3a11347u], (TL) Dmytro Pylypenko/Shutterstock; **202** Rachel Torres/Alamy; **207** Alistair Hobbs/Shutterstock; **210** Danté Fenolio/Science Source; **212, 214** AF archive/Alamy; **217** Guylain Doyle/AGE fotostock; **220** Guylain Doyle/AGE fotostock; **222** Guylain Doyle/AGE fotostock; **224** Wonderlust/Photonica/Getty Images; **225** (BL) Handout/KRT/Newscom, (CL) Oscar White/Corbis, (TL) Christopher Felver/Corbis; **226** Wonderlust/Photonica/Getty Images; **228** Yulkapopkova/Vetta/Getty Images; **230** Icetray/123RF; **251**(BC) Jack Delano/PhotoQuest/Getty Images, (B) Bettmann/Corbis, (CL) Everett Collection Inc/Alamy, (CT) Everett Collection Historical/Alamy, (T) Charles Moore/Black Star/Alamy, (TL) Photoshot; **254** Charles Moore/Black Star/Alamy; **259** (B) National Archives, (C) Everett Collection Inc/Alamy; **259** Photoshot; **260** Stephen F. Somerstein/Getty Images; **260** (TL) Photoshot; **266** Photoshot; **268** Photoshot; **270** Stephen F. Somerstein/Getty Image; **275** Bettmann/Corbis; **280** Bob Adelman/Corbis; **288** Everett Collection Inc/Alamy; **290** Everett Collection Inc/Alamy; **292** Everett Collection Inc/

Alamy; **294** PhotoQuest/Getty Images; **295** National Archives; **297** National Archives; **305** (B) Jack Delano/PhotoQuest/Getty Images, (BC) Bettmann/Corbis, (CT) Everett Collection Historical/Alamy, (T) Andrea Jacobson, The Observatory. MacNeil/Lehrer Productions; **312** Everett Collection Historical/Alamy; **313** (B) Everett Collection Historical/Alamy, (T) Bill O'Leary/The Washington Post/Getty Images; **314** Everett Collection Historical/Alamy; **316** Thall/iStock/Getty Images; **318** Everett Collection Historical/Alamy; **320** Everett Collection Historical/Alamy; **322** ZUMA Press, Inc./Alamy; **323** Bettmann/Corbis; **327** Viramontes, Xavier (1947) ©Copyright Smithsonian American Art Museum, Washington, DC/Art Resource, NY; **327** Xavier Viramontes; **330** Bettmann/Corbis; **332** Bettmann/Corbis; **334** Chris Felver/Getty Images; **335** Jack Delano/PhotoQuest/Getty Images; **337** AP Images; **340** Jack Delano/PhotoQuest/Getty Images; **342** Jack Delano/PhotoQuest/Getty Images; **365** Sotheby's/akg images/Newscom; **374** GL Archive/Alamy; **356** Kichigin/Shutterstock; **357** (BL) Sotheby's/akg images/Newscom, (C) Reuters, (CL) Relativity Media/courtesy Everett Collection, (T) Leo Mason/Leo Mason/Corbis, (TC) Ben Welsh/age fotostock/Alamy, (TL) GL Archive/Alamy; **360** Leo Mason/Leo Mason/Corbis; **365** (BL) Relativity Media/courtesy Everett Collection, **365** (CBL) Relativity Media/courtesy Everett Collection; **365** (CL) Relativity Media/courtesy Everett Collection, (TR) Georgios Kollidas/Shutterstock, (R) GL Archive/Alamy; **367** The Print Collector/Corbis; **368** Peter Phipp/Britain On View/Getty Images; **369** Hugo Philpott/Epa/Newscom; **370** GL Archive/Alamy; **375** Sergii Figurnyi/Fotolia; **376** Relativity Media/courtesy Everett Collection; **400** GL Archive/Alamy; **401** Relativity Media/courtesy Everett Collection; **450** GL Archive/Alamy; **457** BHE FILMS/DINO DE LAURENTIIS CINEMATOGRAFICA/VERONA PROD/Ronald Grant Archive/Mary Evans; **466** GL Archive/Alamy; **479** Cantonatty/Shutterstock; **480** Relativity Media/courtesy Everett Collection; **486** (B) ZU_09/Getty Images, (L) Relativity Media/courtesy Everett Collection, (R) Sotheby's/akg images/Newscom; **501**(B) Courtesy CNN, (C) Reuters, (T) Ben Welsh/age fotostock/Alamy; **504** Ben Welsh/age fotostock/Alamy; **505** Frederick M. Brown/Getty Images; **506** Ben Welsh/age fotostock/Alamy; **508** Ben Welsh/age fotostock/Alamy; **516**(L) Reuters,(R) Courtesy CNN; **517** Reuters; **518** Snvv/Shutterstock; **521** Reuters; **522** Reuters; **524**(B) Nicolas Khayat/KRT/Newscom, (L) Reuters, (R) Courtesy CNN; **528** Courtesy CNN; **529**(B) Courtesy CNN, (T) Reuters; Dinka Jurkovic, Radio Free Europe/Radio Liberty; **542** Soft_light/Shutterstock; **543**(BL) Oleksandr Kalinichenko/Shutterstock, (C) FWStudio/Shutterstock, (BC) A.G.A/Shutterstock, (CL) De Agostini Picture Lib./A. Dagli Orti/akg images, (CTL) Archivart/Alamy, (T )cunaplus/Shutterstock, (TC) Galyna Andrushko/Shutterstock, (TL) Beerkoff/Fotolia; **546** cunaplus/Shutterstock; **551**(B) Oleksandr Kalinichenko/Shutterstock, (CT) De Agostini Picture Lib./A. Dagli Orti/akg images, (T) Beerkoff/Fotolia Kichigin/Shutterstock; **552** Beerkoff/Fotolia; **554** Roman replica of the Athena Farnese (marble), Phidias (c.500 c.432 BC) Museo Archeologico Nazionale, Naples, Italy/Bridgeman Images; **555** Statue of Zeus at Oympia, English School, (20th century)/Private Collection / © Look and Learn/Bridgeman Images; **556** GeoM/Fotolia; **558** Hulton Archive/Handout/Getty Images; **559** The Siege of Troy (oil on canvas), French School, (17th century)/Musee des Beaux Arts, Blois, France/Bridgeman Art Images; **559** The Siege of Troy (oil on canvas), French School, (17th century)/Musee des Beaux Arts, Blois, France/Bridgeman Images; **567** Ivy Close Images/Alamy; **560** Archivart/Alamy; **572** Mary Evans Picture Library/Alamy; **580 581** JOHN WILLIAM/akg images; **584** Scylla attacking Olysseus's ship, Payne, Roger (b.1934)/Private Collection/Look and Learn/Bridgeman Art Images; **584** Scylla attacking Olysseus's ship, Payne, Roger (b.1934)/Private Collection/Look and Learn/Bridgeman Images; **591** Archivart/Alamy; **592** Archivart/Alamy; **594** Hulton Archive/Handout/Getty Images; **595** De Agostini Picture Lib./A. Dagli Orti/akg images; **602** Penelope and the Suitors, 1900 (oil on canvas), Robertson, Victor John (fl.1892 1903)/Private Collection/Photo © Peter Nahum at The Leicester Galleries, London/Bridgeman Art Images; **609** Odysseus punishes the suitors (colour litho), Robinson, Thomas Heath (1869 1954)/Private Collection/The Stapleton Collection/Bridgeman Art Images; **614** North Wind Picture Archives/Alamy; **618** De Agostini Picture Lib./A. Dagli Orti/akg images; **620** De Agostini Picture Lib./A. Dagli Orti/akg images; **622** De Agostini Picture Lib./A. Dagli Orti/akg images;

# ACKNOWLEDGMENTS AND CREDITS

624 (B) Photo by Scott LaPierre, (T) Archivart/Alamy; 632 Archivart/Alamy; 635 Oleksandr Kalinichenko/Shutterstock; 636 USCG; 639 Oleksandr Kalinichenko/Shutterstock; 647 Galyna Andrushko/Shutterstock; 650 Colin McPherson/Corbis; 651 Galyna Andrushko/Shutterstock; 656 Galyna Andrushko/Shutterstock; 658 Galyna Andrushko/Shutterstock; 660(R) Marc Bryan Brown/WireImage/Getty Images, (TL) Matthew Naythons/The LIFE Images Collection/Getty images; 666 FWStudio/Shutterstock; 668 A.G.A/Shutterstock; 661 FWStudio/Shutterstock; 669(B) Tony Mcnicol/Alamy, (C) P Anastasselis/REX/Newscom; (T) Everett Collection Historical/Alamy; 670 A.G.A/Shutterstock; 672 Kovalenko Inna/Fotolia; 674 Shukaylova Zinaida/Shutterstock; 694 Angela Harburn/fotolia; 695 (BC) Everett Collection/Shutterstock, (C) World History Archive/Alamy,(TC) B Christopher/Alamy, (T )djgis/Shutterstock, (TCL) Liukov/Shutterstock, (TL) Falcon Eyes/Shutterstock; 703 Falcon Eyes/Shutterstock; 704 Pirie MacDonald/Corbis; Eyes/Shutterstock; 711 Dezi/Shutterstock; 722 Everett Collection Inc/Alamy; 743(B) Everett Collection/Shutterstock, (BC)World History Archive/Alamy, (T) Liukov/Shutterstock, (TR) B Christopher/Alamy; 746 Photo by Kerry Sherck; 747 Liukov/Shutterstock; 751 Iryna Rasko/Shutterstock; 754 Liukov/Shutterstock; 759(B) Louis Monier/Gamma Rapho/Getty Images, (T) Mark Lennihan/AP Images; 760 (B) Christopher/Alamy; 762 Cultura RM/Art Wolfe Stock/Cultura/Getty Images; 764 Inkwelldodo/Fotolia; 770(B) Sam Simmonds/Polaris/Newscom; (TL) World History Archive/Alamy, (TR) Everett Collection/Shutterstock; 771 World History Archive/Alamy; 773 World History Archive/Alamy; 774(B) Michael Tran/Contributor/FilmMagic/Getty Images, (TL) World History Archive/Alamy, (TR) Everett Collection/Shutterstock; 784 World History Archive/Alamy; Courtesy of University of Maine.

## Credits for Images in Interactive Student Edition Only

### Unit 1

BBC Worldwide Americas, Inc.; BBC Worldwide Learning; Bettmann/Corbis; Charles Eshelman/Getty Images; lithian/Shutterstock; Pat Mor.

### Unit 2

Amos Chapple/Lonely Planet Images/Getty Images; Antonio Busiell/Moment Open/Getty Images; B.Stefanov/Fotolia; Daryl Miller; Dea Lambert/Alamy; Fotosearch/Getty Images; James A. Parcell/The

Washington Post/Getty Images; Oriontrail/iStockphoto/Getty Images; Richard A McMillin/Shutterstock; Saez Pascal/SIPA/Newscom; Saul Loeb/AFP/Getty Images; Serezniy/123RF; Stephen Frink/Corbis; Ullstein bild/Getty Images; AS400 DB/Corbis

### Unit 3

John G. Moebes/Corbis; Bettmann/Corbis; David Margolick; Hulton Archive/Getty Images; Mark Bennington; Sheyann Webb Christburg; WUNC

### Unit 4

DeAgostini/Getty Images; Elizabeth I, Armada Portrait, c.1588 (oil on panel), Gower, George (1540 96) (attr. to)/Woburn Abbey, Bedfordshire, UK/Bridgeman Art Library; Elizabeth I, Armada Portrait, c.1588 (oil on panel), Gower, George (1540 96) (attr. to)/Woburn Abbey, Bedfordshire, UK/Bridgeman Images; Misty Harris;

### Unit 5

Courtesy National Park Service; David Nunuk/All Canada Photos/Getty Images; Doug Allan/Oxford Scientific/Getty Images; Epa european pres  hoto agency b.v./Alamy; Frans Lanting/Mint Images/Getty Images; Jan  R.D. Scott/Moment/Getty Images; Owen Newman/Oxford Sc  tific/Getty Images; Paul Popper/Popperfoto/Getty Images; Perrine D  g/Perspectives/Getty Images; readyimage/Shutterstock; Richard Ellis/ ty Images; Rodney Ungwiluk, Jr./Getty Images; Schomburg Center, PL/Art Resource, NY; Sue Flood/Photodisc/Getty Images; Wayne Lynch/ l Canada Photos/Getty Images

### Unit 6

Solarseven/Shutterstock; Chris Felver/Archive Photos/Getty Images; Dennis Van Tine/ABACAUSA.COM/Newscom; Eric Francis/Getty Images; Eric Schaal/The LIFE Picture Collection/Getty Images; Ron Miller; S_Photo/Shutterstock; Smithsonian Magazine